Martin Luther King, Jr and the Civil Rights Move

Related titles from Palgrave Macmillan

James A. Colaiaco, *Martin Luther King, Jr: Apostle of Militant Nonviolence*

William T. Martin Riches, *The Civil Rights Movement: Struggle and Resistance*, 2nd edition

Brian Ward (ed.), *The Making of Martin Luther King and the Civil Rights Movement*

MARTIN LUTHER KING, JR AND THE CIVIL RIGHTS MOVEMENT

CONTROVERSIES AND DEBATES

Edited by

John A. Kirk

First published 2007 by
PALGRAVE MACMILLAN
Houndmills, Basingstoke, Hampshire RG21 6XS and
175 Fifth Avenue, New York, N.Y. 10010
Companies and representatives throughout the world

PALGRAVE MACMILLAN is the global academic imprint of the Palgrave Macmillan division of St. Martin's Press, LLC and of Palgrave Macmillan Ltd. Macmillan® is a registered trademark in the United States, United Kingdom and other countries. Palgrave is a registered trademark in the European Union and other countries.

ISBN 978-1-4039-9654-1   ISBN 978-0-230-20781-3 (eBook)

DOI 10.1007/978-0-230-20781-3

This book is printed on paper suitable for recycling and made from fully managed and sustained forest sources.

A catalogue record for this book is available from the British Library.

Library of Congress Cataloging-in-Publication Data
Martin Luther King, Jr. and the civil rights movement : controversies and debates / edited by John A. Kirk.
    p. cm.
Includes bibliographical references and index.
ISBN 978-1-4039-9653-4 (cloth)
ISBN 978-0-4039-9654-1 (pbk.)

    1. King, Martin Luther, Jr., 1929–1968. 2. King, Martin Luther, Jr., 1929–1968 – Political and social views. 3. African Americans – Civil rights – History – 20th century – Sources. 4. Civil rights movements – United States – History – 20th century – Sources. 5. United States – Race relations – History 20th century – Sources. 6. African Americans – Biography. 7. Civil rights workers – United States – Biography. 8. Baptists – United States – Clergy – Biography. I. Kirk, John A., 1970–

E185.97.K5M325 2007
323.1196'073–dc22   2006052734

10   9   8   7   6   5   4   3   2   1
16   15   14   13   12   11   10   09   08   07

For Charlene and Sadie

Contents

Acknowledgements

This book is a product of over ten years of teaching a final year under-graduate Special Subject course on 'Martin Luther King, Jr and the Civil Rights Movement' (and even longer spent in researching and writing on King and the movement). I should like to thank all of those students who have taken the course for their input and help over the years and for contributing to the shaping of my understanding of the subject. I am also grateful to my History Department colleague at Royal Holloway, Dr Bruce Baker, who read through the manuscript and made helpful comments, as did an anonymous reviewer for the press. At Palgrave Macmillan, Terka Acton, Felicity Noble, Sonya Barker and Beverley Tarquini, have all provided valuable help in transforming an idea into a finished piece of work. Family, friends, and colleagues, have, as always, played an important role in sustaining me throughout. A special mention, however, goes to my wife Charlene, and to our baby daughter Sadie, for making it all worthwhile.

The publisher and the editor would like to thank the following for use of copyright material:

Blackwell Publishers for Derek H. Alderman, 'Street Names and the Scaling of Memory: The Politics of Commemorating Martin Luther King Jr. within the African American Community', *Area* 35 (2003), pp. 163–73. Reproduced by permission of Blackwell Publishers.

Cambridge University Press for John A. Kirk, 'State of the Art: Martin Luther King, Jr.', *Journal of American Studies* 38 (2004). Reproduced by permission of Cambridge University Press.

Fortress Press for 'There is a Balm in Gilead: The Cultural Roots of Martin Luther King, Jr' by Lewis V. Baldwin. © 1991 Augsbury Fortress. Used by permission.

The Organization of American Historians, for Clayborne Carson, 'Martin Luther King, Jr: Charismatic Leadership in a Mass Struggle', *Journal of*

American History 74: 2 (September 1987), pp. 448–54; Keith D. Miller, 'Martin Luther King, Jr and the Black Folk Pulpit', *Journal of American History* 78: 1 (June 1991), pp. 120–3; © Organization of American Historians, http://www.oah.org. Reprinted with permission.

Orbis Books for James H. Cone, *Martin and Malcolm and America: A Dream or a Nightmare* (Orbis Books, 1991).

Duke University Press for Michael Eric Dyson, 'Martin and Malcolm', in *Transition* 56 (1992), pp. 18–57; © 1992 Oxford University Press. All rights reserved. Used by permission of the publisher. This article was subsequently reprinted in Michael Eric Dyson, *Reflecting Black: African-American Cultural Criticism* (Minneapolis: University of Minnesota Press, 1993, pp. 250–63.

Michael Eric Dyson, for material from *'I May Not Get There with You': The True Martin Luther King, Jr*, by Michael Eric Dyson, pp. 155–67; Copyright © 2000 by Michael Eric Dyson, by permission of The Free Press, a division of Simon & Schuster Adult Publishing Group.

David J. Garrow for 'The Intellectual Development of Martin Luther King, Jr: Influences and Commentaries', *Union Seminary Quarterly Review* 40 (1986), pp. 5–20; and 'From Reformer to Revolutionary', *Reflections on the Legacy*, Democratic Socialists of America (1983), pp. 27–36.

University of North Carolina Press for *The Deacons for Defense: Armed Resistance and the Civil Rights Movement* by Lance Hill; © 2004 by the University of North Carolina Press. Used by permission of the publisher.

Oxford University Press for *The Preacher King: Martin Luther King Jr. and the Word that Moved America* by Richard Lischer; © 1995 by Richard Lischer. Used by permission of Oxford University Press, Inc.; and Adam Fairclough, 'Was Martin Luther King a Marxist?', *History Workshop Journal* 15 (1983), pp. 117–25. Used by permission of Oxford University Press.

Random House and the Wylie Agency for *Killing the Dream* by Gerald L. Posner; © 1998 by Gerald L. Posner. Used by permission of Random House, Inc.

Belinda Robnett, for material from 'African-American Women in the Civil Rights Movement, 1954–1965: Gender, Leadership and Micromobilization', *American Journal of Sociology* 101: 6 (1996), pp. 1661–93, by permission of the University of Chicago Press.

Simon & Schuster for Kenneth O'Reilly, *'Racial Matters': The FBI's Secret File on Black America, 1960–1972*, reprinted with the permission of The Free Press, a division of Simon & Schuster Adult Publishing Group. Copyright © 1989 by Kenneth O'Reilly. All rights reserved.

University of Tennessee Press for *O Freedom! Afro American Emancipation Celebrations* by William H. Wiggins Jr.; © 1987 by the University of Tennessee Press.

Theology Today for James H. Cone, 'Martin Luther King, Jr: Black Theology – Black Church'; © 1984 Theology Today. Originally published in *Theology Today* 41 (1984), pp. 409–20. Reprinted with the author's and the publisher's permission.

Verso Books for William F. Pepper, *An Act of State: The Execution of Martin Luther King* (2002), pp. 6–10. Reprinted with permission of Verso.

Every effort has been made to trace the copyright holders but if any have been inadvertently overlooked the publishers will be pleased to make the necessary arrangements at the first opportunity.

1 Introduction*

The chapters that follow examine a number of the specific issues that have been raised by those writing on Martin Luther King, Jr and the civil rights movement. The purpose of this introductory chapter is twofold. First, it examines the literature on King and the movement that is not covered elsewhere in this book. Second, in doing so it provides a brief biographical overview of King's leadership, and a chronological overview of the civil rights movement, that sets the context for the controversies and debates that follow. Full citations for the works mentioned in this chapter can be found in the Bibliography at the end of the book.

Early histories of the civil rights movement that appeared prior to the 1980s were primarily biographics of Martin Luther King, Jr. Collectively, these works helped to create the familiar Montgomery-to-Memphis narrative framework for understanding the history of the civil rights movement in the United States. This narrative begins with King's rise to leadership during the 1955–6 Montgomery bus boycott in Alabama, and ends with his 1968 assassination in Memphis, Tennessee. Since the 1980s, a number of studies examining the civil rights movement at local and state levels have questioned the usefulness and accuracy of the King-centred Montgomery-to-Memphis narrative as the sole way of understanding the civil rights movement. These studies have made it clear that civil rights struggles already existed in many of the communities where King and the organization that he was president of, the Southern Christian Leadership Conference (SCLC), ran civil rights campaigns in the 1960s. Moreover, those struggles continued long after King and the SCLC had left those communities. Civil rights activism also thrived in many places that King and the SCLC never visited. As a result of these local and state studies, historians have increasingly framed the civil rights movement within the context of a much longer, ongoing struggle for African American freedom and equality, unfolding throughout the twentieth century at local, state and national levels.

Yet although civil rights scholarship has tended to move away from a focus on King, the talismanic leader of the movement is ever-present in the public consciousness. The fiftieth anniversary of the Montgomery bus

* Adapted from John A. Kirk, 'State of the Art: Martin Luther King, Jr', *Journal of American Studies* 38 (2004): 329–47.

boycott in 2005–6, the event that launched King's movement leadership, began a host of fiftieth anniversaries within the Montgomery-to-Memphis timeframe. Just before and during the Montgomery anniversary, the deaths of participants in the bus boycott, Rosa Parks, and King's widow Coretta Scott King, again returned the focus to that seminal event, and served as a reminder that the civil rights movement is inexorably passing from living memory and into history. The ongoing Martin Luther King, Jr Papers Project, under the directorship of Clayborne Carson at Stanford University, California, continues to make King's personal papers, and other King-related primary materials, more accessible to a public audience than ever before. Given the ongoing public and media interest in King and the civil rights movement, the movement anniversaries, and the wider availability of primary sources, it seems ironic that scholarship on King is tending to wane just when it is most needed to place these developments in their proper historical context.

Existing collections on King consist of compendiums of materials (for example, David J. Garrow (ed.), *Martin Luther King, Jr: Civil Rights Leader, Theologian, Orator, Three Volumes* (Brooklyn, NY: Carlson Publishing, 1989)), eclectic conference proceedings (for example, Brian Ward and Tony Badger (eds), *The Making of Martin Luther King and the Civil Rights Movement* (London: Macmillan, 1996) and Peter J. Albert and Ronald Hoffman (eds), *We Shall Overcome: Martin Luther King, Jr, and the Black Freedom Struggle* (New York: Pantheon, 1990)), or are quite narrowly focused on one particular theme or topic (for example, Carolyn Calloway-Thomas and John Louis Lucaites (eds), *Martin Luther King, Jr, and the Sermonic Power of Public Discourse* (Tuscaloosa, AL: University of Alabama Press, 1993) and Lewis V. Baldwin, with Rufus Burrow, Jr, Barbara A. Holmes and Susan Holmes Winfield (eds), *The Legacy of Martin Luther King, Jr: The Boundaries of Law, Politics, and Religion* (Notre Dame, IN: University of Notre Dame Press, 2002)).

Although these books contain valuable scholarship in their own right, they do not provide the necessary wide-ranging critical perspectives on King and the movement for those new to the subject and who want to explore it further. This book fills the existing gap by for the first time bringing together the signally important literature on key controversies and debates that is currently fragmented and scattered in monographs, essays and articles. Each chapter provides a brief introduction to set the context for the various selections. This is followed by a 'Questions for Discussion' section to help in further probing the points that the selections raise, and a 'Further Reading' section for those who want to follow up on them in greater depth and detail. By including a wide variety of topics, the collection seeks to actively bridge, and indeed even to invite, a dialogue between academic scholarship and popular writing on the subject, both of which have brought important insights to the field.

In giving definition and focus to the current body of writings on King, this book not only consolidates our existing understanding of the man and the movement but it also, by revealing the gaps that still remain, suggests what yet needs to be done and in what directions King and movement scholarship might go in the future. No doubt the controversies and debates that I have chosen to include and exclude, and the writings that I have chosen as being representative of them, will itself provoke controversy and debate. This is all for the better. The chapters in this book are designed precisely to invite further reflection, further discussion, and further reading, and they do not pretend nor seek to provide definitive answers to what are often complex questions.

In terms of primary materials, King's books, as well as many of his essays, articles, speeches, and sermons, are currently available in various editions and collections. How useful these sources actually are is a question tackled in Chapter 4, which examines issues related to King's plagiarism, ghost-writing, and voice-merging. The definitive published work covering King's personal papers will be the fourteen-volume set currently being compiled by the King Papers Project. Another important primary source comes from FBI surveillance of King. David Garrow has collected and edited the material gathered from FBI wiretaps on microfilm, which consist of almost 17,000 pages on sixteen reels. Part 1 contains wiretaps of King and part 2 contains wiretaps of Stanley D. Levison, one of King's most trusted SCLC advisors. The FBI also illicitly placed bugging devices in King's hotel rooms. However, at the request of several former SCLC board members concerned about privacy issues, the FBI tapes derived from these bugs are sealed by federal court order until 2027. More on the relationship between King and the FBI can be found in Chapter 9.

A trilogy of books published in the 1980s still set the standard for King biography. Adam Fairclough, *To Redeem the Soul of America* (1987), lends analytical verve to the events surrounding King's presidency of the SCLC and his movement leadership. David Garrow, *Bearing the Cross* (1986), offers exhaustive research and a mastery of the sources. Taylor Branch, *Parting the Waters* (1988), is the first in a trilogy of volumes, finally completed in 2006, that places King's life within the context of the broader civil rights movement and the history of the times on a truly epic scale. These books apart, one of the best, and one of the earliest and frankest assessments of King's life after his assassination, is David L. Lewis, *King: A Critical Biography* (1970). John A. Williams, *The King God Didn't Save* (1970), also provides a critical account of King's life and philosophy. Up until that point, works on King had been more hagiography than biography, including books by Lawrence D. Reddick, *Crusader Without Violence* (1959), Lerone Bennett, Jr, *What Manner of Man* (1964), and William Robert Miller, *Martin Luther King, Jr* (1968). Exceptionally, white author Lionel Lokos, *House Divided* (1968), gives the harshest and most unsympathetic critique of King's movement activism. As King became a more revered figure as a national heroic symbol of the movement in the 1970s, such scathing accounts noticeably diminished. Books by James Alonzo Bishop, *The Days of Martin Luther King* (1971), Stephen B. Oates, *Let the Trumpet Sound* (1982), and Frederick L. Downing, *To See the Promised Land* (1986), are the most notable accounts that fill the gap between David Lewis's book and later studies. The most recent updates of King biography come from Peter J. Ling, *Martin Luther King, Jr* (2002), and Stewart Burns, *To the Mountaintop* (2003). The pick of the shorter studies on *Martin Luther King, Jr* are those written by James A. Colaiaco (1988), Adam Fairclough (1990), John White (1991) and John A. Kirk (2005).

The first volume of the King Papers and the biographies of King provide the best sources for examining his pre-movement life. Born in Atlanta, Georgia, on 15 January 1929, King was steeped in the traditions of the African American Southern Baptist Church. His mother, Alberta Williams King, was the only daughter of successful Atlanta minister Adam Daniel (A.D.) Williams, who was the son of an African American slave preacher. King's father, Martin Luther King, Sr, known affectionately to family and friends as 'Daddy' King, was raised in rural Georgia and was the son of a farmer. An ambitious man, at the age of eighteen Daddy King set off for Atlanta determined to better himself through education. After graduating from the historically black Morehouse College he married into the influential Williams family and later inherited his father-in-law's pulpit at Ebenezer Baptist Church on downtown Auburn Avenue. King spent his early years living with his parents, his older sister Denise, his younger brother Adam Daniel (A.D.), and his maternal grandmother, at 501 Auburn Avenue, just a short distance from Ebenezer.

After graduation from high school in 1944 at the age of fifteen, King followed in his father's and his maternal grandfather's footsteps by enrolling at Morehouse College. Having decided to follow family tradition and pursue a career in the ministry, after graduation from Morehouse in 1948, King went to the predominantly white, northern institution of Crozer Theological Seminary in Chester, Pennsylvania, to study for a divinity degree. Upon graduating from Crozer in 1951, King enrolled at Boston University, again a predominantly white, northern institution, to study for a PhD. While studying at Boston, through a mutual friend King met his future wife, Alabamian Coretta Scott (they married in June 1953), who was at the time studying on a scholarship at Boston's New England Conservatory of Music with aspirations to become a classical singer. Chapter 3 further examines the various influences on King's early life and especially weighs his African American family, church, and religious roots on the one hand, with his academic training in predominantly white institutions on the other.

As King's residential studies at Boston came to a close he began the search for a pastorate where he could work while writing up his PhD dissertation. Through a family friend, King learned of a vacant position at Dexter Avenue Baptist Church in Montgomery, Alabama. Dexter had recently fired its controversial and outspoken pastor Vernon Johns, a reflection of the notoriously tough treatment that the church handed out to its ministers. Unperturbed, King arranged a trial sermon there, which was well received. In April 1954, King accepted Dexter's offer of the post and took up his new job the following September. King completed his PhD thesis and was awarded his doctorate in June 1955 (Chapter 4 looks at King's thesis and his academic work in light of subsequent revelations about his plagiarism). On 17 November 1955, the Kings' first child, Yolanda Denise King, was born. Less than a month later, the Montgomery bus boycott began.

The bus boycott came at a crucial time of change in the ongoing African American struggle for freedom and equality. In May 1954, America's oldest civil rights organization the National Association for the Advancement of Colored People (NAACP), and in particular its Legal Defense and Educational Fund, Inc. (LDF) under the guidance of attorney Thurgood Marshall, won a decisive legal victory after decades of litigation in the courts. In *Brown* v. *Board of Education*, the US Supreme Court outlawed segregation in schools. By dismissing the legal doctrine of 'separate but equal', which had been used to justify segregation since the 1896 *Plessy* v. *Ferguson* decision, the Court paved the way for the dismantling of the entire segregated order in the South. White southerners vowed a campaign of massive resistance to school desegregation. When the Court handed down an ambiguous implementation order for its original ruling in May 1955, it further weakened the prospects of compliance with the law. Positions on segregation and race relations quickly polarized in the South. In August 1955, the murder of fourteen-year-old African American Emmett Till in Money, Mississippi, for allegedly saying 'Bye, baby' to a white woman, caused national outrage. The cold war climate added to the intensity of the times. As the United States sought to influence world opinion, including many nations with peoples of colour, race relations became a point of international, as well as of national, concern.

Much of the scholarship on King has focused upon his involvement in community-based civil rights campaigns. King first came to national prominence as president of the Montgomery Improvement Association (MIA) during the 1955–6 boycott. The boycott began after the arrest of Rosa Parks in December 1955 for failing to give up her seat to a white passenger on a city bus, an act which broke the state's segregation laws. The planned short-term boycott was soon extended in the face of white intransigence, and its aims shifted from winning a modification of segregation on city buses to its complete abolition. Eventually running to thirteen months, media coverage increasingly focused upon King's boycott leadership, and it was this coverage that helped to make him an African American leader of national standing. Chapter 2 focuses on issues relating to King's local and national leadership in the civil rights movement. The boycott ended in December 1956 after the US Supreme Court ordered the desegregation of Montgomery city buses.

Stewart Burns (ed.), *Daybreak of Freedom* (1997), is an edited collection of primary sources that tells the story of the bus boycott. Burns was also one of the joint editors of volume three of the King Papers, which provides an even more comprehensive documentary history of events. J. Mills Thornton, *Dividing Lines* (2002), contains an important analysis of the bus boycott from a local perspective that locates events within the context of white-dominated municipal politics. Catherine Barnes, *Journey from Jim Crow* (1983), places the bus boycott within the larger context of the desegregation of public transportation in the decades before and after events in Montgomery.

There are a number of useful first-hand accounts of the bus boycott. King's book *Stride Toward Freedom* (1958) was the first and others were written over the following decades. One of the best is Jo Ann Robinson, with David Garrow, *The Montgomery Bus Boycott and the Women Who Started It* (1989), which highlights the role played by the Women's Political Council in events. As the title suggests, Robinson's book indicates the crucial role played by women and women's organizations in the civil rights movement, a theme that is discussed further in Chapter 7. Rosa Parks has an autobiography, written with Jim Haskins, *Rosa Parks: My Story* (1992), and a biography written by Douglas Brinkley, *Mine Eyes Have Seen the Glory* (2000), that examine her role in events. Robert Graetz, *A White Preacher's Memoir* (1999) looks at the boycott from the perspective of a sympathetic liberal white minister; Fred D. Gray, *Bus Ride to Justice* (1999), gives the MIA attorney's view; Solomon S. Seay, *I was There by the Grace of God* (1990), gives an account of events by an African American MIA minister; and African American minister U. J. Fields' *The Montgomery Story* (1959) is a noteworthy account since it provides a critical perspective on events in Montgomery from a disgruntled member of the MIA.

In January 1957, King helped to launch the SCLC to capitalize on his own high profile leadership and to coordinate church leaders in other cities in the hope of spreading successful bus boycotts across the South. The biographies of King written by Adam Fairclough and David Garrow look at the origins and founding of the SCLC after the Montgomery bus boycott. Biographies of Bayard Rustin and Ella Baker expand upon the roles played by those two influential figures. There is no autobiography or biography of the third influential figure in the SCLC, the white Jewish New Yorker attorney Stanley Levison.

The founding of the SCLC aside, the period between the end of the Montgomery bus boycott and the beginning of the 1960 sit-in movement is often viewed, as Fairclough titles his chapter on the period in *To Redeem the Soul of America*, as King and the movement's 'Fallow Years'. Efforts by King and the SCLC to spread the bus boycotts to other cities and to instigate mass voter registration campaigns both, for a variety of reasons, met with failure. Sociologist Aldon D. Morris, *The Origins of the Civil Rights Movement* (1984), offers a more upbeat interpretation of the movement during these years. He argues that the organizational foundations for the burst of activism that followed were being laid at a grassroots level in southern communities.

The most dramatic development during this period was at Central High School in Little Rock, Arkansas, where in September 1957 Governor Orval E. Faubus called out National Guard soldiers to prevent the entry of nine African American students. Eventually, President Dwight D. Eisenhower was forced to send in national troops to ensure that the school desegregated. Two civil rights acts were passed by Congress in 1957 and 1960, the first for almost eighty years, but their provisions did little to significantly impact upon African American lives. Apart from King biographies, which often skip quickly over this period, little has been written about King's activities during these years, which included visits to Africa and India, several appearances on the national stage, and a failed attempt upon his life by a mentally ill African American woman while on a book signing trip to New York City.

It was the 1960 Sit-In Movement and the founding of the Student Nonviolent Coordinating Committee (SNCC) and the 1961 Freedom Rides, rather than King, that gave the civil rights movement impetus and direction in the early 1960s. King was only tangentially involved. In October 1960, King participated in a sit-in at the invitation of students in Atlanta. His subsequent arrest and jailing became a campaign issue in the unfolding presidential race between Democrat John F. Kennedy and Republican Richard M. Nixon that year. Kennedy aide Harris Wofford's *Of Kennedy's and Kings* (1980) documents those events, and Clifford M. Kuhn, 'There's a Footnote to History!', provides an important revisionist article that suggests behind-the-scenes political manoeuvring rather than a bullish Kennedy entourage secured King's release. Much to the annoyance of the Congress of Racial Equality (CORE) and SNCC members, the two main civil rights organizations involved in the Freedom Rides, King refused to participate, although he did co-chair a Freedom Rides Coordinating Committee that orchestrated and funded Freedom Rides throughout the summer of 1961. Raymond Arsenault, *Freedom Riders* (2006), provides the most comprehensive account of those demonstrations.

In late 1961 and early 1962, King participated in an emerging local movement in Albany, Georgia, set in motion by SNCC workers there. The campaign is widely viewed as a failure by historians since it did not secure the local gains or elicit the federal intervention that King and the SCLC wanted. The failure has been attributed to the shrewd policing of demonstrations by Albany's police chief Laurie Pritchett, who arrested and jailed demonstrators on charges of obstruction rather than seeking a showdown over segregation, and to internal movement divisions between the SCLC, SNCC, the NAACP, and local people. The Albany movement does not have its own dedicated monograph. There is, however, a volume of the *Journal of South-West Georgia History* (1984) that contains essays on the movement, including a useful overview by John A. Ricks, 'De Lawd Descends and is Crucified'. Journalist Pat Watters, a first-hand observer of events, includes a discussion of them in a book with Reese Cleghorn, *Climbing Jacob's Ladder* (1967), and in his single-authored *Down to Now* (1971). Stephen G. N. Tuck, *Beyond Atlanta* (2001), locates the Albany movement within the context of SNCC organizing in south-west Georgia, and within the broader context of the African American struggle for freedom and equality in the state.

In April 1963, King and the SCLC sought to apply the lessons of defeat in Albany and launched a local campaign in Birmingham, Alabama. The campaign marked a pivotal turning point for King and the civil rights movement. Employing non-violent direct action tactics, King and the SCLC, in concert with local African American activists under the leadership of Rev. Fred Shuttlesworth, president of the SCLC-affiliated Alabama Christian Movement for Human Rights (ACMHR), organized mass demonstrations. Commissioner of Public Safety T. Eugene 'Bull' Connor ordered the use of police dogs and spray from high-powered fire hoses against peaceful protests that provoked a national outcry and forced the Kennedy administration to intervene. President Kennedy appeared on national television to declare civil rights a 'moral issue' and he drew up a Civil Rights Bill to put before Congress. Glenn T. Eskew, *But for Birmingham* (1997), provides the best existing study of the campaign in a local context, looking particularly at the intersection of local and national civil rights movements and the class tensions that existed in Birmingham's African American community. J. Mills Thornton locates events within the context of municipal politics, and points to Connor's desire to retain political office as a motivating force in his actions. Chapter 7 of Brian Ward's *Radio and the Struggle for Civil Rights in the South* offers an innovative account of the role played by black-oriented radio in the campaign. Andrew M. Mannis, *A Fire You Can't Put Out* (1999), examines the life and career of local African American leader Rev Fred Shuttlesworth, Dianne McWhorter, *Carry Me Home* (2001), looks at the role played by the Ku Klux Klan in Birmingham, and Jonathan S. Bass, *Blessed Are the Peacemakers* (2001), looks at the role played by Birmingham's white clergymen, whose criticism of King's non-violent direct action tactics prompted King to write his 'Letter from Birmingham City Jail', one of his most eloquent defences of the use of non-violent direct action and civil disobedience. The use of non-violent direct action in the movement is examined in further detail in Chapter 5. Horace Huntley and

David Montgomery (eds), *Black Workers' Struggle for Equality* (2004), place the 1963 events within the context of ongoing African American union activism in Birmingham, and Charles E. Connerly, *The Most Segregated City in America* (2005), places them within the larger developments in city planning policy. Spike Lee (dir.) *4 Little Girls* (1997), focuses on the bombing of 16th Street Baptist Church after the campaign, which killed four African American girls.

In August 1963, a March on Washington for Jobs and Freedom provided one of the movement's most memorable set pieces. Although King's 'I Have a Dream' speech has come to dominate the march in popular memory, the event was in fact conceived of by A. Philip Randolph and Bayard Rustin. In 1941, Rustin had assisted with Randolph's March on Washington Movement to demand fair employment practices in wartime industries. The threat of the march led to President Franklin D. Roosevelt issuing Executive Order 8802, which banned racial discrimination in hiring and set up of the Fair Employment Practices Committee (FEPC) to enforce the ban. In late 1962, Randolph resurrected the idea in a 'March on Washington for Jobs and Freedom' to coincide with the new burst of African American activism and the hundredth anniversary of President Abraham Lincoln's signing of the Emancipation Proclamation. Thomas Gentile, *March on Washington* (1983), Patrick Henry Bass, *Like a Mighty Stream* (2002), and Lucy G. Barber, *Marching on Washington* (2003), all examine the March on Washington. Taylor Branch's biography of King contains a chapter on the subject, as does Drew Hansen, *The Dream* (2003), a book on King's 'I Have a Dream' speech. Biographies of A. Philip Randolph and Bayard Rustin look at their crucial organizing roles. The autobiographies of Ralph Abernathy, James Farmer, James Forman, Coretta Scott King, John Lewis, Roy Wilkins and Andrew Young all touch upon events.

In May 1964, King and the SCLC launched another campaign in St Augustine, Florida, to put pressure on Congress to pass Kennedy's Civil Rights Bill. At the time the bill was being steered through the legislative process by President Lyndon B. Johnson, who had succeeded Kennedy after his November 1963 assassination. By targeting America's oldest city in the run up to its quadricentennial celebrations, King and the SCLC sought symbolically to highlight the persistence of racism in the United States and the need for federal action. However, there is little evidence to suggest that the demonstrations made any direct impact upon Congress, even though the 1964 Civil Rights Act was eventually passed and signed in July. The act outlawed segregation in all public facilities and accommodations. The local white business community in St Augustine did comply with the terms of the act, but only after King and the SCLC left the city.

As an edited collection of essays by Elizabeth Jacoway and David Colburn, *Southern Businessmen and Desegregation* (1982), demonstrates, white businessmen in St Augustine and in many other localities played a pivotal role in negotiations to end segregation. David Colburn, *Racial Change and Community Crisis* (1985), is a single-authored monograph about King and the SCLC's campaign and makes no bones about its shortcomings. Many in the local African American community, Colburn notes, felt aggrieved that the campaign had stirred racial violence in the city yet had not addressed many of the core economic issues that affected them. Two studies, one by Charles W. Whalen and Barbara Whalen, *The Longest Debate* (1985), and the other by Robert D. Loevy, *To End All Segregation* (1990), look at the difficulties encountered in Congress over the passage of the 1964 Civil Rights Act. Hugh D. Graham, *The Civil Rights Era* (1990), locates the act within evolving federal policy on civil rights in the 1960s and early 1970s.

One of the most important civil rights initiatives during the 1964 presidential election year was the Freedom Summer in Mississippi, conducted by a number of groups that made up the Council of Federated Organizations (COFO), in which SNCC was the dominant force. The summer culminated in an attempt to seat delegates selected in a Freedom Vote under the banner of the Mississippi Freedom Democratic Party (MFDP) at the 1964 Democratic National Convention held in Atlantic City, New Jersey. They insisted that the regular all-white Mississippi Democratic Party was illegitimate because of electoral corruption in the state, which included the widespread denial of African American voting rights. The effort met with a bitter defeat amid political manoeuvring within the Democratic Party hierarchy. King played only a minor role in the Freedom Summer, although he was more prominent in events at Atlantic City, where his refusal to unequivocally back MFDP demands fuelled growing antagonisms with SNCC. Events in Mississippi in 1964 have attracted a large body of writing. The best accounts of the civil rights struggle there are by John Dittmer, *Local People* (1994), and Charles Payne, *I've Got the Light of Freedom* (1995). Of the two, Dittmer has most to say about the MFDP challenge, which is also covered in biographies of MFDP activists Fannie Lou Hamer, Robert Moses and Ella Baker.

King and the SCLC's 1965 Selma campaign and the passage of the 1965 Voting Rights Act are viewed by many commentators as the pinnacle of their achievements. In concert with SNCC and local people, they ran a campaign of non-violent direct action centred upon Selma's attempts to block African American voter registration. The campaign culminated in a showdown on Edmund Pettus Bridge when state law enforcement officers broke up a peaceful march with tear gas and billy clubs. The conflict prompted federal intervention by the Johnson administration and generated an unprecedented degree of nationwide public sympathy and support. Thousands of whites travelled to the city to join a Selma-to-Montgomery march that rounded off the campaign.

David Garrow, *Protest at Selma* (1978), provides the most comprehensive analysis of the Selma campaign and its impact on the passage of the Voting Rights Act. J. Mills Thornton locates events within the context of developments in local municipal politics. Cynthia Griggs Fleming, *In the Shadow of Selma* (2005), looks at the legacies of Selma and examines rural-based freedom struggles. Stephen L. Longenecker, *Selma's Peacemaker* (1987), is an account of events based upon the journal of a local white clergyman, and Mary Stanton, *From Selma to Sorrow* (1998), recalls the life and investigates the death of Viola Liuzzo, a white woman murdered by members of the Ku Klux Klan at the end of the Selma-to-Montgomery march. There are two useful first-hand accounts of the Selma campaign from African American participants. J. L. Chestnut, Jr, with Julia Cass, *Black in Selma* (1991), views events from the perspective of a local African American attorney, and Sheyann Webb and Rachel West Nelson, *Selma, Lord, Selma* (1980), remember their roles from the perspective two local African American school girl participants. Charles Fager, *Selma, 1965* (1974), recalls his involvement in Selma as a white SCLC staff member, and Richard D. Leonard, *Call to Selma* (2002), provides a memoir of his role as a New York Unitarian Universalist minister who answered King's call for the support of white northern liberal clergy on the Selma-to-Montgomery march.

The 1965–6 Chicago campaign marked King and the SCLC's first sustained engagement with racial discrimination in a northern city. In a protracted campaign, they attempted to tackle the problems of economic deprivation and *de facto* segregation that African Americans faced in the city. The campaign culminated in 'Open Housing' marches through white neighbourhoods that met with violent resistance. This brought Mayor Richard J. Daley and other city officials to the negotiating table where they hammered out a Summit Agreement with movement representatives for change in a number of areas. Yet when King and the SCLC left Chicago, little of the agreement was implemented. James R. Ralph Jr, *Northern Protest* (1993), is the best starting point for an overview of the Chicago campaign, with Alan B. Anderson and George W. Pickering, *Confronting the Color Line* (1986), also useful.

In June 1966, just as King and the SCLC were gearing up for the Open Housing marches in Chicago, King was sidetracked by his participation in the Meredith March Against Fear. The march initially represented a one-man protest by James Meredith, who had integrated the University of Mississippi at Oxford amid much controversy and violent white resistance in 1962. Meredith set out on a march from Memphis to Jackson, Mississippi, to assert his right to free movement in the state. Not long after setting off, he was felled and hospitalized by gunshot wounds. King and other civil rights leaders declared their intent to continue the march. New SNCC chair Stokely Carmichael subsequently used the march to publicize the organization's more radical departure, away from integration to an embrace of black nationalism and separatism, and away from non-violence to an advocacy of armed self-defence (see Chapter 5 for more discussion on this topic). This stance crystallized in the slogan of 'black power', which Carmichael popularized on the march.

King's thoughts on the 1966 Meredith March Against Fear and the emergence of black power can be found in Chapter 2 of his book *Where Do We Go From Here?* (1967). Stokely Carmichael and Charles V. Hamilton, *Black Power* (1967), give an introduction to what they see as the various meanings of black power in their co-authored book on the subject. Timothy B. Tyson, *Radio Free Dixie* (1999), makes the important point that figures like NAACP leader Robert F. Williams in North Carolina predated the emergence of black power in many ways, not least in staunchly advocating armed self-defence. William L. Van Deburg, *New Day in Babylon* (1992), provides a comprehensive analysis of black power in its broadest dimensions. Although African American leader Malcolm X was assassinated in 1965, his influence on SNCC and the black power movement was significant. Chapter 6 examines X's career as a point of comparison with King's leadership.

Fewer studies exist on King's final and more radical years from 1965 to 1968, a point that is explored further in Chapter 8. During this period, King's focus began to shift from civil rights to human rights, and from desegregation and voting rights to economic issues. King's April 1967 'Beyond Vietnam' speech at the Riverside Church in New York delivered an unequivocal statement against the war after several years of wavering on speaking out. It marked a final, decisive break with the Johnson administration. The studies of King and the SCLC by Adam Fairclough and David Garrow provide the most extensive discussion on King's stand against the Vietnam War to date. Simon Hall, *Peace and Freedom* (2005), examines the intersection between the civil rights and antiwar movements in the 1960s.

King and the SCLC's planned 1968 Poor People's campaign, which called for an interracial march of the poor on Washington DC and for mass civil disobedience, is covered in Gerald D. McKnight, *The Last Crusade* (1998), which highlights the FBI's harassment of King and its attempts to disrupt the march. Joan Turner Biefuss, *At the River I Stand* (1985), documents the issues and events in the 1968 Memphis sanitation workers' strike, the last community campaign that King was involved in before his assassination. A same-titled documentary of events directed by David Appleby, Allison Graham and Steven Ross (1993) is also extremely useful. Michael Honey (ed.), *Black Workers Remember* (1999) contains a chapter of oral histories by African American Memphis workers involved with the strike, and places that particular event within the wider context of the intersection of African American unionism and civil rights. King's assassination in Memphis while supporting the union workers has been the subject of much controversy and many conspiracy theories as Chapter 9 explains. Equally contentious, as Chapter 10 demonstrates, have been efforts to commemorate King since 1968.

Despite the attention given to Martin Luther King, Jr and the SCLC by historians of the civil rights movement, a number of gaps still remain. Many key advisors to King and influential members of the SCLC such as Stanley Levison, James Bevel, Wyatt Tee Walker, James M. Lawson and Dorothy Cotton, still lack dedicated studies. Critical campaigns such as Albany have yet to be scrutinized in any great depth or detail. Although recent works have gone some way in correcting the neglect of King's later years from 1965 to 1968, there is still too little thorough investigation of them, and in particular of King's stance on the Vietnam War and the issues surrounding the Poor People's campaign. King's formative years after the Montgomery bus boycott from 1957 to 1959 also remain relatively overlooked. Most studies of King's thought and culture have tended to focus quite narrowly on the originality of King's thought and the roots of King's influences. Far fewer studies have expanded upon King's ideas, influences and tactics, and located these within the wider context of the civil rights movement. Themes such as the role of religion and the use of non-violence are the most obvious fertile ground for further study. Surprisingly little has been written on King and the media, particularly given its importance in his campaigns. Richard Lentz, *Symbols, the News Magazines and Martin Luther King, Jr*, (Baton Rouge, LA: Louisiana State University Press, 1990), and Brian Ward, *Radio and the Struggle for Civil Rights in the South*, offer indicative starting points. Essays in Brian Ward (ed.), *Media, Culture and the Modern African American Freedom Struggle* (Gainesville, FL: University Press of Florida, 2001) touch upon popular representations of King and the movement in songs, films, art and literature, areas that have also received relatively little study.

Thus, as movement scholarship continues to expand beyond the scope of King, and to chart new territory in the history of the struggle for African American freedom and equality, there are still plenty of gaps in our existing knowledge and understanding of King and his role in the movement left to explore.

2 Leadership: National and Local Perspectives

Introduction

Questions of leadership are often central to the controversies and debates involving Martin Luther King, Jr. The two selections in this chapter, published over thirty years apart, were written by people of two different generations of movement scholarship and movement activism. August Meier, the author of the first selection, was one of the earliest pioneering white scholars to write on what was then termed 'Negro History' when he graduated with a PhD from Columbia University in New York City in 1957. His thesis laid the groundwork for the publication of his first book, *Negro Thought in America 1880–1915: Racial Ideologies in the Age of Booker T. Washington* (Ann Arbor: University of Michigan Press, 1964). Meier's writings reflect an interest in pre-1960s African American thought and activism. By contrast, African American scholar Clayborne Carson is a product of the movements of the 1960s. This is reflected in his works, which have examined topics such as King, SNCC and Malcolm X. Both Meier's and Carson's scholarship is influenced by their participation in the movements and the events that they write about, an important dimension to the historiography of the civil rights movement and other subjects of recent history.

Given the passage of time between the two essays, there are some striking similarities and agreements which usefully indicate the consensus among historians about the centrally defining aspects of King's leadership. Principally, these are: King's charismatic style of leadership; King's foundations in the African American Southern Baptist Church tradition; King's use of non-violent direct action as protest tactic; King's oratorical skill; King's ability to articulate African American concerns effectively both to African American and to white (mainly northern and liberal) audiences; and King's ability to mediate between different groups and interests within the civil rights movement.

Despite these points of agreement there are also discernible differences. Crucially, the two essays reflect a shifting emphasis in approach to civil rights history between the 1960s and the 1980s. Meier's essay takes a more national-oriented 'top-down' approach to the movement, emphasizing King's ability to act as a negotiator with white power brokers. It is King's 'uniqueness' of talent that is here recognized as being influential. Such an analysis tends towards a model of the civil rights movement which interprets its principal success as the ability to engage the federal government in its cause and to pass national legislation to end legally sanctioned racial discrimination. According to this view, the national legislation began to transform racial practices at a local level that in turn changed the lives of African Americans (mainly in the southern states) on a day-to-day basis. The key triumphs for the movement from this perspective are the passage of the 1964 Civil Rights Act which, among other things, outlawed segregation in public accommodations and facilities, and the passage of the 1965 Voting Rights Act, which removed obstacles to African Americans exercising a free vote and provided federal protection and assistance at the polls in a number of southern states.

Two further points are worthwhile noting about Meier's essay, both of which relate to the fact that it was published in 1965. Firstly, Meier is very forthright about what he sees as King's flaws and shortcomings, as well as King's strengths and abilities. Within a few years after King's 1968 assassination his status as a martyred hero of the movement meant that criticism of his leadership became much more muted. Secondly, Meier tends to emphasize the 'conservative' part of the 'conservative militant' label he ascribes to King. However, as Chapter 8 of this book highlights, King took a more radical stand during the period between 1965 and 1968. It should be borne in mind that Meier's analysis covers only those years up to 1965 and that he was not in a position to view King's career with the benefit of totalizing hindsight.

Carson's selection does have the benefit of hindsight, but it is also shaped by the time in which it was written. Carson writes within a shifting historiographical context that has moved from a national-oriented 'top-down' analysis of the movement to a local-oriented 'bottom-up' approach. Carson sees King's strength lying in his ability to 'mobilize black community resources' rather than to negotiate with influential whites. Instead of being in the possession of 'unique' skills, King is viewed as being 'representative' of local, grassroots African American leadership. Carson claims that King was therefore not necessarily a decisive shaping factor in the civil rights movement and that, moreover, 'If King had never lived, the black struggle would have followed a course of development similar to the one it did.' The whole emphasis of the local-oriented 'bottom-up' approach is based upon a different conception of the civil rights movement than the national-oriented 'top-down' approach. The 'bottom-up' approach insists that the civil rights movement was built upon a multiplicity of leaders and movements at a local level that sustained pressure on whites by mobilizing their own community resources to successfully bring about change. According to this perspective, it was these points of local pressure that drove the movement's success. It contends that although national legislation was important to local change, it was participation in local struggles and the transformative effects this had on individuals and their sense of their own capacity to resist racism and discrimination that lay at the very heart of the movement.

The historiographical debates over 'top-down' versus 'bottom-up' models of the civil rights movement are rooted in debates which unfolded in the movement during the 1960s. King and the SCLC often appeared to be more wedded to the 'top-down' approach. With limited resources, a great deal of store was placed in King's charismatic leadership and set pieces of high profile protest to place pressure on the federal government for change. SNCC, with a committed cadre of volunteers, was drawn to a 'bottom-up' grassroots mobilization strategy of participatory democracy and community empowerment. It argued that this approach could sustain change in local communities far better in the longer term by teaching and training local people to take action and responsibility for themselves rather than waiting for and relying upon a charismatic leader to act on their behalf. Thus Ella Baker, a key figure in the formation of SNCC and the development of its philosophy of grassroots community organizing, later declared: 'The movement made Martin rather than Martin making the movement.'

While it is important to understand the very real differences and distinctions between the national-oriented 'top-down' and local-oriented 'bottom-up' approaches to the civil rights movement, it is equally important to understand their interrelated and often interdependent nature as well. Despite the heated debates, genuine differences and direct competition between King's SCLC and SNCC, there was also a great deal of consensus, similarity, and practical cooperation between the two as well.

Questions for Discussion

1. How does participation in events by historians influence the way they write about those events? Does it provide them with better insight? Does it make them less objective?

2. Assess the advantages and disadvantages of viewing the civil rights movement from a national-oriented 'top-down' perspective.

3. Assess the advantages and disadvantages of viewing the civil rights movement from a local-oriented 'bottom-up' perspective.

4. Was King a man of 'unique' talents or was he simply 'representative' of wider movement leadership? You might like to consider this question after reading this chapter and then return to it again once you have read all of the chapters in this book.

Further Reading

One of the best starting points on King and leadership is a special edition of the *Journal of American History* 74:2 (September 1987): 436–81 which contains 'A Round Table: Martin Luther King Jr' where essays by five scholars, including Carson's selection in this chapter, look at different aspects of King's leadership. There are also a number of relevant essays on the subject in David J. Garrow (ed), *Martin Luther King, Jr: Civil Rights Leader, Theologian, Orator (Three Volumes)* (Brooklyn, NY: Carlson Publishing, 1989). The biographies listed in the Bibliography provide an analysis of King's leadership throughout his career.

Among August Meier's most influential works are: with Francis C. Broderick (ed.), *Negro Protest Thought in the Twentieth Century* (Indianapolis, IN: Bobbs-Merrill, 1965); all of the following co-written with Elliott Rudwick, *CORE: A Study in the Civil Rights Movement, 1942–1968* (New York: Oxford University Press, 1973); *Along the Color Line: Explorations of the Black Experience* (Urbana, IL: University of Illinois Press, 1976); and *Black Detroit and the Rise of the UAW* (New York: Oxford University Press, 1979). Meier also wrote a useful overview of the development of Black History as a field of study, with Elliott Rudwick, *Black History and the Historical Profession, 1915–1980* (Urbana, IL: University of Illinois Press, 1986) and produced a retrospective on his own career, *A White Scholar and the Black Community, 1945–1965: Essays and Reflections* (Amherst, MA: University of Massachusetts Press, 1992). Meier died in 2003.

For Carson's work, see the output of the King Papers Project detailed in the Bibliography, as well as *In Struggle: SNCC and the Black Awakening of the 1960s* (Cambridge, MA.: Harvard University Press, 1981) and, with David Gellen, *Malcolm X: The FBI File* (New York: Carroll and Graff, 1991).

The 'bottom-up' approach to the movement is most evident in the popularity of community studies over the past quarter of a century as a tool for examining local movements. Such studies include: William H. Chafe, *Civilities and Civil Rights: Greensboro, North Carolina and the Black*

Struggle for Freedom (New York: Oxford University Press, 1980); Robert J. Norrell, *Reaping the Whirlwind: The Civil Rights Movement in Tuskegee* (New York: Alfred A. Knopf, 1985); David R. Colburn, *Racial Change and Community Crisis: St Augustine, Florida, 1877–1980* (New York: Columbia University Press, 1985); John Dittmer, *Local People: The Struggle For Civil Rights in Mississippi* (Urbana, IL: University of Illinois Press, 1994); Charles M. Payne, *I've Got the Light of Freedom: The Organizing Tradition and the Mississippi Freedom Struggle* (Berkeley, CA: University of California Press, 1995); Adam Fairclough, *Race and Democracy: The Civil Rights Struggle in Louisiana, 1915–1972* (Athens, GA: University of Georgia Press, 1995); Glenn T. Eskew, *But for Birmingham: The Local and National Movements in the Civil Rights Struggle* (Chapel Hill, NC: University of North Carolina Press, 1997); Abel A. Bartley, *Keeping the Faith: Race, Politics and Social Development in Jacksonville, Florida, 1940–1970* (Westport, CT: Greenwood Press, 2000); Stephen G. N. Tuck, *Beyond Atlanta: The Struggle for Racial Equality in Georgia, 1940–1980,* (Athens, GA: University of Georgia Press, 2001); John A. Kirk, *Redefining the Color Line: Black Activism in Little Rock, Arkansas, 1940–1970* (Gainesville, FL: University Press of Florida, 2002); Cynthia Griggs Fleming, *In the Shadow of Selma: The Continuing Struggle for Civil Rights in the Rural South* (Lanham, MD: Rowman and Littlefield, 2004); J. Todd Moye, *Let the People Decide: Black Freedom and White Resistance Movements in Sunflower County, Mississippi, 1945–1986* (Chapel Hill, NC: University of North Carolina Press, 2004); Andrew M. Manis, *Macon Black and White: An Unutterable Separation in the American Century* (Macon, GA: Mercer University Press and the Tubman African American Museum, 2004); Bobby L. Lovett, *The Civil Rights Movement in Tennessee: A Narrative History* (Knoxville, TN: University of Tennessee Press, 2005); and Peter F. Lau, *Democracy Rising: South Carolina and the Fight for Black Equality since 1865* (Lexington, KY: University Press of Kentucky, 2006).

On the Role of Martin Luther King

August Meier

The phenomenon that is Martin Luther King consists of a number of striking paradoxes. The Nobel Prize winner is accepted by the outside world as *the* leader of the nonviolent direct action movement, but he is criticized by many activists within the movement. He is criticized for what appears, at

From *New Politics* 4 (Winter 1965): 52–9.

times, as indecisiveness, and more often denounced for a tendency to accept compromise. Yet, in the eyes of most Americans, both black and white, he remains the symbol of militant direct action. So potent is this symbol of King as direct actionist, that a new myth is arising about his historic role. The real credit for developing and projecting the techniques and philosophy of nonviolent direct action in the civil rights arena must be given to the Congress of Racial Equality which was founded in 1942, more than a dozen years before the Montgomery bus boycott projected King into international fame. And the idea of mass action by Negroes themselves to secure redress of their grievances must, in large part, be ascribed to the vision of A. Philip Randolph, architect of the March on Washington Movement during World War II. Yet, as we were told in Montgomery on March 25, 1965, King and his followers now assert, apparently without serious contradiction, that a new type of civil rights strategy was born at Montgomery in 1955 under King's auspices.

In a movement in which respect is accorded in direct proportion to the number of times one has been arrested, King appears to keep the number of times he goes to jail to a minimum. In a movement in which successful leaders are those who share in the hardships of their followers, in the risks they take, in the beatings they receive, in the length of time they spend in jail, King tends to leave prison for other important engagements, rather than remaining there and suffering with his followers. In a movement in which leadership ordinarily devolves upon persons who mix democratically with their followers, King remains isolated and aloof. In a movement which prides itself on militancy and 'no compromise' with racial discrimination or with the white 'power structure,' King maintains close relationships with, and appears to be influenced by, Democratic presidents and their emissaries, seems amenable to compromises considered by some half a loaf or less, and often appears willing to postpone or avoid a direct confrontation in the streets.

King's career has been characterized by failures that, in the larger sense, must be accounted triumphs. The buses in Montgomery were desegregated only after lengthy judicial proceedings conducted by the NAACP Legal Defense Fund secured a favorable decision from the U.S. Supreme Court. Nevertheless, the events in Montgomery were a triumph for direct action, and gave this tactic a popularity unknown when identified solely with CORE. King's subsequent major campaigns – in Albany, Georgia; in Danville, Virginia; in Birmingham, Alabama; and in St. Augustine, Florida – ended as failures or with only token accomplishments in those cities. But each of them, chiefly because of his presence, dramatically focused national and international attention on the plight of the Southern Negro, thereby facilitating overall progress. In Birmingham, in particular, demonstrations which fell short of their local goals were directly responsible for a major Federal Civil Rights Act. Essentially, this pattern of local failure and national victory was recently enacted at Selma, Alabama.

King is ideologically committed to disobeying unjust laws and court orders, in the Gandhian tradition, but generally he follows a policy of not disobeying Federal Court orders. In his recent Montgomery speech, he expressed a crude, neo-Marxist interpretation of history romanticizing the Populist movement as a genuine union of black and white common people, ascribing race prejudice to capitalists playing white workers against black. Yet, in practice, he is amenable to compromise with the white bourgeois political and economic Establishment. More important, King enunciates a superficial and eclectic philosophy and by virtue of it he has profoundly awakened the moral conscience of America.

In short, King can be described as a 'Conservative Militant.'

In this combination of militancy with conservatism and caution, of righteousness with respectability, lies the secret of King's enormous success.

Certain important civil rights leaders have dismissed King's position as the product of publicity generated by the mass communications media. But his can be said of the successes of the civil rights nonviolent action movement generally. Without publicity it is hard to conceive that much progress would have been made. In fact, contrary to the official nonviolent direct action philosophy, demonstrations have secured their results not by changing the hearts of the oppressors through a display of nonviolent love, but through the national and international pressures generated by the publicity arising from mass arrests and incidents of violence. And no one has employed this strategy of securing publicity through mass arrests and precipitating violence from white hoodlums and law enforcement officers more than King himself. King abhors violence; as at Selma, for example, he constantly retreats from situations that might result in the deaths of his followers. But he is precisely most successful when, contrary to his deepest wishes, his demonstrations precipitate violence from Southern whites against Negro and white demonstrators. We need only cite Birmingham and Selma to illustrate this point.

Publicity alone does not explain the durability of King's image, or why he remains for the rank and file of whites and blacks alike, the symbol of the direct action movement, the nearest thing to a charismatic leader that the civil rights movement has ever had. At the heart of King's continuing influence and popularity are two facts. First, better than anyone else, he articulates the aspirations of Negroes who respond to the cadence of his addresses, his religious phraseology and manner of speaking, and the vision of his dream for them and for America. King has intuitively adopted the style of the old fashioned Negro Baptist preacher and transformed it into a new art form; he has, indeed, restored oratory to its place among the arts. Second, he communicates Negro aspirations to white America more effectively than anyone else. His religious terminology and manipulation of the Christian symbols of love and non-resistance are partly responsible for his appeal among whites. To talk in terms of Christianity, love, non-violence is reassuring to the mentality of white America. At the same time, the very superficialities of his philosophy – that rich and eclectic amalgam of Jesus, Hegel, Gandhi and others as outlined in his *Stride Toward Freedom* – makes him appear intellectually profound to the superficially educated middle class white American. Actually, if he were a truly profound religious thinker, like Tillich or Niebuhr, his influence would of necessity be limited to a select audience. But by uttering moral cliches, the Christian pieties, in a magnificent display of oratory, King becomes enormously effective.

If his success with Negroes is largely due to the style of his utterance, his success with whites is a much more complicated matter. For one thing, he unerringly knows how to exploit to maximum effectiveness their growing feeling of guilt. King, of course, is not unique in attaining fame and popularity among whites through playing upon their guilt feelings. James Baldwin is the most conspicuous example of a man who has achieved success with this formula. The incredible fascination which the Black Muslims have for white people, and the posthumous near-sanctification of Malcolm X by many naive whites (in addition to many Negroes whose motivations are, of course, very different), must in large part be attributed to the same source. But King goes beyond this. With intuitive, but extraordinary skill, he not only castigates whites for their sins but, in contrast to angry young writers like Baldwin, he explicitly states his belief in their salvation. Not only will direct action bring fulfillment of the 'American Dream' to Negroes but the Negroes' use of direct action will help whites to live up to their Christian and democratic values; it will purify, cleanse and heal the sickness in white society. Whites will benefit as well as Negroes. He has faith that the white man will redeem himself. Negroes must not hate whites, but love them. In this manner, King first arouses the guilt feelings of whites, and then relieves them – though always leaving the lingering feeling in his white listeners that they should support his nonviolent crusade. Like a Greek tragedy, King's performance provides an extraordinary catharsis for the white listener.

King thus gives white men the feeling that he is their good friend, that he poses no threat to them. It is interesting to note that this was the same feeling white men received from Booker T. Washington, the noted early twentieth Century accommodator. Both men stressed their faith in the white man; both expressed the belief that the white man could be brought to accord Negroes their rights. Both stressed the importance of whites recognizing the rights of Negroes for the moral health and well-being of white society. Like King, Washington had an extraordinary following among whites. Like King, Washington symbolized for most whites the whole program of Negro advancement. While there are important similarities in the functioning of both men vis-à-vis the community, needless to say, in most respects, their philosophies are in disagreement.

It is not surprising, therefore, to find that King is the recipient of contributions from organizations and individuals who fail to eradicate evidence of prejudice in their own backyards. For example, certain liberal trade union leaders who are philosophically committed to full racial equality, who feel the need to identify their organizations with the cause of militant civil rights, although they are unable to defeat racist elements in their unions, contribute hundreds of thousands of dollars to King's Southern Christian Leadership Conference (SCLC). One might attribute this phenomenon to the fact that SCLC works in the South rather than the North, but this is true also for SNCC which does not benefit similarly from union treasuries. And the fact is that ever since the college students started their sit-ins in 1960, it is SNCC which has been the real spearhead of direct action in most of the South, and has performed the lion's share of work in local communities, while SCLC has received most of the publicity and most of the money. However, while King provides a verbal catharsis for whites, leaving them feeling purified and comfortable, SNCC's uncompromising militancy makes whites feel less comfortable and less beneficent.

(The above is not to suggest that SNCC and SCLC are responsible for all, or nearly all, the direct action in the South. The NAACP has actively engaged in direct action, especially in Savannah under the leadership of W. W. Law, in South Carolina under I. DeQuincy Newman, and in Clarksdale, Mississippi, under Aaron Henry. The work of CORE – including most of the direct action in Louisiana, much of the nonviolent work in Florida and Mississippi, the famous Freedom Ride of 1961 – has been most important. In addition, one should note the work of SCLC affiliates, such as those in Lynchburg, Virginia, led by Reverend Virgil Wood; in Birmingham led by Reverend Fred Shuttlesworth, and in Savannah, by Hosea Williams.

(There are other reasons for SNCC's lesser popularity with whites than King's. These are connected with the great changes that have occurred in SNCC since it was founded in 1960, changes reflected in the half-jocular epigram circulating in SNCC circles that the Student Nonviolent Coordinating Committee has now become the 'Non-Student Violent Non-Coordinating Committee.' The point is, however, that even when SNCC thrilled the nation in 1960–1961 with the student sit-ins that swept the South, it did not enjoy the popularity and financial support accorded to King.)

King's very tendencies toward compromise and caution, his willingness to negotiate and bargain with White House emissaries, his hesitancy to risk the precipitation of mass violence upon demonstrators, further endear him to whites. He appears to them a 'responsible' and 'moderate' man. To militant activists, King's failure to march past the State Police on that famous Tuesday morning outside Selma indicated either a lack of courage, or a desire to advance himself by currying Presidential favor. But King's shrinking from a possible bloodbath, his accession to the entreaties of the political Establishment, his acceptance of face-saving compromise in this, as in other instances, are fundamental to the particular role he is playing, and essential for achieving and sustaining his image as a leader of heroic moral stature in the eyes of white men. His caution and compromise keep open the channels of communication between the activists and the majority of the white community. In brief: King makes the nonviolent direct action movement respectable.

Of course, many, if not most, activists reject the notion that the movement should be made respectable. Yet, American history shows that for any reform movement to succeed, it must attain respectability. It must attract moderates, even conservatives, to its ranks. The March on Washington made direct action respectable; Selma made it fashionable. More than any other force, it is Martin Luther King who impressed the civil rights revolution on the American conscience and is attracting that great middle body of American public opinion to its support. It is this revolution of conscience that will undoubtedly lead fairly soon to the elimination of all violations of Negroes' constitutional rights, thereby creating the conditions for the economic and social changes that are necessary if we are to achieve full racial equality. This is not to deny the dangers to the civil rights movement in becoming respectable. Respectability, for example, encourages the attempts of political machines to capture civil rights organizations. Respectability can also become an end in itself, thereby dulling the cutting edge of its protest activities. Indeed, the history of the labor movement reveals how attaining respectability can produce loss of original purpose and character. These perils, however, do not contradict the importance of achieving respectability – even a degree of modishness – if racial equality is ever to be realized.

There is another side to the picture: King would be neither respected nor respectable if there were not more militant activists on his left, engaged in more radical forms of direct action. Without CORE and, especially, SNCC, King would appear 'radical' and irresponsible' rather than 'moderate' and 'respectable.'

King occupies a position of strategic importance as the 'vital center' within the civil rights movement. Though he has lieutenants who are far more militant and 'radical' than he is, SCLC acts, in effect, as the most cautious, deliberate and 'conservative' of the direct action groups because of his leadership. This permits King and the SCLC to function – almost certainly unintentionally – not only as an organ of communication with the Establishment and majority white public opinion, but as something of a bridge between the activist and more traditionalist or 'conservative' civil rights groups, as well. For example, it appears unlikely that the

Urban League and NAACP, which supplied most of the funds, would have participated in the 1963 March on Washington if King had not done so. Because King agreed to go along with SNCC and CORE, the NAACP found it mandatory to join if it was to maintain its image as a protest organization. King's identification with the March was also essential for securing the support of large numbers of white clergymen and their moderate followers. The March was the brainchild of the civil rights movement's ablest strategist and tactician, Bayard Rustin, and the call was issued by A. Philip Randolph. But it would have been a minor episode in the history of the civil rights movement without King's support.

Yet curiously enough, despite his charisma and international reputation, King thus far has been more a symbol than a power in the civil rights movement. Indeed his strength in the movement has derived less from an organizational base than from his symbolic role. Seven or eight years ago, one might have expected King to achieve an organizationally dominant position in the civil rights movement, at least in its direct action wing. The fact is that in the period after the Montgomery bus boycott, King developed no program and, it is generally agreed, revealed himself as an ineffective administrator who failed to capitalize upon his popularity among Negroes. In 1957, he founded SCLC to coordinate the work of direct action groups that had sprung up in Southern cities. Composed of autonomous units, usually led by Baptist ministers, SCLC does not appear to have developed an overall sense of direction or a program of real breadth and scope. Although the leaders of SCLC affiliates became the race leaders in their communities – displacing the established local conservative leadership of teachers, old-line ministers, businessmen – it is hard for an observer (who admittedly has not been close to SCLC) to perceive exactly what SCLC did before the 1960s except to advance the image and personality of King. King appeared not to direct but to float with the tide of militant direct action. For example, King did not supply the initiative for the bus boycott in Montgomery, but was pushed into the leadership by others, as he himself records in *Stride Toward Freedom*. Similarly, in the late Fifties and early Sixties, he appeared to let events shape his course. In the last two years, this has changed, but until the Birmingham demonstrations of 1963, King epitomized conservative militancy.

SCLC under King's leadership called the Raleigh Conference of April 1960 which gave birth to SNCC. Incredibly, within a year, the SNCC youth had lost their faith in the man they now satirically call 'De Lawd,' and had struck out on their own independent path. By that time, the Spring of 1961, King's power in the Southern direct action movement had been further curtailed by CORE's stunning Freedom Ride to Alabama and Mississippi.

The limited extent of King's actual power in the civil rights movement was illustrated by the efforts made to invest King with the qualities of a Messiah during the recent ceremonies at the State Capitol in Montgomery. Reverend Abernathy's constant iteration of the theme that King is 'our Leader,' the Moses of the race, chosen by God, and King's claim that he originated the nonviolent direct action movement at Montgomery a decade ago, are all assertions that would have been superfluous if King's power in the movement was very substantial.

It is, of course, no easier today that it has been in the past few years to predict the course of the Negro protest movement, and it is always possible that the current state of affairs may change quite abruptly. It is conceivable that the ambitious program that SCLC is now projecting – both in Southern voter registration and in Northern urban direct action programs – may give it a position of commanding importance in civil rights. As a result of the recent demonstrations in Selma and Montgomery, King's prestige is now higher than ever. At the same time, the nature of CORE and NAACP direct action activities at the moment has created a programmatic vacuum which SCLC may be able to exploit. Given this convergence of circumstances, SCLC leaders may be able to establish an organizational base upon which to build a power commensurate with the symbolic position of their president.

It is indeed fortunate that King has not obtained a predominance of power in the movement commensurate with his prestige. For today, as in the past, a diversity of approaches is necessary. Needed in the movement are those who view the struggle chiefly as a conflict situation, in which the power of demonstrations, the power of Negroes, will force recognition of the race's humanity and citizenship rights, and the achievement of equality. Equally needed are those who see the movement's strategy to be chiefly one of capitalizing on the basic consensus of values in American society by awakening the conscience of the white man to the contradiction between his professions and the facts of discrimination. And just as necessary to the movement as both of these are those who operate skillfully, recognizing and yet exploiting the deeply held American belief that compromise among competing interest groups is the best *modus operandi* in public life.

King is unique in that he maintains a delicate balance among all three of these basic strategy assumptions. The traditional approaches of the Urban League (conciliation of the white businessmen) and of the NAACP (most pre-eminently appeals to the courts and appeals to the sense of fair play in the American public) basically attempted to exploit the consensus in American values. It would of course be a gross oversimplification to say that the Urban League and NAACP strategies are based simply on attempting to capitalize on the consensus of values, while SNCC and CORE act simply as if the situation were purely a conflict situation.

Implicit in the actions of all civil rights organizations are both sets of assumptions – even where people are not conscious of the theoretical assumptions under which, in effect, they operate. The NAACP especially encompasses a broad spectrum of strategies and types of activities, ranging from time-tested court procedures to militant direct action. Sophisticated CORE activists know very well when a judicious compromise is necessary or valuable. But I hold that King is in the middle, acting in effect as if he were basing his strategy upon all three assumptions described above. He maintains a delicate balance between a purely moral appeal and a militant display of power. He talks of the power of the bodies of Negro demonstrators in the streets, but unlike CORE and SNCC activists, he accepts compromises at times that consist of token improvements, and calls them impressive victories. More than any of the other groups, King and SCLC can, up to this point at least, be described as exploiting all three tactical assumptions to an approximately equal degree. King's continued success, I suspect, will depend to a considerable degree upon the difficult feat of maintaining his position at the 'vital center' of the civil rights movement.

Viewed from another angle King's failure to achieve a position of power on a level with his prestige is fortunate because rivalries between personalities and organizations remain an essential ingredient of the dynamics of the movement and a precondition for its success as each current tries to out do the others in effectiveness and in maintaining a good public image. Without this competitive stimulus, the civil rights revolution would slow down.

I have already noted that one of King's functions is to serve as a bridge between the militant and conservative wings of the movement. In addition, by gathering support for SCLC, he generates wider support for CORE and SNCC, as well. The most striking example is the recent series of demonstrations in Selma where SNCC had been operating for nearly two years with only moderate amounts of publicity before King chose that city as his own target. As usual, it was King's presence that focused world attention on Selma. In the course of subsequent events, the rift between King and SNCC assumed the proportions of a serious conflict. Yet people who otherwise would have been hesitant to support SNCC's efforts, even people who had become disillusioned with certain aspects of SNCC's policies during the Mississippi Summer Project of 1964, were drawn to demonstrate in Selma and Montgomery. Moreover, although King received the major share of credit for the demonstrations, it seems likely that in the controversy between King and SNCC, the latter emerged with more power and influence in the civil rights movement than ever before. It is now possible that the Administration will, in the future, regard SNCC as more of a force to be reckoned with than it has heretofore.

Major dailies like the *New York Times* and the *Washington Post*, basically sympathetic to civil rights and racial equality, though more gradualist than the activist organizations, have congratulated the nation upon its good fortune in having a 'responsible and moderate' leader like King at the head of the nonviolent action movement (though they overestimate his power and underestimate the symbolic nature of his role). It would be more appropriate to congratulate the civil rights movement for *its* good fortune in having as its symbolic leader a man like King. The fact that he has more prestige than power; the fact that he not only criticizes whites but explicitly believes in their redemption; his ability to arouse creative tension combined with his inclination to shrink from carrying demonstrations to the point where major bloodshed might result; the intellectual simplicity of his philosophy; his tendency to compromise and exert caution, even his seeming indecisiveness on some occasions; the sparing use he makes of going to or staying in jail himself; his friendship with the man in the White House – all are essential to the role he plays, and invaluable for the success of the movement. It is well, of course, that not all civil rights leaders are cut of the same cloth – that King is unique among them. Like Randolph, who functions very differently, King is really an institution. His most important function, I believe, is that of effectively communicating Negro aspirations to white people, of making non-violent direct action respectable in the eyes of the white majority. In addition, he functions within the movement by occupying a vital center position between its 'conservative' and 'radical' wings, by symbolizing direct action and attracting people to participate in it without dominating either the civil rights movement or its activist wing. Viewed in this context, traits that many activists criticize in King actually function not as sources of weakness, but as the foundations of his strength.

Martin Luther King, Jr: Charismatic Leadership in a Mass Struggle

Clayborne Carson

The legislation to establish Martin Luther King, Jr.'s birthday as a federal holiday provided official recognition of King's greatness, but it remains the responsibility of those of us who study and carry on King's work to define his historical significance. Rather than engaging in officially approved nostalgia, our remembrance of King should reflect the reality of his complex

From *Journal of American History* 74: 2 (September 1987): 448–54.

and multifaceted life. Biographers, theologians, political scientists, sociologists, social psychologists, and historians have given us a sizable literature of King's place in the Afro-American protest tradition, his role in the modern black freedom struggle, and his eclectic ideas regarding nonviolent activism. Although King scholars may benefit from and may stimulate the popular interest in King generated by the national holiday, many will find themselves uneasy participants in annual observances to honor an innocuous, carefully cultivated image of King as a black heroic figure.

The King depicted in serious scholarly works is far too interesting to be encased in such a didactic legend. King was a controversial leader who challenged authority and who once applauded what he called 'creative maladjusted nonconformity.'[1] He should not be transformed into a simplistic image designed to offend no one – a black counterpart to the static, heroic myths that have embalmed George Washington as the Father of His Country and Abraham Lincoln as the Great Emancipator.

One aspect of the emerging King myth has been the depiction of him in the mass media, not only as the preeminent leader of the civil rights movement, but also as the initiator and sole indispensible element in the southern black struggles of the 1950s and 1960s. As in other historical myths, a Great Man is seen as the decisive factor in the process of social change, and the unique qualities of a leader are used to explain major historical events. The King myth departs from historical reality because it attributes too much to King's exceptional qualities as a leader and too little to the impersonal, large-scale social factors that made it possible for King to display his singular abilities on a national stage. Because the myth emphasizes the individual at the expense of the black movement, it not only exaggerates King's historical importance but also distorts his actual, considerable contribution to the movement.

A major example of this distortion has been the tendency to see King as a charismatic figure who single-handedly directed the course of the civil rights movement through the force of his oratory. The charismatic label, however, does not adequately define King's role in the southern black struggle. The term *charisma* has traditionally been used to describe the godlike, magical qualities possessed by certain leaders. Connotations of the term have changed, of course, over the years. In our more secular age, it has lost many of its religious connotations and now refers to a wide range of leadership styles that involve the capacity to inspire – usually through oratory – emotional bonds between leaders and followers. Arguing that King was not a charismatic leader, in the broadest sense of the term, becomes somewhat akin to arguing that he was not a Christian, but emphasis on King's charisma obscures other important aspects of his role in the black movement. To be sure, King's oratory was exceptional and many people saw King as a divinely inspired leader, but King did not receive and did not want the kind of unquestioning support that is often associated with charismatic leaders. Movement activists instead saw him as the most prominent among many outstanding movement strategists, tacticians, ideologues, and institutional leaders.

King undoubtedly recognized that charisma was one of many leadership qualities at his disposal, but he also recognized that charisma was not a sufficient basis for leadership in a modern political movement enlisting numerous self-reliant leaders. Moreover, he rejected aspects of the charismatic model that conflicted with his sense of his own limitations. Rather than exhibiting unwavering confidence in his power and wisdom, King was a leader full of self-doubts, keenly aware of his own limitations and human weaknesses. He was at times reluctant to take on the responsibilities suddenly and unexpectedly thrust upon him. During the Montgomery bus boycott, for example, when he worried about threats to his life and to the lives of his wife and child, he was overcome with fear rather than confident and secure in his leadership role. He was able to carry on only after acquiring an enduring understanding of his dependence on a personal God who promised never to leave him alone.[2]

Moreover, emphasis on King's charisma conveys the misleading notion of a movement held together by spellbinding speeches and blind faith rather than by a complex blend of rational and emotional bonds. King's charisma did not place him above criticism. Indeed, he was never able to gain mass support for his notion of nonviolent struggle as a way of life, rather than simply a tactic. Instead of viewing himself as the embodiment of widely held Afro-American racial values, he willingly risked his popularity among blacks through his steadfast advocacy of nonviolent strategies to achieve radical social change.

He was a profound and provocative public speaker as well as an emotionally powerful one. Only those unfamiliar with the Afro-American clergy would assume that his oratorical skills were unique, but King set himself apart from other black preachers through his use of traditional black Christian idiom to advocate unconventional political ideas. Early in his life King became disillusioned with the unbridled emotionalism associated with his father's religious fundamentalism, and, as a thirteen year old, he questioned the bodily resurrection of Jesus in his Sunday school class.[3] His subsequent search for an intellectually satisfying religious faith conflicted with the emphasis on emotional expressiveness that pervades evangelical religion. His preaching manner was rooted in the traditions of the black church, while his subject matter, which often reflected his wide-ranging philosophical interests, distinguished him from other preachers who relied on rhetorical devices that manipulated the emotions of listeners. King used charisma as a tool for mobilizing black communities, but he always used it in the context of other forms of intellectual and political leadership suited to a movement containing many strong leaders.

Recently, scholars have begun to examine the black struggle as a locally based mass movement, rather than simply a reform movement led by national civil rights leaders.[4] The new orientation in scholarship indicates that King's role was different from that suggested in King-centered biographies and journalistic accounts.[5] King was certainly not the only significant leader of the civil rights movement, for sustained protest movements arose in many southern communities in which King had little or no direct involvement.

In Montgomery, for example, local black leaders such as E. D. Nixon, Rosa Parks, and Jo Ann Robinson started the bus boycott before King became the leader of the Montgomery Improvement Association. Thus, although King inspired blacks in Montgomery and black residents recognized that they were fortunate to have such a spokesperson, talented local leaders other than King played decisive roles in initiating and sustaining the boycott movement.

Similarly, the black students who initiated the 1960 lunch counter sit-ins admired King, but they did not wait for him to act before launching their own movement. The sit-in leaders who founded the Student Nonviolent Coordinating Committee (SNCC) became increasingly critical of King's leadership style, linking it to the feelings of dependency that often characterize the followers of charismatic leaders.[6] The essense of SNCC's approach to community organizing was to instill in local residents the confidence that they could lead their own struggles. A SNCC organizer failed if local residents became dependent on his or her presence; as the organizers put it, their job was to work themselves out of a job. Though King influenced the struggles that took place in the Black Belt regions of Mississippi, Alabama, and Georgia, those movements were also guided by self-reliant local leaders who occasionally called on King's oratorical skills to galvanize black protestors at mass meetings while refusing to depend on his presence.

If King had never lived, the black struggle would have followed a course of development similar to the one it did. The Montgomery bus boycott would have occurred, because King did not initiate it. Black students probably would have rebelled – even without King as a role model – for they had sources of tactical and ideological inspiration besides King. Mass activism in southern cities and voting rights efforts in the deep South were outgrowths of large-scale social and political forces, rather than simply consequences of the actions of a single leader. Though perhaps not as quickly and certainly not as peacefully nor with as universal a significance, the black movement would probably have achieved its major legislative victories without King's leadership, for the southern Jim Crow system was a regional anachronism, and the forces that undermined it were inexorable.

To what extent, then, did King's presence affect the movement? Answering that question requires us to look beyond the usual portrayal of the black struggle. Rather than seeing an amorphous mass of discontented blacks acting out strategies determined by a small group of leaders, we would recognize King as a major example of the local black leadership that emerged as black communities mobilized for sustained struggles. If not as dominant a figure as sometimes portrayed, the historical King was nevertheless a remarkable leader who acquired the respect and support of self-confident, grass-roots leaders, some of whom possessed charismatic qualities of their own. Directing attention to the other leaders who initiated and emerged from those struggles should not detract from our conception of King's historical significance; such movement-oriented research reveals King as a leader who stood out in a forest of tall trees.

King's major public speeches – particularly the 'I Have a Dream' speech – have received much attention, but his exemplary qualities were also displayed in countless strategy sessions with other activists and in meetings with government officials. King's success as a leader was based on his intellectual and moral cogency and his skill as a conciliator among movement activists who refused to be simply King's 'followers' or 'lieutenants.'

The success of the black movement required the mobilization of black communities as well as the transformation of attitudes in the surrounding society, and King's wide range of skills and attributes prepared him to meet the internal as well as the external demands of the movement. King understood the black world from a privileged position, having grown up in a stable family within a major black urban community; yet he also learned how to speak persuasively to the surrounding white world. Alone among the major civil rights leaders of his time, King could not only articulate black concerns to white audiences, but could also mobilize blacks through his day-to-day involvement in black community institutions and through his access to the regional institutional network of the black church. His advocacy of nonviolent activism gave the black movement invaluable positive press coverage, but his effectiveness as a protest leader derived mainly from his ability to mobilize black community resources.

Analyses of the southern movement that emphasize its nonrational aspects and expressive functions over its political character explain the black struggle as an emotional outburst by discontented blacks, rather than recognizing that the movement's strength and durability came from its mobilization of black community institutions, financial resources, and grass-roots leaders.[7] The values of southern blacks were profoundly and permanently transformed not only by King, but also by involvement in sustained protest activity and community-organizing efforts, through thousands of mass meetings, workshops, citizenship classes, freedom schools, and informal discussions. Rather than merely accepting guidance from above, southern blacks were resocialized as a result of their movement experiences.

Although the literature of the black struggle has traditionally paid litle attention to the intellectual content of black politics, movement activists of the 1960s made a profound, though often ignored, contribution to political thinking. King may have been born with rare potential, but his most significant leadership attributes were related to his immersion in, and contribution to, the intellectual ferment that has always been an essential part of Afro-American freedom struggles. Those who have written about King have too often assumed that his most important ideas were derived from outside the black struggle – from his academic training, his philosophical readings, or his acquaintance with Gandhian ideas. Scholars are only beginning to recognize the extent to which his attitudes and those of many other activists, white and black, were transformed through their involvement in a movement in which ideas disseminated from the bottom up as well as from the top down.

Although my assessment of King's role in the black struggles of his time reduces him to human scale, it also increases the possibility that others may recognize his qualities in themselves. Idolizing King lessens one's ability to exhibit some of his best attributes or, worse, encourages one to become a debunker, emphasizing King's flaws in order to lessen the inclination to exhibit his virtues. King himself undoubtedly feared that some who admired him would place too much faith in his ability to offer guidance and to overcome resistance, for he often publicly acknowledged his own limitations and mortality. Near the end of his life, King expressed his certainty that black people would reach the Promised Land whether or not he was with them. His faith was based on an awareness of the qualities that he knew he shared with all people. When he suggested his own epitaph, he asked not to be remembered for his exceptional achievements – his Nobel Prize and other awards, his academic accomplishments; instead, he wanted to be remembered for giving his life to serve others, for trying to be right on the war question, for trying to feed the hungry and clothe the naked, for trying to love and serve humanity. 'I want you to say that I tried to love and serve humanity.'[8] Those aspects of King's life did not require charisma or other superhuman abilities.

If King were alive today, he would doubtless encourage those who celebrate his life to recognize their responsibility to struggle as he did for a more just and peaceful world. He would prefer that the black movement be remembered not only as the scene of his own achievements, but also as a setting that brought out extraordinary qualities in many people. If he were to return, his oratory would be unsettling and intellectually challenging rather than remembered diction and cadences. He would probably be the unpopular social critic he was on the eve of the Poor People's Campaign rather than the object of national homage he became after his death. His basic message would be the same as it was when he was alive, for he did not bend with the changing political winds. He would talk of ending poverty and war and of building a just social order that would avoid the pitfalls of competitive capitalism and repressive communism. He would give scant comfort to those who condition their activism upon the appearance of another King, for he recognized the extent to which he was a product of the movement that called him to leadership.

The notion that appearances by Great Men (or Great Women) are necessary preconditions for the emergence of major movements for social changes reflects not only a poor understanding of history, but also a pessimistic view of the possibilities for future social change. Waiting for the Messiah is a human weakness that is unlikely to be rewarded more than once in a millennium. Studies of King's life offer support for an alternative optimistic belief that ordinary people can collectively improve their lives. Such studies demonstrate the capacity of social movements to transform participants for the better and to create leaders worthy of their followers.

Notes

1. Martin Luther King, Jr., speech at the University of California, Berkeley, tape recording, 17 May 1967, Martin Luther King, Jr., Papers Project (Stanford University, Stanford, CA).
2. Martin Luther King, Jr., described this episode, which occurred on the evening of 27 January 1956, in a remarkable speech delivered in September 1966. It is available on a phonograph record. Dr King's Entrance into the Civil Rights Movement. *Martin Luther King, Jr.: In Search of Freedom* (Mercury SR 61170).
3. Martin Luther King, Jr., 'An Autobiography of Religious Development' [*c*. 1950], Martin Luther King, Jr., Papers (Mugar Library, Boston University). In this paper, written for a college class, King commented: 'I guess I accepted Biblical studies uncritically until I was about twelve years old. But this uncritical attitude could not last long, for it was contrary to the very nature of my being.'
4. The new orientation is evident in William H. Chafe, *Civilities and Civil Rights: Greensboro. North Carolina, and the Black Struggle for Equality* (New York, 1980); David R. Colburn, *Racial Change and Community Crisis: St. Augustine, Florida, 1877–1980* (New York, 1985); Robert J. Norrell, *Reaping the Whirlwind: The Civil Rights Movement in Tuskegee* (New York, 1985); and John R. Salter. *Jackson, Mississippi: An American Chronicle of Struggle and Schism* (Hicksville, NY 1979).
5. The tendency to view the struggle from King's perspective is evident in the most thoroughly researched of the King biographies, despite the fact that the book concludes with Ella Baker's assessment: 'The movement made Martin rather than Martin making the movement.' See David J. Garrow, *Bearing the Cross: Martin Luther King. Jr., and the Southern Christian Leadership Conference* (New York; 1980), esp 625. See also David L. Lewis, *King: A Biography* (Urbana, 1978); Stephen B. Oates, *Let the Trumpet Sound* (New York, 1982); and Adam Fairclough, *To Redeem the Soul of America. The Southern Christian Leadership Conference and Martin Luther King, Jr.* (Athens, 1987).

6. See Clayborne Carson, *In Struggle: SNCC and the Black Awakening of the 1960s* (Cambridge, MA, 1981); and Howard Zinn, *SNCC: The New Abolitionists* (Boston, MA, 1965).
7. For incisive critiques of traditional psychological and sociological analyses of the modern black struggle, see Doug McAdam, *Political Process and the Development of Black Insurgency, 1930–1970* (Chicago, 1982); and Aldon D. Morris. *Origins of the Civil Rights Movement: Black Communities Organizing for Change* (New York, 1984).
8. James M. Washington (ed.), *A Testament of Hope: The Essential Writings of Martin Luther King, Jr.* (San Francisco, 1986), p. 267.

3 Influences: African American Church, White Academy

Introduction

This chapter and the next are closely linked in that they both look at different aspects of the larger debate about King's ideas and their expression. In this chapter, the focus is on how African American traditions transmitted through family and church, and white traditions transmitted through academic study, impacted upon King. It is now generally accepted that African American traditions were more influential in shaping King's development, but how historians arrived at this consensus, and exactly how historians identify these influences, remain important to King scholarship. In identifying King's influences, the question of which primary sources historians use has been crucial. Both of the selections in this chapter address this point and it is examined in greater detail in the next chapter.

In Chapter 6 of his first book, *Stride Toward Freedom* (1958), King outlined his intellectual debts accrued through his studies at Morehouse College (1944–8), Crozer Theological Seminary (1948–51) and Boston University (1951–55). King cited a string of mainly white Western activists, writers, philosophers and theologians as his intellectual influences. Early scholarship followed King's prompts and traced the ways in which the various thinkers he had cited shaped his movement activism. One of the earliest and most accomplished of these studies is Kenneth L. Smith and Ira G. Zepp, Jr, *Search for the Beloved Community: The Thinking of Martin Luther King, Jr* (1974). A more recent update is John J. Ansbro, *Martin Luther King, Jr: The Making of a Mind* (1983).

In the first selection in this chapter, David J. Garrow provides a useful synopsis of Smith and Zepp's study and its conclusions, together with his own insightful commentary on their findings. From the outset, he raises the problem of primary sources, noting that King's books were heavily ghost-written (that is, penned by other people under King's name). Garrow questions how accurately these books reflect King's own thoughts and ideas. He also points out that many studies of King's intellectual influences have focused more upon his formal academic studies rather than the informal influences of family and friends, and church and religion. As a result they provide a skewed picture of King's intellectual development.

In tracing King's academic career, Garrow notes that his early studies at Morehouse were relatively undistinguished. Only when King entered Crozer Theological Seminary did he begin to take his studies more seriously. Garrow moves on to provide a useful summary introduction to the various influences often cited as making an impact upon King. These include, for example, George W. Davis's 'evangelic liberalism'; Walter Rauschenbusch's 'social gospel'; Karl Marx's critique of capitalism; Mohandas K. Gandhi's 'non-violent satyagraha'; Reinhold Neibuhr's 'Christian realism'; Edgar S. Brightman's 'personalism'; and G. W. F. Hegel's 'dialectical method' of analysis.

Garrow makes the important point that as well as neglecting King's influences prior to his formal schooling, many studies have also tended to overlook the relationship between King's academic training and how the ideas he encountered there were shaped by his actual involvement in the civil rights movement. The concept of Gandhian non-violence is a good example in this respect. While at Crozer, King largely dismissed the idea that Gandhian non-violence could provide an effective form of protest. During the Montgomery bus boycott, King admitted that he knew 'very little' about Gandhi. Indeed, King even applied for an arms permit during the boycott so that he could carry a weapon for self-defence. Only by participating in the movement over time did King come to see the practical applications of non-violence.

Garrow is at pains to point out that what is centrally missing from many analyses of King's intellectual development is the role of the African American church and African American religion. In the second selection, James Cone takes up this point and expands upon it. In the late 1960s and early 1970s, Cone helped to pioneer the idea of 'black theology' which sought to construct a 'theology of black liberation' to make the message of the Bible relevant to the African American struggle for freedom and equality. Black theology seeks to counteract the fact that Christianity in the United States has been a white-dominated religion that has often been integral to justifying racial oppression. For example, in the antebellum South a theology of white supremacy was constructed to defend the practice of slavery as biblically mandated. In contrast, African American counternarratives of Bible stories have continually stressed themes of liberation and freedom from oppression. Black theology revisited those traditions within the specific context of the emergence of the black power movement in the mid- to late- 1960s and developed a more systematic reading of the Bible's liberation narratives. Rather than reject Christianity for Islam as Malcolm X and the Black Muslims did, black theology instead looked to reinvent Christianity from an African American perspective.

Despite the fact that King did not develop his own systematic theology of civil rights, Cone argues that the African American church and African American religion profoundly shaped and influenced King to a much greater degree than King's emphasis on mainly white Western philosophers and theologians suggests. Cone contends that King explained his ideas in the context of white Western traditions when he was primarily trying to communicate with a white audience that could identify with those traditions. However, that rhetoric merely provided a 'conceptual structure to a primary commitment determined by the black church community'. Put simply, it was King's family roots in the African American religious and African American Southern Baptist Church traditions that provided the lens through which he understood and appropriated the ideas and rhetoric of white thinkers in his later academic studies. Throughout his life, it was these African American traditions, rather than the training of the white academy and the ideas that he encountered there, to which King returned and from which he drew inspiration.

Cone says that it is difficult to conceptualize African American cultural influences upon King in the same way as white Western intellectual influences because King expressed his debts to the two in very different ways. Cone argues that whereas King articulated the influences of white thinkers in his written works and public speeches that were directed at white audiences, the influence of African American traditions is witnessed more in King's oral delivery of speeches and sermons, which was evident when King addressed predominantly African American audiences. This echoes a long-standing tradition in African American culture where, Cone states, 'Our theologies have been presented in the forms of sermons, songs, prayers, testimonies, and stories of slavery and oppression.' Cone's emphasis on oral traditions being more important than written traditions in African American culture again raises important questions about the sorts of sources that we use to understand King. Clearly, if Cone's arguments hold true, visual and oral sources will give us a far more accurate understanding of King than written texts will.

Questions for Discussion

1. Identify and assess the early influences of family, religion and church on King.

2. Identify and assess the influences of the ideas that King encountered in his academic studies.

3. Why have historians traditionally relied on written texts as primary sources? What challenges does examining cultures based on oral traditions present?

Further Reading

A number of studies have been written on what might be broadly termed as King's thought and culture. On King and religion see Kenneth L. Smith and Ira G. Zepp, *Search for the Beloved Community: The Thinking of Martin Luther King, Jr* (Lanham, MD: University Press of America, 1986); Noel Leo Erskine and Bernice A. King, *King Among Theologians* (Cleveland, OH: Pilgrim Press, 1995); Luther D. Ivory, *Toward a Theology of Radical Involvement: The Theological Legacy of Martin Luther King, Jr* (Nashville, TN: Abingdon Press, 1997), and Russell Moldovan, *Martin Luther King, Jr: An Oral History of his Religious Witness and his Life* (Lanham, MD: International Scholars, 1999). David L. Chappell, *A Stone of Hope: Prophetic Religion and the Death of Jim Crow* (Chapel Hill, NC: University of North Carolina Press, 2004) locates King within the wider story of prophetic religion in the civil rights movement.

John J. Ansbro, *Martin Luther King, Jr: The Making of a Mind* (Maryknoll, NY: Orbis Books, 1983), has been reprinted as *Martin Luther King, Jr: Nonviolent Strategies and Tactics for Social Change* (Lanham, MD: Madison Books, 2000) to focus more on non-violence, but still in the main explores King's intellectual influences. Hanes Walton, *The Political Philosophy of Martin Luther King, Jr* (Newport, CT: Greenwood Press, 1972) and Richard H. King, *Civil Rights and the Idea of Freedom* (New York: Oxford University Press, 1992) are both concerned with King's political philosophy. Ervin Smith, *The Ethics of Martin Luther King, Jr* (New York: Edwin Mellen Press, 1981) examines King's concept of ethics and Michael G. Long, *Against Us, But For Us: Martin Luther King, Jr and the State* (Macon, GA: Mercer University Press, 2002) looks at King's concept of the state. Lewis V. Baldwin has written extensively on King's cultural roots and King's cultural legacy in *There is a Balm in Gilead: The Cultural Roots of Martin Luther King, Jr* (Minneapolis, MN: Fortram Press, 1991), *To Make the Wounded Whole: The Cultural Legacy of Martin Luther King, Jr* (Minneapolis, MN: Fortram Press, 1992) and *The Legacy of Martin Luther King: The Boundaries of Law, Politics and Religion* (Notre Dame, IN: University of Notre Dame Press, 2002).

The role of ideas in the wider civil rights movement is not something that has attracted a great deal of attention. The best starting points are Richard H. King, *Civil Rights and the Idea of Freedom*, Ted Ownby (ed.), *The Role of Ideas in the Civil Rights South* (Jackson, MS: University Press of Mississippi, 2002) and Carol Posgrove, *Divided Minds: Intellectuals and the Civil Rights Movement* (New York: W. W. Norton, 2001).

The role of the African American church has an extensive literature. One of the best and most recent starting points is C. Eric Lincoln and Lawrence Mamiya, *The Black Church in the African-American Experience* (Durham, NC: Duke University Press, 1990). On the development of black theology see James Cone's work. A useful summary is Cone's 'Black Theology in American Religion', *Journal of the American Academy of Religion* 53: 4 (December 1985): 755–71. Longer works include: *A Black Theology of Liberation* (Philadelphia, PA: Lippincott, 1970); *The Spirituals and the Blues: An Interpretation* (New York: Seabury Press, 1972); *God of the Oppressed* (New York: Seabury Press, 1975); *For My People: Black Theology and the Black Church* (Maryknoll, NY: Orbis Books, 1984); and *Risks of Faith: The Emergence of a Black Theology of Liberation, 1968–1998* (Boston, MA: Beacon Press, 1999).

The Intellectual Development of Martin Luther King, Jr: Influences and Commentaries

David J. Garrow

Most analyses of the intellectual development of Martin Luther King, Jr., concentrate on the formative influences that supposedly shaped the major themes in King's thought. Many commentaries have argued that one or another predominant influence was ignored or slighted by other commentators, and, unfortunately, much of the literature can be characterized as a multi-party tug of war, with different scholars seeking to claim King for Walter Rauschenbusch's social gospel, for Boston University's personalism, for Mohandas K. Gandhi's satyagrahic nonviolence, or for Reinhold Niebuhr's Christian realism. Although there are varying degrees of accuracy in these contending claims, most of this scholarly battle for King's intellectual soul has proceeded with an amazing lack of attention to the two traditions which actually exerted the greatest formative influences on King's

From *Union Seminary Quarterly Review* 40 (1986): 5–20.

thought and action: the biblical inheritance of the story of Jesus Christ, and the black southern Baptist church heritage into which King was born.

The regrettable limitations of the literature on King's thought have been magnified by scholars' widespread blindness to the fact that dependable analysis of King's thinking must be based on wide-ranging usage of his hundreds of unpublished sermons and speeches, materials that paint a far more dependable picture of King's beliefs than the heavily edited and sometimes ghost-written works that were published in book or magazine form under King's name during his lifetime. Scholars have no expectation that presidents and prime ministers personally write every word of their public addresses, but most commentators on King, while often engaging in the most precise textual exegeses of King's publications, have failed to understand that a man whose daily schedule over ten years' time was even more hectic than that of most heads of state simply did not have the time to draft or sometimes even revise the works which were put forward under his name. This naive over-reliance on the least dependable King texts, coupled with the limited usage that commentators have made of the much more dependable, and often extemporaneous, unpublished King texts, has unfortunately led to a situation in which much existing scholarship on King is of little serious, long-term value, and in which truly dependable studies of his thought are just getting underway or beginning to appear. It is of crucial importance as this promising new era begins that illusions about past debates and contributions be minimized.[1]

Another regrettable, though less crucial, problem in scholarship on King has been the widespread failure to pay adequate heed to the two most valuable analytical works written to date: Ira G. Zepp, Jr.'s impressive 1971 dissertation on 'The Intellectual Sources of the Ethical Thought of Martin Luther King, Jr., ...,' and Kenneth L. Smith and Zepp's co-authored 1974 book, *Search for the Beloved Community: The Thinking of Martin Luther King, Jr.*[2] Written well before the copious King Papers at the Martin Luther King, Jr. Center for Nonviolent Social Change in Atlanta first were opened to researchers, Zepp and Smith nonetheless made far more productive use of the King materials at Boston University's Mugar Library than did other scholars. Nonetheless, in ensuing years, even well-known writers on King's life and thought have at times published pieces that make no reference whatsoever to these most thorough and insightful volumes.[3]

Zepp and Smith give a fair and balanced, if at times incomplete, portrayal of the major intellectual traditions upon which Martin King drew. They rightly suggest that it was King's three years at Crozer Theological Seminary (1948–1951), much more so than either his undergraduate experience at Morehouse College (1944–1948) or his graduate years at the Boston University School of Theology (1951–1954), that witnessed King's academic maturation and the development of a first-rate intellectual curiosity and self-testing. Nonetheless, while surveying the contributions that evangelical liberalism and the social gospel, Gandhian nonviolence, Niebuhrian realism and Boston University's personalism all made to King's development, Zepp and Smith do not adequately appreciate how King's evaluation and partial adoptions of different intellectual doctrines were profoundly rooted in his social presuppositions and faith experience. Those presuppositions and experiences were themselves the product of King's upbringing in a family and a church that inculcated the biblical stories, especially for this son and grandson of preachers, and that fully represented the strong faith heritage of the black southern Baptist church.

Most surveys of King's intellectual development, including Smith and Zepp's, begin not with King's childhood exposure to the Bible or his youthful years watching his father pastor Atlanta's Ebenezer Baptist Church, but with the written texts to which he was exposed, first at Morehouse College and then, more importantly, at Crozer. Most biographies of King overstate the impact of Morehouse President Benjamin E. Mays, and sometimes that of religion professor George Kelsey, on young King. They also underemphasize the importance of 'Daddy' King's ministerial role and usually overlook two other Morehouse professors and close family friends, Lucius M. Tobin and Samuel W. Williams, who joined King's father in officiating at 'M.L.'s' ordination to the ministry in the early spring of 1948 during his senior year in college.[4]

Almost all accounts play down the fact that King's student record at Morehouse was undistinguished and that faculty members viewed him as an underachiever. Dean B. R. Brazeal acknowledged King's 'comparatively weak high school background,' and President Mays called him capable of 'substantial B work' but 'not brilliant.' Professor Kelsey termed King's record 'short of what may be called "good," ' but designated him 'one of those boys who came to realize the value of scholarship late in his college career. His ability exceeds his record at Morehouse.'

King's achievements at Crozer proved Kelsey's judgment correct. Kelsey also viewed King as 'quite serious about the ministry and as having a call rather than a professional urge.'[5] On his application to Crozer, King said he had chosen the ministry because of 'an inescapable urge to serve society' and 'a sense of responsibility which I could not escape.' In a longer explanation just a few years later, King said:

> I had felt the urge to enter the ministry from my latter high school days, but accumulated doubts had somewhat blocked the urge. Now it appeared again with an inescapable drive. My call to the ministry was not a miraculous or supernatural something; on the contrary, it was an inner urge calling me to serve humanity. I guess the influence of my father also had a great deal to do with my going in the ministry. This is not to say that he ever spoke to me in terms of being a minis-

ter, but that my admiration for him was the great moving factor. He set forth a noble example that I didn't mind following.[6]

Beyond the examples of Daddy King, Reverends Tobin and Williams, and academicians Mays and Kelsey, one of the most influential of King's experiences during his three years at Crozer was his close relationship with the Reverend J. Pius 'Joe' Barbour, a King family friend and Morehouse graduate who had been the first black to attend Crozer and who pastored Calvary Baptist Church in Chester, Pennsylvania. While Crozer opened King's intellectual horizons and allowed him to demonstrate fully his academic abilities, Barbour's close father–son stewardship helped King remain firmly rooted in the heritage from which he had come.[7]

King's new commitment to academic excellence and intellectual curiosity was quite visible to his close Morehouse friend Walter McCall, who arrived at Crozer one semester after King. 'The dramatic change came in him when he entered the seminary. He began to take his studies more seriously ... he devoted time to his books night and day.' A white Georgian who roomed across the hall from King, DuPree Jordan, agreed. 'He was very studious; he spent a lot more time on his lesson assignments than most of us did.'[8]

The assignments that most stimulated King's interest were those he received from Professor George W. Davis, with whom he took thirty-four of his 110 course hours during his three years at Crozer. As Smith and Zepp relate in detail, Davis was an evangelical liberal heavily influenced by William Newton Clarke and William Adams Brown and also affected by the mysticism of Rufus Jones and Edgar S. Brightman's emphasis on the value of human personality in Christian faith. Laying Davis's principal beliefs alongside the later writings of King, Smith and Zepp contend that

> Most of the major themes of Martin Luther King were the themes of evangelical liberalism. His stress upon the fatherhood of God and the brotherhood of man, the centrality of religious experience, the concern of God for all of life, the rights of man and moral feeling, the humanity of Jesus and his emphasis upon love, the dynamic nature of history and God's actions therein, his essential optimism about human nature and history, the tolerance and openness of the liberal spirit, his tolerance toward pluralism of world religions – all of these were key themes of evangelical liberalism embraced quite early in his intellectual pilgrimage.

Davis, they emphasize, 'introduced King to the major motifs of King's mature thought.'[9]

Smith and Zepp are right to emphasize the profound importance of Davis in King's development, an importance that has been underestimated by most other commentators. Smith and Zepp also emphasize that it was Davis who first introduced King to the writings of Walter Rauschenbusch, the activist pastor and social gospel exponent whose influence on King has been noted, and at times overstated, by many subsequent commentators. A major characteristic of Rauschenbusch and the social gospel movement was an interest in social justice and the effects of social institutions and processes. In many ways the social gospel movement was a reaction against the excessively individualistic ethical vision of much Protestant thought that had been influenced by the Calvinist tradition. Social gospel thought was notably optimistic, and believed that much progress toward the 'inclusive human community' that would represent God's will could be achieved if the church would adopt a social as well as personal role. Rauschenbusch 'saw a major conflict between the teachings of Jesus and the major institutions of capitalism in the United States. He believed that the church would be more effective in combating the evils of society if it abandoned the indirect approach through individuals and made a direct assault upon unjust institutions.' The social gospellers believed that social as well as personal salvation was attainable and a millenial peace could be achieved because human limitations were eradicable through proper education and moral instruction.

Rauschenbusch's three major influences on King, Smith and Zepp state, were his advocacy of a prophetic role for religion, of an active social change role for the church, and his belief that the kingdom of God was an attainable ideal – an ideal that King in later years often spoke of as 'the beloved community.' All three influences reinforced and strengthened the emphasis on socially relevant religion that King had always heard Mays and Kelsey stress at Morehouse.[10]

The commentary on Rauschenbusch in King's *Stride Toward Freedom* emphasizes the attraction King felt toward Rauschenbusch's advocacy of a socially-active church, but underlying even that positive response were two other dimensions in the writings of Rauschenbusch that deeply and profoundly appealed to King as a young divinity student at Crozer. First, King's attraction to the social gospel's openly optimistic view of society's chances for progress and humanity's possible perfectibility was not simply a matter of abstract preference. 'It is,' King wrote in an autobiographical essay at that time, 'quite easy for me to lean more toward optimism than pessimism about human nature mainly because of my childhood experiences.' It is 'quite easy,' King added, 'for me to think of the universe as basically friendly.'[11]

In essence, then, King's first profound intellectual attractions, to George Davis's evangelical liberalism and Walter Rauschenbusch's social gospel thought, had their explicit and, indeed, conscious roots in the incipient worldview that King acquired during his upbringing in a close-knit, loving family and the Ebenezer church environment that daily shaped the Kings' lives. Biographical writers repeatedly have stressed the privileged and relatively protected life that young King enjoyed in Atlanta's Auburn Avenue community, despite the harsh strictures of racial discrimination and segregation, but few if any commentators have fully appreciated the underlying link that existed between the predispositions King drew from his youth and the ideas he was drawn to as a young man.

A second, though less fully documentable, attraction that King felt toward Rauschenbusch's writings concerned the social gospel's strong critique of the evils of capitalism. 'Most of us are not capitalists, we're just potential capitalists,' one surprised fellow student, Francis Stewart, recalls King having told a white Baptist women's group at a church in Chester. In one seminar at Crozer, King presented an excellent and positive report on R. H. Tawney's classic Marxist study, *Religion and the Rise of Capitalism*, and in another paper King spoke of 'my present anti-capitalistic feelings.' J. Pius Barbour, reflecting back on his own private conversations with King during those years, asserted firmly that King 'was economically a Marxist. . . . He thought the capitalistic system was predicated on exploitation and prejudice, poverty, and that we wouldn't solve these problems until we got a new social order.' King had spent one Christmas vacation reading the works of Karl Marx, and 'he believed that Marx had analyzed the economic side of capitalism right,' Barbour recalled.[12]

Daddy King also was aware of M. L.'s economic views. 'Politically,' King, Sr. wrote, 'he often seemed to be drifting away from the basics of capitalism and Western democracy that I felt very strongly about.' That strong theme in King's thinking was also clear to friends he made in Boston after graduating from Crozer in 1951 at the top of his class. Coretta Scott, the young Alabama music student whom King met in Boston in early 1952 and married fifteen months later, later recalled the subjects King brought up during their early dates. 'I remember him talking about his concern for the masses. He talked about the unequal distribution of wealth and he said, 'it's so unfair that a small percentage of the population could control all of the wealth.' He felt that there could be a more equitable distribution of wealth.' In particular, Mrs. King remembered, Martin was unhappy with the acquisitiveness he saw in his father. 'He said, "My old man is a capitalist and I don't believe in capitalism as it is practiced in the United States".... He felt that that was very unjust and he said that his father loved money and that he thought in terms of his own family more than' the rest of humanity.[13]

Although those repeated, early manifestations of King's anti-capitalistic economic thought have been minimized if not completely ignored by most students of his life, another early political influence has been so over-emphasized and overstated as to distort seriously many of the commentaries on King's intellectual development. These accounts portray King as a complete believer in the precepts of Gandhian nonviolence as early as his second year at Crozer. Some writers have suggested that a crucial influence was a lecture that well-known pacifist A. J. Muste gave at Crozer in early November, 1949. Although King certainly attended the talk, one of his fellow students remembered the event because of how strenuously King had disagreed with Muste's views. Muste and King got in 'a pretty heated argument,' Francis Stewart later recalled. 'King sure as hell wasn't any pacifist then.'[14]

One year later, during the winter of 1950–51, King heard Howard University President Mordecai Johnson, just back from a trip to India, speak in Philadelphia about how Gandhi's nonviolent satyagraha had brought about revolutionary changes in Indian society. That lecture spurred King's interest, but his first exposure to Gandhi's writings, in a course that fall with George Davis on the psychology of religion, already had given King a fundamentally critical attitude toward Gandhian nonviolence. King expressed his doubts in a paper he submitted to Kenneth Smith, who had just begun teaching at Crozer. Picking up on a recent article in the *Crozer Quarterly* by political theorist John H. Hallowell which attacked Muste's pacifism, King argued that Gandhi's success in India did not mean that the pacifist approach could work everywhere. Pacifists, King emphasized, 'fail to recognize the sinfulness of man.' Though they focused upon the problems of war and violence, they did not appreciate that those were merely symptoms of man's sinfulness. 'Since man is so often sinful,' King wrote, 'there must be some coercion to keep one man from injuring his fellows.' Aggression and injustice must be resisted, not tolerated, though the respondents 'must not seek revenge.' An active stance, not a passive one, must be adopted in the face of injustice. Seven years later, looking back upon the evolution of his thought, King remarked that 'When I was in theological school I thought the only way we could solve our problem of segregation was an armed revolt.'[15]

The fact that King did not at any time during his divinity and graduate school educaton adopt a belief in pacifism, Gandhi, or nonviolence is further underlined by events that took place during the early months of the Montgomery bus boycott in 1955–56. When white harassment and violence was targeted against the protest leaders and their homes, King and his closest colleague, Ralph Abernathy, decided to take up side arms. 'We felt we ought to be ready,' Abernathy later explained. 'I asked King if he had any means of protection for him and his family. He said the only weapon he had was a butcher knife. He asked, 'What do you have?' I said, 'The only thing I have is a razor.' We decided that we should go downtown together and buy some weapons for our protection.' Accompanied by a third minister, King and Abernathy visited the county sheriff's office to request pistol permits, but the applications were denied. Several days later, as white violence continued, King and several colleagues called upon Alabama Governor James E. Folsom, widely known for his relative liberalism on matters of race. 'What we really want to ask of you,' King told Folsom, 'is protection of the state. We have no confidence in the city police.' Folsom said he would have state officers keep an eye on King's home, but King had a further request. 'What we would like to have, is to have you issue a permit to keep a gun in my car.' The governor responded that he would have to discuss that with the Montgomery County sheriff, and King's group departed.[16]

Several weeks later, as representatives of several pacifist political organizations arrived in Montgomery to speak with King and other boycott leaders, one of the representatives, Bayard Rustin, along with a journalist friend, William Worthy, visited King's home. Rustin took a seat on a couch and Worthy started to sit in an armchair. Rustin looked over and saw a pistol on the seat. 'Watch out, Bill, there's a gun in that chair.' Worthy put the pistol aside, and when King came in, Rustin queried him about the presence of the gun. The movement intended to harm no one unless violently attacked, King explained.[17]

Glenn Smiley, a Fellowship of Reconciliation staff member, was another exponent of nonviolence who visited Montgomery and spoke at length with King during the early months of the protest. Smiley took along an armful of books on nonviolence for their first meeting, and asked King about his familiarity with the doctrine. 'I said to Dr. King,' Smiley recalled, ' "I'm assuming that you're very familiar and have been greatly influenced by Mahatma Gandhi.' And he was very thoughtful, and he said, 'As a matter of fact, no. I know who the man is, I have read some statements by him, and so on, but I will have to truthfully say' – and this is almost a direct quote ... – 'I will have to say that I know very little about the man." ' King stated that he nonetheless admired Gandhi, and Smiley described to King how the essence of nonviolence was a refusal to retaliate against evil, a refusal based on the realization that 'the law of retaliation is the law of the multiplication of evil.' That session was only the first of many such long conversations between the two men about nonviolence and the Gandhian tradition, conversations that had a profound effect on both King's thought and his language. 'He didn't even use the word at first,' Smiley later stressed regarding King's adoption of nonviolence. 'He used "passive resistance" almost entirely.'[18]

Although commentaries that seek to argue King's adherence to or appreciation of Gandhian nonviolence prior to the spring of 1956 are hence quite erroneous,[19] one major intellectual influence that did come upon King during his last year at Crozer, an influence which in the long run was the most important academic doctrine in King's developing thought, is sometimes underemphasized by students of his life. That influence was the Christian realism of Reinhold Niebuhr, whose effect was quite clear in the critique of pacifism that King submitted to Professor Smith. In fact, both of the senior year courses King took with Smith exposed King to Niebuhr's writings and to Niebuhr's sharp critique of Rauschenbusch's social gospel optimism, a critique that Smith enthusiastically endorsed. Niebuhr believed that Rauschenbusch's emphasis upon the power of Christian love to advance the cause of social justice was misplaced and naive, that 'it did not measure adequately the power and persistence of man's self-concern.' Human selfishness, Niebuhr stressed in his 1932 book *Moral Man and Immoral Society*, was the major barrier to justice in society, and people in privileged groups were the most persistent in obstructing any efforts to improve society. 'Disproportion of power in society is the real root of social injustice,' Niebuhr argued, and 'economic power is more basic than political power.' Because of these prolonged and persistent inequalities, 'relations between groups must therefore always be predominantly political rather than ethical.' Social gospel thought was blind to these hard and painful truths about modern society.[20]

The arguments of Niebuhr and the friendly prodding of Smith moved King away from his earlier attachment to the most optimistic aspects of Rauschenbusch's social gospel and George Davis's evangelical liberalism. Looking back, King later confessed that he had become 'absolutely convinced of the natural goodness of man and the natural power of human reason.' Niebuhr's more persuasive realism, however, showed him 'the complexity of human motives and the reality of sin on every level of man's existence.' Most importantly, Niebuhr's realistic view of power in society spoke directly to King's natural interest in Christian perspectives that accounted for the pervasiveness of racial discrimination and segregation. Just as Rauschenbusch's championing of an active social role for religion had spoken to King's desire to involve the church in struggles against American racism, Niebuhr's emphasis on the reality of human sin, particularly in the realm of social power, offered King an instructive and appealing doctrinal explanation for the actuality of racial injustice. Christian love alone clearly could not eliminate discrimination and achieve basic social change. His deep attraction to Niebuhrian realism, King wrote, 'may root back to certain experiences that I had in the south with a vicious race problem. Some of the experiences that I encountered there made it very difficult for me to believe in the essential goodness of man.'[21]

It is beyond the scope of this paper to sketch out in full detail how King's later life experiences during the civil rights movement repeatedly reminded him of the essential accuracy of Niebuhr's social philosophy and of the need for political coercion in combating society's injustices; careful study of King's hundreds of unpublished sermons and speeches from his movement years, however, reveals his growing realization of black America's need to pursue an aggressively coercive, Niebuhrian political strategy. These works also contain regular, extemporaneous references to Niebuhr and the analyses of *Moral Man* in particular. Indeed, while the incredibly hectic nature of King's later years virtually precluded him from undertaking any serious, time-consuming writing about weighty intellectual doctrines,

King's political development can easily, accurately and fairly be labeled an increasingly Niebuhrian evolution.[22]

Upon graduation from Crozer in 1951, King chose Boston University's School of Theology from among several doctoral programs he had considered. The principal attraction of Boston, King later explained, was the presence of Edgar S. Brightman, whose book *A Philosophy of Religion* had been a main text in two of George Davis's courses and whom Davis recommended highly to King. Brightman, along with other principal members of the Boston theology faculty such as L. Harold DeWolf and Peter Bertocci, was a leading proponent of personalism. As the name suggested, personalism held that the human personality, i.e., all individual persons, was the ultimate intrinsic value in the world. That emphasis was extremely attractive to King, for it placed human equality, and respect for all human individuals, at the center of the social value system. 'The dignity and worth of all human personality,' an affirmation which was the central tenet of personalism, was a phrase that King often used extemporaneously in his sermons and addresses over the following fifteen years. Just as was the case with those doctrines of Rauschenbusch and Niebuhr that King found most attractive, in the case of personalism, too, it was the consonance between King's already-developed views and the principal theme of personalism that led King to adopt and give voice to that tenet so firmly and consistently.[23]

The second and equally, if not more, important doctrinal influence on King during his Boston studies came from G. W. F. Hegel. Hegel's dialectical method of thesis, antithesis and synthesis became one of the most central tools in King's intellectual repertoire. As Harold DeWolf later observed, 'regardless of subject matter, King never tired of moving from a one-sided thesis to a corrective, but also one-sided antithesis and finally to a more coherent synthesis beyond both.'[24]

One early reflection of King's new attraction to the Hegelian dialectical method was a Boston essay in which he dealt with each of the two major doctrines he had been attracted to while at Crozer. Now King argued that one must adopt *both* the ethical love emphasis of Rauschenbusch *and* the realists' stress upon political power. 'The balanced Christian,' King wrote, 'must be both loving and realistic. ... as an individual in complex social relations he must realistically meet mind with mind and power with power.' The answer should not be an 'either/or' choice, it should be 'both/and.' A love ethic could work well in direct relationships, but in the larger social setting coercive power was necessary to increase social justice. 'Whereas love seeks out the needs of others, justice ... is a check (by force, if necessary) upon ambitions of individuals seeking to overcome their own insecurity at the expense of others.' Liberal theology and the social gospel, King said, confuse 'the ideal itself with the realistic means which must be employed to coerce society into an approximation of that ideal. ... Men are controlled by power, not mind alone.' Despite the attractions of balance and inclusivity that the dialectical combination offered, King still leaned towards Niebuhr's analysis. Niebuhr was 'unqualifiedly pessimistic about the future of things,' but 'his analysis of the complexity of the social situation is profound indeed, and with it I would find very little to disagree.' In the years ahead, King's comments would indicate a growing appreciation for the hard-eyed insights of the Niebuhrian perspective.[25]

In subsequent circumstances, King often employed the thesis-antithesis-synthesis format to search for a middle way between what he defined as competing extremes. Most importantly, as the Montgomery protest matured and King spent more time mulling the advice and input of outside advisers Smiley and Rustin, he came to view Gandhian nonviolence as precisely such a middle course – an active path of resistance that avoided the sins of passivity and despair in the face of injustice, but a form of resistance that also avoided the multiplication of evil that Smiley had argued would stem from a hateful response or retaliatory violence. 'Like the synthesis in Hegelian philosophy,' King wrote in 1958, 'the principle of nonviolent resistance seeks to reconcile the truths of two opposites – acquiescence and violence – while avoiding the extremes and immoralities of both.'[26] In time King would virtually institutionalize a dialectical discussion and decision-making format within the counsels of the Southern Christian Leadership Conference (SCLC) by encouraging different aides and assistants to champion fundamentally opposite points of view. After allowing all participants to have their say and attack each other's points of view, King almost without fail would speak up and outline an intermediate decision which incorporated what he had identified as the best aspects of each of the contending perspectives. No small number of SCLC strategy sessions and staff discussions thus represented the concrete application of a principle that King first encountered as an abstract formulation in Boston.

While it is beyond the scope of this essay to sketch out in full form just how common and extensive King's application of that format became in later years, it is one of the most important intellectual influences on his later political and movement decision-making. Students of his movement activities need to appreciate this influence in order to understand fully the often-criticized moderation that movement colleagues privately believed King displayed when tough choices had to be made. King's deep-seated penchant for identifying at the outset two supposed extremes, and his concentration upon ascertaining an intermediate middle way, meant not only that his analytical approach was oriented toward moderation, but also, and equally importantly, that it was fundamentally inclined towards compromise. Only more extensive analysis, coupled with the most careful and precise historical review of King's movement decision-making, will enable the full development of this extremely important insight into King's manner of thinking.

...

The central argument of this essay has been that any balanced and insightful analysis of the intellectual influences upon Martin King must take place within the context of a clear understanding and appreciation of the fundamentally Christian, biblical roots from which King's most basic beliefs and assumptions sprang. Similarly, any full appreciation of the absolute centrality of King's faith experience to his entire life, and especially to his civil rights leadership role, must also proceed with those roots and that heritage clearly in mind.

...

While George Davis's liberalism, Walter Rauschenbusch's social gospel, Gandhian nonviolence, Boston personalism, and the Hegelian dialectic all exerted fundamental influence upon the shaping of Martin King, latter-day academic analyses of King's thinking and development must no longer make the grievous mistake of ignoring or minimizing the two most formative influences in King's life: the Bible and the church.

Notes

1. Two particular, often-cited King items that must be used with the greatest caution are 'Pilgrimage to Nonviolence,' pages 90 through 107 in *Stride Toward Freedom* (New York: Harper & Brothers, 1958), and *Why We Can't Wait* (New York: New American Library, 1964), with the exception of chapter 5, the 'Letter from Birmingham Jail,' the most dependable version of which appears in the *New Leader*, 24 June 1963, pp. 3–11. On the problems with 'Pilgrimage,' see Zepp, 'Intellectual Sources' (n. 2 below), esp. 143–9 and 340; and James P. Hanigan, *Martin Luther King, Jr., and the Foundations of Nonviolence* (Lanham, MD: University Press of America, 1984), pp. 67, 160.
2. Zepp, 'The Intellectual Sources of the Ethical Thought of Martin Luther King, Jr., As Traced in His Writings with Special Reference to the Beloved Community,' Unpublished PhD dissertation, St. Mary's Seminary and University, 1971; Smith and Zepp, *Search for the Beloved Community: The Thinking of Martin Luther King, Jr.* (Valley Forge, PA: Judson Press, 1974).
3. See, e.g., Stephen B. Oates, 'The Intellectual Odyssey of Martin Luther King,' *Massachusetts Review* 22 (Summer 1981): 301–20, and *Let the Trumphet Sound: The Life of Martin Luther King, Jr* (New York: Harper & Row, 1982); and John J. Ansbro, 'Martin Luther King's Conception of Agape,' *Gandhi Marg* (2nd series) 2 (January 1981): 556–71. Although Ansbro's subsequent book, *Martin Luther King, Jr: The Making of a Mind* (Maryknoll, NY: Orbis Books, 1982), makes several incidental references to Smith and Zepp, Zepp's and Smith's analyses remain considerably more insightful, complete and dependable than either Ansbro's volume or the earlier work of Hanes Walton, Jr., *The Political Philosophy of Martin Luther King, Jr* (Westport, CT: Greenwood Publishing Co., 1971). Critical commentaries on the Ansbro book appear in *Fellowship*, January–Feburuary 1984, pp. 32–3, by James H. Cone, and the *Journal of American*

History, 70 (March, 1984): 925–6, by Steven F. Lawson. Also see Ansbro's response in the March, 1984 *Fellowship*, p. 21; and a further Ansbro piece, 'Martin Luther King's Civil Disobedience – A Rejoinder,' *Gandhi Marg* (2nd series) 3 (March 1982): 709–21, which is speaking to Louis Waldman, 'Civil Rights – Yes; Civil Disobedience – No (A Reply to Dr. Martin Luther King),' *New York State Bar Journal* 37 (August 1965): 331–7.

4. David Garrow, *Bearing the Cross: Martin Luther King, Jr., and the Southern Christian Leadership Conference, 1955–1968* (New York: William Morrow & Co., forthcoming 1986) chapter 1.

5. B. R. Brazeal to Charles E. Batten, 23 March 1948, Benjamin E. Mays to Charles E. Batten, 28 February 1948, and George Kelsey to Charles E. Batten, 12 March 1948, author's files.

6. Martin Luther King, Jr., 'Application …,' n.d. [ca. early February, 1948], author's files King, 'An Autobiography of Religious Development,' n.d. [ca. 1949], King Papers, Boston University (and reprinted in full in Mervyn A. Warren, 'A Rhetorical Study of the Preaching of Dr. Martin Luther King, Jr., Pastor and Pulpit Orator,' Unpublished PhD dissertation, Michigan State University, 1966, pp. 269–84).

7. J. Pius Barbour Interview (David L. Lewis, September 1968, Chester, PA); David Lewis, *King: A Critical Biography* (New York: Praeger Publishers, 1970), pp. 26–36; Hanigan, *King*, pp. 116–18.

8. McCall Interview (Herbert Holmes, 31 March 1970, Atlanta, GA), p. 20, King Center; Jordan Interview (David Garrow, 14 January 1984, Atlanta, GA).

9. Smith and Zepp, *Search*, pp. 21–31, esp. 29.

10. Smith and Zepp, *Search*, pp. 33–45, esp. 41. Also see Carlyle Marney, 'The Significance of Walter Rauschenbusch for Today,' *Foundations* 2 (January 1959): 13–26; Robert T. Handy, ed., *The Social Gospel in America, 1870–1920* (New York: Oxford University Press, 1966), pp. 253–63; Donovan E. Smucker, 'The Rauschenbusch Story,' *Foundations* 2 (January 1959): 4–12; Henry W. Bowden, 'Walter Rauschenbusch and American Church History,' *Foundations* 9 (July–September 1966); 234–50; and James E. Tull, *Shapers of Baptist Thought* (Valley Forge, PA: Judson Press, 1972), pp. 183–207. Rauschenbusch's major books were *Christianity and the Social Crisis* (New York: Macmillan, 1907), *Christianizing the Social Order* (New York: Macmillan, 1912), and *A Theology for the Social Gospel* (New York: Macmillan, 1917).

11. King, *Stride*, pp. 91–2; King, 'An Autobiography …,' n. 6 above. Later analyses that stress Rauschenbusch's influence on King include Paul R. Garber, 'Martin Luther King, Jr.: Theologian and Precursor of Black Theology,' unpublished PhD dissertation, Florida State University, 1973, pp. 67–85; John H. Cartwright, 'The Social Eschatology of Martin Luther King, Jr.,' in Cartwright (ed.), *Essays in Honor of Martin Luther King, Jr.* (Evanston, IL: Leifer Bureau of Social and Religious Research, Garrett Evangelical Theological Seminary, 1977), pp. 1–13; and Drexel T. Brunson, 'The Quest for Social Justice: A Study of Walter Rauschenbusch and His Influence on Reinhold Niebuhr and Martin Luther King, Jr.,' Unpublished PhD dissertation, Florida State University, 1980.

12. Francis Stewart Interview (David Garrow, 29 March 1984, Atlanta, GA): Kenneth L. Smith, 'Martin Luther King, Jr.: Reflections of a Former Teacher,' *Bulletin on Crozer Theological Seminary 57* (April 1965): 2–3; King, 'An Autobiography …,' n. 6 above; Barbour Interview (Lewis), n. 7 above; Lewis, *King*, p. 354.

13. Martin Luther King, Sr., *Daddy King: An Autobiography* (New York: William Morrow & Co., 1980), p. 147; Coretta Scott King Interview (Charlotte Mayerson, 15 July 1968, Manchester, NH, III, pp. 51–55). Also see James P. Hanigan, 'Martin Luther King, Jr. and the Ethics of Militant Nonviolence,' unpublished PhD dissertation, Duke University,

1973, p. 9; Merglone Pitre, 'The Economic Philosophy of Martin L. King, Jr.,' *Review of Black Political Economy* 9 (Winter 1979): 191–8; and Adam Fairclough, 'Was Martin Luther King a Marxist?,' *History Workshop* 15 (Spring 1983): 117–25.

14. Stewart Interview (Garrow), n. 12 above; also see King, *Stride*, p. 95; Lewis, *King*, p. 35; and Jo Ann O. Robinson, *Abraham Went Out: A Biography of A. J. Muste* (Philadelphia, PA: Temple University Press, 1981), pp. 277–8. Efforts to build King's few early references to Henry David Thoreau (see *Stride*, pp. 51, 91) into an argument for a major early Thoreauvian influence on King are similarly unsuccessful; see the intelligent comments offered by Douglas A. Walker, 'The Thoreauvian Legacy of Martin Luther King,' Unpublished MA thesis, Texas Christian University, 1970; and George E. Carter, 'Martin Luther King: Incipient Transcendentalist,' *Phylon* 40 (December 1979): 318–24.

15. King, *Stride*, p. 96; Smith and Zepp, *Search*, pp. 47–69; King, 'War and Pacifism,' n.d. [ca. spring 1951], King Papers, Boston University, Box 15; King in *Peace News*, 31 January 1958, p. 2, and *Hindustan Times*, 30 January 1958.

16. Ralph D. Abernathy, 'The Natural History of a Social Movement: The Montgomery Improvement Association,' Unpublished MA thesis, Sociology Department, Atlanta University, August 1958, pp. 60–1 (copy in author's files); 'Negro Leader Fails to Get Pistol Permit,' *Montgomery Advertiser*, 4 February 1956, p. B3; Cliff MacKay, 'Terror in Alabama,' *Afro-American*, 11 February 1956, pp. 1, 8. Indeed, the most thorough review of King's copious Crozer and Boston class notebooks revealed only two references to Gandhi. Hanigan, *King*, p. 156.

17. Bayard Rustin Interviews (T. H. Baker, 17 & 30 June 1969, New York: Lyndon B. Johnson Library; James Mosby, 13 February 1970, New York: Moorland-Spingarn Research Center, Howard University; David Garrow, 22 April 1982, New York).

18. Glenn Smiley Interview (David Garrow, 6 April 1984, North Hollywood, CA). Also see Smiley Interview (Katherine M. Shannon, 12 September 1967, Nyack, NY, Moorland-Spingarn Research Center, Howard University), and Smiley's extensive contemporaneous correspondence concerning King and the Montgomery events, located in the Fellowship of Reconciliation Papers, Swarthmore College Peace Collection.

19. As Hanigan has nicely put it, 'King was not a disciple of Gandhi. He was a disciple of Jesus Christ.' *King*, p. 158. Commentaries that emphasize, and usually over-emphasize, the impact of Gandhi on King Include George Hendrick, 'Gandhi and Dr. Martin Luther King,' *Gandhi Marg* 3 (January 1959): 18–22; James H. Smylie, 'On Jesus, Pharoahs, and the Chosen People: Martin Luther King as Biblical Interpreter and Humanist,' *Interpretation* 24 (January 1970): 74–91; Donald H. Smith, 'An Exegesis of Martin Luther King, Jr.'s Social Philosophy,' *Phylon* 31 (Spring 1970): 89–97; William R. Duggan, 'Three Men of Peace,' *Crisis* 81 (December 1974): 331–7; Om Dikshit, 'The Impact of Mahatma Gandhi on Martin Luther King, Jr.,' *Negro History Bulletin* 38 (February–March 1975): 342–4; and John Eubanks, 'Nonviolence and Social Change,' *Journal of Religious Thought* 35 (Fall–Winter 1978–79): 9–18.

20. Smith and Zepp, *Search*, pp. 71–97; Niebuhr, *Moral Man and Immoral Society* (New York: Charles Scribner's Sons, 1932), pp. xxiii, 163, 210; Niebuhr, 'Walter Rauschenbusch in Historical Perspective,' *Religion in Life* 27 (Autumn 1958): 527–36, at 533.

21. Martin Luther King, Jr., 'Pilgrimage to Nonviolence,' *Christian Century* 77 (13 April 1960): 439–41, at 439; King, 'How Modern Christians Should Think of Man,' n.d., King Papers, Boston University, Box 15. Also see Emmett C. Burns, 'Love, Power, and Justice as Central Elements in a View of Social Change: A Comparison and Evaluation of the Thought of Reinhold Niebuhr and Martin Luther King, Jr.,' Unpublished PhD dissertation, University of Pittsburgh, 1974.

22. See, e.g., Martin Luther King, Jr., 'Address to Operation Breadbasket Meeting at Chicago Theological Seminary,' 25 March 1967, King Papers, King Center.

23. Warren, 'A Rhetorical Study,' p. 85, citing an August 31, 1966 interview with King; Smith and Zepp, *Search*, pp. 99–118; Joseph H. Thompson, 'Martin Luther King, Jr. and Christian Witness: An Interpretation of King Based on a Theological Model of Prophetic Witness,' Unpublished PhD dissertation, Fordham University, 1981, esp. p. 108. Also see Warren E. Steinkraus, 'Martin Luther King's Personalism and Nonviolence,' *Journal of the History of Ideas* 34 (January–March 1973): 97–111, and Leo Sandon, Jr's excellent 'Boston University Personalism and Southern Baptist Theology,' *Foundations* 20 (April–June 1977), 101–8. While King makes many repeated bows towards personalism in his unpublished Boston University dissertation ('A Comparison of the Conceptions of God in the Thinking of Paul Tillich and Henry Nelson Wieman,' 1955), the manuscript supplies few if any insights into King's own thinking. Unfortunately, in later years some Boston theologians have badly overstated the formative influence their instruction and personalism had on King. See, e.g., L. Harold DeWolf, 'Martin Luther King, Jr., as Theologian,' *Journal of the Interdenominational Theological Center* 4 (Spring 1977): 1–11, at 9–10; and Walter G. Muelder, 'Communitarian Christian Ethics: A Personal Statement and a Response,' in Paul Deats, Jr (ed.), *Toward a Discipline of Social Ethics* (Boston: Boston University Press, 1972), pp. 295–320, at 299 and 314, and, more strongly, Muelder, 'Martin Luther King, Jr.'s Ethics of Nonviolent Action,' unpublished paper, 1985, King Center.

24. DeWolf, 'Martin Luther King,' p. 8. Also see Bennie E. Goodwin, 'Martin Luther King, Jr.: American Social Educator,' Unpublished PhD dissertation, University of Pittsburgh, 1974, pp. 66–7, 132; and Hanigan, *King*, pp. 80, 100–1.

25. Martin Luther King, Jr., 'Reinhold Niebuhr's Ethical Dualism,' 9 May 1952, King Papers, Boston University, Box 15. King added that 'the more aggressively one relates the gospel to life, the more sensitively he realizes that the social unit can accommodate only justice, not agape.' Some excellent comments on why Hegel's dialectical method was attractive to King appear in Ralph Levering's forthcoming essay, 'Martin Luther King, Jr.: A Christian's Quest for Social Transformation,' in Charles DeBenedetti (ed.), *Peace Heroes in Twentieth Century America* (Bloomington: Indiana University Press, 1986).

26. King, *Stride*, pp. 213 14.

Martin Luther King, Jr: Black Theology – Black Church

James H. Cone

Even though there are important differences between King and me, I think that they can best be understood from within the context of the black church rather than in the context of

From *Theology Today* 41 (1984): 409–20.

*white liberal and neo-orthodox theologies of North America
and Europe. Such views as represented by King and me, as
well as many others, can be found throughout the black religious tradition. There is no need to turn to white Western
theology for an explanation.*

Not much has been written about Martin Luther King, Jr., and the relation
of his theology to the black church and the rise of black theology during
the late 1960s. Many assume that the black church made no decisive impact
upon his intellectual life. To explain his theology, most interpreters turn
to his teachers at Crozer Theological Seminary and Boston University.[1]
The implication of this procedure is that his theological perspective was
defined exclusively by the intellectual impact of white Western theology
and philosophy rather than the black church. While I do not deny the
influence of his seminary and university teachers, I think the influence
of the black church was much more decisive in shaping his theological
perspective.

Because many misunderstand the origin of King's theology in the black
church, they also misunderstand his relation to black theology. Many
assume that black theology and Martin Luther King, Jr. have completely different theological and political perspectives. Persons who
hold this viewpoint often explain the difference by saying that King
was concerned primarily with love, non-violence, and the reconciliation between blacks and whiles. But black theology, in contrast to
King, seldom mentions love or reconciliation between blacks and whites
and explicitly rejects non-violence with its endorsement of Malcom X's
contention that blacks should achieve their freedom 'by any means
necessary.' Some claim that black theology is a separatist and an
extremist interpretation of the Christian faith. But King was an integrationist and a moderate who believed that whites can and should be
redeemed.

During a decade of writing and teaching Black Theology, the most
frequent question that has been addressed to me, publically and privately,
by blacks and especially whites, has been: 'How do you reconcile the separatist and violent orientation of black theology with Martin Luther King's
emphasis on integration, love, and non-violence?' I have always found
it difficult to respond to this question because those who ask it seem
unaware of the interrelations between King, black theology, and the black
church.

While it is not my primary intention to compare King and black theology, I do hope that an explication of his theology in the context of the
black church will show, for those interested in a comparison, that black
theology and King are not nearly as far apart as some persons might be
inclined to think.

I

Martin Luther King, Jr. was a product of the black church. When the question is asked, 'Who is Martin King?' or 'What is his theology?' neither question can be answered properly without giving major attention to the context of King's origin, which is the black church.

Martin King was the son of a Baptist preacher, and he entered the ministry during his student years at Morehouse College. While he was deeply influenced by his teachers at Crozer Theological Seminary and Boston University, the black church was much more decisive in determining his theology, even though he seldom referred to it when he attempted to explain the course of his intellectual development. When asked about the sources of his theological perspective, he referred to such persons as Henry David Thoreau, Mahatma Gandhi, Reinhold Niebuhr, Walter Rauschenbusch, L. Harold DeWolf, and Edgar Sheffield Brightman.

I think it is unquestionably true that these philosophers and theologians, as well as other writers and teachers whom King encountered in graduate school, had a profound effect upon the content, shape, and depth of his theological perspective. They provided the intellectual structure for him to express his ideas about love, non-violence, the value of the human person, and the existence of a moral order in the universe. When King was asked to give an explanation for an action or belief, the question usually came from the white community, and he almost always answered the question by appealing to intellectual sources that were regarded as persuasive authorities in the community from which the questions were derived. Martin King seldom had to defend his perspective to black people, and when he was required, as with the advocates of Black Power,[2] white intellectual resources were never mentioned, because that would have been a sure way to lose the argument.

References to the intellectual tradition of Western philosophy and theology were primarily for the benefit of the white public so that King could demonstrate to them that he could think as well or better than any other seminary or university graduate. Furthermore, King knew that he could not receive substantial support from the white community until he explained to their satisfaction what he believed and why. If he had appealed directly to the black church tradition as the primary source of his theological and political perspective, no one in the white community would have taken him seriously, since the black church is usually not thought of as being the origin of intellectual ideas regarding theology or social change.

But I contend that King's failure to refer directly to the black church as the chief source for his theological perspective does not mean that it is not, in fact, the chief source. What then is the evidence for my claim regarding the primacy of the black church in Martin King's theology? It is difficult to answer this question, because we are accustomed to looking for evidence in printed sources and also from people who knew him personally. While the evidence for my claim does not necessarily contradict what King said about himself or what others say about him, it is not primarily dependent upon their testimonies. My evidence is indirect, and it can only be understood by people who believe that there is an interplay between their social context and the ideas they promote.

To contend that King's graduate teachers and the books he read in graduate school accounted for the whole of his theological perspective is to discount completely his early home and church context and thereby suggest that he arrived at Crozer Seminary and Boston University with a blank mind. Even if we do not hold with Karl Marx's contention that 'consciousness is from the beginning a social product,' we cannot claim the opposite, that is, that 'life is determined by consciousness,' and still appropriately account for the whole of a person's perspective. We must say with Marx 'that circumstances make men just as much as men make circumstances.'[3] If circumstances are relevant in the assessment of a person's ideas and actions, we must then inquire about Martin King's circumstances so that we can understand properly the distinctive contribution of his theology.

Using Boston University and Crozer Theological Seminary as the primary resources for understanding King's ideas and actions ignores the enormous impact of the black church upon his life and thought. It is like using the theology of John Wesley as the primary determinant for explaining who Richard Allen was, and why he founded the African Methodist Episcopal Church. We know that such an explanation may be useful in a dialogue with white United Methodists or British Methodists but not in explaining the historical and theological significance of Richard Allen or of the church he founded. To understand Richard Allen and the significance of his church, it is necessary to know something of his slave circumstances, and what that meant for African people in North America during the late eighteenth and early nineteenth centuries.[4] A similar observation can and should be made regarding Martin King's theology.

II

What were the circumstances that determined the perspective of King's theology and politics? The most significant circumstances that shaped King's theology, in my judgment, were the oppression of black people and the liberating message of the black church. These two realities – the oppression of blacks and the black church's liberating message of the Gospel – provided King with the intellectual challenge to develop a theology that was Christian and also relevant for the social and political needs of black people.

That was why he entered the ministry while a student at Morehouse and later accepted a call to be pastor of Dexter Avenue Baptist Church in Montgomery, rather than seeking a teaching post at a white seminary or university. In fact, King turned down many teaching offers at major white universities and seminaries, and he also refused several invitations to pastor white churches, because of his primary commitment to the black church and its message of liberation for black people.

The black church was also the context out of which Martin King accepted the call to be the leader of the Montgomery Bus Boycott. After his success in Montgomery, King founded the Southern Christian Leadership Conference (SCLC) which received its support primarily from black preachers and their churches. In order to keep his identity firmly tied to the black church as he served as the president of SCLC, he became the co-pastor of Ebenezer Baptist Church in Atlanta. Martin King's close ties with the black church in preference over the alternatives indicate that his primary commitment was to that community. Anyone, therefore, who wishes to understand his life and thought must make the black church the primary source for the analysis.

The best way of deciding what was primary for King's life and thought is to ask, 'What tradition did he turn to in moments of crisis during his ministry?' Where one turns when one's back is up against the wall and when everything seems hopeless will tell us far more about our theology than what is often printed in articles and books. When King encountered the harsh contradictions of white violence and when he had run out of rational alternatives on how best to defeat it non-violently, where did he turn for insight, courage and hope that things can and will be otherwise? Did he turn to Brightman, DeWolf, Niebuhr, or Gandhi? Of course not. None of these intellectual resources were useful to him in the context of crisis.

In moments of crisis when despair was about to destroy the possibility of making a new future for the poor, King turned to the faith contained in the tradition of the black church. Whether one speaks of Montgomery, Albany, Birmingham, Selma, or Chicago, the crises arising from his struggle to implement justice never produced despair in his theological and political consciousness. The reason is not found in his intellectual grasp and exposition of white liberal theology but in the faith and life of the black church. With the resources of this religious tradition, he had a foundation that could sustain him in his struggle for justice. Had not his people been struggling for freedom for over three hundred and fifty years, and despite many disappointments and apparent defeats? Does not the faith of the black church empower black Christians to 'keep on keeping on' even though the odds might be against them?

This is the context for understanding the often heard faith claim, 'I ain't no ways tired.' This affirmation of faith is not derived from the faith of middle class blacks or whites and their capitalistic orientation. Rather this faith is derived from the meeting of God in the pains and struggles of poor blacks who refuse to accept despair as the logical consequence of their oppression, because they firmly believe that 'God can make a way out of no way.'

It was Martin King's identity with the tradition of this black faith that enabled him to overcome crisis moments during his fight for justice. While he was not always sure how to make this faith intellectually convincing to his friends and supporters in the white community, he knew that his own people were already aware of the inability of white concepts to explain the certainty of black faith. That was why it was so easy for him to get a little carried away when speaking in a black church. Their enthusiastic responses to his sermons on justice and non-violence, saying 'amen,' 'right-on,' 'speak the truth,' let him know that they were in solidarity with him, and that they would follow him wherever he led them. They had already demonstrated their presence with him in Montgomery, Birmingham, and Selma. Furthermore, King also knew that their belief in him was in no way dependent upon his theological perspective as defined by white theological resources. Black people followed King, because he embodied in word and deed the faith of the black church which has always claimed that oppression and the Gospel of Jesus do not go together.

III

The white public and also many white scholars have misunderstood King, because they know so little about the black church community, ignoring its effect upon his life and thought. An example of this misguided interpretation are the books by Kenneth Smith and Ira Zepp, Jr., *Search for the Beloved Community: The Thinking of Martin Luther King, Jr.* (Judson, 1974), and John Ansbro, *The Mind of Martin Luther King, Jr.* (Orbis, 1982). These authors analyze the thought of Martin King as if the black church community had no decisive impact on him, indeed as if thought itself is limited to the white intellectual community. While these books are useful in telling us what King learned in graduate school and what intellectual resources he used in communicating his ideas to the white community, they are not helpful in identifying the heart of King's theology and faith that sustained him in his fight for justice.

When one uses exclusively the perspectives of white theologians to interpret Martin King, it is difficult to explain the consistency of his thinking and actions. How is it possible for King to reconcile his use of the neo-orthodox theology of Reinhold Niebuhr and the Boston Personalism of Edgar S. Brightman? King appeals to so many resources for his ideas that it is conceptually impossible to reconcile them into one coherent whole when these white philosophers and theologians are used as the primary source of their origin and analysis. That is why many of King's interpreters find it nearly impossible to explain the whole of his theological perspective in a consistent and wholistic manner.

What is true for the interpreters of Martin King is also true for many interpreters of my own perspective on black theology. As King used evangelical liberalism and Boston Personalism in defining his theology, many of my interpreters claim that I use the so-called neo-orthodox theology of Karl Barth. When I also begin to use Tillich, Marx, [Dietrich] Bonhoeffer, and other white interpreters for the presentation of my ideas, my interpreters get a little confused in explicating the consistency of my perspective, because the different ideas I use for interpreting black theology do not belong in the same theological school of thought.

What is most interesting is that even I myself used to think that the sources for explaining my theology were Barth, Bonhoeffer, and Tillich, because these were the theologians who made the most conscious intellectual impact on me during my seminary days. When I graduated from Garrett Theological Seminary and Northwestern University after writing a PhD dissertation on Karl Barth's anthropology, I naturally turned to him for communicating my deepest feelings about the theological implications of the black struggle for freedom. At that time, Barth and others like him were the only intellectual resources at my command for explicating the theological meaning of the black struggle, even though the truth of it did not arise from the experience of white neo-orthodox theologians.

Since the publication of *Black Theology and Black Power* (1969), I have come to realize the limitation of this procedure and have attempted to correct it as much as possible, while not denying the usefulness of ideas from all cultures. I now know that even though I may not have recognized it, the black church was and still is the most dominant element for a proper understanding of my own theological perspective. While I do not rule out other influences, they are not in any way decisive. I can discard Barth and Tillich as easily as I can choose to use them. They, as well as others, are merely instrumental in giving conceptual structure to a primary commitment determined by the black church community.

IV

With the black church community in mind, one can then understand both the similarities and differences between King's theology and my own perspective on black theology. Although our differences on violence versus non-violence, love and reconciliation, and the possibility of change in the white community are real, they are differences between two persons who are deeply committed to the same faith of the black church. Our differences are not so great as is usually believed. They are more semantic than substantive, and can best be understood by investigating our different circumstances in the black community and the audiences to which we address our viewpoints.

King was not nearly as non-violent as many claimed, and his faith in whites and the accomplishment of his movement was not uncritical. For example, when he spoke about black progress in the area of Civil Rights, he knew that all was not as well as whites liked to think and that for the masses of blacks the movement had left their situation of oppression untouched. In a 1965 interview with Alex Haley, King said:

> Though many would prefer not to, we must face the fact that progress for the Negro – to which white moderators like to point in justifying gradualism – has been relatively insignificant, particularly in terms of the Negro masses. What little progress has been made – and that includes the Civil Rights Act – has applied primarily to the middle-class Negro. Among the masses, especially in the Northern ghettoes, the situation remains the same, and for some it is worse.'5

Speaking about his disappointment regarding Southern white ministers, King said: 'The most pervasive mistake I have made was in believing that because our cause was just, we could be sure that the white ministers of the South, once their Christian consciences were challenged, would rise to our aid. . . . I ended up, of course, chastened and disillusioned.'6

Both of these quotations show that Martin King did face the failure of the Civil Rights movement to reach the masses of black people. He also realized that whites, even liberal clergy, could not always be counted on to act out in life what they claim in their confessions of faith or in their theological textbooks.

My own perspective on black theology, unlike Martin King, begins with the assumption that the people who benefit from the unjust social, political, and economic order are not likely to be the ones who will change it radically. I do not make this claim because I think that whites are by nature more evil than any other group of people. I make this claim because of the Christian doctrine of sin which says that individuals or groups will claim more than what they ought to, if they can get away with it. I think that the reality of sin has already been validated by history. I do not believe that any group of people will do right, because of the demands of faith alone.

As Reinhold Niebuhr forcefully demonstrated in his *Moral Man and Immoral Society*, individuals may stand outside of themselves and therefore act against their interests as defined by the existing social arrangements. But groups seldom, if ever, can transcend their interests for the sake of another. Martin King was certainly aware of Niebuhr's analysis, but it apparently made little impact on his theological consciousness, since his optimism regarding whites could not be shaken radically. King's optimism, however, is not derived primarily from the theological liberalism of Bostonian Personalism or of the Social Gospel movement.

I think King received this faith in whites from the black church tradition which has always extended its openness to reconciliation to the white community. What is most amazing about the black community as a whole and the black church in particular is their willingness to forgive whites regarding their brutality during slavery, lynching, and even oppression today in the ghettoes of the urban cities. But despite our willingness to extend the right hand of fellowship, whites continue their massive assault upon the humanity of our people, and get angry with us if we say we don't like it. It seems that whites have been allowed to do what they wish to us so long that they regard such inhumane invasion of black humanity as synonymous with their freedom.

With regard to what black people can expect from white people in our struggle for freedom, there are some genuine differences between King and me. I do not believe that whites or any other group holding power will voluntarily empower those who are powerless. Freedom is not a gift but must be taken. While the Gospel of God can and does empower people to change sides in the struggle for freedom, we must realize that many people publicly testify that they are for the poor but are in fact against them.

Even though there are important differences between King and me, I think that they can best be understood from within the context of the black church rather than in the context of white liberal and neo-orthodox theologies of North America and Europe. Such views are represented by King and me, as well as many others, can be found throughout the black religious tradition. There is no need to turn to white Western theology for an explanation. King's perspective has its antecedents in Frederick Douglass, while my view is partly found in the life and writings of Henry Highland Garnet, both of whom were contemporaries in the nineteenth century and stressed somewhat different views regarding the place of whites in the black struggle of freedom.[7]

V

What was the main content of King's thought which he derived from the black church tradition? This question is not easy to answer because the black church has not done much systematic reflection in the area of theology. Our theologies have been presented in the forms of sermons, songs, prayers, testimonies, and stories of slavery and oppression. In these sources we have given our views of God and the world, and how each may be understood in relation to our struggle for freedom. We did not write essays on Christian doctrine because our descendants came as slaves from Africa and not as free people from Europe. Many blacks were prevented from learning to read and write either by the circumstances of our birth or by the legal restrictions defined by the Government. Therefore, we had to do theology in other forms than rational reflections. We sang and preached our theology in worship and other sacred contexts. The central meaning disclosed in these non-rational sources is found in both their *form* and *content* and is identical with *freedom* and *hope*.

The influence of the black church and its central theme of freedom and hope can be seen in the language of King's speaking and writing. Everything he said and wrote sounds like a black sermon and not rational reflection. To be sure, King finished first in his class at Crozer and also wrote a PhD dissertation at Boston on Henry Nelson Wieman's and Paul Tillich's conceptions of God. But it is significant to note that he did not adopt the style of theological presentation from any of his white theological mentors. He may have referred to white theologians and philosophers when he needed to explain his views to a white public, but the style of his presentation was unmistakably from the tradition of black preaching.

Like his predecessors and contemporaries in the black church, King preached his theology, because the theme of freedom and hope had to be reflected in the movement and rhythm of his voice, if he expected a black congregation to take his message seriously. The eschatological hope of freedom is not only an idea to be analyzed in the conceptual language of white theologians and philosophers. It is primarily an event to be experienced when God's word of freedom breaks into the lives of the gathered community through the vehicle of the sermon's oration. No one understood the relationship between style and meaning in the context of the black church any better than Martin King.

In the black church, the meaning is found not primarily in the intellectual content of the spoken word but in the *way* the word is spoken and its effect upon those who hear it. That was why King could speak on Plato, Augustine, or even Boston Personalism, about which most blacks know nothing and care even less, and still move the congregation to tears and shouts of praise, even though they did not understand the content of his discourse. What they understood was the appropriate tone and movement of his speech which the people believe is the instrument for the coming presence of God's spirit, thereby empowering them with the hope for freedom. The people believe that freedom is coming because a foretaste of it is given in the sermon event itself. When King spoke of his dream at the 1963 March on Washington, and when he spoke the night before his assassination in Memphis of his hope that we will reach the Promised Land, black people did not believe him because of the cogency of his logic but rather because of the spirit of empowerment generated by the style of his sermon oration. The people believed him because they contended that they experienced in their hearts the Spirit of God's liberating presence.

I think style is important in doing theology, and I try to reflect it in my own theology. How can black theology claim to be derived from the black community if it does not reflect in its style the language of the people? If black people do not recognize themselves in the language of theology, how can theology really claim blackness as its identity? For any theology to be truly black, its blackness must be expressed in the form in which it is written. This point was impressed on my own theological consciousness by the black critics of my early books, *Black Theology and Black Power* (1969) and *A Black Theology of Liberation* (1970). With the publication of *The Spirituals and the Blues* (1972), *God of the Oppressed* (1975), *My Soul Looks Back* (1982), and other subsequent writings, I have tried to incorporate not only the *content* of liberation in theology but also in the very form of the language itself. Martin King has been helpful in the accomplishment of this task.

VI

In addition to the style of King's theology pointing toward freedom and hope, the same theme is also found in the *content* of his message. The influence of the black church on the content of King's theology is not easy to demonstrate. Anyone can easily notice the influence of the black church on his sermonic delivery and in the form of his writings. But that is not the case with the content of his message, since he does not explicitly refer to the black church. What is clear, however, is that the central theme of freedom and hope do define the content of King's life and message. It is summarized in his March on Washington speech:

I have a dream that my four little children will one day live in a nation where they will not be judged by the color of their skin but by the content of their character. . . . With this faith we will be able to transform the jangling discords of our nation into a beautiful symphony of brotherhood. With this faith we will be able to work together, to pray together, to struggle together, to go to jail together, to stand up for freedom together, knowing that we will be free one day.

The words were spoken in 1963, but few of us today can speak with the confidence of Martin King, because events since that time are difficult to reconcile with his optimism. Between 1965 and 1968, even King had to move away from the optimism defined in the 1963 Washington speech, because his sermons and speeches did not dislodge the entrenchment of white power as he appeared to think. But despite the failure of his sermons and speeches to move whites to change the social, political, and economic situation, the content of his message of freedom and hope did move blacks to action. Without the response of the black church people, King would have had his hope for freedom destroyed, because even liberal whites seemed incapable of embodying the hope and freedom about which he preached.

In the black church, King knew that the people had a hope that stretched back to the beginnings of the black Christian community in the eighteenth and nineteenth centuries. All he had to do was restate that hope for freedom in the songs and language of the people and they would respond to the content of the message. That was why King used the language of the so-called 'Negro Spirituals' in his sermons in black churches. His sermons always contained the hope for freedom, and he always related it to his current struggles to attain freedom in this world. But when it seemed as if freedom was difficult to realize in this world, Martin King did not despair but moved its meaning to an eschatological realm as defined by the black church's claim that 'the Lord will make a way somehow.' The night before he was assassinated, King, in a black church worship service, restated that hope with the passion and certainty so typical of the black preacher: 'I may not get there with you, but I want you to know tonight that we as a people will get to the promised land. . . . Mine eyes have seen the glory of the coming of the Lord.'

King's emphasis on the eschatological hope of freedom as defined by 'the coming of the Lord' was not derived from white theologians and philosophers, but from his own religious tradition. These words of faith and hope were derived from the black tradition as defined by our pain and suffering. People who have not lived in the context of hundreds of years of slavery and suffering are not likely to express an eschatological hope of freedom. Hope in God's coming eschatological freedom is always derived from the suffering of people who are seeking to establish freedom on earth but have failed to achieve it. In their failure to establish freedom in their existing present, black people prevented despair from becoming the defining characteristic of their lives by looking forward to God's coming, eschatological freedom.

As with King, black theology, and the black church generally, we blacks do not deny that trouble is present in black life. What we deny is that it has the last word, for we believe, in the words of Charles Tindley, that 'we will understand it better by and by.'

Trials dark on every hand, and we cannot understand.
All the ways that God would lead us to the Blessed Promised Land
But he guides us with his eye and we'll follow till we die.
For we'll understand it better by and by.

By and by, when the morning comes,
All the saints of God are gathered home
We'll tell the story how we overcome
For we'll understand it better by and by.

Notes

1. See especially Kenneth L. Smith and Ira G. Zepp, Jr, *Search for the Beloved Community: The Thinking of Martin Luther King, Jr.* (Valley Forge: Judson Press, 1975) and John J. Ansbro, *The Mind of Martin Luther King, Jr.* (Maryknoll, NY: Orbis 1982). King's biographers make a similar assumption. See especially David L. Lewis, *King: A Critical Biography* (Baltimore: Penguin Books, 1970). Martin King himself is partly responsible for this one-sided interpretation of his thinking because he seldom refers to the black church as the source of his theology. See especially his 'Pilgrimage to Nonviolence' in *Stride Toward Freedom: The Montgomery Story* (New York: Harper, 1958), pp. 90–107.
2. See especially his response to Black Power radicals in *Where Do We Go From Here: Chaos or Community* (Boston, MA: Beacon, 1967), ch. 11.
3. Marx, 'The German Ideology,' in Robert C. Tucker (ed.), *The Marx–Engels Reader*, 2nd edn (New York: Norton, 1978), pp. 158, 165.
4. For information regarding Richard Allen and the African Methodist Episcopal Church, see Carol V. R. George, *Segregated Sabbaths: Richard Allen and the Rise of Independent Black Churches, 1760–1840* (New York: Oxford University Press, 1973).
5. Alex Haley, 'Playboy Interview with Martin Luther King,' *Playboy*, XII, Jan. 1965, pp. 70–1.
6. Ibid., p. 66.
7. For an interpretation of nationalism and integration in the history of black religious thought, see Gayraud S. Wilmore, *Black Religion and Black Radicalism*, 2nd edn (Maryknoll, NY: Orbis Books, 1983); see also Francis L. Broderick, 'The Gnawing Dilemma: Separatism and Integration, 1865–1925,' in Nathan Huggins, Martin Kilson, and Daniel Fox (eds.), *Key Issues in the Afro-American Experience*, vol. II (New York: Harcourt Brace Jovanovich, 1971).

4 Authorship: Plagiarism, Ghost-Writing and Voice-Merging

Introduction

In the previous chapter both David Garrow and James Cone raise the question of the relationship between the sources that historians use and their interpretations of King. This problem was magnified in 1990 when Clayborne Carson, as director of the King Papers Project, broke the news that King had 'used the words of others without giving them credit' in some of his college essays and in large chunks of his Boston University PhD thesis. King's plagiarism, as others quickly labelled it, raised a storm of controversy. The plagiarism debate has been examined by contemporaries of King, academic scholars, and experts in plagiarism, in a special edition of the *Journal of American History*.

The academic plagiarism debate set the context in the 1990s for other questions about the relative merits and authenticity of primary sources related to King. The first selection in this chapter looks at this debate in relation to King's published books and the practice of ghost-writing. In an extract from a longer work about King's cultural roots, Lewis V. Baldwin directly addresses the points raised by Garrow and Cone. Baldwin contends that, although King's books were admittedly largely ghost-written, King did personally read and approve the publication of work penned under his name. If King had been unhappy with anything that his ghost-writers had produced he would have had the opportunity to correct or to veto it (although how closely King scrutinized this work is still open to question). Baldwin asserts that King's books do therefore accurately reflect his views and can be legitimately and usefully examined as primary sources. Moreover, Baldwin points out that ghost-writing is widely practised by many major public figures and that if we discount the validity of King's works because of this practice, there are many other works by famous people that we would have to strike from the historical record as well.

The use of King's sermons as primary sources has also come under close scrutiny. In the second selection, Keith D. Miller, in an essay included in the *Journal of American History* plagiarism roundtable, and which represents a synopsis of his arguments developed at length elsewhere, points out that King's sermons 'borrowed, modified, and synthesized themes, analogies, metaphors, quotations [and] illustrations' from the sermons of Harry Emerson Fosdick and other nineteenth-century white liberal preachers. Miller terms this practice 'voice-merging' and argues that it is part of a distinct African American 'black folk pulpit' oral tradition of melding the words of others into new forms without necessarily acknowledging their origin. If James Cone's essay in the last chapter asserts that it was primarily King's academic training that allowed him to articulate his arguments to white audiences, Miller argues then that the shared religious texts and traditions of white and African American churches played a crucial role in this respect too.

In the third selection, Richard Lischer claims that Keith Miller's work may exaggerate the extent of King's 'borrowing' in his sermons by emphasizing their written content rather than their actual performance from the pulpit (note that Lischer's use of the word 'homiletics' here refers to the art of preaching). It was, Lischer insists, echoing James Cone's point in the previous chapter, the performance and delivery of King's sermons and speeches before an audience, rather than the actual words that he used, which was the most important factor in generating their meaning. On the printed page, King's sermons give little sense of his actual style of delivery, of the timbre and tone of his voice, of the historical context in which they were delivered, or of the crucial 'call and response' aspect of the sermon, whereby the replies of the audience become integral to the sermon's direction and meaning.

Moreover, Lischer claims that Miller may exaggerate the extent to which King actually did borrow from the words of other sermons in the first place. He argues that since preachers, African American and white, drew from a relatively small pool of biblical allusions and ideas that have been exhaustively mined, what constitutes an 'original' interpretation of them and what constitutes a 'copy' is very often blurred. Following on from that point, Lischer critiques Cone's assertion that King essentially had two different voices, one for speaking to white audiences and one for speaking to African American audiences. Lischer agrees with Miller that it was shared texts common to both whites and to African Americans in the United States, both religious and secular – for the latter see as examples the Declaration of Independence, the Constitution and the Emancipation Proclamation – that allowed King to effectively bridge the racial divide in his use of language.

It is important to distinguish between the practice of 'plagiarism,' 'ghost-writing,' and 'voice-merging', and the contexts within which they operate. Plagiarism is a serious academic offence that constitutes cheating. When King wrote within an academic context, he was aware of the rules that governed such work. Blatantly breaking those rules is therefore impossible to excuse. Ghost-writing is a greyer area. While it is true that a number of public figures use ghost-writers, this can be done in a variety of ways. As historian Richard King has noted, 'We know how to recognize the signals of its presence – from thanks for editorial help in the acknowledgements to explicit mention in phrases such as "as told to" or "with the help of".' However, M. L. King, as with many other public figures, did not use these prompts in his work and he did in fact pass the words off as his own. There is an element of deception involved in this, even if it is an accepted practice within the publishing industry. Voice-merging is a more acceptable practice since it operates within a shared and acknowledged tradition of the black folk pulpit. King and his audience understood that his words were being borrowed from other sermons, many of which they already recognized, and they understood that this was an accepted practice within that particular preaching tradition. So although plagiarism, ghost-writing and voice-merging all share the same common denominator of using the words of others without attribution, it is the rules and contexts within which they operate that determine the acceptability of those practices.

Questions for Discussion

1. What is plagiarism and what problems does it raise?

2. What is ghost-writing and what problems does it raise?

3. What is voice-merging and what problems does it raise?

4. Compare and contrast plagiarism, ghost-writing and voice-merging. Identify the similarities and differences between them.

Further Reading

The best starting point for King and plagiarism is the collection of essays in a special edition of the *Journal of American History* 78 (June 1991): 11–123, 'Becoming Martin Luther King, Jr: Plagiarism and Originality: A Round Table'. Theodore Pappas, *Plagiarism and the Culture War: The Writings of Martin Luther King, Jr and Other Prominent Americans* (Tampa, FL: Hallberg, 1998) examines King's plagiarism from the perspective of the American Right although his somewhat self-righteous glee at exposing King's shortcomings quickly proves wearing. Eugene D. Genovese, *The Southern Front: History and Politics in the Cultural Cold War* (Columbia: University of Missouri Press, 1995) is another book highly critical of King's plagiarism. Michael Eric Dyson, *I May Not Get There with You: The True Martin Luther King, Jr* (New York: Free Press, 2000), in Chapter 7, ' "Somewhere I Read of the Freedom of Speech": Constructing a Unique Voice', offers a more measured, thoughtful and insightful response to the plagiarism controversy.

On King's sermons and preaching traditions see Keith D. Miller, *Voice of Deliverance: The Language of Martin Luther King, Jr, and Its Sources* (New York: Free Press, 1992), and Richard Lischer, *The Preacher King: Martin Luther King, Jr and the Word that Moved America* (New York: Oxford University Press, 1995). Richard H. King, *Civil Rights and the Idea of Freedom* (New York: Oxford University Press, 1992) in Chapter 5 provides a critique of Miller's work and a thoughtful analysis of the various plagiarism, ghost-writing and voice-merging debates. An essay collection edited by Carolyn Calloway-Thomas and John Louis Lucaites, *Martin Luther King, Jr, and the Sermonic Power of Public Discourse* (Tuscaloosa, AL: University of Alabama Press, 1993), and a monograph by Fredrik Sunnemark, *Ring Out Freedom! The Voice of Martin Luther King, Jr and the Making of the Civil Rights Movement* (Bloomington, IN: Indiana University Press, 2004), further explore King's use of rhetoric. Drew D. Hansen, *The Dream: Martin Luther King, Jr and the Speech that Inspired a Nation* (New York: HarperCollins, 2003), examines King's famous 'I Have a Dream' speech at the 1963 March on Washington.

There is a Balm in Gilead: The Cultural Roots of Martin Luther King, Jr

Lewis V. Baldwin

The contents of this work rest on the notion that King's published books and essays are as reliable as his largely unpublished, spontaneously delivered sermons, speeches, and mass meeting addresses for understanding him and for interpreting the evolution and changing emphases in his thought. David Garrow has consistently warned scholars away from primary reliance on King's published books and essays, noting that these sources were largely

From *There is a Balm in Gilead: The Cultural Roots of Martin Luther King, Jr* (Minneapolis: Fortress Press, 1991), pp. 11–14.

ghostwritten by Al Duckett, Harris Wofford, Stanley Levison, Bayard Rustin, and other advisers to King. Garrow points specifically to *Why We Can't Wait* (1964), which was almost completely ghostwritten by Duckett, to *Stride toward Freedom* (1958), and to *Where Do We Go from Here: Chaos or Community?* (1967), which include extensive pieces of material prepared by Wofford, Levison, Rustin, and others.[1] The 'King' one sees in these sources, according to Garrow, 'is at some considerable distance, in many particulars, from the King one sees in the largely unpublished, spontaneously delivered sermons in black churches and mass meeting addresses at Southern community rallies.' Garrow establishes the reliability of the wealth of King's extemporaneous, unpublished texts on the grounds that 'there's no editorial revisions or "toning up" of the language by King advisers in these manuscript texts.'[2] He concludes that the 'naive over-reliance' of scholars 'on the least dependable King texts, coupled with the limited usage that commentators have made of the much more dependable, and often extemporaneous, unpublished King texts, has unfortunately led to a situation in which much existing scholarship on King is of little serious, long-term value, and in which truly dependable studies of his thought are just getting underway or beginning to appear.'[3]

James H. Cone has stressed as strongly as Garrow the unreliability of King's published works for providing a dependable analysis of his life and thought. Cone insists that 'Working for the movement 20 hours a day, traveling 325,000 miles and making 450 speeches a year, it was not possible for King to write everything that was published under his name.'[4] Like Garrow, Cone declares that the unpublished materials at Atlanta's King Center and Boston University's Mugar Memorial Library provide vastly more support, both substantively and linguistically, for the contention that King was a product of black folk culture in the South.[5]

Garrow and Cone have been engaged in a serious effort to do revisionist scholarship on Martin Luther King, Jr. However, I am not convinced of the soundness of their arguments concerning the limitations of King's published texts. In cases where ghostwriters prepared King's books, essays, and speeches, they took words out of his mouth instead of putting words into his mouth. It is unreasonable for anyone to expect a man of King's greatness and level of social involvement to write every word of his books, essays, and speeches.[6] But such works were published with his approval, and there is no evidence that he disclaimed any of these texts. I personally have found no important discrepancies between what appears in King's edited and sometimes ghostwritten works and what is included in his extemporaneous, unpublished texts. King's personality and the basic outlines of his thought are evident in both. Garrow and Cone make too much of the fact that many of King's texts were heavily edited and ghostwritten, and if the standards and limitations they have applied to King's published works are applied to those of other great men and women in our history, the history books would have to be largely rewritten in order to be reliable. My contention is that any dependable picture of King's personality, thinking, and activities must draw on both his published and unpublished texts.

Notes

1. A letter from David J. Garrow, to Lewis V. Baldwin, 24 September 1984; a letter from David J. Garrow, to Lewis V. Baldwin, 2 February 1985; and David J. Garrow, 'The Intellectual Development of Martin Luther King, Jr.: Influences and Commentaries,' *Union Seminary Quarterly Review* 40, no. 4 (January 1986): 5–6.
2. Garrow, letter to Baldwin, 24 September 1984.
3. Garrow, 'The Intellectual Development of Martin Luther King, Jr.,' 5. Garrow regards King's published books as being carefully prepared 'for presentation to a largely northern, largely white, and largely well-educated audience of potential contributors.' Scholarly works such as Hanes Walton, Jr.'s *The Political Philosophy of Martin Luther King, Jr.* (1971) and Ansbro's *Martin Luther King, Jr.: The Making of a Mind* (1982), which have drawn heavily on King's published works, are dismissed by Garrow as 'workman-like exegeses of the "King" that he, and his advisers, thought most attractive to the northern audience whose support the movement needed, but that "King" is a spiritual stick-figure, so to speak, compared to the actual man.' See a letter from Garrow, to Baldwin, 24 September 1984.
4. James H. Cone, 'The Theology of Martin Luther King, Jr.,' *Union Seminary Quarterly Review* 40, no. 4 (January 1986): 39, n. 30. This point is also forcefully made in Garrow, 'The Intellectual Development of Martin Luther King, Jr.,' 5.
5. Cone, 'The Theology of Martin Luther King, Jr.,' 21–39; and a letter from Garrow, to Baldwin, 24 September 1984.
6. However, King did occasionally mention in his interviews and in letters addressed to others the considerable time he spent working on his books – comments that Garrow and Cone have apparently ignored. For example, in March 1967, King said in an interview, 'I spent the months of January and February completing my book' or 'working on the chapters of my book,' which is 'entitled, *Where Do We Go from Here: Chaos or Community?*' See Martin Luther King, Jr, 'Transcript of a Press Conference at Liberty Baptist Church,' Chicago, IL. (The King Center Archives, 24 March 1967), 1.

Martin Luther King, Jr and the Black Folk Pulpit

Keith D. Miller

Clearly, Clayborne Carson, Ralph E. Luker, and their staff at the Martin Luther King, Jr., Papers Project are engaged in the most painstakingly thorough and laudable investigation ever made into Martin Luther King, Jr.'s years as a graduate student.

From *Journal of American History* 78: 1 (June 1991): 120–3).

The most important question that Carson and his colleagues raise is not why King plagiarized but how his magisterial language developed. Even the preliminary findings of the project help refute the fallacious answer offered by a squadron of King scholars.[1]

Virtually an entire generation of researchers has repeatedly argued that King's intellectual development, ideas, and oratory grew from his philosophical and theological studies in graduate school. Biographers and academics have persistently claimed that King's reading of famous Euro-American philosophers (especially G. W. F. Hegel) and theologians (especially Walter Rauschenbusch, Reinhold Niebuhr, and Paul Tillich) inspired his thought and his language and thus the civil rights movement itself.

This view is wrong.

What is most striking about Carson's report is its dramatic demonstration of the *absence* of influence by well-known Western philosophers and theologians (whom I call the Great White Thinkers) on the mature King who led the civil rights movement. Surely Carson's evidence indicates that King's dissertation did not deeply engage his intellectual interests. Neither did several of his term papers. Moreover, he absolutely ignored the assumptions and rules about language that the university had patiently coached him to observe, including the bedrock rule of print culture: 'Thou shall not use someone else's language without acknowledgement.'

While the discovery by Carson and his colleagues has made headlines, we should not be surprised to learn that King's intellectual evolution and language have little to do with the largely abstruse conceptions of the Great White Thinkers. Instead, as I demonstrate in a new book, King's world view and discourse sprang from two major sources: the sermons of Harry Emerson Fosdick and other liberal white preachers, and the African-American folk pulpit of King's father and grandfather, both of whom were folk preachers.[2] Though systematically scorned, ignored, patronized, or dismissed by most King researchers and most other students of religion, African-American folk religion shaped King more than any other influence.

Prevented from learning how to read and write, slaves developed a highly oral tradition of folk preaching. Black folk preachers could not own their sermons because they did not write them down. Instead, they borrowed sermons from each other on the assumption that everyone creates language and no one owns it. For example, 'The Eagle Stirs Her Nest' and 'Dry Bones in the Valley,' two sermons King heard as a child, were initially delivered at least as early as the 1860s, have been recorded many times, and can still be heard in black churches.[3] A large community shares those two sermons (and, for that matter, spirituals such as 'Swing Low, Sweet Chariot'), for only with the arrival of print have people come to view language as private property to be copyrighted, packaged, and sold as a commodity.

In the folk pulpit, one gains an authoritative voice by adopting the persona of previous speakers as one adapts the sermons and formulaic expressions of a sanctified tradition. Like generations of folk preachers before him, King often borrowed, modified, and synthesized themes, analogies, metaphors, quotations, illustrations, arrangements, and forms of argument used by other preachers. Like other folk preachers, King typically ended his oral sermons (and almost every major speech) by merging his voice with the lyrics of a spiritual, hymn, or gospel song.

As a very young undergraduate, seminarian, and doctoral candidate, King ventured outside the universe of African-American orality to negotiate his way through the unfamiliar terrain of intellectualized print culture. Thoroughly schooled in folk homiletics, he resisted academic commandments about language and many ideas espoused by his professors and the Great White Thinkers. As part of his resistance, he began the process of creatively translating into print the folk procedures of voice merging and self-making. He had trouble at first. Composing graduate papers and a dissertation about erudite metaphysical topics, he wrote a peculiarly crabbed, stilted, self-conscious prose that does not sound remotely like the King his friends knew or the later King. (For that reason, his dissertation and other graduate papers have never before been published.)

Fortunately King escaped the confines of his professors' strange, artificial tongue and their ivory-tower theological formalism. After leaving the academy, he sounded exactly like himself as he seized Fosdick's and others' sermons for the purpose of transferring black demands for freedom into an idiom acceptable to his main audience – white listeners.

The King Project provides examples of how this process began. Discussing the first set of boxed excerpts, Carson explains that King 'even adopted [Edgar S.] Brightman's first person pronoun' when King wrote: 'We must grant freely, how ever, that final intellectual certainty about God is impossible.'[4] Actually, King's merging of his voice and identity with that of Brightman, a respected theologian, roughly resembles the practice of folk preacher E. O. S. Cleveland, who merged his voice with the lyrics of a popular gospel song:

> THANK GOD, I Know How To Fly. Yes – I KNOW How To Fly. Yes Yes – Yes – I KNOW HOW TO FLY. DO YOU KNOW HOW TO FLY? ...

> Some glad morning when this life is o'er, I'll fly away
> To a home on God's celestial shore, I'll fly away.[5]

The last two lines above and several concluding lines of Cleveland's sermon form the lyrics of the song 'I'll Fly Away.' But who is the 'I' of 'THANK GOD, I Know How to Fly'? The 'I' designates Cleveland, but this 'I' becomes the narrative voice of 'I'll Fly Away' as Cleveland fuses his identity with the speaker of 'I'll Fly Away.' In roughly similar fashion, King practices voice merging when he merges his 'we' with Brightman's 'we' and blends his narrative identity with that of Brightman.

King's voice merging continued when he returned to the South and developed black preachers' traditional message of deliverance into the central theme and overarching framework for the entire civil rights movement. He remained a folk preacher throughout his public career. In the final two sentences of his last speech, he thundered, 'I'm not fearing any man. Mine eyes have seen the glory of the coming of the Lord!' The last sentence forms the opening line of 'The Battle Hymn of the Republic,' both a patriotic standard and a popular hymn. In King's speech, 'mine eyes' designates King's eyes but also the eyes of the narrator of the song; the personal pronoun 'mine' signifies both King and the narrator. Through this remarkable act of voice merging and self-making, King, like Cleveland, creates an authoritative, expansive self by merging his identity with that of the narrator of a religious song. King converges his voice and his identity not only with the narrator but also with Union soldiers who vocalized the lyrics as they walked into the Civil War and with every choir member and churchgoer who ever sang the words. In that speech and in countless previous addresses (including 'I Have a Dream'), the mature King created a voice and a self by expertly fusing his persona with those of earlier selves sanctioned by hallowed religious and nationalist traditions.

Resisting his professors' rules about language and many notions of the Great White Thinkers, King crafted highly imaginative, persuasive discourse through the folk procedures of voice merging and self-making. Reanimating the slaves' world view, he prodded John F. Kennedy and most of white America to listen for the first time to the slaves' time-honored cry for racial equality. By doing so, he gave whites their best – and possibly last – chance to solve what had always been this nation's gravest and most tortuous problem: racial injustice. King's paradoxical ability to revive the words of others in order to become himself enabled the United States to begin the task of healing the grievous wound of racism. Voice merging kept Jefferson's dream alive.

Notes

1. Martin Luther King, Jr., Papers Project. 'The Student Papers of Martin Luther King, Jr.: A Summary Statement on Research,' *Journal of American History*, 78 (June 1991).
2. Keith D. Miller, *Voice of Deliverance: The Language of Martin Luther King, Jr., and Its Sources* (New York, 1991).
3. Bruce Rosenberg, *The Art of the American Folk Preacher* (New York, 1970), 28, 155–62, 200–8.
4. Martin Luther King, Jr, 'The Place of Reason and Experience in Finding God.' [Sept. 13, 1949–Nov. 23, 1949], folder 17, box 112, Martin Luther King, Jr, Papers (Mugar

Memorial Library, Boston University); cited in King Project, 'Student Papers of Martin Luther King,' excerpts, set A; ibid.

5. E. O. S. Cleveland, *The Eagle Stirring Her Nest* (n.p., 1946) (Schomburg Center for Research in Black Culture. New York Public Library, New York, NY), 71.

The Preacher King: Martin Luther King, Jr and the Word that Moved America

Richard Lischer

...

What is the creative dynamic at work in King the preacher? Is it tradition or plagiarism? Keith Miller, who has thoroughly documented the sources of King's published sermons and other writings, announces his own position with the comment: 'Certainly an awareness of King's plagiarism does little to increase one's admiration for King.' Miller is making a legitimate criticism of King's failure to give credit to [Phillips] Brooks, [Harry Emerson] Fosdick, Howard Thurman, [J. Wallace] Hamilton, [George] Buttrick, and others in *Strength to Love* [a book of King's sermons published in 1963]. But before we begin adjusting our admiration for Dr. King, should we not consider the full force of his preaching and not merely the printed records of some of his early sermons? How did he use what he received and, having used it, was the event that he created a *copy* of someone else's published sermon?

Any appraisal of King's preaching on the basis of his sermons published in *Strength to Love* will reveal something of his citation habits, but it is bound to distort the essence of his preaching, not only because the book does not portray his mature thought or homiletical style but because *no* book can capture oral performance. Even if we had a later volume of his sermons, it could not convey the essence of his preaching, for the sermon's meaning occurs in the voicing of the word. The sermons in *Strength to Love* have been ripped from their context, which was the church's defiant worship in the midst of social and political upheaval in the South. King and his publishers decontextualized his sermons in order to give them a timeless and universal quality, which King should have known is the very antithesis of a sermon. In these sermons, the issue of race appears as an application or addendum to the prudent observations of a midcentury American liberal. The sermons in *Strength to Love* contain no intimate reports of the battle

From *The Preacher King: Martin Luther King, Jr and the Word that Moved America* (New York: Oxford University Press, 1995), pp. 108–13.

raging over integration, no trace of weariness, defiance, or disillusionment. They tell no stories from the pool halls and barber shops of Auburn Avenue. In them no authoritative voice from his Daddy's chair says, 'Make it plain, M. L.' The published sermons do not convey the extemporized celebrations of the gospel or the formulaic altar calls characteristic of King's later preaching at Ebenezer and of black preaching in general. They do not get *down* or soar to an ecstatic climax. They do not *deliver*. The printed sermons offer no access to the oral event whose power is real and felt but unrepeatable. They contain scarcely a memory of his voice.

Miller's analysis not only overlooks the eventfulness of King's sermons, it actually exaggerates the extent to which King relied on the words of other preachers. When passages from King's sermons are lined up in parallel columns beside their sources, the configuration on the page conveys the impression of massive borrowing, of a preacher who was neither original nor ethical in his use of secondary sources. But when King's whole sermons are read alongside the whole sermons of the influential preachers, it becomes clear that for the most part King used his peers – Fosdick, Buttrick, Thurman, Hamilton – the way preachers have always used the sermons of others: for an idea, a phrase, an outline.

A survey of the prominent preachers reveals how much homiletical material they held in common and how routinely they all borrowed from one another. To cite a most flagrant instance, it is instructive to notice how many preachers *published* imitations of Fosdick's famous antiwar sermon, 'The Unknown Soldier,' organizing their sermons around the very same rhetorical device. Or, to cite another example, when one considers how many sermons were 'out there,' say, on 'the nature of man,' one is taken with how *little* King borrowed from Claude E. Hill, Lynn Harold Hough, Sidney E. Mead, J. Wallace Hamilton, Harry Emerson Fosdick, and Fulton Sheen, each of whom published a sermon on the paradox of human nature during the period in which King was allegedly scouring the homiletical magazines for ideas. In the 1949–1950 edition of *Best Sermons*, a volume young King would have known, there are no fewer than eight sermons on the paradox of human nature. King's later 'What is Man?' does not so much copy from any of them as *join* them as one more sermonic reflection on the Bible and popular anthropology. King's sermon alludes to the popular piece on the chemical insignificance of the human animal whose ingredients are worth a total of ninety-eight cents. *Many* of the sermons on human nature in that period ring in the same illustration, just as many of them quote Sir James Jeans's comment that 'the universe seems to be nearer to a great thought than to a great machine.' That is the way preaching works. The anonymous banality as well as Sir James's profoundity were *there* for use – some would say, plundering – and the preachers, who like comedians are always looking for good material, put them to use.

In 1992 one of the most formidable black preachers of our century, Sam Proctor, and, like King, a graduate of 'Barbour University,' visited Duke University Chapel and, without citation, used as the premise of his sermon Harry Emerson Fosdick's 'Making the Best of a Bad Mess.' 'For this cause left I thee in Crete,' Paul says to Titus, 'that thou shouldest set in order the things that were wanting.' Fosdick's homiletical moral is that according to the Bible, Crete was a terrible place, filled with liars, evil beasts, and gluttons (Titus 1:12), but that it was just the sort of place that Christianity seeks to redeem. Just as Paul left Titus in such a bad mess, so God sends young Christians today to make the best of hopeless situations. Whether Fosdick invented or received his sermon's premise was irrelevant to King, who used the same idea in the 1950s and '60s and to Proctor who repreached it in the 1990s. Aside from the formulas about 'Crete,' King's sermon bears no relation to Fosdick's, and Proctor's bears none to King's. What is certain is that countless other preachers will continue to drain the swamp that is 'Crete' well into a new millennium.

Not all similarities between sermons are the result of conscious imitation. Miller consistently underestimates the body of theological knowledge available to seminary-trained preachers and often mistakes King's allusions to commonly held knowledge for intentional borrowing. For example, it seems pointless to try to trace, as Miller does, King's frequent dissertation on the three Greek meanings of love to a particular source. Anyone who has been to seminary more than a semester knows all about that. (King's handwritten class notes on *agape, philia,* and *eros,* taken in systematic Theology I, are available to scholars in the Boston University Library.) Likewise, it is futile to make much of the similarities between four preachers' account of the Prodigal Son as if they copied from one another. More than four preachers have tarried pregnantly over the phrase, 'And when he came to himself.' Miller should not be surprised that good preachers dwell on phrases like 'my father's house' or 'outstretched arms,' which are a part of the permanent script of Christian consciousness throughout the world.

Even when Miller has overstated his case, he has made his point. King's printed sermons *do* resemble the sermons of others. Preachers tend to echo the work of others – the black expression is 'I can hear Taylor *in* you' – because they learn to preach by imitating others. The published sermons that Miller scrutinizes are in fact the polished versions of King's own training sermons. Although in the preface to *Strength to Love* he says that he preached them at Dexter and Ebenezer, most of them originated in his pre-Dexter period of apprenticeship. They are the products of learning by imitation and preaching as rhetorical drill, methods he grew up with and learned from Pius Barbour and others. At Dexter King enjoyed only one year of normal pastoral duties and sermon preparation. The appearance of *Strength to Love* in 1963 effectively 'froze' his published homiletical style. He never produced another book of sermons.

King's method of preaching should not be evaluated on the basis of the sermons in this volume. This is to arrest his theology and style at a period in which he was heavily dependent on liberal theology and homiletics and had not publicly revealed his own black voice. Such a reading encourages speculation as to why King tried to sound so 'white' in his preaching, as though King were only pretending to be a liberal as a strategic device for ingratiating himself with white audiences. Miller theorizes that King suppressed his black roots, quoted the talismans of Western civilization, and thoroughly immersed himself in the liberal homiletical conventions of his day because he wanted to associate the claims of his Movement with what is best in Western culture. Miller writes, 'By adapting and readapting sermonic boilerplate and by refining and retesting his best original material, King successfully placed the strands of his homiletical arguments against segregation into a web of ideas and phrases that the moderate and liberal white Protestant community had already approved.' That is only to say he wanted to make his claim with words and ideas that his audience understood and accepted. This is hardly a novel rhetorical strategy on King's part, and it hardly deserves description in as ominous and reproachful a tone as Miller uses.

In a later essay, Miller adds a further spin to his theory by describing King's extensive use of Western philosophy and liberal homiletics as an enormous exercise in 'self-making' by which he carefully constructed a public self at variance with his own cultural background and intelligence. In a recent presidential primary, one candidate accused his opponent of 'reinventing himself' every few years. The comment was neither given nor received as a compliment. Where does one draw the line between the self-making that occurs in any public speech and self-making as out-and-out fraud? In his analysis of King, Miller leans toward the fraudulency end of the spectrum without, however, meaningfully addressing the *borrowed* quality of many of America's public documents and speeches – whether Jefferson's borrowings in the *Declaration*, Lincoln's reliance on Theodore Parker's 'of all, for all, and by all,' or [John F.] Kennedy's well-publicized dependence on Theodore Sorenson. Why figures such as these were not also involved in public 'self-making' is not made clear. In point of fact, King followed conventional methods of composition used in politics and homiletics. He immersed himself in the ideas of others and donned the costumes necessary to his cause. King successfully raided liberal culture, which, if one is to accept Miller's account, he could not possibly have digested – despite six years of postgraduate training in it – and has now achieved 'iconic status' as an American hero.

It is not only true but a truism that one part of King's many-sided genius was his ability to communicate with white liberals. But the duplicity theory of King's rhetoric simply reduces a complex and accomplished communicator to the sum of his sources. It does not appreciate how fully and unreservedly King at one period in his life joined the circle of liberal preachers in America. The duplicity theory does not do justice to the depth of King's exposure to and appreciation of liberal Protestant theology, and it does not explain why, if he was only mouthing white platitudes in order to ingratiate himself with liberals, he preached portions of these liberal 'white' sermons of Brooks, Fosdick, and others in his own black congregations in Montgomery and Atlanta. Nor does it explain why he gave essentially the same liberal speeches at predominantly black colleges and seminaries. If King embraced liberalism as a political ploy, why were its sentiments scattered throughout the sermons of [Benjamin] Mays, [Vernon] Johns, [J. Pius] Barbour, and other leading black preachers? What was *their* agenda? We are truer to the complexity of King if we admit that the sermons in *Strength to Love* represent his training wheels in theology and homiletics, which, by the time they were published, he had already outgrown.

The duplicity theory focuses exclusively on what it sees as King's self-conscious attempt to copy the style and values of the mid-twentieth-century liberal pulpit. It not only minimizes his appreciation of liberalism, but, by failing to give a *comprehensive* account of King's preaching, it omits its all-important prophetic dimension. Miller's theory leaves the impression that King was so preoccupied with associating himself with political and social liberalism that he never broke with it, never disassociated the Movement from it, and indeed never raged against it. But King's legendary ability to communicate with more than one audience did not compromise his moral vision or quiet his prophetic rage.

The duplicity theory operates with a rigid notion of 'self' and 'style.' Its premise is that there is but one true self that projects one true style. Any variation from this singularity is assigned to fraudulency rather than complexity. If, as one of King's associates once observed, 'Dr. King spoke and everybody could understand in his own language,' the only possible explanation of this phenomenon, according to the duplicity theory, lies in King's intention to depart from his own true self and style in order to deceive his audience. He fabricates another self. But what if the *self* is known only on its surfaces, and what if *style* bears no obligation to correspond to some metaphysical entity called an inner self, which is unknowable to outsiders anyway, but rather has a responsibility to adapt and mutate according to the demands of a particular audience at a given time? When these questions are addressed to King, one hears a rich variety of stylistic and thematic adaptations tailored to the needs of several sorts of white and black constituencies. When the questions of self and style are related to King's role in American history, one recalls [W. E. B.] Du Bois's (and King's) moving testimony to the Negro's desire to be *both* fully black and fully American. That anyone could have thought this possible, for however brief a period of time, seems inconceivable to contemporary interpreters of King.

Notes

1. *p. 75*: *"one's admiration of King"*: Keith D. Miller, "Influence of a Liberal Homiletic Tradition on *Strength to Love* by Martin Luther King, Jr." Th.M. thesis, School of Theology, Boston University (1985), p. 195.

2. *p. 76*: *the nature of man*: see *The Pulpit* (Chicago: Christian Century Foundation, 1948–55). April 1948, May 1950, January 1955; J. Wallace Hamilton's sermons. "Remember Who You Are" and "Horns and Halos in Human Nature," in J. Wallace Hamilton, *Horns and Halos in Human Nature* (Westwood, NJ: Fleming in H. Revell, 1954), pp. 46–67; Harry Emerson Fosdick, "The Mystery of Life," in Harry Emerson Fosdick, *The Secret Victorious Living* (New York: Harper and Brothers, 1934), pp. 129–38; Fulton Sheen, "The Psychology of a Frustrated Soul," in Joseph Fort Newton (ed.), *Best Sermons, 1949–1950* (New York, Harcourt Brace, 1950), pp. 28–34.

3. *p. 76*: *ninety-eight cents*: "What is Man?" January 12, 1958, Martin Luther King, Jr. Center for Nonviolent Social Change Archives, Atlanta, Georgia (hereinafter cited as MLK, Atlanta). For the Jesus quotation see Martin Luther King, Jr., *Strength to Love*, (Philadelphia: Fortress Press, 1988 [1963]), p. 71.

4. *p. 77*: *a "bad mess" in Crete*: Henry Emerson Fosdick, "Making the Best of a Bad Mess," in Harry Emerson Fosdick, *Hope of the World* (New York: Harper 1933), pp. 117–25. For King's version see "Making the Best ..." (April 1966), Audiotape, Howard Divinity School Library, Howard University, Washington, D.C. Proctor's sermon is available in audio and videotape from Duke University Chapel.

5. *p. 77*: *"Three loves"*: Keith D. Miller, "Martin Luther King, Jr. Borrows a Revolution: Argument and Audience, and Implications of a Secondhand Universe," *College English* 48:2 (February 1986), 250–51. On the Prodigal Son, see Miller, "Influence of Liberal Homiletic," pp. 73–4, 250.

6. *p. 77*: *"period of apprenticeship"*: King, *Strength to Love*, p. 7.

7. *p. 78*: *white Protestants had "already approved"*: Miller, "Martin Luther King, Jr. Borrows a Revolution," p. 256, Miller's theory draws on theologian James H. Cone's assertion that the primary audience for Martin Luther King was white America. See James H. Cone, "Martin Luther King, Jr. Black Theology – Black Church," *Theology Today* 40:4 (January 1984): 409–20, in which he asserts, "References to the intellectual tradition of Western philosophy and theology were primarily for the benefit of the white people so that King could demonstrate to them that he could think as well or better that any other seminary or university graduate" (p. 411). In a recent book, Cone writes, "King used liberal, Protestant theology to articulate the religious dimensions of what he believed about America, because he knew that its language about God was more acceptable to white people than the spirituality of black people" (James H. Cone, *Martin and Malcolm and America: A Dream or a Nightmare?* (Maryknoll, NY: Orbis Books, 1991), p. 132). In the area of preaching, African-American scholarship has not dealt with King's use of sources. Many would agree with the accomplished black preacher and former King colleague J. T. Potter: "Seldom, I think, black preaching has a mentor in the black community" (interview by Richard Lischer, March 7, 1988).

8. *p. 78*: *"self-making" and "iconic status"*: Keith D. Miller, "Composing Martin Luther King, Jr.," *PMLA* 105:1 (January 1990): 70–1, 79.

9. *p. 78*: *Lincoln and Parker*: See Garry Wills, *Lincoln Gettysburg: The Words That Remade America* (New York: Simon and Schuster, 1992), p. 107.

10. *p. 79*: *"everybody could understand"*: John Gibson interview, Ralph J. Bunche Oral History Collection, Moorland-Spingarn Research Center, Howard Univesity, Washington, D.C.

11. *p. 79*: *self* and *style*: These are Richard A. Lanham's assertions in *Style: An Anti-Textbook* (New Haven, CT: Yale University Press, 1974), pp. 115–16, 124.
12. *p. 79*: *both black and American*: W. E. B. du Bois, *The Souls of Black Folk* in *Three Negro Classics* (New York: Avon Books, 1965 [1900], p. 215. See Martin Luther King, Jr., *Where Do We Go from Here: Chaos or Community?* (New York: Harper and Row, 1967): "The old Hegelian synthesis still offers the best way to many of life's dilemmas. The American Negro is neither totally African nor totally Western. He is Afro-American, a true hybrid, a combination of two cultures" (p. 53).

5 Tactics: Non-violence, Violence and Armed Self-defence

Introduction

In recent years a number of studies have challenged the idea that the defining tactic of the civil rights movement was non-violent direct action. Instead, they have focused on the practice of violence and armed self-defence. The first selection in this chapter is by the author of one of those studies, Lance Hill, who has written on Louisiana's armed self-defence group, the 'Deacons for Defense'. Hill argues that the 'myth' of non-violence plays to the model that the civil rights struggle was won from the 'top down', with peaceful African American protests persuading a white-dominated federal government and nation to reform its overtly racist practices. In reality, Hill claims, 'segregation yielded to force as much as it did to moral suasion.' Hill defines a 'non-violent' phase of the movement stretching from 1954 to 1963 which, he argues, was supplanted after the 1963 Birmingham 'riots' by the violence of civil unrest and armed self-defence. This rising violence was crucial to the (in Hill's words) 'moderates' who practised nonviolence, since it handed them greater leverage in insisting that their demands be met to avoid the movement being taken over by violent 'militants'. Hill concludes that 'in an ideal world, rational argument and moral suasion should settle all conflicts. But that is not the history of the civil rights movement.'

Hill writes (one might argue appropriately, given his subject matter) in a very emotive, confrontational and often polemical style. What he infers in his writing is as intriguing as his overt arguments and it is worthwhile paying close attention to the language that he uses. One of Hill's central points, that movement violence gave greater leverage in negotiations to those who advocated peaceful protest, is certainly true and would meet with little argument. Some of his other conclusions are more controversial.

Hill's neat chronology of a transformation from a non-violent to a violent movement in 1963 might be viewed as overly simplistic. For a start, one might construct a similar model (and some have) that uses the 1965 Watts riots in Los Angeles or the 1966 rise of the 'black power' slogan as chronological turning points in that respect. More importantly, some would question the validity of a strictly chronological demarcation for the transformation from a non-violent to a violent movement. As historian Timothy B. Tyson has demonstrated in his contributions to the debate, African American activists such as Robert F. Williams in North Carolina were practising armed self-defence before, during, and after, the rise and fall in the popularity of non-violent direct action.

The language Hill uses is at times problematic. For example, he equates the word 'pacifism' with 'nonviolent direct action'. King and other proponents of non-violent direct action would dispute this and make a clear distinction between the two: 'Pacifism' implies 'non-resistance' whereas 'nonviolent direct action' implies 'active resistance'. An added confusion here is that Gandhi often referred to the technique as 'passive resistance'. However, non-violence is not simply about standing idly by in the face of oppression but about directly confronting it head on, although without resorting to the same tactic of violence often used by oppressors. Hill also adds on to the dichotomy of non-violence versus violence a string of other oppositions. Non-violence, it is implied, is a tactic of 'women and children' whereas violence is a tactic of 'men'. This is patently not true, since many men participated in non-violent demonstrations and many women and children practised armed-self defence too. The inference does reflect the machismo of armed-self defence in the movement in particular and of gun culture in the United States more generally. Whether protest is gender-neutral or gender-specific is an important corollary debate here which is examined further in Chapter 7. Whether protest has a class basis, in the implied opposition between middle-class non-violence and working-class violence, is also worth reflecting upon. So too is the issue of what constitutes a 'moderate' as opposed to a 'militant'.

Although John A. Colaiaco's essay in the second selection was written almost twenty years earlier than Hill's book on the Deacons for Defense, it is placed here in non-chronological order because it in many ways anticipates and acts as a rebuttal to some of Hill's challenges to the use of non-violent direct action. In particular, the line: 'What King's critics often failed to realize was that non-violent direct action is not a passive, but a militant and essentially coercive means of bringing about social change.' Ironically, one of the criticisms that King faced from white opponents who derided the tactic of non-violent direct action was that it was far too militant and fostered too much violence. In contrast, critics within the movement complained that non-violent direct action was too 'moderate' and too 'passive'. Certainly, King's campaigns involved a degree of violence, although King was at pains to point out, as Colaiaco notes, that non-violent demonstrations simply acted as a lightning conductor for white hostility and brought to the surface the often latent violence that underpinned segregation in the South. Non-violent direct action meant that African Americans could to some degree manipulate the focus of white violence and direct it to their own advantage, for example by gaining sympathetic media coverage. One result of this conscious manipulation of confrontation was that remarkably few people were killed or seriously injured in these demonstrations, certainly not in comparison to the violent urban riots in the 'long hot summers' after 1965. Non-violence also addressed the reality that African Americans were overall, both in the South and in the United States, outnumbered and outgunned. In practical terms, King believed that the widespread use of African American violence would prove suicidal.

Coloaico's analysis is not without flaws. Principally, in the light of subsequent scholarship, it is clear that his portrayal of just how smooth and premeditated King's strategy of non-violence actually was is exaggerated. King and other senior figures in the SCLC developed their strategy of mass nonviolent direct action demonstrations by trial and error and they did not always go to plan. Any form of confrontational protest brings with it the risk of violence spiralling out of control. The line between a 'demonstration' and a 'riot' can sometimes become blurred. Non-violent direct action did not guarantee success and King and the SCLC encountered as many failures and ambiguous outcomes as they did successes.

Non-violent direct action, and violence and armed self-defence, need not be seen as mutually exclusive strategies of protest. The two ran in tandem throughout the 1950s and 1960s, even though the emphasis on one or the other tended to shift at different times and in different places. It should also be noted that individuals did not simply fall into camps that advocated either non-violence or violence and armed self-defence. King remained committed to the ideal, as well as to the idea, of non-violence. Many more activists viewed non-violence, violence and armed self-defence as belonging to a battery of tactics, which also included, for example, litigation and boycotts as well.

Questions for Discussion

1. Consider the advantages and disadvantages of armed self-defence as a tactic in the civil rights movement.

2. Consider the advantages and disadvantages of non-violent direct action as a tactic in the civil rights movement.

3. Do protest tactics have gender and class dimensions to them? If so, can you identify what these are?

4. 'Should individuals be prevented from exercising their constitutional rights merely because their actions might provoke violence?' (John Colaiaco). Discuss.

Further Reading

Most of the books on King and non-violence deal with the intellectual, philosophical and ethical dimensions of the tactic, such as John J. Ansbro, *Martin Luther King, Jr: The Making of a Mind* (Maryknoll, NY: Orbis Books, 1983), reprinted as *Martin Luther King, Jr: Nonviolent Strategies and Tactics for Social Change* (Lanham, MD: Madison Books, 2000); James P. Hanigan, *Martin Luther King, Jr and the Foundations of Nonviolence* (Lanham, MD: University Press of America, 1984); William D. Watley, *Roots of Resistance: The Nonviolent Ethic of Martin Luther King, Jr* (Valley Forge, PA: Judson Press, 1985); and Greg Moses, *Revolution of Conscience: Martin Luther King, Jr, and the Philosophy of Nonviolence* (New York: Guilford Press, 1997). Sudarshan Kapur, *Raising Up A Prophet: The African American Encounter with Gandhi* (Boston, MA: Beacon Press, 1992) demonstrates that King's non-violence unfolded within the context of a longer tradition of African American encounters with Gandhism, and Joseph Kip Koser, 'Richard Gregg, Mohandas Gandhi, and the Strategy of Nonviolence', *Journal of American History* 91: 4 (March 2005): 1318–48 explores the origins and development of the tactic. There are no monographs that have yet provided a focused and searching analysis of the tactic of non-violent direct action as a tool of protest in the civil rights movement. Adam Fairclough, 'Martin Luther King, Jr and the Quest for Nonviolent Social Change', *Phylon* 47 (1986): 1–15, gives a useful brief overview, as does the introduction to David J. Garrow, *Protest at Selma: Martin Luther King, Jr, and the Voting Rights Act of 1965* (New Haven, CT: Yale University Press, 1978).

Works on armed-self defence have grown rapidly in recent years. A useful overview is Emilye J. Crosby, ' "This Nonviolent Stuff Ain't No Good. It'll Get Ya Killed": Teaching About Self-Defense in the African American Freedom Struggle', in Julie Buckner Armstrong, Houston B. Robertson and Rhonda Y. Williams (eds), *Teaching the American Civil Rights Movement: Freedom's Bittersweet Song* (New York: Routledge, 2002): 159–73.

Lance Hill, *The Deacons for Defense: Armed Resistance and the Civil Rights Movement* (Chapel Hill, NC: University of North Carolina Press,

2004) and Greta De Jong, *A Different Day: African American Struggles for Justice in Rural Louisiana, 1900–1970* (Chapel Hill, NC: University of North Carolina Press, 2002) both focus on Louisiana.

Timothy B. Tyson, *Radio Free Dixie: Robert F. Williams and the Roots of Black Power* (Chapel Hill, NC: University of North Carolina Press, 1999) and 'Robert F. Williams, "Black Power," and the Roots of the African-American Freedom Struggle', *Journal of American History* (Sept. 1998): 540–70, Craig S. Pascoe, 'The Monroe Rifle Club: Finding Justice in an "Ungodly and Social Jungle Called Dixie" ' in Michael A. Bellesiles (ed.), *Lethal Imagination: Violence and Brutality in American History* (New York: New York University Press, 1999): 393–424, and Marcellus C. Barksdale, 'Robert F. Williams and the Indigenous Civil Rights Movement in Monroe, North Carolina, 1961', *Journal of Negro History* 69: 2 (Spring 1984): 73–89 all focus on Robert F. Williams and the Monroe Rifle Club in North Carolina. Robert Williams, *Negroes with Guns* (Detroit: Wayne State University Press, 1998) is the most recent reprint of a first-hand account originally published in 1962.

Akinyele Umoja, 'The Ballot and the Bullet: A Comparative Analysis of Armed Resistance in the Civil Rights Movement', *Journal of Black Studies* 29 (March 1999): 558–78; ' "We Will Shoot Back!": The Natchez Model and Paramilitary Organization in the Mississippi Freedom Movement', *Journal of Black Studies* 32: 3 (January 2002): 271–94; and '1964: The Beginning of the End of Nonviolence in the Mississippi Freedom Movement,' *Radical History Review* 85 (Winter 2003): 201–26, look at events in Mississippi, and Simon Wendt, 'God, Gandhi, and Guns: The African American Freedom Struggle in Tuscaloosa, Alabama, 1964–1965', *Journal of African American History* 89: 1 (Winter 2004): 36–56 looks at a case study in Alabama.

The Deacons for Defense: Armed Resistance and the Civil Rights Movement

Lance Hill

...

According to conventional wisdom, nonviolence provided the impetus for change during the civil rights movement. In some quarters it has become heresy to suggest otherwise. Historians, for the most part, continue to labor under this truism. But the experience of the Deacons – and the other 'God's Devils' of the period – stubbornly contradict the myth of nonviolence.

From *The Deacons for Defense: Armed Resistance and the Civil Rights Movement* (Chapel Hill, NC: University of North Carolina Press, 2004), pp. 258–73.

Nonviolence as the motive force for change became a reassuring myth of American moral redemption – a myth that assuaged white guilt by suggesting that racism was not intractable and deeply embedded in American life, that racial segregation and discrimination were handily overcome by orderly, polite protest and a generous American conscience, and that the pluralistic system for resolving conflicts between competing interests had prevailed. The system had worked and the nation was redeemed.

It was a comforting but vacant fiction. In the end, segregation yielded to force as much as it did to moral suasion. Violence in the form of street riots and armed self-defense played a fundamental role in uprooting segregation and economic and political discrimination from 1963 to 1965. Only after the threat of black violence emerged did civil rights legislation move to the forefront of the national agenda. Only after the Deacons appeared were the civil rights laws effectively enforced and the obstructions of terrorists and complicit local law enforcement agencies neutralized.[1]

Nonviolence did have its day. Nonviolence unquestionably defined the black freedom movement from 1954 to 1963 – through the Montgomery Bus Boycott, the lunch counter sit-ins, and the Freedom Rides. But by the end of 1962 Martin Luther King and the more militant nonviolent organizations had fallen victim to state repression and terrorism. The Student Nonviolent Coordinating Committee (SNCC), CORE, and Southern Christian Leadership Conference (SCLC) had all failed to secure local reform, voting rights, or protective federal legislation. Appeals to the conscience of whites had foundered in the South and were having limited success in the North. By the beginning of 1963 the Kennedy administration was backtracking on promised civil rights legislation. Terrorism and legal repression so demoralized the movement that activists concluded that federal intervention was their only salvation. Activists were learning that the myth of nonviolence rested on a perilous underestimation of racism and a misplaced confidence in the American conscience and democratic institutions.

Then came the Birmingham campaign in 1963 and, more important, the Birmingham riots. The first riot occurred on 3 May after police opened up with water cannons on protesters. Young black men, nonpacifists who had previously lingered on the sidelines, now retaliated with bricks and bottles. On 4 May three thousand blacks, most of whom were uninvolved in nonviolent marches, assembled in downtown Birmingham and clashed with police again.[2] Three days later a peaceful protest sparked more displays of force by nonmovement blacks, including several hundred who encircled two police officers.[3] Finally, in the early hours of 12 May a massive riot broke out in response to two Ku Klux Klan bombings the night before. For the first time in the history of the civil rights movement, working-class blacks took to the streets in a violent protest against police brutality and Klan terror. The young blacks who defied King's strictures irreversibly altered the strategy of the civil rights movement, raising the specter of massive black civil violence and ultimately forcing the first real concession in the form of the Civil Rights Act. From Birmingham forward, every peaceful nonviolent protest carried the threat of black violence. The Birmingham riots marked the end of nonviolence and the advent of a movement characterized by both lawful mass protest and defensive violence.[4]

The May riots were followed by another riot in Birmingham on 15 September 1963 in response to the bombing of the 16th Street Baptist Church. All of these riots were essentially acts of *defensive violence*, that is to say, collective acts intended to protect the black community from police or white terrorist violence. In this sense, these forcible collective protests were part of the same countermovement against nonviolence represented by the Deacons and their armed self-defense philosophy. The tactic of collective force spread rapidly after the May riots in Birmingham. In the summer of 1963 – in the middle of what is traditionally viewed as the nonviolent phase of the movement – black civil violence against police and white vigilantes exploded in Lexington, North Carolina; Savannah, Georgia; Charleston, South Carolina; and Cambridge, Maryland. During 1964–65 more black riots erupted in southern cities, including a second uprising in Cambridge and disorders in St Augustine, Florida; Natchez, McComb, and Jackson, Mississippi; Jacksonville, Florida; Henderson, North Carolina; Princess Anne, Maryland; and Bogalusa, Louisiana. Numerous 'near-riots' occurred in Nashville, Atlanta, and other cities.[5]

Urban rebellions in the South placed enormous pressure on national policymakers, but they also dramatically affected local power relations. Significantly, the southern riots contributed to civil rights victories in many cities – in some cases, months before the Civil Rights Act went into effect. Desegregation settlements were quickly negotiated in Charleston, Savannah, Cambridge, Lexington, and St Augustine. McComb, Mississippi, lived under a siege by white terrorists from 1962 to 1964, despite two separate SNCC campaigns. After a series of bombings in September 1964, McComb blacks abandoned nonviolence and staged a riot. Within days, President Johnson brought pressure to bear on state officials, and the Klan was soon out of business. 'Whatever the speculation,' writes John Dittmer, 'the fact remains that until the end of September the Klan had its way in McComb, and the bombers were arrested only after blacks engaged in retaliatory violence and after both the president and the governor had threatened to send troops to occupy McComb.'[6]

The phenomenon of the defensive street riot also casts light on the role of black men in the freedom movement. Throughout the South, most black men boycotted the civil rights movement; the campaigns in Birmingham, New Orleans, Bogalusa, and Jonesboro became movements of women and children.[7] Many civil rights leaders explained the absence of men as some character failing – apathy, alienation, or fear.[8] Yet black men did participate in the black freedom movement in the Deep South – but not under the discipline of nonviolent organizations.

The numerous instances of black violence in response to police brutality and Klan terror constituted a form of collective political behavior – one that attracted thousands of black men. These collective acts of force were, in every sense, an integral part of the African American freedom movement. But for many leaders of the national civil rights organizations, the nonviolent movement was the *only* movement. When SCLC's James Bevel tried to disperse rioters who were taunting Bull Connor's troops in downtown Birmingham, Bevel shouted, 'If you are not going to respect the policemen, you're not going to be in the movement.' Contrary to Bevel, the crowd was very much a part of the movement – but a movement beyond the control of the pacifists.[9]

This conflation of nonviolence with 'the movement' blinded many to a new social movement unfolding before their eyes. 'No longer can white liberals merely be proud of those well-dressed students, who are specialists in non-violent direct action,' wrote Bayard Rustin in the days after Birmingham. 'Now they are confronted with a Negro working class that is demanding equal opportunity and full employment.'[10]

Even the role of black students in the movement was changing. During the 1964 Freedom Summer, SNCC lamented the lack of participation by southern black men and college students. But earlier that year, nearly one thousand black Mississippi students – men and women – risked life and limb in a militant demonstration and riot against police at Jackson State College. Although police wounded three protesters, the students were determined to march the following day and confront the police again; they were deterred only when Charles Evers and James Meredith intervened.[11] The hundreds of young people who participated in these protests were no less courageous or motivated than the passive resisters and no less part of a movement. But their actions made it clear that they believed that repression would only yield to force. One study concluded that black working class parents of CORE volunteers were less concerned with the possibility that their children would end up in jail and more concerned with the perils of pacifism. 'Most of the working parents – like with the CORE members – just object to the nonviolence,' said one CORE leader. 'That's what they disapproved of most. They wished we were taking guns.'[12] It was the genius of the Deacons that they recognized this sentiment and offered black men a way to participate in the movement while maintaining their concept of male honor and dignity.

'The lesson of Birmingham,' Malcolm X once observed, 'is the Negroes have lost their fear of the white man's reprisals and will react with violence, if provoked.'[13] One of the great ironies of the civil rights movement was that black collective force did not simply *enhance* the bargaining power of moderates; it was the very *source* of their power. This was evident even at the March on Washington, long heralded as the apogee of the nonviolent movement. Although the day at the reflecting pool was tranquil, the weeks preceding the march provoked considerable anxiety over fears of violence. The city banned liquor sales, President Kennedy mobilized 4,000 troops and placed another 15,000 paratroopers on alert in North Carolina. Authorities in Washington, according to one King biographer, feared that 'Negroes might sack the Capitol like Moors and Visigoths reincarnate.'[14]

Later in the day of the march, King met with Kennedy, accompanied by several other civil rights leaders and labor leader Walter Reuther. Reuther's remarks to the president offer a glimpse at how the fear of violence was shaping white opinion. Reuther took it upon himself to advise Kennedy on how to get the business community to support the pending civil rights legislation. In Detroit, Reuther said, he had pigeonholed automobile executives and told them bluntly, 'Look, you can't escape the problem. And there are two ways of resolving it; either by reason or riots.' As King looked on, Reuther pushed home his point. 'Now the civil war that this is gonna trigger is not gonna be fought at Gettysburg,' Reuther warned. 'It's gonna be fought in your backyard, in your plant, where your kids are growing up.'[15]

Black violence, in the form of riots and militant armed self-defense, fundamentally changed the meaning of nonviolence and the role of King and moderate leaders; it provided moderates with a negotiating power that they had never enjoyed before.[16] It was the threat of black violence, not redemptive suffering and moral suasion, that was now making the political establishment take notice of nonviolent protest. King understood the changing dynamics and readily deployed apocalyptic images of black violence in his speeches and writings. In his famous 'Letter from Birmingham City Jail' written in April 1963, King posed nonviolence as the only alternative to an impending violent revolt that was being fomented by the forces of 'bitterness and hatred' in the black movement. If nonviolence 'had not emerged I am convinced that by now the streets of the South would be flowing with floods of blood,' wrote King. 'And I am further convinced that if our white brothers dismiss as "rabble rousers" and "outside agitators" – those of us working through the channels of nonviolent direct action . . . millions of Negroes, out of frustration and despair, will seek solace and security in black ideologies, a development that will lead inevitably to a frightening racial nightmare.'[17]

King added that the black man had 'many pent-up resentments and latent frustrations' that needed to be released through nonviolent marches, sit-ins, and Freedom Rides. 'If his repressed emotions do not come out in these nonviolent ways,' he warned, 'they will come out in ominous expressions of violence. This is not a threat; it is a fact of history.'[18]

Following the March on Washington, King returned to his Birmingham theme. 'Unless some immediate steps are taken by the US government, to restore a sense of confidence and the protection of life, limb, and property,' he told an audience, 'my pleas [for nonviolence] will fall on deaf ears and we shall see in Birmingham and Alabama the worst racial holocaust the nation has ever seen.' At times, King's message was multilayered and seemingly contradictory, conveying different meanings to different audiences. His preachments against violence were intended for blacks, while his allusions to retributive violence were intended for whites.[19]

King's words were not wasted on the nation's leaders. What the Kennedy administration feared was not peaceful protest, but the black violence that might accompany it.[20] After the Birmingham riots, Attorney General Robert Kennedy expressed concern that police violence 'could trigger off a good deal of violence around the country, with Negroes saying that they've been abused for all these years and they are gonna have to start following the ideas of the Black Muslims and not go along with the white people.' President Kennedy, in his famous 11 June 1963 speech calling for civil rights legislation, spoke of 'a rising tide of discontent that threatens the public safety.' Social chaos would be the price of complacency. 'The fires of frustration and discord are burning in every city, North and South, where legal remedies are not at hand,' Kennedy warned. 'Redress is sought in the streets, in demonstrations, parades, and protests which create tensions and threaten violence and threaten lives.' Unless Congress acted, the only remedy blacks had was 'in the street.' In his message to Congress one week later the president revisited his apocalyptic images, speaking of the 'fires of frustration and discord' now burning 'hotter than ever' and conjuring up images of a nation wracked by 'rancor, violence, disunity, and national shame.' Kennedy's argument was explicit: nonviolent protest had become violent, and civil rights legislation was the only way to end the protests and avert black violence.[21]

Force and coercion also contributed to the 1965 Voting Rights Act. Although African Americans protested peacefully in Selma, Alabama, by 1965 most whites believed that the nonviolent civil rights movement had disappeared. The summer before, riots had erupted in Harlem; Rochester, New York; Jersey City, Paterson, and Elizabeth, New Jersey; Chicago; and Philadelphia – in which 2,483 rioters were arrested and more than 1,000 stores destroyed. By the time of the Selma march, many white Americans feared that behind every gospel-singing nonviolent protester stood a menacing street thug ready to hurl a firebomb.[22]

...

Violence is a controversial and emotional subject. Americans would like to believe that change has always been peaceful and orderly. We like to believe that each generation learns from the past, and we fear that young people will learn the wrong lessons from history; that in an age of numbing violence, a story about people who took the law into their own hands is a misguided fable.

...

In an ideal world, rational argument and moral suasion should settle all conflicts. But that was not the history of the civil rights movement. We can predict with the precision of science that problems of inequality and ethnic competition for power and resources will persist well into the future. What the Deacons tell us is that when appeals to reason and morality fail, oppressed people will turn to coercive methods of disruption, force, and violence. We delude ourselves as a nation if we think we can remain indifferent to these inequities and injustices without paying a price. We have the historical hindsight and the means to stop this cycle of violence.

Notes

1. Sidney Hook maintained that nonviolence is never effective by itself: that the threat of violence is what influences those in power, and reform is futile without violence. The popular myth that Gandhi led a nonviolent anticolonial revolution in India is belied by the violence that surrounded his movement. Gandhi constantly launched campaigns he could not control. For example, during the boycott of the visit of the prince of Wales in 1921, Gandhi's followers noted in Bombay while chanting their leader's name. In 1922 Gandhi called off a noncooperation campaign when volunteers attacked a police station and killed twenty-one police and Chaukidars. Hook cited in S. P. Aiyar, "The Anatomy of Mass Violence in India," in S. P. Aiyar (ed.), *The Politics of Mass Violence in India* (Bombay: P. C. Manaktalas and Sons, 1967, p. 28. See also Y. D. Phadke, "Historical Background of Mass Violence in India," in S. P. Aiyar (ed.), *The Politics of Mass Violence in India*, pp. 50–1.

2. Glenn T. Eskew, *But for Birmingham: The Local and National Movements in the Civil Rights Struggle* (Chapel Hill, NC: University of North Carolina Press, 1997), pp. 268, 270–1.

3. Ibid., p. 278 (riot of 7 May); Lester Sobel (ed.), *Civil Rights, 1960–1966* (New York: Facts of File, 1967), p. 181.

4. Eric Arnesen's book on black dockworkers, *Waterfront Workers of New Orleans: Race, Class, and Politics, 1863–1923* (New York: Oxford University Press, 1991), is a case study on how the judicious use of force helped secure black working-class economic gians. In the last decade there has been more interest in the role of organized labor in the civil rights movement. See Michael K. Honey, *Southern Labor and Black Civil Rights: Organizing Memphis Workers* (Urbana: University of Illinois Press, 1993).

5. For the Lexington, N.C., riot of 5 June 1963, see Theodore C. Sorenson, *Kennedy* (New York: Harper and Row, 1965), p. 493, and Sobel, *Civil Rights*, 204; for the Cambridge, Md., riot of 11 June 1963, see Sobel, *Civil Rights*, 196–97; for the Jackson State College, Jackson, Miss., riot of 4 February 1964, see *NYT*, 4, 5 February 1964, and John Dittmer, *Local People: the Struggle for Civil Rights in Mississippi* (Urbana: University of Illinois Press, 1994), p. 238, for the Jacksonville, Fla., riot of 23–24 March 1964, see "Shocking Police Action Spurs Negro Students to Strike Back," *Jet*, 9 April 1964, 14–19. Michael Newton, *Invisible Empire: The Ku Klux Klan in Florida* (Gainesville: University of Florida Press, 2001), p. 173; and Sobel, *Civil Rights*, 252–53; for the Henderson, N.C., riot of 12 July 1964, see Sobel, *Civil Rights*, 253, and Thomas F. Parker, (ed.), *Violence in the US, vol. I: 1956–1967* (New York: Facts on file, 1974, p. 75; for the Princess Anne, Md.,

riot of 26 February 1964, see Sobel, *Civil Rights*, 253; for the 1964 McComb, Miss., riot, see Dittmer, *Local People*, 305–10. Violence erupted in the wake of NAACP leader Medgar Evers's assassination in Jackson on 12 June 1963 as a crowd of rock-throwing blacks, chanting "We want the murderer," marched on the downtown business district, resulting in twenty-seven arrests. See Sobel, *Civil Rights*, 191; Douglas O. Linder, "Bending Toward Justice: Heroes in Great Trials Involving the Rights of Black Americans," http://www.law.umkc.edu/faculty/projects/ftrials/trialheroes/doaressay.html, pp. 2–3; Jackson State erupted a second time on to May 1967, when more than one thousand students engaged in a pitched battle against police and the National Guard. See Dittmer, *Local People*, 413. The Cambridge riots began on 11 June 1963, and the National Guard was not withdrawn until 1964. Cleveland Sellers, with Robert Terrell, *The River of No Return: The Autobiography of a Black Militant and the Life and Death of SNCC* (New York: William Morrow, 1973), pp. 66 and 74, reported that blacks were extensively armed in the spring of 1964 in Cambridge, Md., and that during the April riot a group of armed black men held off advancing National Guard troops with gunfire. For the St. Augustine, Fla., riot, see Newton, *Invisible Empire*, 173.

6. Dittmer, *Local People*, 310.
7. On the dearth of adult African American men in the movement, see Sally Belfrage, *Freedom Summer* (London: Andre Deutsch), p. 76. In the Mississippi Delta, SNCC's constituency was primarily the very young and the very old. See Dittmer, *Local People*, 125. As early as the Nashville sit-ins in 1961, young black men were fighting back, says SNCC leader James Forman. There was regrettably "limited participation of young blacks in the student movmeent precisely because of its nonviolent character." James Forman, *The Making of Black Revolutionaries* (Washington, D.C.: Open Hand Publishing, 1985), pp. 376, 95.
8. One researcher found that black CORE activists, frustrated by their organizing failure, often blamed working class blacks, whom they thought were "too cowardly to stand firm, too brainwashed by the white culture, and too apathetic to support the militant movement." Inge Powell Bell, *CORE and the Strategy of Nonviolence* (New York: Random House, 1968), pp. 99–100.
9. Eskew, *But for Birmingham*, 271.
10. Milton Viorst, *Fire in the Streets: America in the 1960s* (New York: Simon and Schuster, 1979), pp. 222–3.
11. On the lack of involvement by black students, see Dittmer, *Local People*, 245, and *NYT*, 4, 5 February 1964.
12. Bell, *CORE*, 99. Bell concluded that there was an inverse relationship between socio-economic status and participation in the movement by black students. Black middle-class students were less likely to participate in protests, often succumbing to pressure from status-conscious parents who regarded jail as a "badge of disgrace." CORE tended to attract more children of the working class, whose parents were less concerned with the stigma of jail.
13. "Freedom Now," *Time*, 17 May 1963, 23–25.
14. Taylor Branch, *Parting the Waters: Martin Luther King and the Civil Rights Movement, 1954–63* (New York: Simon and Schuster, 1988), p. 872.
15. Ibid., 885.
16. Herbert M Haines, *Black Radicals and the Civil Rights Mainstream, 1954–1970* (Knoxville: University of Tennessee Press, 1989), makes a strong argument for the "radical flank effect" on mainstream movments, though I would argue that the radical flank effect theory misreads the role of radicals in the black freedom movment. William L. Van DeBurg, *New Day in Babylon: The Black Power Movement and American Culture, 1966–1975* (Chicago: University of Chicago Press, 1992), offers an excellent analysis of

the positive impact of Black Power consciousness; he also argues, like Haines, that Black Power rhetoric enhanced the bargaining position of moderates (p. 306). I am arguing that black civil violence did not merely *enhance* the power of moderates: it was the primary source of their negotiating power. The events of the movment demonstrated time and again that the white power structure was unwilling to make any meaningful concessions unless there was a threat of black civil violence. The threat of violence transformed the very role of moderates; they ceased to be moderates when they began to benefit from white fears of black violence. After Birmingham, it was impossible to employ nonviolence in the moral and noncoercive way that Gandhi intended; the threat of violence was ever-present in the minds of whites. The fear of black cilvil violence was the driving force for the passage of the Civil Rights Act of 1964 and the Voting Rights Act of 1965. Moreover, nonviolent reformers who derived their bargaining power from the threat of violence were not, in the strict sense, practicing the teachings of Gandhi.

17. MLK, "Letter from Birmingham City Jail," 48–49.
18. Ibid., 49.
19. Robert D. Loevy, *To End All Segregation: The Politics of the Passage of the Civil Rights Act of 1964* (Lanham, MD: University Press of America, 1990, pp. 63–4. A few weeks later King told a gathering of Howard University, "If the civil rights legislation does not pass, I say to you that this ugly sore on the body politic of segregation suddenly will become malignant, and this nation may live in a long sight of darkness and violence." "Dr. King, Others Forecast Violence in Rights Struggle," *Jet*, 21 November 1963, 5.
20. Malcolm X saw a direct link between the Birmingham riots and Kennedy's new civil rights initiative. Malcolm aruged that King had met failure in the Albany desegregation campaign in 1962 and was failing again in Birmingham until "Negroes took to the streets"— forcing Kennedy to expedite the Civil Rights Act. Malcolm X, "Message to the Grass Roots," 10 November 1963, in *Malcolm X Speaks* (New York: Grove Press, n.d., pp. 13–14.
21. *Public Papers of the President of the United States: John F. Kennedy, 1963* (Washington, D.C.: Government Printing Office, 1964), pp. 397–98, 483–94. "Everybody looks back on it and thinks that everybody was around this [civil rights] for the last three years," Robert Kennedy once said, "but what aroused people generallyt in the country and aroused the press was the Birmingham riots in May of 1963." Quoted in Hianes, *Black Radicals*, 159, and Eskew, *But for Birmingham*, 392 (n. 24). The 12 May riot is detailed in Eskew, 300–303, and Sobel, *Civil Rights*, 184. President Kennedy's national television address on the heels of the Birmingham riots said nothing about rights or racial justice but instead sounded a "pox on both houses" theme. "The Federal Government will not permit it to be sabotaged by a few extremists on either side who think they can defy both the law and the wishes of responsible citizens by inciting or inviting violence," said Kennedy, equating Klan and police terror with the black response in Birmingham. "I call upon the citizens of Birmingham, both Negro and white, to live up to the standards their responsible leaders set last week in reaching the agreement, to realize that violence only breeds more violence. ... There must be no repetition of last night's incidents by any group." John F. Kennedy, "Radio and Television Remarks Following Renewal of Racial Strife in Birmingham," 12 May 1964, 9:00 P.M., *Public Papers*, 397–98 (quotation, p. 397). One month later Kennedy appeared before the U.S. Conference of Mayors and once again invoked the threat of black civil violence. He reminded the mayors that during the summer "large numbers of Negroes will be out of work" and the "events in Birmingham have stepped up the tempo of the nationwide drive for full equality—and rising summer temperatures are often accompanied by rising human emotions." If the nation did nothing it would be "inviting pressure and increasing tension, and inviting possible violence." Kennedy, "Address in Honolulu before the United States Conference of

Mayors," 6 June 1963, *Public Papers*, 454–59. In his 19 June message to Congress introducing the civil rights bill, Kennedy made eight separate references to the threat of violence, six that specifically appealed to white fears of black civil violence. He ended his address by warning blacks that "violence is never justified; and while peaceful communication, deliberation and petition of protest continue, I want to caution against demonstrations which can lead to violence." Kennedy, "Special Message to the Congress on Civil Rights and Job Opportunities," 19 June 1963, *Public Papers,* 483–94 (quotation, p. 493)

22   *Violence in the City: An End of a Beginning: A Report by the Governor's Commission on the Los Angeles Riots,* http://www.usc.edu/libraries/archives/cityinstress/mccone/part3.html (2 December 1965). White fears of black violence were pervasive by 1964. In the *New York Times Magazine* in November 1964, philosopher and author Eric Hoffer opined: "The Negro seems to say: 'Lift up my arms. I am an abandoned and abused child. Adopt me as your favourite son. Feed me, clothe me, educate me, love me and baby me. You must do this right away or I shall set your house on fire, or rot at your doorstep and poison the air you breathe.'" Conservative cartoonist Al Capp responded to Hoffer's article, saying, "It says aloud what most of America is saying through clenched teeth." Hoffer and Capp quoted in Benjamin Muse, *The American Negro Revolution: From Nonviolence to Black Power, 1963–1967* (Bloomington: Indiana University Press, 1968) p. 107.

Martin Luther King, Jr and the Paradox of Nonviolent Direct Action

James A. Colaiaco

My friends, I must say to you that we have not made a single gain in civil rights without determined legal and nonviolent pressure ... Freedom is never voluntarily given by the oppressor; it must be demanded by the oppressed.

Martin Luther King, Jr, 'The Letter from Birmingham Jail' (1963)

I

When the definitive history of the American civil rights movement is eventually written, one of the central themes will be that Martin Luther King, Jr. ranks among the greatest political strategists of all time. During the decade of 1955 to 1965, America was the scene of a social revolution that transformed the politics of the entire nation. King organized an army of nonviolent blacks that succeeded in exposing the evils of white racism and

From *Phylon* 47 (Spring 1986): 16–28.

overthrowing the legal system of segregation that had prevailed for generations in the South. King's method of militant nonviolent direct action, inspired by the achievement of Mohandas K. Gandhi in India, disrupted the segregationist order by means of marches, mass demonstrations, sit-ins, boycotts and, whenever necessary, civil disobedience. In the short span of ten years more was accomplished than in the previous one hundred, including the enactment of the Civil Rights Act of 1964 and the Voting Rights Act of 1965. While King was not the first to employ the nonviolent method in an attempt to resolve the race problem in America, he was the most successful in mobilizing masses of blacks to protest nonviolently for the fulfillment of their basic civil rights.

Although dedicated to nonviolence, King drew much criticism because his protest campaigns often were accompanied by violence. In the wake of the successful Birmingham campaign in 1963, journalist Reese Cleghorn wrote that King knew well that 'the "peaceful demonstrations" he organized would bring, at the very least, tough repressive measures by the police. And although he hoped his followers would not respond with violence – he has always stressed a nonviolent philosophy – that was a risk he was prepared to take.'[1] Although *Time* magazine chose King as 'Man of the Year' in 1964, its feature article contained the following observation: 'King preaches endlessly about nonviolence, but his protest movements often lead to violence.'[2] When King was awarded the Nobel Peace Prize in December 1964, the *U.S. News & World Report*, in an article entitled 'Man of Conflict Wins a Peace Prize.' remarked that many Americans believed it 'extraordinary that this prize should go to a man whose fame is based upon his battle for civil rights for Negroes – and whose activities often led to violence.'[3] In an April 1965 article in the conservative *National Review*, entitled 'The Violence of Noviolence,' Frank Meyer attacked what he regarded as the 'violent essence' of King's method. He charged that King's campaigns depended upon 'the provocation of violence' and a 'violent assault upon representative, constitutional government.'[4]

Such criticism persisted throughout King's public career. In another *National Review* article, published shortly after King announced plans for a spring 1968 Poor People's Campaign, involving massive civil disobedience in the nation's capital, Meyer assailed what he termed King's 'insurrectionary methods,' and solemnly warned of impending 'anarchy.'[5] Another critic, Lionel Lokos, in a book assessing King shortly after his assassination in 1968, charged that King's success depended upon both the threat and the provocation of violence, and argued that he left his nation 'a legacy of lawlessness.'[6] Lokos concluded: 'It has often been remarked that while Martin Luther King himself was virtually Nonviolence on a Pedestal, violence somehow never seemed far behind him.'[7] Even staunch supporters of King conceded that his success was largely dependent upon the provocation of violence. Civil rights activist Jan Howard, a participant in the Selma voting-rights campaign in 1965, maintained that although dedicated to nonviolence as a means of action, the civil rights movement needed violence to sustain it.[8] Historian Howard Zinn also admitted that civil rights were often won at the price of violence, but he contended that the degree of violence resulting from protests was insignificant compared to the justice achieved.[9]

The controversy over King's method arose from the paradox inherent in the strategy of nonviolent protest. Although King repeatedly preached that violence was immoral, his critics were correct in noting that his nonviolent method was most successful when it provoked violence from defenders of the racist order. In a revealing article for the *Saturday Review*, written during the Selma protest, King articulated the strategy of a successful nonviolent direct action campaign:

1 Nonviolent demonstrators go into the streets to exercise their constitutional rights.
2 Racists resist by unleashing violence against them.
3 Americans of conscience in the name of decency demand federal intervention and legislation.
4 The Administration, under mass pressure, initiates measures of immediate intervention and remedial legislation.[10]

King's critics quoted the above scenario as an example of self-incrimination.[11] They were surprised indeed to find King admitting that nonviolence draws its strength as a technique from the violent reactions of opponents. King and his followers always hoped to achieve their goals peacefully; but since the racist community was usually unyielding, civil rights protesters found that when they used nonviolent soul force, they often were met by physical force. Nevertheless, they were prepared to endure the violence they provoked rather than inflict physical injury upon their opponents. Racists contended that the black protesters should be blamed because their actions precipitated violence and disturbed law and order. Until the protesters arrived, the racists lamented, peace reigned in the community. But this argument rests on the erroneous assumption that the absence of overt conflict in a community means justice is present. The purpose of King's nonviolent direct action campaigns was to compel racist communities to reveal their injustice and brutality, and to compel the government, whether local or federal, to institute legislative reform.

What King's critics often failed to realize was that nonviolent direct action is not a passive, but a militant and essentially coercive means of bringing about social change. At the beginning of his public career, when King was propelled into international fame by his leadership of the Montgomery bus boycott in 1956, he was inclined to stress the importance of converting his racist opponents by reason and love. But after the wave of student sit-ins throughout the South in 1960, and the Freedom Rides in 1961 – which forced Southern communities to comply with federal law – King increasingly perceived the coercive essence of nonviolent direct action. As he developed a more realistic view of humanity and the nature of political power, he saw that most racists were compelled rather than converted. Nonviolent direct action was successful in the South because it exerted political, economic and moral pressure upon the segregationist order. It was this coercive element in King's nonviolent method that provoked violence from racists.

Critics of King concentrated upon the violence that his method stirred, giving scant consideration to the violence inflicted upon the victims of racist oppression. In almost every instance, it was the racists who committed the violence, while the nonviolent protesters provided the occasion for the racists to reveal their true nature. In effect, the racists said to the blacks: 'For the sake of law and order, you must submit to a social system even though you believe it to be unjust. If you protest, however nonviolently, I will retaliate violently and blame you for provoking me.' On the other hand, when the blacks did not protest, their passivity was interpreted to mean that they were content with their subservient condition. For generations, passive blacks had been virtually invisible – to use novelist Ralph Ellison's well-known description. As a result of the nonviolent protests led by Martin Luther King, Jr, blacks were no longer invisible; they literally had thrust themselves upon the national consciousness.

While it is true that the nonviolent protest movement was to a large extent sustained by the violent racist response it generated, one must realize that this violence was intrinsic to the racist social fabric. Such violence was not always apparent. Beneath the calm facade of the segregationist law and order lay the more subtle and often hidden violence of institutional racism. When not overtly subduing its victims with dogs and clubs, a racist society depends upon a latent form of violence, hidden under the guise of law and order. As long as blacks were willing to accept their oppression, they remained victims of a psychological form of violence, one that stripped them of their dignity as human beings. Denied fundamental civil rights, decent housing, and an adequate education, generations of black Americans were broken in spirit by the silent violence of the racist system. But when the nonviolent protesters employed direct action to confront racism, this hidden violence was exposed. King maintained that by resisting, the black man would 'force his oppressor to commit his brutality openly – in the light of day – with the rest of the world looking on.'[12] The civil rights movement was able to defeat the segregationist order in the South because the violence that it provoked from racists stirred the nation's conscience by making evident the injustice that had always existed, but under the cloak of legitimacy. Each nonviolent protester became a target, magnetizing the hatred of racists and exposing them to public view through the media. Clearly, to blame the nonviolent protesters for the violence that accompanied King's campaigns in the South is a prime example of distorting reality by blaming the victims.

II

An analysis of the history of the civil rights movement in America reveals that blacks most often made significant gains only after they employed non-violent direct action to disrupt the segregationist order, provoking a crisis. As Charles V. Hamilton has observed correctly: 'A politics of crisis is a prominent part of the black political experience.'[13] Before the emergence of Martin Luther King, Jr, the dominant means of winning civil rights was the legalism practiced by the National Association for the Advancement of Colored People (NAACP). Since its foundation in 1909, the NAACP had used a combination of public education, legislative lobbying, and court action as means to achieve greater equality for black Americans. Its strategy was to undermine the legal structure of segregation gradually by plodding away case by case through the courts. During the 1940s and 1950s, the Association won a series of impressive victories, climaxed by the Supreme Court decision in *Brown* v. *Board of Education* on May 17, 1954, declaring segregation in the public schools unconstitutional. But in the years immediately following the *Brown* decision, the great expectation of blacks that segregation was on the verge of defeat went unfulfilled. Public schools and accommodations remained segregated as the Southern states mounted a strategy of 'massive resistance.'[14] White Citizens' Councils were instituted and new life was breathed into the Klan. Meanwhile the federal government, adopting a policy of extreme caution, was reluctant to enforce the *Brown* decision. Perhaps the most flagrant expression of Southern resistance occurred on March 12, 1956, when 101 Southern members of Congress signed the 'Southern Manifesto,' condeming *Brown* as 'contrary to established law and to the Constitution,' and appealing to their states to use 'all lawful means to bring about a reversal of this decision' and to 'prevent the use of force in its implementation.'[15] Such blatant contempt for the law on the part of the South had a deplorable consequence. 'The true meaning of the Manifesto,' wrote Anthony Lewis of the *New York Times,* 'was to make defiance of the Supreme Court and the Constitution socially acceptable in the South – to give resistance to the law the approval of the Southern Establishment.'[16]

In the face of such a deliberate and concerted effort to defy the law, it became apparent that legislation and court action alone would be insufficient to achieve full citizenship for black Americans. Obviously, law and court decisions must be enforced in order to be meaningful. The law merely declares and defines rights; it does not fulfill them. During the 1950s and early 1960s, the Federal Bureau of Investigation and the Justice Department stood by while federal laws were defied, and civil rights workers were brutally beaten, jailed, and sometimes murdered. Although civil rights laws were enacted in 1957 and 1960, promising greater equality to blacks, these laws were either poorly enforced or ignored. Hence, a method had to be developed that would coerce the Southern states to comply with the law of the land, and induce the President and Congress to be more active in supporting civil rights. The method, forged in the crucible of the Montgomery bus boycott and developed into a fine art during King's Birmingham campaign in 1963, was mass nonviolent direct action. Under the leadership of Martin Luther King, Jr and the Southern Christian Leadership Conference (SCLC) – the organization King founded in 1957 to coordinate direct-action campaigns – the nonviolent method would revolutionize race relations in the South.

History confirms that the federal government long had been derelict in its duty to protect the rights of black citizens in the South. Usually, it enforced civil rights laws only after being compelled to do so. Although the *Brown* decision outlawed segregation in the public schools, a crisis was necessary in Little Rock, Arkansas, in 1957, imposing the threat of widespread violence, before President Eisenhower dispatched federal troops to enforce a federal district court order to desegregate the city's Central High School. Although the Supreme Court had ruled against segregation in interstate travel, first in 1946 in *Morgan v. Virginia*, and again in 1960 in *Boynton* v. *Virginia*, only after violence was committed against valiant Freedom Riders in 1961 did the Kennedy Administration intervene and the Interstate Commerce Commission (ICC) issue a decree supporting the court decisions. James Farmer, National Director of The Congress on Racial Equality (CORE) at the time and organizer of the Freedom Rides, recalled a strategy of deliberate confrontation: 'Our philosophy was simple. We put pressure and create a crisis and then they react. I am absolutely certain that the ICC order wouldn't have been issued were it not for the Freedom Rides.'[17] In 1962, President Kennedy sent deputy marshalls and federalized the National Guard to quell a riot in which two persons died and 375 were injured, after the University of Mississippi, in defiance of a federal court order, attempted to bar the enrollment of James Meredith.

Martin Luther King, Jr's successful nonviolent direct-action campaigns followed a recognizable pattern: the provocation of a crisis – accompanied by racist violence against nonviolent protesters – followed by federal intervention. King's unsuccessful campaign in Albany, Georgia in 1962, where Chief of Police Laurie Pritchett pursued a strategy of meeting nonviolence with nonviolence, peacefully arrested hundreds of demonstrators, underscored the fact that in order to achieve victory against segregation, the provocation of racist violence was essential. Only after violence was inflicted upon black demonstrators in Birmingham in 1963 was the federal government compelled to intervene and national attention focused upon the evils of racism in the Deep South. During the planning stages of the Birmingham campaign – called Project C (the 'C' stood for confrontation) – King's principal SCLC assistant, Wyatt Tee Walker, explained: 'We've got to have a crisis to bargain with. To take a moderate approach, hoping to get white help doesn't work. They nail you to the cross. ... You've got to have a crisis.'[18] Writing from his Birmingham jail cell, King revealed that the purpose of nonviolent direct action was 'to create such a crisis and foster such a tension that a community which has constantly refused to negotiate is forced to confront the issue. It seeks to so dramatize the issue that it can no longer be ignored.'[19] Shortly after King's release from jail, the Birmingham campaign reached a climax when thousands of school children were led in demonstrations that succeeded in bringing the city to its knees. Essential to the success of King in Birmingham was the violent response of Sheriff Eugene 'Bull' Connor, who epitomized the worst in Southern racism. King had learned that capturing media attention was necessary for victory in the battle for civil rights. While the demonstrators in Birmingham remained committed to nonviolence, millions of Americans were shocked by scenes on television and in the press, of city police, led by Connor, subjecting blacks to night sticks, high-pressure fire hoses, and attack dogs. After weeks of demonstrations, a settlement was reached, with federal assistance, that met essentially all the blacks' demands. After more violence erupted, not only by whites, but also by blacks who were not part of King's nonviolent army, President Kennedy sent federal troops to the outskirts of Birmingham and announced publicly that the federal government would guarantee the settlement. King's Birmingham campaign succeeded in compelling the federal government to intervene in support of black protesters, and was instrumental in the creation of the bill that would become the Civil Rights Act of 1964. President Kennedy was only partly jesting when he confided to King shortly after the Birmingham settlement: 'Our judgment of Bull Connor should not be too harsh. After all, in his way, he has done a good deal for civil rights-legislation this year.'[20]

In the spring of 1964, King led a campaign to desegregate public accommodations in St Augustine, Florida, America's oldest city. After weeks of mass meetings and nonviolent marches – which were met by savage white violence – the city sheriff obtained a local court injunction banning night marches. Night marches to the Old Slave Market in St Augustine's public square had become increasingly effective in dramatizing the contrast between the nonviolent dignity of blacks and the brutality of white racists. Within a few weeks, King and the Southern Christian Leadership Conference (SCLC) were granted a federal court injunction permitting night marches on the grounds that the ban was in violation of First and Fourteenth Amendment rights. Though white racist violence continued, it abated after SCLC lawyers, armed with the recently passed 1964 Civil Rights Act, were successful in securing a federal court order enjoining St Augustine hotels, motels, and restaurants to desegregate.[21] Although the St Augustine campaign did not fully achieve its goals, it nevertheless had a national impact. The racist violence it provoked focused attention once again on the grievances of blacks, stimulating federal court action in support of civil rights, and providing publicity that facilitated passage of the 1964 Civil Rights Act by Congress. These achievements, born of a nonviolent protest campaign that kindled a violent response, are a prominent illustration of the benefits derived from the paradox inherent in nonviolent direct action.

The following year, 1965, King and the SCLC launched a voting-rights campaign in Selma, Alabama, which became the climax of the civil rights movement in the South. Here too, King's success depended upon the ability of a nonviolent protest to create a crisis. As he observed: 'Demonstrations, experience has shown, are part of the process of stimulating legislation and law enforcement. The federal government reacts to events more quickly when a situation cries out for its intervention.'[22] Selma was an ideal place for a nonviolent direct-action campaign. Not only had the vast majority of its black citizens been denied the right to vote, but Sheriff Jim Clark's well-known record of brutality against civil rights workers had made him as much a symbol of white racism as Birmingham's Connor. After weeks of demonstrations and sporadic racist violence, protesters finally were able to provoke a crisis on March 7, 'Bloody Sunday,' when Alabama state police violently prevented them from marching across the Edmund Pettus Bridge and on to the state capitol in Montgomery to petition Governor George Wallace to enforce voting rights. After further protests, including another tense confrontation on the Edmund Pettus Bridge, President Johnson responded to the growing national outrage on March 15 by issuing an emotional appeal to Congress to support his proposed voting-rights legislation. Within a week, the President dispatched federal troops to Alabama to protect the historic voting-rights march from Selma to Montgomery, culminating in a stirring address to the entire nation by Martin Luther King, Jr. The Selma campaign bore substantial fruit, providing the major stimulus for the passage of the Voting Rights Act of 1965.

In Birmingham, St Augustine, and Selma, King and the SCLC proved to be consummate masters of the art of crisis politics. They aroused sympathy for the cause of blacks and national anger at the methods used to suppress them. Essential to King's success was his ability to attract media attention to the plight of black Americans and manipulate his opponents into playing directly into his hands. Though King would denounce the immoral practices recommended by Machiavelli for the successful politician, an analysis of his campaigns reveals that while he appeared to be the lamb, in reality his nonviolent method embodied much of the lion and the fox.

III

Citizens of a nation dedicated to the ideals of liberty, justice, and equality are understandably disturbed by the fact that a severe crisis was usually necessary before the federal government would intervene in the states and localities to defend basic civil rights. The frustration of millions of black Americans was articulated by a line in the speech of John Lewis, chairman of the Student Nonviolent Coordinating Committee (SNCC), delivered during the March on Washington on August 28, 1963: 'I want to know: which side is the federal government on?'[23] Under the US Constitution, all citizens, regardless of race, color, or creed, are guaranteed the First Amendment rights to speak freely, assemble peacefully, and petition the government for a redress of grievances. The Fourteenth Amendment guarantees the right of equal protection of the laws and prohibits any state from depriving a citizen of life, liberty, or property without due process of law. The Fifteenth Amendment protects the right of all citizens to vote. A democracy seeks to balance two values. On the one hand, law and order must be preserved and violence controlled in order that people's rights will not be endangered. On the other hand, individual citizens must be free to act peacefully to protect their rights. They must be free to dissent, to organize, to demonstrate. The question is: should individuals be prevented from exercising their constitutional rights merely because their actions might provoke violence? In other words, must individuals surrender their right to protest because of the threat of disorder? This is a complex issue, with no easy answer. Of course, the state must preserve order. But if the mere possibility of violence is sufficient to sanction the denial of the constitutional right to protest, all an oppressor must do to prevent the institution of remedial reform is to indicate beforehand that response to protests will be violent. While King's campaigns in the South often stirred racist violence, they did not depart from the requirements of the Constitution. Unlike the racists, who continued to act in defiance of federal law and Supreme Court decisions, King and the SCLC manifested a profound respect for the principle of law and order. They did not seek to destroy the social fabric; they sought instead to make it more just. Hence, whenever their protests involved civil disobedience to what they regarded as unjust segregation laws, they willingly accepted the legal penalty for their principled disobedience.

Despite express constitutional guarantees, blacks in the South frequently were beaten and arrested for picketing and demonstrating peacefully, and deprived of the right to vote. The primary responsibility for the enforcement of the Constitution and the laws of the nation lies with the Executive branch of the federal government. The duty of the President is to 'preserve, protect, and defend the Constitution of the United States' (Article II), which is 'the supreme law of the land' (Article VI). Nevertheless, the

Executive branch, as has been noted, has been reluctant to fulfill its responsibility.

In order to understand why King found it necessary to provoke crises to compel federal intervention on behalf of the rights of black citizens, one must understand certain principles of the American federal system. The issue of enforcing civil rights in the South posed a difficult dilemma for the federal government. The great architects of the US Constitution perceived that since power tends to corrupt, there should be a federal system of government – separating power, in the interest of liberty, between a central national or federal government and individual state governments. Under this system, the states' rights doctrine dictates that police power is reserved first to the local authorities. Consequently, the federal government assumed the authority to intervene in the states – either by court injunction, arrests, or federalizing a state National Guard – only when a federal court order was violated, such as at Little Rock in 1957, or when it was demonstrated that a state could no longer maintain order, such as in Birmingham in 1963 and Selma in 1965. Unless compelled by these criteria, the federal government had refused to intervene in the states to enforce civil rights. But this was no solution for the numerous instances of violence committed against blacks locally in the South. To leave protection entirely in the hands of the state and local authorities, except in cases of intense crisis, was insufficient, for it was often these same authorities who were responsible for the violation of civil rights.

King and the SCLC were counselled on the complexities of federalism by their legal advisors, including members of the NAACP Legal Defense Fund, Inc., seasoned veterans in the struggle for the equality of blacks. Indeed, King learned to take advantage of the dual system of federal-state law that federalism provided. Thus, civil disobedience to state segregation laws was justified on the grounds of an appeal to the higher law of the nation. At the same time, King and his staff understood the importance of maintaining a separation of power between the federal government and the states. But they also perceived that the South long had exploited the states' rights doctrine as a means of protecting its racist policies. During the late 1950s and early 1960s, the repeated demands of civil rights advocates that the federal government pursue a more active policy in enforcing civil rights in the South presented a formidable challenge to the traditional assumptions and rules of federal-state relations.

During the Kennedy Administration, pressure for federal intervention increased as violence against civil rights workers escalated in the Deep South. President Kennedy was determined to proceed with the utmost caution in the field of civil rights.[24] Though black voters had been essential to his slim victory in the election of 1960, he did not want to risk alienating Southern Democrats in Congress, or jeopardize the rest of his ambitious legislative program by calling for the passage of another civil rights act.

In response to insistent pleas that the federal government play a stronger role in promoting civil rights, the Administration confined itself largely to supporting a voter registration drive sponsored by the leading civil rights organizations.

The Kennedy Administration sought to explain and justify its caution. Attorney General Robert Kennedy had strong reservations against a civil rights policy that would place what he regarded as too much power in the hands of the Justice Department. In 1963, he requested that the House Judiciary Committee not grant broad injunctive power to the Attorney General in civil rights cases because 'one result might be that State and local authorities would abdicate their law enforcement responsibilities, thereby creating a vacuum, in authority which could be filled only by Federal force. This in turn – if it is to be faced squarely – would require creation of a national police force.'[25] The fullest articulation of the Administration's position was presented by Burke Marshall, Assistant Attorney General and head of the Civil Rights Division of the Justice Department. In a series of lectures delivered at Columbia University in 1964, published as *Federalism and Civil Rights*, Marshall echoed Robert Kennedy's fear that effective federal intervention to enforce civil rights would necessitate the institution of a national police force, with dangerous consequences for the federal system. Justice Robert Jackson had warned that 'the establishment of the supremacy of the national over the local police authorities' might lead to a totalitarian state.[26] Yale University law professor Alexander Bickel declared that a national police force would be 'destructive of the values of a free society.' In sum, the Administration's main contention was that more active intervention on its part to enforce civil rights might destroy the delicate balance between the federal and state powers that the Founding Fathers thought essential for the preservation of liberty. In an interview with Anthony Lewis in 1964, Robert Kennedy expressed grave misgivings when asked whether the federal government might assume primary responsibility for law enforcement in the states: 'I just wouldn't want that much authority in the hands of either the FBI, or the Department of Justice, or the President of the United States.'[27]

Civil rights activists long had pleaded with the federal government to investigate and prosecute cases of racist brutality in the South. According to Marshall, were the federal government to initiate civil rights suits on behalf of private citizens, it would exceed the legitimate limits of its power. The fundamental assumption of the federal system is that constitutional rights are 'individual and personal, to be asserted by private citizens as they choose, in court, speaking through their chosen counsel.'[28] Moreover, he argued that in order to secure an injunction to protect a citizen's rights, the Justice Department must have specific statutory authority, such as that granted under the Civil Rights Acts of 1957 and 1960 for cases dealing with voting rights.

It was not long before advocates of civil rights subjected the Administration's position to a thorough refutation. Some twenty-nine professors from six of the nation's leading law schools sought to establish a firm legal basis for greater federal intervention in defense of civil rights.[29] Citing the *Debs* case of 1895 as precedent, in which the Supreme Court ruled that the federal government may enforce the law when necessary by injunction in any part of the nation, they argued that the Justice Department could seek injunctions to protect the civil rights of individuals in the Deep South without specific statutory authority.[30] Moreover, they cited Title 10, Section 333 of the United States Code, which reads in part:

> The President, by using the militia or the armed forces, or both, *or by any other means* (italic added), shall take such measures as he considers necessary to suppress, in a State, any domestic violence, unlawful combination, or conspiracy, if it – (1) so hinders the execution of the laws of that State, and of the United States within the State, that any part or class of its people is deprived of a right, privilege, immunity, or protection named in the Constitution and secured by law, and the constituted authorities of that State are unable, fail, or refuse to protect that right, privilege or immunity, or to give that protection; or (2) opposes or obstructs the execution of the laws of the United States or impedes the course of justice under those laws ...[31]

The foregoing section of the US Code was used by the Kennedy Administration to justify sending federal troops to Birmingham in 1963. Moreover, the Supremacy Clause of the US Constitution (Article VI) empowered the federal government to intervene whenever a state failed to protect constitutionally guaranteed rights, such as the rights to vote and to demonstrate. As Haywood Burns has pointed out, the federal government usually justified its refusal to intervene more actively in civil rights matters by blurring the distinction between authority and policy.[32] The Kennedy Administration clearly had the authority to intervene all along; it simply chose not to do so.

As far as a national police force was concerned, civil rights lawyers pointed out that in effect one already existed in the FBI, which was authorized to investigate and arrest criminals who violated federal laws.[33] If the FBI can make on the spot arrests of those guilty of bank robbery, narcotics violations, and espionage, why can it not arrest those guilty of violating federal civil rights laws? One of the most persuasive arguments for greater federal intervention was developed by Howard Zinn, who contended that the Fourteenth Amendment had been enacted specifically to place the authority to enforce civil rights in the hands of the federal government whenever a state failed to enforce them.[34] Hence, the federal government had jurisdiction over violations of the

Fourteenth Amendment, and its refusal to protect civil rights within the states was an abdication of its legal authority and a violation of the Constitution it was entrusted to uphold. Nevertheless, despite the cogent arguments of civil rights lawyers, the federal government persisted in its policy of intervening directly in the Southern states to uphold civil rights only after a severe crisis arose, such as in Birmingham and Selma. Were it not for these crises, stirred by King's creative strategy of nonviolent direct action, the segregationist system would have been perpetuated for millions of Southern blacks while the national government chose to sacrifice civil rights to a distorted view of federalism.

IV

By 1965, King's method of militant nonviolent direct action had succeeded in arousing the nation to the evils of racism in the South and influencing directly the enactment of historic civil rights legislation. The Civil Rights Act of 1964 and the Voting Rights Act of 1965 transformed the face of the South and exerted a profound effect upon the entire nation. The nonviolent direct-action method enabled oppressed blacks to act constructively towards attaining freedom for themselves and vindicating their dignity as American citizens. Meanwhile, the progress made against segregation in the South had also awakened the blacks of the North. In August 1965, six days of rioting in the Watts section of Los Angeles signalled the end of the era of nonviolence, and served as a grim warning that the problems of the nation's ghettos could no longer be ignored. When King took his nonviolent method to the large Northern ghettos, where the problems were more complex and deeply rooted, he was less effective, for the oppressors were better prepared and more sophisticated, and racism more subtle and intractable. As King and the SCLC learned in Chicago in 1966, it was much easier to desegregate a lunchcounter or a bus station in the South than to eradicate ghetto poverty, unemployment, deplorable housing, and inadequate schools. It was also easier to provoke a crisis in a small Southern city, where nonviolent demonstrations could virtually paralyze a community, than in a vast metropolis like Chicago, where similar demonstrations were readily absorbed and neutralized. Moreover, beginning in 1965, thousands of lower-class ghetto blacks found the violent rhetoric of Black Power more appealing than nonviolence. But once blacks adopted the tactics of violence, they were less successful in exposing the often hidden violence of institutional racism and in compelling the fulfillment of their just demands. King's militant nonviolent method was successful in the South because blacks could be trained in nonviolent tactics that when applied to the racist system created the friction necessary to provoke a crisis and expose the brutality of the oppressors. If Martin Luther King, Jr's non-violent method was paradoxical because it often provoked a violent response, the supporters of the racist system were responsible for the paradox.

Notes

1. Reese Cleghorn, 'Martin Luther King, Jr. Apostle of Crisis,' in C. Eric Lincoln, *Martin Luther King, Jr, Profile* (New York, 1970). p. 114.
2. 'Man of the Year,' *Time* 3 January 1964, p. 13.
3. 'How Martin Luther King Won the Nobel Peace Prize,' *US News & World Report*, February 8, 1965, p. 76.
4. Frank Meyer, 'The Violence of Nonviolence,' *National Review*, April 20, 1965, p. 327.
5. Frank Meyer, 'Showdown with Insurrection,' *National Review*, January 16, 1968, p. 36.
6. Lionel Lokos, *The Life and Legacy of Martin Luther King* (New Rochelle, New York, 1968), p. 460.
7. Ibid., p. 225.
8. Jan Howard, 'The Provocation of Violence: A Civil Rights Tactic?' *Dissent*, 13 (January–February, 1966): 94–9.
9. Howard Zinn, 'The Force of Nonviolence,' *The Nation*, March 17, 1962, pp. 227–33.
10. Martin Luther King, Jr, 'Behind the Selma March,' *Saturday Review*, 48 (April 3, 1965): 16.
11. For examples, see Lokos, op. cit., p. 75; and Frank Meyer, op. cit., p. 327.
12. Martin Luther King, Jr., *Why We Can't Wait* (New York, 1964), p. 27.
13. Charles V. Hamilton (ed.), *The Black Experience in American Politics* (New York, 1973), p. 157.
14. See Francis M. Wilhoit, *The Politics of Massive Resistance* (New York, 1973).
15. Ibid., pp. 52–3.
16. Anthony Lewis, *Portrait of a Decade: The Second American Revolution* (New York, 1964), p. 45.
17. Quoted in Victor S. Navasky, *Kennedy Justice* (New York, 1971) p. 233.
18. Quoted in Harvard Sitkoff, *The Struggle for Black Equality, 1954–1980* (New York, 1981), pp. 128–9.
19. Martin Luther King, Jr., 'Letter from Birmingham Jail,' *Why We Can't Wait*, p. 81; for an analysis of King's famous letter, see James A. Colaiaco, 'The American Dream Unfulfilled: Martin Luther King. Jr. and the Letter from Birmingham Jail,' *Phylon*, 45 (March 1984): 1.
20. King, *Why We Can't Wait*, p. 144.
21. See Alan F. Westin and Barry Mahoney, *The Trial of Martin Luther King* (New York, 1974), pp. 161–4.
22. Stephen B Oates, *Let the Trumpet Sound: The Life of Martin Luther King, Jr.* (New York, 1982), p. 326.
23. The text of Lewis' speech, which was altered just prior to delivery to mollify its criticism of the federal government, is reprinted in Philip S Foner (ed.), *The Voice of Black America* (New York, 1975) vol. 2, pp. 359–61.

24. See Carl Brauer, *John F. Kennedy and the Second Reconstruction* (New York, 1977); and Victor Navasky, op. cit.
25. Arthur M. Schlesinger, Jr, *Robert Kennedy and His Times* (New York, 1979), p. 330.
26. Ibid., p. 328.
27. Ibid., p. 329.
28. Burke Marshall, *Federalism and Civil Rights* (New York, 1964), p. 50.
29. Haywood Burns, 'The Federal Government and Civil Rights,' in Leon Friedman (ed.), *Southern Justice* (New York, 1965), p. 236.
30. Howard Zinn, *The Southern Mystique* (New York, 1964), pp. 205–6
31. Haywood Burns, op. cit., p. 237.
32. Ibid., p. 236.
33. Howard Zinn, op. cit., p. 207; and Burns, op. cit., p. 238.
34. Zinn, op. cit., pp. 207–8.

6 Comparisons: Martin Luther King, Jr and Malcolm X

Introduction

Martin Luther King, Jr and Malcolm X have become popular shorthand symbols for polar ideological and other differences within the African American struggle for freedom and equality. There is King's integrationism versus Malcolm X's separatism and nationalism; Christian preacher versus minister of Islam; non-violence versus violence and armed self-defence; South versus North; moderate versus militant; reformer versus radical; middle-class versus working-class; university educated academic versus self-taught prison inmate; lighter-skinned versus darker-skinned; even, Michael Eric Dyson wryly notes in his selection, short versus tall.

In fact, King and X only met once, and briefly, in Washington DC on 26 March 1964, while they were attending the US Senate's debate on the Civil Rights Bill. Their cordial greeting and chat revealed that despite their differences there was little personal animosity between the two men. In the first selection, James Cone begins with that meeting between King and X and goes on to suggest that the most profound difference between them is the 'integrationism' versus 'nationalism' divide. 'Integrationists', Cone asserts, are those who believe that it is possible to reconcile being an African descendant and being American at the same time, and who believe that justice can be achieved within a white-dominated society by appealing to shared religious values and shared American values of 'freedom and democracy'. 'Nationalists' meanwhile embrace their African identity while rejecting American values. They believe that the historic persistence of racism and discrimination against African Americans, by legal, social, political and economic means, through the eras of slavery, segregation, and afterwards, demonstrates an irreconcilable tension between being black and receiving fair treatment in a white-dominated American society. Their solution is to separate from that society in some form or other.

Cone traces the development of integrationist thought from the early founding of independent African American church denominations which adopted, and then critiqued, white Christianity, such as the African Methodist Episcopal (AME) Church, the African Methodist Episcopal Zion (AMEZ) Church and various African American Baptist churches; to African American abolitionist Frederick Douglass, a former slave who eloquently campaigned against slavery in the nineteenth century; to civil rights organizations such as the NAACP, the National Urban League (NUL) and CORE, which paved the way for the later emergence of King's SCLC.

Cone then traces the development of nationalist thought from the slave conspiracies and revolts of the seventeenth, eighteenth and nineteenth centuries; to the free-born Martin Delany, a journalist and medical practitioner whose book *The Condition, Elevation, Emigration, and Destiny of the Colored People of the United States, Politically Considered* (1852) is one of the earliest articulations of African American nationalism and separatism; to Henry McNeal Turner, an AME Church bishop, and a prominent leader in the late-nineteenth and early twentieth century 'Back to Africa' movement; to Jamaican Marcus Garvey, whose Harlem-based United Negro Improvement Association (UNIA) became the first mass membership African American protest organization in the 1920s; to Elijah Muhammad's Nation of Islam (NOI), also popularly known as the 'Black Muslims,' to which Malcolm X belonged.

Having defined these two traditions, however, Cone acknowledges that they merely represent 'two broad streams of black thought' instead of clear-cut differences and he concedes that 'no black thinker has been a pure integrationist or a pure nationalist'. Rather, Cone views integrationism and nationalism as complementary ideas that belong to a much wider and more significant tradition of African American resistance to white supremacy. Like many academics who have spurned the simple popular dichotomies that allegedly divide King and X, Cone makes the case, both here and in the larger study to which this selection belongs, that the two men were ultimately more alike than they were different, that they were on the same side in wanting greater African American freedom and equality, and that, particularly by the end of their lives, their paths were converging, with King becoming increasingly radical and X becoming more 'moderate' after his break with the NOI.

The ambiguities of integrationist and nationalist thought are on display in Cone's respective narratives of those traditions. While his sketches do provide a useful starting point for identifying and unpicking the two strands of thought, the omission of African American leaders such as Booker T. Washington and W. E. B. Du Bois are telling. A former slave, Washington was the foremost African American leader in the United States from the 1890s until his death in 1915. In the face of segregation and disfranchisement laws being passed in the South in the 1890s, Washington advocated a temporary separation of the races, aligning him with nationalist traditions, but only so that African Americans could develop the appropriate skills and education to enter white society, aligning him with integrationist traditions. Washington's rival, the free born, Harvard-educated Du Bois, who became the most prominent African American in the United States after Washington's death, is similarly difficult to categorize. As a founder member of the Niagara Movement, which was a forerunner of the NAACP, Du Bois is aligned with integrationist traditions (although it should be noted that Du Bois always harboured scepticism about white involvement in these enterprises), while his later involvement with black nationalism and Pan-Africanism aligns him more with nationalist and internationalist traditions.

In the second selection in this chapter, Michael Eric Dyson reviews the book from which Cone's selection is drawn. Dyson provides a thoughtful commentary on Cone's career and scholarship and usefully sketches out Cone's analysis of the differences and similarities between King and X. He also provides an important critique of Cone's central thesis about the similarities between King and X overriding their differences. The delicate balance in this respect lies in fostering an appreciation of the similarities between the two men 'without homogenizing [them] into a mythic unity'. Pivotally, Dyson questions whether race can be viewed as a primary common denominator in struggles for African American freedom and equality above and beyond the latent divisions and differences existing within the African American population. For example, Dyson questions if a common African American heritage meant that King and X had more in common than the differences suggested by their respective Christian and Islamic beliefs. Furthermore, did their privileged position as men mean that they had more in common with white men than with African American women? Are identifications based along social class lines more or less important than race? Likewise, Dyson concedes, King and X 'were deeply divided not only about their tactics of social protest, but about their anthropological, social and psychological understanding of human beings'. Dyson concludes that 'the complexity and diversity of racial experiences cautions against advocating racial unity based on the presumption of homogeneity.'

One of the things worth keeping in mind about the debate over the differences and similarities between King and X is the fact that both changed considerably throughout their lives. The assassinations which brought a premature end to both men's lives at the still relatively young age of 39 years means that we cannot for certain know how each man would have continued to develop had he lived. Moreover, thrust into the media spotlight early in their lives in times of dramatic change and upheaval, the two men matured in public view even as they struggled to come to terms with and to understand the events that shaped them. The constant growth and development of the two men in their short lives means that we are always faced with the prospect of trying to compare two points that were never fixed but continually in flux.

Questions for Discussion

1. How useful are the labels of 'integrationist' and 'nationalist' for understanding African American leadership traditions?

2. Identify the differences and similarities between Martin Luther King, Jr and Malcolm X. Which do you think are the most significant?

3. How important is race as a defining identity in the United States? Is it as important as religion, gender, and class, for example? Can you think of other categories that might be added to this list?

Further Reading

The best starting point for an extended discussion on King and Malcolm X in the broadest context is James H. Cone, *Martin, Malcolm and America: A Dream or Nightmare?* (Maryknoll, NY: Orbis Books, 1991). Also useful is David Howard-Pitney, *Martin Luther King, Jr, Malcolm X, and the Civil Rights Struggle of the 1950s and 1960s: A Brief History with Documents* (Boston, MA: Bedford St. Martin's Press, 2004). Lewis V. Baldwin and Amiri YaSin Al-Hadid, *Between Cross and Crescent: Christian and Muslim Perspectives on Malcolm and Martin* (Gainesville, FL: University Press of Florida, 2002) have examined the two men within their religious contexts, as has Larry L. MacOn, *The Religious Ethics of Martin Luther King, Jr and Malcolm X* (Euclid, OH: Lakeshore Communications, 2000). Allan Aubrey Bocsak, *Coming In Out of the Wilderness: A Comparative Interpretation of the Ethics of Martin Luther King, Jr and Malcolm X* (Kampen: Uitgeversmaatschappij J. H. Kok, 1976) looks at the comparative ethics of the two men.

King has been compared with a wide variety of other figures as well as Malcolm X. These include studies by Julius R. Scruggs, *Baptist Preachers with Social Consciousness: A Comparative Study of Martin Luther King, Jr and Harry Emerson Fosdick* (Philadelphia, PA: Dorrance Books, 1978); Walter E. Fluker, *They Looked for a City: a Comparative Analysis of the Ideal of Community in the Thought of Howard Thurman and Martin Luther King, Jr* (Lanham, MD: University Press of America, 1989); Mary King, *Mahatma Gandhi and Martin Luther King, Jr: The Power of Nonviolent Direct Action* (Paris: UNESCO Publishing, 1999); A. L. Herman, *Community, Violence, and Peace: Aldo Leopold, Mohandas K. Gandhi, Martin Luther King Jr, and Gautama the Buddha in the Twenty-First Century* (Albany, NY: State University of New York Press, 1999).

On Malcolm X, the best starting point is Malcolm X, with Alex Haley, *The Autobiography of Malcolm X* (New York: Grove Press, 1965). Spike Lee (dir.), *Malcolm X* (Pathe Films, 1992) uses the autobiography as the basis for his biopic. Both book and film, however, have their limitations as primary sources as Nell Irvin Painter, 'Malcolm X Across the Genres', *American Historical Review* 98: 2 (April 1993): 432–9 and Gerald Horne, ' "Myth" and the Making of *Malcolm X*', *American Historical Review* 98: 2 (April 1993): 440–50 point out. George Breitman, *Malcolm X Speaks* (New York: Pathfinder Press, 1965) and *By Any Means Necessary: Speeches, Interviews, and a Letter by Malcolm X* (New York: Pathfinder Press, 1970) provides more direct access to Malcolm X related primary material. One of the earliest and best biographies of Malcolm X is Peter Goldman, *The Death and Life of Malcolm X* (London: Gollancz, 1974) now updated and supplanted by Bruce Perry, *Malcolm: The Life of a Man Who Changed Black America* (Barry Town, NY: Station Hill Press, 1990). Manning Marable is currently working on what promises to be the definitive biography of Malcolm X, provisionally titled *Malcolm X: A Life of Reinvention* (New York: Viking Penguin, forthcoming). Marable is director of the Malcolm X Project *http://www.columbia.edu/cu/ccbh/mxp/*, the closest equivalent to the King Papers Project. Louis A. DeCaro has written two books that look at the religious aspects of Malcolm X's life and career: *On the Side of My People: The Religious Life of Malcolm X* (New York: New York University Press, 1996) and *Malcolm and the Cross: The Nation of Islam, Malcolm X, and Christianity* (New York: New York University Press, 1998). Michael Eric Dyson, *Making Malcolm: The Myth and Meaning of Malcolm X* (New York: Oxford University Press, 1995) provides a counterpoint to his meditation on King in *I May Not Get There with You: The True Martin Luther King, Jr* (New York: Free Press, 2000).

There is an extensive literature on other African American leaders. There are a number of studies providing introductory profiles and comparisons such as Peter J. Paris, *Black Leaders in Conflict: Joseph H. Jackson, Martin Luther King, Jr, Malcolm X, Adam Clayton Powell, Jr* (New York: Pilgrim Press, 1978); John White, *Black Leadership in America: From Booker T. Washington to Jesse Jackson* (Harlow: Longman, 1985); and Manning Marable, *Black Leadership: Four Great American Leaders and the Struggle for Civil Rights* (New York: Penguin, 1999).

A number of books published in the 1960s and 1970s located black nationalist traditions within the context of the emergence of the civil rights and black power movements. Among them were: Essien Udosen Essien-Udom, *Black Nationalism: A Search for Identity in America* (Chicago, IL: University of Chicago Press, 1962) and *Black Nationalism: The Rise of the*

Black Muslims in the USA. (Harmondsworth: Penguin Books, 1966); Theodore Draper, *The Rediscovery of Black Nationalism* (New York: Viking Press, 1970); Victor Ullman, *Martin R. Delaney: The Beginnings of Black Nationalism* (Boston, MA: Beacon Press, 1971); Thomas P. Vincent, *Black Power and the Garvey Movement* (Berkeley, CA: Ramparts Press, 1971); and Sterling Stuckey, *The Ideological Origins of Black Nationalism* (Boston, MA: Beacon Press, 1971). The best recent book on the subject is William L. Van Deburg (ed.), *Modern Black Nationalism from Marcus Garvey to Louis Farrakhan* (New York: New York University Press, 1997).

Booker T. Washington, *Up from Slavery: An Autobiography* (originally published in 1901 and available in various reprints) is a first-hand account of his life and his definitive two-volume biography is by Louis R. Harlan, *Booker T. Washington: The Making of a Black Leader, 1856–1900* (New York: Oxford University Press, 1972) and *Booker T. Washington: The Wizard of Tuskegee, 1901–1915* (New York: Oxford University Press, 1983). W. E. B. Du Bois, *The Souls of Black Folk* (originally published in 1903 and available in various reprints) is his most famous and most often quoted work on African American history, politics, and culture, and the two-volume biography by David Levering Lewis, *W. E. B. Du Bois: Biography of a Race, 1868–1919* (New York: Henry Holt and Co., 1993) and *W. E. B. Du Bois: The Fight for Equality and the American Century, 1919–1963* (New York: Henry Holt and Co., 2000) is the equivalent of Harlan's biography on Washington. Marcus Garvey's writings can be sampled in the compilation by his widow Amy Jacques Garvey (ed.), *Philosophy and Opinions of Marcus Garvey, Or Africa for the Africans* (originally published in two volumes in 1923 and 1925 and now available in various one-volume reprints). Tony Martin, *Race First: The Ideological and Organizational Struggles of Marcus Garvey and the Universal Negro Improvement Association* (Westport, CT: Greenwood Press, 1976), is the closest to a standard biography with Judith Stein, *The World of Marcus Garvey: Race and Class in Modern Society* (Baton Rouge, LA: Louisiana State University Press, 1986), and Rupert Lewis's *Marcus Garvey: Anti-Colonial Champion* (London: Karia Press, 1987) the most current valuable updates.

Martin and Malcolm and America: A Dream or a Nightmare?

James H. Cone

...

The meeting of Martin and Malcolm has profound, symbolic meaning for the black freedom movement. It was more than a meeting of two prominent leaders in the African-American community. It was a meeting of two great resistance traditions in African-American history – integrationism and nationalism. Together Martin, a Christian integrationist, and Malcolm, a Muslim nationalist, would have been a powerful force against racial injustice. When they were separated, their enemies were successful in pitting them against each other and thereby diluting the effectiveness of the black freedom movement. Both Martin and Malcolm were acutely aware of the dangers of disunity among African-Americans. They frequently spoke out against it and urged African-Americans to forget their differences and to unite in a common struggle for justice and freedom. Why then did Martin and Malcolm not set an example by joining their forces together into a black united front against racism? The answer to this question is found partly in the interrelationship of integrationism and nationalism in African-American history. These two resistance traditions also provide the historical context for a deeper understanding of Martin's dream and Malcolm's nightmare.

Integrationism and Nationalism in African-American Intellectual History

No one stated the dilemma that slavery and segregation created for Africans in the United States as sharply and poignantly as W. E. B. Du Bois. In his classic statement of the problem, he spoke of it as a 'peculiar sensation,' a 'double-consciousness,' 'two souls, two thoughts, two unreconciled strivings; two warring ideals in one dark body, whose dogged strength alone keeps it from being torn asunder.' The 'twoness' that Du Bois was describing stemmed from being an African *in* America. 'Here, then, is the dilemma,' he wrote in 'The Conservation of Races.' 'What, after all, am I? Am I an American or am I a Negro? Can I be both?'[1]

From *Martin and Malcolm and America: A Dream or a Nightmare?* (New York: Orbis Books, 1991), pp. 1–17.

Integrationist thinkers may be defined as those who answer 'Yes' to the question, 'Can I be both?' They believe it is possible to achieve justice in the United States and to create wholesome relations with the white community. This optimism has been based upon the 'American creed,' the tradition of freedom and democracy as articulated in the Declaration of Independence and the Constitution, and is supported, they believe, by the Jewish and Christian Scriptures. The integrationist line of thought goes something like this: If whites really believe their political and religious documents, then they know that black people should not be enslaved and segregated but rather integrated into the mainstream of the society. After all, blacks are Americans, having arrived even before the Pilgrims. They have worked the land, obeyed the laws, paid their taxes, and defended America in every war. They built the nation as much as white people did. Therefore, the integrationists argue, it is the task of African-American leaders to prick the conscience of whites, showing the contradictions between their professed values and their actual treatment of blacks. Then whites will be embarrassed by their hypocrisy and will grant blacks the same freedom that they themselves enjoy.

On the other hand, nationalist thinkers have rejected the American side of their identity and affirmed the African side, saying 'No, we can't be both.' They have contended that 244 years of slavery, followed by legal segregation, social degradation, political disfranchisement, and economic exploitation means that blacks will never be recognized as human beings in white society. America isn't for blacks; blacks can't be for America. The nationalists argue that blacks don't belong with whites, that whites are killing blacks, generation after generation. Blacks should, therefore, separate from America, either by returning to Africa or by going to some other place where they can create sociopolitical structures that are derived from their own history and culture.

Integrationism and nationalism represent the two broad streams of black thought in response to the problem of slavery and segregation in America. Of course, no black thinker has been a pure integrationist or a pure nationalist, but rather all black intellectuals have represented aspects of each, with emphasis moving in one direction or the other, usually at different periods of their lives. What emphasis any black thinker made was usually determined by his or her perspective on America, that is, whether he or she believed that blacks would soon be included in the mainstream of American life on a par with whites. When blacks have been optimistic about America – believing that they could achieve full equality through moral suasion and legal argument – they have been integrationists and have minimized their nationalist tendencies. On the other hand, despair about America – believing that genuine equality is impossible because whites have no moral conscience or any intention to apply the laws fairly – has always been the seedbed of nationalism. To understand Martin King's and Malcolm X's perspectives on

America and their relation to each other, it is important to see them in the light of these two different but interdependent streams of black thought.

Integrationism before Martin King

Integrationists have had many able advocates since the founding of the republic. Among them were the great abolitionist Frederick Douglass, many prominent black preachers, and representatives of the National Association for the Advancement of Colored People (NAACP), the National Urban League, and the Congress of Racial Equality (CORE).

Frederick Douglass was the outstanding advocate of integrationism during the nineteenth century. Born a slave, Douglass escaped from slavery and became an international figure with his powerful speeches and writings in defense of the full citizenship rights of blacks. For him the existence of slavery was a staggering contradiction of the principles of the Constitution and the concept of humanity.

Unlike the white abolitionist William Lloyd Garrison, who denied his allegiance to a Constitution ratified by slaveholders, Douglass embraced it as an 'anti-slavery document' and then proceeded to quote it as supporting evidence for the abolition of slavery. The Constitution reads, ' "We the people"; not we the white people,' Douglass proclaimed; 'and if Negroes are people, they are included in the benefits for which the Constitution of America was ordained and established.'[2]

No one was as persuasive as Frederick Douglass in pointing out to whites the hypocrisy of extolling the 'principles of political freedom and of natural justice' articulated in the Declaration of Independence while holding blacks as slaves. His well-known Independence Day speech in Rochester, New York, on the topic 'What to the Slave Is the Fourth of July?' was calculated to cut deeply into the conscience of whites who thought of themselves as civilized. 'To [the slave], your celebration is a sham,' he proclaimed to a stunned white audience. 'Your denunciation of tyrants, brass-fronted impudence; your shouts of liberty and equality, hollow mockery. ... There is not a nation on the earth guilty of practices more shocking and bloody than are the people of the United States.'[3]

Douglass's scathing words did not mean that he had given up on America and would accordingly seek separation from the land of his birth. He was offered an opportunity to stay in England where he was given many honors, but he rejected the idea. Douglass believed that blacks could find justice in the United States and safely intertwine their future with that of the white majority. He was severely critical of blacks and whites who proposed the colonization of blacks in Africa or some other place. 'It's all nonsense to talk about the removal of eight million of the American people from their homes in America to Africa,' he said. 'The destiny of the colored Americans ... is the destiny of America. We shall never leave you. ... We are here. ... To imagine that we should ever be eradicated is absurd and ridiculous. We can be modified, changed, assimilated, but never extinguished. ... This is our country; and the question for the philosophers and statesmen of the land ought to be, What principle should dictate the policy of the nation toward us?'[4]

Although Douglass experienced many disappointments in his fight for justice, he never lost his love for America or his belief that blacks would soon achieve full freedom in the land of their birth. 'I expect to see the colored people of this country enjoying the same freedom [as whites],' he said in 1865, 'voting at the same ballot-box ..., going to the same schools, attending the same churches, traveling the same street cars, in the same railroad cars, ... proud of the same country, fighting the same foe, and enjoying the same peace, and all its advantages.'[5]

Optimism about blacks achieving full citizenship rights in America has always been the hallmark of integrationism. This optimism has been based not only on the political ideals of America but also upon its claim to be founded on Christian principles. Blacks have believed that the Christian faith requires that whites treat them as equals before God. No group articulated this point with more religious conviction and fervor than black preachers.

According to black preachers, Christianity is a gospel of justice and love. Believers, therefore, must treat all people justly and lovingly – that is, as brothers and sisters. Why? Because God, the creator of all, is no respecter of persons. Out of one blood God has created all people. On the cross Jesus Christ died for all – whites and blacks alike. Our oneness in creation and redemption means that no Christian can condone slavery or segregation in the churches or the society. The integration of whites and blacks into one community, therefore, is the only option open for Christians.

As early as 1787, Richard Allen (an ex-slave and a Methodist minister) led a group of blacks out of St George Methodist Church in Philadelphia, and in 1816 he founded the African Methodist Episcopal (AME) Church. He did this because he and his followers refused to accept segregation in the 'Lord's house.' A few years later, James Varick and other blacks in New York took similar action and organized the African Methodist Episcopal Zion (AMEZ) Church. Black Baptists also formed separate congregations.

Independent black churches were not separatist in the strict sense. They were not separating themselves from whites because they held a different doctrinal view of Christianity. Without exception, blacks used the same articles of faith and polity for their churches as the white denominations from which they separated. Separation, for blacks, meant that they were rejecting the *ethical* behavior of whites – they were rejecting racism that was based on the assumption that God created blacks inferior to whites. Blacks also wanted to prove that they had the capability to organize and to operate a denomination just like whites. In short, black Christians were bearing witness to their humanity, which they believed God created equal to that of whites. The motto of the AME Church reflected that conviction: 'God our Father, Christ our Redeemer, Man our Brother.' 'When these sentiments are universal in theory and practice,' the AME bishops said in 1896, 'then the mission of the distinctive colored organization will cease.'[6]

Not all black Christians chose the strategy of separation. Instead, some decided to stay in white denominations and use them as platforms from which to prick the conscience of whites regarding the demands of the gospel and to encourage blacks to strike a blow for freedom. 'Liberty is a spirit sent out from God,' proclaimed Henry Highland Garnet, a Presbyterian minister, 'and like its great Author, is no respector of persons.'[7]

Following the Civil War, the great majority of black Christians joined black-led churches among the Methodists and Baptists. The independence of these churches enabled their pastors to become prominent leaders in the black struggle for integration in the society. Prominent Baptists included Adam Clayton Powell, Sr, and Jr, of the Abyssinian Baptist Church (New York), Martin Luther King, Sr, of Ebenezer Baptist Church (Atlanta), William Holmes Borders of the Wheat Street Baptist Church (Atlanta), and Vernon Johns of the Dexter Avenue Baptist Church (Montgomery). Reverdy C. Ransom, an AME minister, was a 'pioneer black social gospeler.' Other significant voices included Benjamin E. Mays, president of Morehouse College, and Howard Thurman, dean of Rankin Chapel and professor of theology at Howard University. All spoke out against segregation and racism in the white churches and the society, insisting that the integration of blacks and whites into one community was the demand of the Christian faith. In his book *Marching Blacks*, Adam Powell, Jr, accused white churches of turning Christianity into 'churchianity,' thereby distorting its essential message of 'equality' and 'brotherhood.' 'No one can say that Christianity has failed,' he said. 'It has never been tried.'[8]

How can whites claim to be Christians and still hold blacks as slaves or segregate them in their churches and the society? That has been the great paradox for black Christians. Since whites attended their churches regularly, with an air of reverence for God, and studied the Bible conscientiously, blacks expected them to see the truth of the gospel and thereby accept them into their churches and the society as brothers and sisters. Many black Christians believed that it was only a matter of a little time before Jesus would reveal the gospel truth to whites and slavery and segregation would come tumbling down like the walls of Jericho. That was the basis of the optimism among black Christians.

Too much confidence in what God is going to do often creates an other-worldly perspective which encourages passivity in the face of injustice and suffering. That happened to the great majority of blacks from the time of the Civil War to the coming of Martin Luther King, Jr. The organized fight for justice was transferred from the churches to secular groups, commonly known as civil rights organizations, especially the NAACP, the National Urban League, and CORE. Each came into existence for the sole purpose of achieving full citizenship rights for African-Americans in every aspect of American society. They often have used different tactics and have worked in different areas, but the goal has been the same – the integration of blacks into the mainstream of American society so that color will no longer be a determining factor for success or failure in any human endeavor.

Founded by prominent whites and blacks in 1909, the NAACP was the first and has been the most influential civil rights organization. Branded as radical before the 1960s, it has been a strong advocate of integration, using the courts as the primary arena in which to protest segregation. The NAACP is best known for its successful argument before the United States Supreme Court against the doctrine of 'separate but equal' schools for blacks and whites, claiming that such schools are inherently unequal and therefore unconstitutional. The 17 May 1954 school desegregation decision has often been called the beginning of the black freedom movement of the 1950s and 1960s.

One year after the founding of the NAACP, the National Urban League was organized. Less aggressive than the NAACP, the Urban League was founded 'for the specific purpose of easing the transition of the Southern rural Negro into an urban way of life. It stated clearly that its role was to help these people, who were essentially rural agrarian serf-peasants, adjust to Northern city life.' Using the techniques of persuasion and conciliation, the Urban League appealed to the 'enlightened self-interest' of white business leaders 'to ease the movement of Negroes into middle class status.'[9]

A generation later, in 1942, the Congress of Racial Equality was founded in Chicago. The smallest and most radical of the three groups, CORE is best known for introducing the method of nonviolent direct action, staging sit-ins in restaurants and freedom rides on buses. This new dimension of the black struggle for equality had a profound effect on the civil rights move-ment in the 1950s and 1960s and particularly on Martin King.

Unlike the black churches, which had few white members and no white leaders, the civil rights organizations included whites in every level of their operations. For example, a white person has often served as the president of the NAACP, and each of the three organizations has had a significant number of whites serve on its board of directors. They claimed that the implementation of integration must apply to every aspect of the society, including their own organizations. The inclusion of whites also limited their independence and made them vulnerable to the nationalist critique that no black revolution can be successful as long as its leadership is dependent upon white support.

Black Nationalism before Malcolm X

The roots of black nationalism go back to the seventeenth-century slave conspiracies, when Africans, longing for their homeland, banded together in a common struggle against slavery, because they knew that they were not created for servitude. In the absence of historical data, it is not possible to describe the precise ideology behind the early slave revolts. What we know for sure is that the Africans deeply abhorred slavery and were willing to take great risks to gain their freedom.

This nationalist spirit was given high visibility in the slave revolts led by Gabriel Prosser, Denmark Vesey, and Nat Turner during the first third of the nineteenth century. But it was also found in the rise of mutual-aid societies, in the birth and growth of black-led churches and conventions, and in black-led emigration schemes. Unity as a people, pride in African heritage, the creation of autonomous institutions, and the search for a territory to build a nation were the central ingredients which shaped the early development of the nationalist consciousness.

There have been many articulate voices and important movements of black nationalism throughout African-American history. Among them were David Walker and Martin Delany during the antebellum period and Henry McNeal Turner, Marcus Garvey, Noble Drew Ali, and Elijah Muhammad during the late nineteenth and early twentieth centuries.

The central claim of all black nationalists, past and present, is that black people are primarily Africans and not Americans. Unlike integrationists, nationalists do not define their significance and purpose as a people by appealing to the Declaration of Independence, the Constitution, Lincoln's Emancipation Proclamation, or even the white man's religion of Christianity. On the contrary, nationalists define their identity by their resistance to America and their determination to create a society based on their own African history and culture. The posture of rejecting America and accepting Africa is sometimes symbolized with such words as 'African,' 'black,' and 'blackness.' For example, Martin Delany, often called the father of black nationalism, boasted that there lived 'none blacker' than himself. While Douglass, in typical integrationist style, said, 'I thank God for making me a man simply,' he reported that 'Delany always thanks Him for making him a black man.'[10]

The issue for nationalists was not only human slavery or oppression. It was also the oppression of *black* people by *white* people. Nothing aroused the fury of nationalists more than the racial factor in human exploitation.

Their identity as black touched the very core of their being and affected their thoughts and feelings regarding everything, especially their relations with white people. Nationalists, unlike integrationists, could not separate their resentment of servitude from the racial identity of the people responsible for it. 'White Americans [are] our *natural enemies*,' wrote David Walker in his *Appeal* in 1829. 'By treating us so cruel,' we 'see them acting more like devils than accountable men.' According to Walker, 'whites have always been an unjust, jealous, unmerciful, avaricious and blood-thirsty set of beings, always seeking after power and authority.'[11]

Black nationalism was defined by a loss of hope in America. Its advocates did not believe that white people could ever imagine humanity in a way that would place black people on a par with them. 'I am not in favor of caste, nor a separation of the brotherhood of mankind, and would as willingly live among white men as black, if I had an *equal possession and enjoyment* of privileges,' Delany wrote in 1852 to the white abolitionist William Lloyd Garrison; he went on: 'but [I] shall never be reconciled to live among them, subservient to their will – existing by mere *sufferance*, as we, the colored people, do, in this country. ... I have no hopes in this country – no confidence in the American people.'[12]

This difference in emotional orientation between nationalists and integrationists led to disagreement in their definition of freedom and their strategies for achieving it. For nationalists, freedom was not black people pleading for integration into white society; rather it was separation from white people so that blacks could govern themselves. For many nationalists, separation meant emigration from the United States to some place in Africa or Latin America. 'Every people should be the originators of their own designs, the projector of their own schemes, and creators of the events that lead to their destiny – the consummation of their own desires,' Delany wrote in his best-known work, *The Condition, Elevation, Emigration, and Destiny of the Colored People of the United States* (1852). 'No people can be free who themselves do not constitute an essential part of the *ruling element* of the country in which they live,' said Delany. 'The liberty of no man is secure, who controls not his political destiny. ... To suppose otherwise, is that delusion which at once induces its victim, through a period of long suffering, patiently to submit to every species of wrong; trusting against probability, and hoping against all reasonable grounds of expectation, for the granting of privileges and enjoyment of rights, that will never be attained.'[13]

The ebb and flow of black nationalism, during the nineteenth century and thereafter, was influenced by the decline and rise of black expectations of equality in the United States. When blacks felt that the achievement of equality was impossible, the nationalist sentiment among them always increased. Such was the case during the 1840s and 1850s, largely due to the Fugitive Slave Act (1850) and the Dred Scott Decision (1857).

During the Civil War and the Reconstruction that followed it, black hopes soared and even Delany stopped talking about the emigration of blacks and began to participate in the political process in South Carolina, running for the office of lieutenant-governor.

Black expectations of achieving full citizenship rights, however, were short-lived. The infamous Hayes Compromise of 1877 led to the withdrawal of federal troops from the South, thereby allowing former white slaveholders to deal with their former slaves in any manner they chose. The destructive consequences for blacks were severe politically, economically, and psychologically. Accommodationism emerged as the dominant black philosophy, and Booker T. Washington became its most prominent advocate. Washington replaced Frederick Douglass as the chief spokesperson for blacks, and ministers were his most ardent supporters.

During the period of the 'nadir' and the 'long dark night' of black people's struggle for justice in America, Henry McNeal Turner, a bishop in the AME Church, and Marcus Garvey of the Universal Negro Improvement Association (UNIA) articulated nationalist perspectives that were more directly linked with the subsequent philosophy of Malcolm X. Like Malcolm's, their perspectives on America were derived from the bottom of the black experience. They spoke a language that was full of racial pride and denunciation of white America. It was intended to elevate the cultural and psychological well-being of down-trodden blacks burdened with low self-esteem in a society dominated by the violence of white hate groups and the sophisticated racism of the Social Darwinists.

A native of South Carolina, Turner grew up on the cotton fields with slaves and learned to read by his own efforts. He was a proud and fearless man, and his nationalism was deepended as he observed the continued exploitation of blacks by whites, North and South, during and following Reconstruction. When the Supreme Court ruled in 1883 that the Civil Rights Act of 1875 was unconstitutional, Turner felt that that 'barbarous decision' dissolved the allegiance of black people to the United States. 'If the decision is correct,' he wrote, 'the United States Constitution is a dirty rag, a cheat, a libel, and ought to be spit upon by every negro in the land.'[14]

The betrayal of Reconstruction, the 'enactment of cruel and revolting laws,' lynching and other atrocities, reenslavement through peonage, and political disfranchisement encouraged Turner to conclude that blacks would never achieve equality in the United States. He became an ardent advocate of emigration to Africa. 'There is no more doubt in my mind,' Turner said, 'that we have ultimately to return to Africa than there is of the existence of God.'[15]

Although Turner was elected a bishop in the AME Church, he was not the typical holder of that office. The more whites demeaned blackness as a mark of inferiority, the more Turner glorified it. At a time when black and white Christians identified God with European images and the AME

Church leaders were debating whether to replace the word 'African' in their name with 'American,' Turner shocked everyone with his declaration that 'God is a Negro.'[16]

Although Turner addressed his message to the sociopolitical problems of the black masses in the rural South, he did not create an organization to implement his African dream. That distinction fell to Marcus Garvey.

On 23 March 1916, one year after Turner's death, Marcus Garvey came to the United States from his native Jamaica. While Turner's base was the rural South, Garvey worked in the urban North, mainly in Harlem. While the geography was different, the people were essentially the same, being mostly immigrants from the South in search of the American dream of economic security, social advancement, and political justice. Instead they entered a nightmare of racism and poverty which they thought they had left behind in the South.

Garvey understood the pain of color discrimination because he experienced it personally and observed it in the lives of other blacks in Jamaica and also during his travels in Central America, Europe, and the United States. It seemed that everywhere he traveled blacks were being dominated by others. 'Where is the black man's Government?' he asked. 'Where is his King and his kingdom? Where is his President, his country, and his ambassador, his army, his navy, his men of big affairs?' Unable to find them, Garvey, with the self-assurance of a proud black man, then declared: 'I will help to make them.'[17]

Garvey knew that without racial pride no people could make leaders and build a nation that would command the respect of the world. This was particularly true of blacks who had been enslaved and segregated for three hundred years. In a world where blackness was a badge of degradation and shame, Garvey transformed it into a symbol of honor and distinction. 'To be a Negro is no disgrace, but an honor, and we of the Universal Negro Improvement Association do not want to become white.'[18] He made blacks feel that they were somebody and that they could do great things as a people. 'Up, you mighty race,' Garvey proclaimed, 'you can accomplish what you will,' and black people believed him.

As whites ruled Europe and America, Garvey was certain blacks should and would rule Africa. To implement his African dream, he organized the UNIA, first in Kingston, Jamaica, and later in New York. 'Africa for the Africans' was the heart of his message. In 1920 Garvey called the first International Convention of Negro Peoples of the World, and 25,000 delegates from twenty-five countries met in New York City. A redeemed Africa, governed by a united black race proud of its history, was the theme which dominated Garvey's speeches. 'Wake up Ethiopia! Wake up Africa!' he proclaimed. 'Let us work towards the one glorious end of a free, redeemed and mighty nation. Let Africa be a bright star among the constellation of nations.' 'A race without authority and power is a race without respect.'[19]

No one exceeded Garvey in his criticisms of the philosophy of integration, as represented by the members of the NAACP and other middle-class black leaders and intellectuals. He believed that any black organization that depended upon white philanthropy was detrimental to the cause of Africa's redemption and the uplifting of the black race. 'No man will do as much for you as you will do for yourself.'[20] By depending on whites, blacks were saying that they could not do it alone, thereby creating a sense of inferiority in themselves.

According to Garvey, integration is a self-defeating philosophy that is promoted by pseudo-black intellectuals and leaders. He accused integrationists of wanting to be white and completely ignoring the socioeconomic well-being of poor blacks at the bottom. W. E. B. Du Bois, then the editor of the NAACP's *Crisis* magazine, was one of Garvey's favorite targets of criticism. Garvey urged his followers that 'we must never, even under the severest pressure, hate or dislike ourselves.'[21] His criticism of the NAACP and Du Bois was very similar to Malcolm X's attack upon the same organization and its executive director, Roy Wilkins, during the 1960s. Black nationalists are defined by race confidence and solidarity, and they are often intemperate in their criticisms of black integrationists, for they believe integrationists compromise the self-respect and dignity of the race by wanting to mingle and marry white people – the enemy.

In 1920, Garvey's UNIA claimed a membership of four million and a year later six million, with nine hundred branches. While most scholars insist that the numbers were inflated, no one denies that Garvey organized the largest and most successful mass movement of blacks in the history of the United States. Garvey did what all black nationalists after him have merely dreamed of doing, and that is why they continue to study his life and message for direction and inspiration.

Concerned about Garvey's popularity, the government, with the help of black integrationist leaders, convicted him of mail fraud. Upon his imprisonment and deportation, black nationalism entered a period of decline. But the problems of oppression and identity which gave rise to it did not disappear.

In addition to Marcus Garvey's UNIA, two movements were important in defining the nationalism that influenced Malcolm X: the Moorish Science Temple founded by Noble Drew Ali in Newark, New Jersey, and the Nation of Islam – the 'Black Muslims' – founded in Detroit in 1930 by the mysterious Wallace D. Fard and later headed by his disciple, Elijah Poole, a former Baptist minister from Sandersville, Georgia. Elijah Poole as Elijah Muhammad achieved his authority in the Black Muslim religion because he convinced Black Muslim believers, including Malcolm, that Allah came to North America 'in the person of Wallace D. Fard,' taught him for three and a half years, and then chose him as his Messenger.

Both movements rejected Christianity and white people and affirmed the religion of Islam and an African-Asian identity. Both movements were primarily religious, having less political emphasis than Garvey's UNIA. Although the Moorish Science Temple is still in existence, it was important mainly as a forerunner of the Nation of Islam. The Nation of Islam received many members from the Moorish Science Temple following the assassination of Noble Drew Ali.

The Nation of Islam was the most important influence on the life and thought of Malcolm X. Its importance for Malcolm was similar to the role of the black church in the life of Martin King. While Garvey influenced Malcolm's political consciousness, Elijah Muhammad defined his religious commitment. Elijah Muhammad was the sole and absolute authority in defining the doctrine and practice of the Nation of Islam. While affirming solidarity with worldwide Islam, he proclaimed distinctive doctrines. The most important and controversial one was his contention that whites were by nature evil. They were snakes who were incapable of doing right, devils who would soon be destroyed by God's righteous judgment. White people, therefore, were identified as the sole cause of black oppression.

In Black Muslim theology the almighty black God is the source of all good and power. To explain the origin of the evil of black oppression, Muhammad rejected the Christian recourse to divine mystery or God's permissive will, instead setting forth his own distinctive explanation, which focused on the myth of Yacob. Out of the weak individuals of the black race, Yacob, a renegade black scientist, created the white race, thereby causing all of the evil which has flowed from their hands: 'The human beast – the serpent, the dragon, the devil, and Satan – all mean one and the same: the people or race known as the white or Caucasian race, sometimes called the European race. Since by nature they were created liars and murderers, they are the enemies of truth and righteousness, and the enemies of those who seek the truth.'[22] This myth was important for Malcolm's view that the whites are evil by nature. The myth and its doctrinal development came exclusively from Elijah Muhammad.

The logical extension of this doctrine is that since black people are by nature good and divine, they must be separated from whites so they can avoid the latter's hour of total destruction. The solution to the problem of black oppression in America, therefore, is territorial separation, either by whites financing black people's return to Africa or by providing separate states in America.

Although the Nation of Islam and other nationalist movements (especially Garvey's) were the dominant influence in shaping Malcolm's life and thought, he was also indebted to the integrationist protest tradition. The same kind of cross current of nationalist and integrationist influences bore upon the career of Martin King, though he was indebted far less to the nationalist tradition. No sharp distinction can be drawn between the traditions, because representatives of both were fighting the same problems – the power of 'white over black' and its psychological impact upon the self-esteem of its victims. Nationalists and integrationists were aware of the truth of each other's viewpoint, even though they did not always acknowledge it. Integrationists realized the danger of complete assimilation into American society. Like nationalists, they did not want to destroy the cultural and spiritual identity of blacks. That was perhaps the major reason why black churches and fraternal and sororal organizations remained separate from whites. Despite their repeated claim about 11:00 a.m. on Sunday morning being the most segregated hour of the week, black ministers in black denominations made no real efforts to integrate their churches. They knew that if they did, their power as blacks would have been greatly curtailed and their own cultural and spiritual identity destroyed. The advocates of integration, therefore, focused their energies primarily on the political and economic life of America. They believed that justice was possible if whites treated blacks as equals under the law.

Likewise, black nationalists realized the danger of complete isolation from the political and economic life of America. That was perhaps the major reason for the frequent shifts in their philosophy. Black nationalism was not primarily a Western, 'rational' philosophy, but rather a black philosophy in search of its African roots. It was a cry for self-esteem, for the right to be recognized and accepted as human beings. Its advocates knew that blacks could not survive politically or economically in complete separation from others, especially whites in the United States. Neither could any other people (including whites) survive in isolation from the rest of the world. Everyone was interdependent. The black masses, therefore, did not follow nationalists because of their call for separation from America. Rather it was because of the nationalists' ability to speak to their 'gut level' experience, that is, to express what it *felt* like to be black in white America.

Integrationists and nationalists complemented each other. Both philosophies were needed if America was going to come to terms with the truth of the black experience. Either philosophy alone was a half-truth and thus a distortion of the black reality in America. Integrationists were *practical*. They advocated what they thought could be achieved at a given time. They knew that justice demanded more. But why demand it if you can't get it? Why demand it if the demand itself blocks the achievement of other desirable and achievable goals? In their struggle for justice, they were careful not to arouse the genocidal instincts inherent in racism. Thus they chose goals and methods which many whites accepted as reasonable and just. The strengths and weaknesses of the integrationist view are reflected in the life and ministry of Martin King.

Nationalists were *desperate*. They spoke for that segment of the African-American community which was hurting the most. Thus, they often did not consider carefully the consequences of their words and actions. The suffering of the black poor was so great that practical or rational philosophies did not arouse their allegiance. They needed a philosophy that could speak to their existence as black people, living in a white society that did not recognize their humanity. They needed a philosophy that empowered them to 'respect black' by being prepared to die for it. Overwhelmed by misery, the black poor cried out for relief, for a word or an act that would lift them to another realm of existence where they would be treated as human beings. In place of an American dream, nationalists gave the black poor an African dream. The strengths and the weaknesses of this perspective were reflected in the life and ministry of Malcolm X.

Martin King and Malcolm X were shaped by what Vincent Harding has called the 'Great Tradition of Black Protest,'[23] a tradition that comprised many variations of nationalism and integrationism. Their perspectives on America were influenced by both, even though they placed primary emphasis on only one of them. Both integrationism and nationalism readied Martin and Malcolm for leadership in the black freedom movement of the 1950s and 1960s – with Martin proclaiming an American dream from the steps of the Lincoln Memorial and Malcolm reminding him of an American nightmare in the streets of Harlem.

Notes

1. W. E. B. Du Bois, *The Souls of Black Folk* (1903; reprint, New York: Fawcett Premier Book, 1968), pp. 16, 17; W. E. B. Du Bois, 'The Conservation of Races' (1897), in Julius Lester (ed.), *The Seventh Son: The Thought and Writings of W. E. B. Du Bois* (New York: Vintage Book, 1971), vol. 1, p. 182.
2. Philip S. Foner (ed.), *Frederick Douglass: Selections from His Writings* (New York: International Publishers, 1964), p. 57.
3. Ibid., pp. 52–3.
4. Cited in Lerone Bennett, Jr., *Pioneers in Protest* (Chicago: Johnson Publishing, 1968), pp. 208–9.
5. Foner (ed.), *Frederick Douglass*, p. 44.
6. Cited in Peter J. Paris, *The Social Teaching of the Black Churches* (Philadelphia: Fortress Press, 1985), p. 25, n. 26.
7. Henry Highland Garnet, *An Address to the Slaves of the United States of America* (1843), reprinted with David Walker's *Appeal* (1829), in *Walker's Appeal & Garnet's Address to the Slaves of the United States of America* (New York: Arno Press/New York Times, 1969), p. 93.
8. Adam Clayton Powell, Jr., *Marching Blacks*, rev. edn (New York: Dial Press, 1973), p. 194.
9. Kenneth B. Clark, 'The Civil Rights Movement: Momentum and Organization', *Daedalus*, 95 (Winter 1966), p. 245.
10. Cited in Theodore Draper, *The Rediscovery of Black Nationalism* (New York: Viking Press, 1970), p. 22; for an interpretation of the origin of black nationalism, see August Meier, 'The Emergence of Negro Nationalism', Parts I and II, *Midwest Journal*, vol. 45 (Winter 1951 and Summer 1953), pp. 96–104 and 95–111.

11. *Walker's Appeal and Garnet's Address,* pp. 71, 73, 27–8; see also Sterling Stuckey, *The Ideological Origins of Black Nationalism* (Boston, MA: Beacon Press, 1972), pp. 97, 99, 55–6.

12. Carter G. Woodson (ed.), *The Mind of the Negro as Reflected in Letters Written during the Crisis, 1800–1860* (1926; reprint, New York: Russell & Russell, 1969), p. 293.

13. Martin Robinson Delany, *The Condition, Elevation, Emigration, and Destiny of the Colored People of the United States* (1855; reprint, New York: Arno Press/New York Times, 1969), p. 209; see also John H. Bracey, Jr., August Meier, and Elliott Rudwick (eds), *Black Nationalism in America* (Indianapolis: Bobbs-Merrill, 1970), p. 89.

14. Henry McNeal Turner, 'The Barbarous Decision of the Supreme Court' (1883), in Edwin S. Redkey (ed.), *Respect Black: The Writings and Speeches of Henry McNeal Turner* (New York: Arno Press/New York Times, 1971), p. 63.

15. Ibid., p. 165; Edwin S. Redkey, *Black Exodus: Black Nationalist and Back-to-Africa Movements, 1890–1910* (New Haven, CT: Yale University Press, 1969), p. 29.

16. Henry McNeal Turner, 'God is a Negro' (1898), in Redkey (ed.), *Respect Black,* pp. 176–7.

17. Amy Jacques Garvey (ed.), *Philosophy and Opinions of Marcus Garvey* (New York: Arno Press/New York Times, 1969), vol. 2, p. 126.

18. Ibid., pp. 325–6.

19. Ibid., vol. 1, pp. 5, 2.

20. Cited in E. David Cronon, *Black Moses: The Story of Marcus Garvey and the Negro Improvement Association* (Madison: University of Wisconsin Press, 1955), p. 173.

21. Garvey (ed.), *Philosophy and Opinions,* vol. 2, p. 326.

22. Cited in Louis E. Lomax, *When the Word is Given . . .* (New York: Signet Book, 1964), p. 56. The classic study on the Nation of Islam is C. Eric Lincoln, *The Black Muslims in America* (Boston, MA: Beacon Press, 1961, rev. edn., 1973). See also E. U. Essien-Udom, *Black Nationalism: The Search for an Identity in America* (Chicago: University of Chicago Press, 1962); James Baldwin, *The Fire Next Time* (New York: Dell, 1962). An early significant study is Erdmann Doane Beynon, 'The Voodoo Cult Among Negro Migrants in Detroit', *American Journal of Sociology,* May 1938, pp. 894–907. See also Monroe Berger, 'The Black Muslims', *Horizon,* Winter, 1964, pp. 48–65. The best source for the teaching of Elijah Muhammad is his *The Supreme Wisdom: The Solution to the So-Called Negroes' Problem* (Chicago: University of Islam, 1957); also his *Message to the Blackman* (Chicago: Muhammad's Temple No. 2).

23. Vincent Harding, *There is a River: The Black Struggle for Freedom in America* (New York: Harcourt Brace Jovanovich, 1981), p. 83.

Reflecting Black: African-American Cultural Criticism

Michael Eric Dyson

Martin Luther King, Jr, and Malcolm X are the towering icons of contemporary African-American culture. Of course, King has transcended the boundaries of race. His iridescent image has been seized upon to illumine

From *Reflecting Black: African-American Cultural Criticism* (Minneapolis: University of Minnesota Press, 1993), pp. 250–63.

an astonishing array of social projects – and commercial products – whose humanitarian pedigree is thought to be vouchsafed by symbolic solidarity with an American hero. But the international fame and nearly universal respect he now commands have not diminished his appeal among common black people who will never know either. Millions of black homes continue to display portraits of King, his graceful humility radiating a perennial blessing to their domestic space. For many blacks, King's progressive civil protest, in which American ideals of justice engendered civil disobedience and social compromise, has become the definitive model for social transformation.

But for a generation of black youth reared on sound bites of history that mimic the rap culture that has shaped them, the voice of Malcolm X supplies the authentic timbre of social rebellion. And his serene but ominous countenance peering from countless posters forms the perfect portrait of black anger at American pride and prejudice. Unlike King, however, the hues of Malcolm's charisma have for the most part remained dark and radical. His reputation is shaped by the specific appeal to racial identity and cultural pride, heroic gestures in an era of political surrender and resurgent racism.

Rap artists, black youth culture's self-styled postmodern urban griots, dispense social criticism and history lessons with Malcolm's hot breath sampled between their fiery lyrics. Radical and black nationalist intelligentsia employ Malcolm's words as the touchstone of an independent and critical black cultural consciousness. And even black people for whom King's example provides an ideological north star draw solace from Malcolm at moments of uncertainty about the sanity of American culture or the sincerity of American democracy.

That Martin and Malcolm, therefore, represent two distinct traditions of response to homegrown American racism is undeniable. Captured in the useful but imprecise shorthand developed to distinguish the ways black people have resisted racism for more than two centuries, King's position represented an integrationist approach to the American dilemma, advocating equal inclusion of blacks in the drama of national privilege. And for most of his life Malcolm X advocated a separatist and nationalist strategy for black survival, seeking a space free from white racial violence. But what is even more intriguing, although more subtle and complex, is the way in which King's and Malcolm X's strategies, ideologies, and principles of racial combat seemed at *crucial points* to be of a piece, the fragmented components of a narrative whole of racial redemption.

This is a complicated point to make without homogenizing King and Malcolm X into a mythic unity, without creating consonance where there is none, and without imposing a grid on racial experience. The challenge to anyone who would interpret King and Malcolm X is to appreciate both overlap and opposition, but only after tracing the contours of their ideologies, exploring the nuances of their respective visions of racial transformation, and investigating the varied intellectual and social resources they brought to bear to the traditions in which they took part.

To this task James Cone seems particularly well suited. Born and reared in the Deep South, Cone has spent most of his career as a teacher and scholar in northern institutions. Educated as an undergraduate at a historically black college, Cone gained his doctorate degree at a white university, where he was trained in the thought of neo-orthodox German theologian Karl Barth. Soon thereafter, Cone came to reject many of the premises of white Western theology. In its place, he articulated a theology that reflected black religious experience and reshaped theological language in light of the guiding principle of black liberation and resistance to oppression. Indeed, Cone is widely regarded as the father of black theology.

In his incipient expression of intellectual dissent from traditional theology, the ground-breaking *Black Theology and Black Power*,[1] Cone proved to be the angry young man of the religious academy. He took traditional theology to task for its vicious complicity in the oppression of blacks by supplying theological comfort and philosophical justification to white racism. Although he failed to take seriously the important exceptions to his theological diatribe (a failure duly noted by equally blind white theologians), Cone's often shrill tone struck a highly responsive chord in important sectors of the theological academy.

But more importantly, Cone made theology suddenly attractive, and in some cases irresistible, for a whole generation of black religious intellectuals and church persons who questioned the power of their discipline and faith to facilitate social transformation after King's death. Cone integrated elements of traditional black church life (discourse about justice, God, and judgment) with radical social ideas (black power, a black God, and trenchant criticism of white racism). Here was a black man trained like Martin who spoke like Malcolm, an X in King's clothing.

In more than twenty years and several books since then, Cone has refined his vision of the scope and tasks of the black theological enterprise. He has introduced a vibrant idiom in theological language from his academic base as Charles Briggs Distinguished Professor of Systematic Theology at New York's Union Theological Seminary. Cone has lectured across the hemisphere, his books have been translated into several languages, and his ideas have spawned dissertations, conferences, and books in many parts of the world.

Like King and Malcolm X, Cone is a revolutionary figure, and like them, he has endured the pain and risk of growth. He has integrated new strands into his arguments over the years to address his former weaknesses, particularly on issues of gender and social theory. Each new book has reflected his continuing dialogue with an expanded group of interlocutors. Cone's latest book, *Martin & Malcolm & America: A Dream or a Nightmare*, takes us forward by looking backward. He examines two figures who have influenced black Americans, and more specifically, the shape and character of his own thought. In a sense, his book is a public reckoning with his own intellectual and personal heritage. It is, in many ways, an impressive achievement and perhaps his best book.[2]

Cone's book is organized in a methodical fashion, with his characteristic clarity of expression on generous display. While obfuscatory and insular jargon hold sway in so many academic disciplines, Cone never lets the language he is using get in the way of the story he is telling. Other fine studies have compared King and Malcolm X, along with other black religious and intellectual figures, such as Peter Paris's *Black Leaders in Conflict* and Robert Franklin's *Liberating Visions*.[3] With the exception of Louis Lomax's *To Kill a Black Man*,[4] Cone's is the first book-length study devoted exclusively to comparing the two figures.

Although the trajectory of their social acceptance has been wildly different, King and Malcolm X scaled the heights of cultural popularity only after their apocalyptic martyrdoms. Although he is now shrouded in myth and legend, King's popularity plummeted in the years prior to his death because of his opposition to the Vietnam War, the rise of Black Power, and his turn toward matters of class inequality. And when he was assassinated, Malcolm was diligently redefining his ideological identity and winning increasing popularity among an audience previously denied him because of his role in the Nation of Islam. But it has taken nearly a quarter century for his appeal to fully emerge and for his image, voice, and message to find a new place in the black cultural imagination. As Cone observes:

> Twenty-five years after his assassination, there is a resurgence of interest in him, especially among the young who were not born when he died. Malcolm's name, words, and face appear on buttons, T-shirts, and the covers of rap records. His life has become the basis of films, plays, and even operas. He is now being quoted by mainstream black leaders, who once despised him. Conferences, seminars, and parades are being held in his honor, and streets, schools, and organizations are being named after him. People are making annual pilgrimages to his birthplace and grave site.

Although research on King is voluminous and growing daily, the literary attention paid to Malcolm is only now swelling to match his renewed popularity. Bruce Perry's recent biography of Malcolm X and Spike Lee's upcoming film about him will most certainly stimulate more interest in the man's legacy, as will Cone's fine comparative study.

Cone's text also deftly explores the differences between King and Malcolm X, which upon cursory glance appear conspicuous. After all, their differences from birth might be considered a study in suggestive polarities: south/north, middle-class/poor, light-skinned/dark-skinned, tall/short, educated/auto-didact, and slow-southern-cadency/rapid-fire-oratory. And

Cone goes to great lengths to show how substantial their differences were. He shows us how the social, political, and economic forces that produced them, as well as the geographic regions that were the scene of their major contributions, reveal a great deal about the character and limitations of their respective contributions. King was reared in a comfortable, middle-class home in Atlanta that nurtured his sense of self-worth in the bosom of a vibrant black religious faith. Malcolm X's first memory in 1929, ironically the year of King's birth, was a nightmare, a terrifying remembrance of the burning of his family home in Lansing, Michigan, by white vigilantes.

Cone's introductory chapter shows how King and Malcolm X participated in venerable traditions of integrationist and nationalist social thought and practice, and hence were neither completely nor finally the inventions of mass media or white society. Each was fundamentally a creative and singularly gifted political and social actor within a rich and particular ideological heritage. Although Cone delineates the specific marks of each tradition on King and Malcolm X, he also concedes that the rhetoric of nationalism and integrationism were used to express complex beliefs that were sometimes combined by black leaders and intellectuals in their struggles against slavery and oppression:

> Of course, no black thinker has been a pure integrationist or a pure nationalist, but rather all black intellectuals have represented aspects of each, with emphasis moving in one direction or the other, usually at different periods of their lives. ... When blacks have been optimistic about America – believing that they could achieve full equality through moral suasion and legal argument – they have been integrationist and have minimized their nationalist tendencies. On the other hand despair about America – believing that genuine equality is impossible because whites have no moral conscience or any intention to apply the laws fairly – has always been the seedbed of nationalism.

Cone's abbreviated genealogy of conflicting and sometimes converging black ideological traditions provides a helpful scheme for comprehending continuities between past advocates of resistance to racist oppression and his twin subjects, King and Malcolm X. It may also result in closer attention to the significant and suggestive dissimilarities between King and Jesse Jackson, Malcolm X and Louis Farrakhan – dissimilarities that are often overlooked in the avid search for successor messiahs in our era of racial desperation.

Cone skillfully contrasts the impact of their early lives on the development of their thought in sketching a kind of existential ecology of the origins of King's dream and Malcolm X's nightmare. King's embrace of crucial elements of a Booker T. Washington version of accommodationism and a Frederick Douglass version of integrationism, supported by his father's and grandfather's philosophies, found expression in his early leadership style. And his absorption of the ideals of Christian brotherhood and universal love preached in the black church shaped his understanding of acceptable forms of protest and resistance to racism.

Cone's point here, set against the stream of one school of King interpretation, is that the black church was the primary influence on King's life and thought, and that only later did white Protestant liberal theology, Gandhi, Niebuhr, and strands of the social gospel play a role. In intellectual biographies of King, such as Kenneth Smith's and Ira G. Zepp's *Search for the Beloved Community* and John J. Ansbro's *Martin Luther King, Jr.: The Making of a Mind*,[5] the latter influences have been accorded primacy. Other recent studies of King have acknowledged the decisive role of black church faith and culture in shaping King's thought, such as Lewis Baldwin's *There Is a Balm in Gilead* and Fred Downing's *To See the Promised Land.*.[6] And in a few scattered essays, Cone has argued for the preeminence of black Christian values and practice in understanding the moral vision and social protest of King, an argument he elaborates in the course of his book:

> The *faith of the black experience* began to shape King's idea of God during childhood, and it remained central to his perspective throughout his life. This point needs emphasis because many interpreters have failed to acknowledge the *decisive* role of the black religious tradition upon King's thinking. Without denying other important influences – liberal Protestantism, Gandhi, Niebuhr, among others – we still must emphasize that no tradition or thinker influenced King's perspective as much as the faith which blacks created in their fight for dignity and justice.

Moreover, King's virtually unlimited optimism about the possibilities of interracial coalitions defeating racism developed only after he conquered his 'antiwhite feeling' in college, where he encountered whites in interracial organizations. As Cone points out, King's desire to explore the merits of integrationism almost blinded him to the necessity for addressing racism in his graduate work:

> It is important to note that he did not even mention racism in most of his graduate papers that dealt with justice, love, sin, and evil. In six years at Crozer and Boston, King never identified racism as a theological or philosophical problem or mentioned whether he recognized it in the student body and faculty . . . Like most integrationists of his time, and in contrast to Malcolm and the nationalists, Martin appeared to be glad merely to have the opportunity to prove that Negroes could make it in the white man's world.

Here, and throughout his book, Cone gives the sharpest criticism of King's psychological disposition toward white society articulated since John A. Williams's *The King God Didn't Save* and David Lewis's *King: A Biography*.[7]

While avoiding the more exaggerated effects of Williams's self-conscious debunking of the King myth and supplying a more nuanced reading of the black religious roots of King's thought than found in Lewis's treatment, Cone vigorously challenges and critiques King's weaknesses.

He is just as balanced toward Malcolm X. Cone discusses Malcolm X's origins in Omaha, tracing the influence of his parent's nationalist activity on his worldview. Like King, Malcolm X's father was a Baptist preacher, although on a much more modest scale, preaching as an itinerant or 'jackleg' minister. Malcolm X's father was president of the Omaha branch of Garvey's UNIA, while his mother was the group's reporter. During his childhood, Malcolm X was subject not only to white violence, but also to a vicious circle of domestic violence as his father beat his mother and they both abused their children. Malcolm lost his father early, and it is not clear whether his death was accidental or murder. What is clear, though, is that Earl Little's death had a traumatic effect on Malcolm X's family, leaving mother Louise Little to rear eight children during the depression. She eventually suffered a mental break-down, and the children were placed in several foster homes.

After experiencing the ravages of integrated schooling, Malcolm dropped out of high school to live with his half sister in Boston. Malcolm had already begun to steal in Nebraska because of extreme hunger, and he expanded his hustling repertoire in Boston. He used cocaine and established a burglary ring to support his expensive habit. After he was caught and sent to prison, Malcolm X displayed a resentful attitude until his conversion to the teaching of Elijah Muhammad, founder of the Nation of Islam.

As Cone explains, Malcolm X was drawn to the Nation because of its definition of the white man as the devil and its strong emphasis on pride in black culture and history. Malcolm's many difficulties with whites in adolescence and his experiences in Boston's ghetto prepared him to reject nonviolence and integration and to accept a strong separatist philosophy as the basis for black survival in racist America:

> Malcolm's experience in the ghetto taught him that the black masses could be neither integrationist nor nonviolent. Integration and non-violence assumed some measure of political order, a moral conscience in the society, and a religious and human sensitivity regarding the dignity and value of all persons. But since the masses in the ghettos saw no evidence of a political order that recognized their humanity or a moral conscience among white people, an appeal to integration and nonviolence sounded like a trick to delude and disarm poor blacks, so whites would not have to worry about a revengeful response to their brutality.

In the first section of his book, Cone gives us a good sense of how King and Malcolm X were formed and what differences their respective social origins made on the way they thought about race and American society.

Cone devotes two chapters to exploring King's and Malcolm X's understanding of America through the metaphors of dream and nightmare, metaphors that would define their different approaches to racial justice. Cone probes the social sources of King's American Dream, linking King's vision to the white public, 'because he believed they had the material resources and moral capacity to create a world based on the principles that they claimed to live by.' Cone also explains that King urged black people to enact their redemptive roles in American society by pursuing self-respect, high moral standards, whole-hearted work, leadership, and nonviolence. Despite severe challenges to King's faith in the plausibility of American democracy, especially after the bombing of a church in Birmingham that killed four innocent black girls, he continued to believe that the American Dream would soon be fulfilled.

From the very beginning, however, Malcolm X understood that the conditions of black Americans were a nightmare of racial injustice, urban poverty, and drug addiction, all presided over by the negligence and hypocrisy of white liberals and unprincipled racists. Here and throughout, Cone makes clear that Malcolm X's unbridled anger toward white racism provided a strong counterpoint to King's integrationist philosophy, making King's views, once deemed radical, seem acceptably moderate by comparison. Once Malcolm X left the Nation, however, he discovered that many integrationists were more radical and militant than he had formerly believed. Still, Malcolm continued to enliven the role of the angry black in order to provide a sharp enough contrast to King that white people would gladly listen to his demands.

For most of Malcolm's life, King avoided him. Of course, Malcolm had developed a side career of verbally assaulting 'so-called Negro' leaders, taking special delight in tagging King with a jumble of colorful but caustic monikers, including 'religious Uncle Tom, traitor, chump and the Reverend Dr. Chickenwing.' For his part, King believed that Malcolm X's promulgation of black anger and his statements about the 'reciprocal bleeding' of whites and blacks were irresponsible and morally wrong. King also believed that violence as a tactic of survival was suicidal in light of the fact that blacks were only 10 percent of the population and therefore grossly overmatched and underarmed.

Cone probes Malcolm's conception of divine justice, predicated upon a philosophy of an eye for an eye, and explores his advocacy of self-knowledge, self-love, self-defense, racial separatism, and most of all, racial unity, 'the dominant theme of his ministry.' After he examines the impact of King's and Malcolm X's faith and theology on their versions of the American dream and nightmare, Cone details the unraveling of King's faith in American justice and Malcolm X's reexamination of a strong version of separatist black nationalism after his break with Muhammad.

King's confrontation with persistent racism caused him to reject his former optimism about the capacity or willingness of whites to practice social justice. Although Cone details King's growing pessimism about the structural racism and economic inequality of American society, he doesn't tell us that this prompted King to advocate 'nonviolent sabotage,' which included blocking the normal functioning of the government as a sign of deep social frustration and moral outrage. Cone reveals that King also began to ponder the virtues of 'temporary segregation' as a means of reconstituting the economic health of black communities, since American society had not shown serious interest in reordering social priorities and redistributing wealth.

In his mature stride, King also increased his emphasis on black pride, appealing to a theme that had been implicit in much of his work but now, because of the challenges to nonviolence posed by Black Power, required an explicit articulation. Such moves caused David Halberstam to call King a 'nonviolent Malcolm X,' a characterization King rejected. Nonetheless, his later thinking is detailed by Cone in a way that leaves no doubt that King's shift to progressive and radical social thought was a permanent feature of his mature civil protest.

But, as Cone shows, Malcolm X too was changing. His break with Muhammad had freed Malcolm to become publicly political, an opportunity that Malcolm X used to attempt to join forces with King and progressive elements of the traditional civil rights community. But Malcolm's reputation of advocating violent self-defense had been so deeply entrenched that even his move away from Muhammad didn't prevent the white media from viewing Malcolm as a rabid racist and destructive demagogue. As Cone notes, this troubled Malcolm X, who had a genuine desire to forsake his recent past and articulate his racial demands to a wider audience. Rebuffed and scorned, Malcolm entered into a phase of radical rabble-rousing, still specifying the absurdity of white racism, while displaying a newfound openness to limited white support of black freedom. Even after his journey to Mecca, however, Malcolm never surrendered his advocacy of black unity as a precondition to black freedom, a unity that could never result if even well-intentioned whites participated in black organizations.

X's stress on unity is a theme that resonates with Cone's own thinking and shapes his understanding of King and Malcolm X throughout his book. It also limits his understanding of the two figures. In a discussion of the impact of the faith of the black experience on King's idea of God, Cone says:

> As different as Martin's and Malcolm's religious communities were, Martin's faith, nonetheless, was much closer to Malcolm's than it was to that of white Christians, and Malcolm's faith was much closer to Martin's than it was to that of Muslims in the Middle East, Africa, or Asia; that was true because both of their faith commitments were

derived from the *same* experience of suffering and struggle in the United States. Their theologies, therefore, should be interpreted as different religious and intellectual responses of African-Americans to their environment as they searched for meaning in a nation that they did not make.

But is this accurate? Is it true that the experience of black suffering and struggle is the primary basis of unity, even when the differences between black people are strong and persistent? While Cone may be right to suggest that King and Malcolm X were closer to one another than they were to white Christianity and orthodox Islamic belief, this must be proved by citing historical evidence. As Cone has so convincingly shown us, King and Malcolm X were deeply divided not only about their tactics of social protest, but about their anthropological, social, and psychological understanding of human beings.

It is, therefore, conceivable that a white person who embraced King's understanding of human community, love, interracial coalition, and the limitations of injustice of white racial practices might indeed have more in common with King than a black person who held highly divergent views about such issues, despite a shared experience of racial suffering. The case of Supreme Court Justice Clarence Thomas and other black conservatives proves that there is no necessary or automatic similarity in the interpretation of the 'black experience' and that suffering due to racism is no guarantee of unanimity on the means to achieve racial justice. Thus, King would have had (and I believe he did have) more in common with say, [white socialist writer] Michael Harrington, than he would have had with [African American conservative writer] George Schuyler when it came to issues of racial and economic justice.

Cone himself provides ample support for the belief that King and Malcolm X, as a result of their concrete set of historical experiences, were indeed converging on a similar, although by no means identical, view of racial justice and economic health for black people. But as Cone also makes clear, they had enormous and long-standing barriers to overcome to achieve even limited ideological parity. For instance, Malcolm's earlier views of violence, as Cone points out, 'were hardly different from that of the whites he criticized.' And in criticizing King and Malcolm X for their abominable views on women, Cone points out how they had more in common with white men than with black women:

While Martin and Malcolm challenged white values regarding race, their acceptance of black male privilege prevented them from seeing the connection between racism and sexism. While both differed sharply with most white men when it came to matters involving race, they shared much of the typical *American* male's view of women. Martin's and Malcolm's views regarding women's place were not significantly different from those of men of other races.

The call for racial unity is usually premised on the assumption that the experience of black suffering will itself guarantee similarity of perspective. But the complexity and diversity of racial experiences cautions against advocating racial unity based on the presumption of homogeneity. Neither does it bode well for trying to explain the genuine and irresolvable differences between King and Malcolm X, no matter how much we appeal to their same experience of suffering and struggle. Besides, other dimensions of struggle to which King and Malcolm became more sensitive, such as class inequality, mean that the experience of suffering, although crucial and certainly central, is not the exclusive or exhaustive basis of racial unity.

Because Cone believes that both King and Malcolm X promoted self-knowledge and respect for one's history and culture as the basis for unity – without which there could be no freedom – the view of unity based on sameness of experience fails to capture other enabling forms of racial solidarity. Furthermore, it imposes a narrow view of their uses of history and culture, especially in King's case. Such a view leads Cone to stress the necessity and crucial ingredients of self-esteem in combating black disunity and the corrosive racism that destroys black culture without supplying a trenchant criticism of the social forces that help construct and define self-regard. Regarding the latter, Cone concludes:

> It is not easy to survive in a society that says that you do not count. Many do not survive. With the absence of black pride, that 'I am somebody' feeling, many young African-Americans have no respect for themselves or for anybody else. ... Malcolm X is the best medicine against genocide. He showed us by example and prophetic preaching that ... we can take that long walk toward freedom. Freedom is first and foremost an inner recognition of self-respect, a knowledge that one was not put on this earth to be a nobody. African-Americans can do the same today. We can fight for our dignity and self-respect.

While Cone's claims are undeniable, what is needed at this point is a complex and detailed cultural criticism in light of the social vision and religious values that King and Malcolm X promoted, values that Cone has expressed in his own work. It seems odd that Cone prescribes self-respect and self-esteem without giving a sharp or substantial analysis of the social resources for such qualities and the political and economic reasons that prevent their flourishing in many urban black communities across the country. It is precisely here that we want the full analytical power of black theology and the best available insights of progressive social theory brought to bear upon the various crises that confront black Americans in tracking a path for those who take the mature King and Malcolm X seriously. Here Cone's treatment falls noticeably short.

Nevertheless, Cone's study of King and Malcolm X is admirable. Cone gives a life-sized portrait of two figures who have grown larger than life. And with the phenomenal resurgence of interest in Malcolm, Cone has not been afraid to criticize him for his often lethal sexism, his advocacy of impractical strategies of violence, and his almost exclusive focus on race, which was only decentered after his break from the Nation of Islam.

The imaginative virtue of Cone's book is that he has shown that Martin and Malcolm needed each other, that their ideas and social strategies brought them to a strange but effective symbiosis. His title, employing his subjects' first names, is a symbol of the first-name familiarity we feel with these great men and a striking emblem of their genuine humility. As we struggle to take measure of their extraordinary accomplishments, Cone's book will be indispensable in charting how two supremely human and heroic figures occupied and defined their times with empowering vision and sacrificial action.

Notes

1. James H. Cone, *Black Theology and Black Power* (New York: Seabury Press, 1969).
2. James H. Cone, *Martin & Malcolm & America: A Dream or a Nightmare* (New York: Orbis, 1991).
3. Peter Paris, *Black Leaders in Conflict*, 2nd edn (Louisville, KY: Westminister Press/ John Knox Press, 1991); and Robert M. Franklin, *Liberating Visions: Human Fulfillment and Social Justice in African-American Thought* (Minneapolis, MN: Augsburg Fortress, 1989).
4. Louis Lomax, *To Kill a Black Man* (Los Angeles: Holloway House, 1968).
5. Kenneth Smith and Ira G. Zepp, *Search for the Beloved Community: The Thinking of Martin Luther King, Jr.* (Valley Forge, PA.: Judson Press, 1974); and John J. Ansbro, *Martin Luther King, Jr.: The Making of a Mind* (New York: Orbis, 1982).
6. Lewis Baldwin, *There is a Balm in Gilead: The Cultural Roots of Martin Luther King, Jr.* (Minneapolis, MN: Augsburg Fortress, 1991); and Frederick L. Downing, *To See the Promised Land: The Faith Pilgrimage of Martin Luther King, Jr* (Macon, GA: Mercer University Press, 1986).
7. John A. Williams, *The King God Didn't Save* (New York: Coward-McCann, 1970); and David Lewis, *King: A Biography*, 2nd edn (Urbana, IL: University of Illinois Press, 1978).

7 Relationships: Women and Gender, Sex and Sexuality

Introduction

The literature on African American and white women's contributions to the civil rights movement has expanded dramatically in recent years and has restored their contributions to the once almost exclusively male-dominated historical record. Studies of gender roles – that is, the role played by concepts of femininity and masculinity in shaping the nature of movement activism and involvement – have been fewer in number. Studies of sex and sexuality – that is, the role played by sex and sexual preferences in shaping movement activism and involvement – have been fewer still.

In the previous chapter, Michael Eric Dyson's selection notes that both King and Malcolm X have been criticized for their decidedly unliberated views of women, although in this respect they differed little from their African American and white male peers of the time. While disappointingly little attention has been paid to how conceptions of masculinity shaped King's and Malcolm X's movement activism, ample evidence has been presented of their commitment to traditional gender roles. For King, this started at home with his wife Coretta who, despite her considerable willingness to become involved in the movement, was expected to play the role of dutiful wife and mother and to run the household while her husband was away on movement business. Mrs King became much more publicly visible in social and political activism after her husband's death.

As Belinda Robnett demonstrates in the first selection, King's expectations of gender roles in his home life extended into his movement activism. Discerning readers will note that Robnett is the only woman contributor to the selections in this book, a fair and accurate reflection of the overwhelmingly male-dominated King scholarship, which tells an interesting story in its own right. In fact, Robnett's work is not about King in particular but rather more generally about the ways that women were systematically excluded from formal leadership roles in the movement. Robnett notes that the exclusion of women from such positions of leadership was evident from King's earliest involvement in the movement in the Montgomery bus boycott. Although it was the action of Rosa Parks that precipitated the bus boycott, and it was the idea of Jo Ann Robinson, president of the Women's Political Council, to hold a boycott in the first place, men subsequently dominated the Montgomery Improvement Association (MIA) which took charge of its day-to-day running. This was not only a reflection of the gender expectations of the time but more specifically a replication of a male-dominated African American Southern Baptist Church hierarchy that the ministerial leadership of the MIA transposed onto the organization. The same was true of the similarly male- and ministerial-dominated SCLC. Even seasoned women activists with essential skills that might well have made the SCLC a more effective organization, such as Ella Baker, Septima Clark and Dorothy Cotton, were held back purely because of blinkered male prejudice over appropriate gender roles.

However, as Robnett also reveals, King and the SCLC were not the only ones tainted in this respect. Sexism ran rife throughout the movement, even in organizations that were supposedly dedicated to more enlightened demo-cratic ideals, such as SNCC. Men dominated the leadership and decision-making in that organization too and were likewise constricted by their preconceived notions about gender roles. Robnett argues that the exclusion women faced within movement organizations led them to carve out their own separate and distinctive niche of movement activism. Instead of seeking titled positions which limited their abilities within male-dominated organi-zations, they gravitated towards fieldwork and looked to exercise influence in grassroots community-based organizing. In doing so, they formed a dis-tinct category of movement 'bridge leaders', an important concept that informs Robnett's wider scholarship on the subject. In essence, bridge lead-ership provides a link between movement organizations and their potential grassroots membership, along with an important forum for mediation between the formal and informal aspects of movement activism. One conse-quence of this, Robnett points out, was that women 'felt their experiences in the movement to be liberating rather than constrained by their gender'. Indeed, for many women, participation in the civil rights movement was a crucial formative experience that led to the later development of and partic-ipation in an emergent women's movement in the mid- to late-1960s.

Given that the civil rights movement's high profile years were in the 1960s, a decade much touted as an era of 'sexual liberation', movement scholarship has been relatively coy about the role played by sex and sexuality in movement activism. The main focus to date have been studies of the 1964

Mississippi Freedom Summer that highlight the complicating factors of race and sex in that project and the questions it raised and discussions it promulgated within SNCC. Aside from that topic, it has been revelations about King's sexual philandering that have made the most headlines. Rumours of King's promiscuity circulated for many years, prompted by the FBI's covert surveillance of King and its attempts to pass on allegedly lurid details of his sex life to the press, which numerous editors refused to print. However, as Michael Eric Dyson notes in the second selection, confirmation of such rumours came from a surprising source: one of King's closest friends and confidants, Ralph D. Abernathy. Abernathy's 1989 autobiography contained a number of salacious details about King, while being noticeably more circumspect about his own frailties and shortcomings. Abernathy claimed that he was trying to paint a more human picture of King with all his faults laid bare. Others accused him of jealousy and betrayal.

The central question such revelations have raised is this: How does the knowledge of King's infidelity impact upon his legacy as a movement leader? For some, it comprehensively undermines King's moral authority. For others, it is a regrettable but nevertheless relatively marginal factor in King's overall accomplishments. There have been ready defenders of King's actions as Dyson's selection suggests. The 'preacherly culture' to which King belonged had a tradition of womanizing that often turned a blind eye to such misdemeanours. The tensions and strains of the movement led to an increased inclination to seek escape through physical intimacy. King was often away from home for days if not weeks on end because of his involvement with the movement and his high profile status and personal charisma brought temptation and opportunity to stray constantly his way. Yet for all these defences, the fact is that King broke his own code as a committed Christian not to commit adultery. As Dyson points out, King was painfully aware of the contradictions between what he practised and what he preached in this regard.

Another point that Dyson raises in his discussion is the possibility that the FBI surveillance of King might reveal evidence of King's bisexuality. Although the actual evidence for this is extremely tenuous, garnered as it is from the hearsay of FBI agents who may not be the most reliable source, what is interesting is that such revelations may be more damaging to King than his adultery. There is clearly a moral hierarchy at work here and one of the least charted themes in movement scholarship is the dynamics of sexuality and especially male homosexuality (and even more so lesbianism) and movement activism. The most insightful work to date in this area is John D'Emillio's biography of Bayard Rustin and Mississippi activist Aaron Henry's memoir. King's own paranoia about being labelled as a homosexual was revealed in a 1960 episode when African American New York congressman Adam Clayton Powell Jr threatened to expose (an entirely fabricated) homosexual affair between King and Rustin if plans to picket the

Democratic and Republican National Conventions that year were not called off. King quickly moved to distance himself from Rustin, who up to that point had been one of his closest advisors within the SCLC. Much to Rustin's surprise and annoyance, King accepted his resignation when it was proffered.

The controversies and debates that relate to women and gender, and to sex and sexuality, provide an indication of the far-reaching impact that the civil rights movement had. By giving birth to a new wave of social activism and involvement, and by providing a template and inspiration for other marginalized groups within American society, it paved the way for the emergence of a 'movement culture' in the 1960s and 1970s. Not only did it impact upon the women's rights movement and the gay rights movement, but it also impacted upon and influenced Native American, Latino and Asian American rights movements, as well as the American environmentalist movement, among others. Beyond the United States, the movement also belonged to wider postwar global struggles over decolonization and human rights that it both learned from and helped to shape.

Questions for Discussion

1. How and why did men and women play different roles in the civil rights movement?

2. Why do you think that more attention has been given to the way that gender shaped women's roles in the movement than to the way that it shaped men's roles in the movement?

3. Do revelations about King's sexual promiscuity undermine his historical legacy? Should public figures be judged by their private lives?

4. Assess the relationship between the civil rights movement and other movements for freedom and equality in the United States and in the wider world.

Further Reading

A good starting point for examining the role played by women in the civil rights movement is the collection of essays by Vicki Crawford, Jacqueline Rouse and Barbara Woods (eds), *Women in the Civil Rights Movement: Trailblazers and Torchbearers, 1941–1965* (Brooklyn, NY: Carlson Publishing, 1990) and Bettye Collier-Thomas and V. P. Franklin (eds), *Sisters in the Struggle: African American Women in the Civil Rights–Black Power Movement* (New York: New York University Press, 2001). These provide a number of profiles of influential women as a starting point for the numerous autobiographies and biographies available. There are also a number of useful historical examinations of African American women, including Michele Wallace, *Black Macho and the Myth of the Superwoman* (New York: Dial Press, 1978); bell hooks, *Ain't I a Woman? Black Women and Feminism* (Boston: South End Press, 1981); Angela Davis, *Women, Race and Class* (New York: Random House, 1981); Paula Giddings, *When and Where I Enter: The Impact of Black Women on Race and Sex in America* (New York: William Morrow, 1984); Jacqueline Jones, *Labor of Love, Labor of Sorrow: Black Women, Work and the Family from Slavery to Present* (New York: Basic Books, 1985); Stephanie J. Shaw, *What a Woman Ought to Be and Do: Black Professional Women Workers During the Jim Crow Era* (Chapel Hill, NC: University of North Carolina Press, 1996); Deborah Gray White, *Too Heavy a Load: Black Women in Defense of Themselves, 1894–1994* (New York: W. W. Norton, 1999); and Lynne Olson, *Freedom's Daughters: The Unsung Heroines of the Civil Rights Movement from 1830 to 1970* (New York: Charles Scribner's, 2001).

Most of the above works deal mainly with African American women. There are collections which deal specifically with white women's experiences such as Debra L. Schultz, *Going South: Jewish Women in the Civil Rights Movement* (New York: New York University Press, 2001) and Gail S. Murray (ed.), *Throwing Off the Cloak of Privilege: White Southern Women Activists in the Civil Rights Era* (Gainesville, FL: University Press of Florida, 2004). For useful first-hand accounts of white women's experiences in the 1964 Mississippi Freedom Summer, see Sally Belfrage, *Freedom Summer* (London: Deutsch, 1965), and Mary King, *Freedom Song: A Personal Story of the 1960s Civil Rights Movement* (New York: William Morrow, 1987). Mary King was later one of the leading figures in the women's movement. Her co-authorship with Casey Hayden of 'Sex and Caste: A King of Memo' (1965), together with an earlier anonymous 'SNCC Position Paper: Women in the Movement' (1964) provide examples of the link between the civil rights and women's movements. These short pieces can be found in Alexander Bloom and Wini Breines (eds), *Takin' it to the Streets: A Sixties Reader* (New York: Oxford University Press, 1995): 44–51. One helpful study that examines the links between civil rights activism and the women's movement is Sara Evans, *Personal Politics: The Roots of Women's Liberation in the Civil Rights Movement and the New Left* (New York: Alfred A. Knopf, 1979).

The fact that there is some division in the studies of African American and white women's contributions to the movement is a reflection of the disputes over race and gender that took place within the civil rights and women's movements. Many African American women pointed out that the women's movement was overwhelmingly dominated by and oriented to white middle-class concerns. African American feminism thus developed in different ways, charted in Kimberly Springer, *Living for the Revolution: Black Feminist Organizations, 1968–1980* (Durham, NC: Duke University Press, 2005).

A good introduction not just to women's activism but also the shaping role of gender is Belinda Robnett, *How Long? How Long? African American Women in the Struggle for Civil Rights* (New York: Oxford University Press, 1997). Peter J. Ling and Sharon Monteith (eds), *Gender in the Civil Rights Movement* (New York: Garland Publishing, 1999; reprinted New Brunswick, NJ: Rutgers University Press, 2004) provides a collection of essays on the subject. The first book to give an extensive analysis of the shaping role of masculinity within the movement is Steve Estes, *I Am a Man: Race, Manhood, and the Civil Rights Movement* (Chapel Hill, NC: University of North Carolina Press, 2005). On the intersection of homosexuality and movement activism see Aaron Henry, with Constance Curry, *Aaron Henry: The Fire Ever Burning* (Jackson, MS: Mississippi University Press, 2000) and John D'Emillio, *Lost Prophet: The Life and Times of Bayard Rustin* (New York: Free Press, 2003). On the broader context of homosexuality in the South see John Howard, *Men Like That: A Southern Queer History* (Chicago, IL: University of Chicago Press, 1999).

On sexuality in the US see John D'Emilio and Estelle Freedman, *Intimate Matters: A History of Sexuality in America* (New York: Harper and Row, 1988). On gay and lesbian liberation, see John D'Emilio, *Sexual Politics, Sexual Communities: The Making of a Homosexual Minority in the United States, 1940–1970* (Chicago, IL: University of Chicago Press, 1983); Barry D. Adam, *The Rise of a Gay and Lesbian Movement* (Boston, MA: Twayne Press, 1987); Lillian Faderman, *Odd Girls and Twilight Lovers: A History of Lesbian Life in Twentieth Century America* (New York: Columbia University Press, 1991); Eric Marcus, (ed.), *Making History: The Struggle for Gay and Lesbian Equal Rights, 1945–1990: A Oral History* (New York: HarperCollins, 1992); Martin Duberman, *Stonewall* (New York: Dutton, 1993); and H. N. Hirsch (ed.), *The Future of Gay Rights in America* (New York: Routledge, 2005). On the intersection between civil rights and gay liberation see Eric Brandt (ed.), *Blacks and Gays and the Struggle for Equality* (New York: New Press, 1999).

A brief but helpful introduction to the relationship between the civil rights movement and other struggles for freedom and equality is Judith Rollins, 'Part of a Whole: The Interdependence of the Civil Rights Movement and Other Social Movements,' *Phylon* 47:1 (1986): 61–70. The rights movement literature is vast and the following is only a sampling of works to indicate starting points.

Native Americans: Stan Steiner, *The New Indians* (New York: Harper and Row, 1968); Alvin M. Josephy, Jr, *Red Power: The American Indian's*

Fight for Freedom (New York: McGraw-Hill, 1971); John William Sayer, *Ghost Dancing the Law: The Wounded Knee Trials* (Cambridge, MA: Harvard University Press, 1997); and Dennis Banks, with Richard Erobes, *Ojibwa Warrior: Dennis Banks and the Rise of the American Indian Movement* (Norman, OK: University of Oklahoma Press, 2004).

Latino/Chicano: F. Arturo Rosales, *Chicano! The History of the Mexican American Civil Rights Movement* (Houston, TX: Arte Publico Press, 1996); Susan Ferriss and Ricardo Sadoval, *The Fight in the Fields: Cesar Chavez and the Farmworkers Movement* (New York: Harcourt Brace, 1997); George Mariscal, *Brown-Eyed Children of the Sun: Lessons from the Chicano Movement, 1965–1975* (Albuquerque: University of New Mexico Press, 2005); and Miguel Melendez, *We Took to the Streets: Fighting for Latino Rights with the Young Lords* (New Brunswick, NJ: Rutgers University Press, 2005).

Asian Americans: Angelo N. Anchetta, *Race, Rights and the Asian American Experience* (New Brunswick, NJ: Rutgers University Press, 1998); Mitchell T. Maki, Harry H. L. Kitano and S. Megan Berthold (eds), *Achieving the Impossible Dream: How Japanese Americans Obtained Redress* (Urbana, IL: University of Illinois Press, 1999); John S. W. Park, *Elusive Citizenship: Immigration, Asian Americans and the Paradox of Civil Rights* (New York: New York University Press, 2004); and Diane Carol Fujino, *Heartbeat of Struggle: The Revolutionary Life of Yuri Kochiyama* (Minneapolis, MN: University of Minnesota Press, 2005).

American environmentalism: Philip Shabecoff, *A Fierce Green Fire: The American Environmentalist Movement* (New York: Hill and Wang, 1992); Kirkpatrick Sale, *The Green Revolution: The American Environmental Movement, 1962–1992* (New York: Hill and Wang, 1993); Riley E. Dunlap and Angela D. Mertig (eds), *American Environmentalism: The US Environmental Movement, 1970–1990* (New York: Taylor and Francis, 1992); and Mark H. Lytle, *Gentle Subversive: Rachel Carson and the Rise of the Environmental Movement* (New York: Oxford University Press, 2006). For a compendium of movement speeches see Josh Gottheimer (ed.), *Ripples of Hope: Great American Civil Rights Speeches of the African American, Asian American, Gay, Latino and Women's Movements* (New York: Basic Civitas Books, 2003).

African-American Women in the Civil Rights Movement, 1954–65: Gender, Leadership, and Micromobilization

Belinda Robnett

...

Gender as a Category for Exclusion from Formal Leadership

That women were excluded from formal leadership positions during the time of the civil rights movement should come as no surprise. The women's liberation movement in the United States did not develop until the late sixties and early seventies. Within this context, notions of feminism and equal representation of women were not considerations in movement participation. Therefore, any analysis of gendered power relations is necessarily post hoc. This should not, however, preclude analysis. It is clear that the expectations were for men to occupy the formal leadership positions. In all of the movement organizations, women's representation as formal leaders was scant.

The MIA, for example, whose organization was patterned after the church, was established with only one woman officer, the financial secretary. Women participated in committees where they were outnumbered by men. For example, Rosa Parks was the only woman to serve on the committee to write the MIA constitution, and Irene West was the only woman on the nine-member committee to establish a bank and savings association. Erna Dungee, Alda Caldwell, and Euretta Adair were on the finance committee with four men. Women did chair certain committees, such as the welfare committee and the membership committee. Both areas were also the responsibility of women in the church.[1] Women within the welfare committee were responsible for the well-being of those who might suffer economic reprisals for movement participation. It was not that women were prevented from participating in important ways but that their participation options were limited.

In an interview, Johnnie Carr, a member of the MIA, agreed that, while women could chair a committee or hold office as a secretary, they would not be elected president: 'Well, it was not a stated thing but just an understood thing. ... Now of course when you spoke out against things like that,

From *American Journal of Sociology* 101: 6 (May 1996), pp. 1661–93.

a lot of times you were even criticized by other women that felt like … this is not what we ought to be doing.' She continued, 'I think we just accepted the servant [role] and done what we could because we felt like togetherness was the point.'[2]

It was not that women could not be viewed as possessing leadership qualities; such qualities were viewed in positive terms within the community. Rather, it was that these qualities were suitable for local activities and committee duties. Though Jo Ann Robinson, Irene West, and later Johnnie Carr were members of the board, most women's activities included fundraising, membership recruitment, and community welfare.[3] Jo Ann Robinson was an instrumental leader in the Montgomery bus boycott, which is often thought of as the beginning of the civil rights movement. The boycott was organized as a means of forcing desegregation on the buses. Yet, Robinson's position within the MIA did not reflect her leadership abilities. Her actions were certainly no less critical to the success of the boycott than were those of the male officers. Yet, as Dorothy Cotton recalls, the recognition of women's leadership often took the form of a 'paternalistic pat on the head.'[4]

At the mass meetings, which were generally minister led, women's activities were acknowledged with anecdotal stories that portrayed their courage in not riding the buses. Committee chairs of the membership and welfare committees were often given three-minute slots to give updates on the progress of these endeavors. The belief in the ministers' authority as leaders was born out in the MIA newsletter, edited by Jo Ann Robinson but subject to approval by Martin Luther King, Jr., which did not contain much information on the activities of women and tended to focus on the ministers.[5]

This pattern of gender exclusion from formal leadership positions was also true of the SCLC. Males, in particular ministers, dominated the upper ranks of the SCLC hierarchical structure. At the executive staff level, there were only two areas where women actively participated, the Citizenship Education Program and the fund-raising department. Until 1965, there were either no women on the board of directors, or one woman. In 1964, Marian B. Logan of New York City served as the only female member of the board. By 1965, there were three women on the board: Logan, Erna Dungee, and Victoria Gray. Thirty-nine males constituted the rest of the board roster.[6]

Likewise, women, even when they were privy to board and executive staff meetings, found themselves left out of decision-making processes regarding organization, structure, and future strategies. Ella Baker, despite her experience as a seasoned activist and freelance consultant to civil rights groups, was hired as the acting director of the newly formed SCLC. Since the ministers did not feel that a woman was a suitable director for their organization, they hired her on a temporary basis while they searched for a more appropriate replacement. During her tenure, she was consistently frustrated by the dominance of the Baptist ministers and their lack of confidence in her skills. In commenting on why she decided to leave the SCLC, she replied, 'In the first place, I had known, number one, that there would never be any role for me in a leadership capacity with SCLC. Why? First, I'm a woman. Also, I'm not a minister.' She continued,

> In the first place, the combination of being a woman, and an older woman, presented some problems. Number one, I was old enough to be the mother of the leadership. The combination of the basic attitude of men, and especially ministers, as to what the role of women in their church setups is – that of taking orders, not providing leadership – and the ego that is involved – the ego problems involved in having to feel that here is someone who had the capacity for a certain amount of leadership and, certainly, had more information about a lot of things than they possessed at that time – this would never had lent itself to my being a leader in the movement there.'[7]

This feeling of not being allowed to rise in the ranks of the SCLC leadership was echoed by Septima Clark, a key activist in the SCLC. She recalled, 'I was on the Executive Staff of SCLC, but the men on it didn't listen to me too well. They liked to send me into many places because I could always make a path in to get people to listen to what I have to say. But those men didn't have any faith in women, none whatsoever. They just thought that women were sex symbols and had no contribution to make. That's why Rev. Abernathy would say continuously, "Why is Mrs. Clark on this staff?" '[8]

Clark's and Baker's comments reflect the degree to which women's positions were controlled by the belief that male ministers should be the primary source for formal leadership. At most of the conventions the only women to participate regularly were Septima Clark and Dorothy Cotton, both of whom ran the education area of the SCLC, and Diane Nash Bevel, the youth group coordinator. Clark and Cotton were usually afforded a few minutes to report on the progress of the Citizenship Education Program, while Bevel ran a youth group workshop. At board meetings as well as executive staff meetings, women's verbal comments were scarce and usually treated without serious consideration, especially if they were policy suggestions.[9]

Dr King, in a letter intended as a preface to Septima Clark's autobiography, *Echo in My Soul*, indicates his view of women's positions in the struggle for civil rights. He wrote, '*Echo in My Soul* epitomizes the continuous struggle of the Southern Negro woman to realize her role as a mother while fulfilling her forced position as community teacher, intuitive fighter for human rights and leader of her unlettered and disillusioned people.'[10] The young Baptist minister believed that women, while capable of leadership, did not and should not exercise this ability by choice. A woman's position was more naturally suited as a support to her husband and as a mother to her children.

Dr King's ambivalence toward women extended into his dealings with other women on his staff as well. Carole F. Hoover was the daughter of a minister in Chattanooga, Tennessee, who began working for the SCLC in 1962 and served as an aide to Wyatt T. Walker, the executive assistant. In 1964 Walker was relocated, leaving Hoover uncertain of her status. Repeated attempts to discuss her situation with Dr King failed, and in a letter to him she wrote,

> I regret that I have to communicate by this means with you, however, it seems that it is impossible for me to be afforded an opportunity to talk with you. ... I need to know specifically what my responsibility will be and also my job classification. ... My second concern stems from the fact that I am so obviously excluded from meetings where programming, policy and future plans for the organizations are dealt with. Consequently, I am poorly informed which is bad, because I am constantly before groups for promotions, fund raising and other things where it is mandatory to be equipped with information on our present program. At present, I do not know what cities we will be in this summer for direct action. I feel that if I am to remain on the staff at least I should be informed.[11]

Carole Hoover was not a part of the executive staff, though her position clearly required such participation (by 1965 she was included in these meetings).[12] That women were systematically excluded from positions in formal leadership is obvious. Such exclusion was not, however, limited to minister-led organizations.

The Student Nonviolent Coordinating Committee, which was primarily a secular, nonhierarchical organization, also tended to exclude women from the formal leadership. Although there were rotating chairs and an executive committee, between 1960 and 1965, all of the chairs and executive secretaries were men. Likewise, the majority of those who served on the executive committee were men. Virtually all project directors were men until 1964.[13] So men tended to dominate official positions of power, though in SNCC there was no clear line of authority. Theoretically, SNCC leaders were to take the form of organizers who would inspire local leadership.

In the beginning, the membership in SNCC was primarily composed of men. In correspondence sent to the SNCC office in 1962, a prospective woman volunteer writes, 'Many of us are interested in the possibility of going to the South but are hesitant because from the information we have received about SNCC we could find only male students' names in the accounts of students working there.'[14] In response, Horace Julian Bond, a SNCC field secretary, replied, 'Although we do not presently have any girls on our field staff, we do have a very capable office manager who is very female. Diane Nash one of the leaders of the Nashville Student Movement, was a leader on SNCC's staff until her recent marriage. Glen Green, Joy Reagan, Bertha Gober, and other college girls have been members of the staff in the past as well.' He continued, 'In addition, let me say that if we were able to hire a girl to type some of our correspondence, I wouldn't have made as many mistakes as I have.'[15]

From the beginning, a core of men remained central in various positions of power. Such male leaders as James Forman, John Lewis, Marion Barry, Bob Moses, Worth Long, Courtland Cox, Ivanhoe Donaldson, and later Stokely Carmichael, were either chairs of SNCC or representatives on the executive committee. Women tended to rotate in or out of the executive committee positions and to align themselves with either the Forman, Moses, or Carmichael camp.[16]

Though women were viewed as capable and often participated in ways that endangered their lives, certain gender-based restrictions on their participation remained. In 1964, the Atlanta staff, which included administration, the 'Student Voice,' photography, research, Northern coordination, Southern coordination, communications, office managers, telephone operators, the financial department, Freedom Singers, and others, was predominately male. Carol Merritt was the only woman in the administrative area, where she directed the education program. The executive secretary, program director, administrative assistant, chairman, and Freedom Summer coordinator were all men. There were no women in the 'Student Voice' area and only one or two women in the other areas. The only exceptions to this pattern are the telephone operators and the financial department, who were exclusively women.

Ruby Doris Smith Robinson's position in charge of personnel was placed in the 'other' category.[17] This position actually gave her a great deal of power within SNCC since she was responsible for hiring and firing volunteers and for signing checks that went to the various projects.[18] There were also women campus travelers who solicited funds and volunteers. These included Jean Wheeler, Enoch Johnson, Joyce Brown, and Judy Richardson.[19] In a 1964 job description of personnel in the Atlanta office, it is clear that job title and job descriptions adhered to gender-based divisions of labor. For example, the executive director, the 'unofficial' office manager, and the staff coordinator were all men. The descriptions of their jobs included words that indicated authority over others, while women's job descriptions, such as those of Forman's secretary and of the women coordinators, included the verbs 'answers' and 'handles.' The receptor of women's authority was generally an object, namely correspondence.[20]

In a 1964 office staff meeting, Julian Bond, the director of communications, indicated his dislike of working with women, which was honored with the appointment of a man as his coworker. As the staff minutes state, 'Julian doesn't like working with women. … Would like to have Mike Sayer as requested earlier.' There was no attempt to confront this issue by either the men or women present at the meeting.[21] Later that year in an executive committee meeting that included four women and 14 men, the group discussed the possibility of training a SNCC member to become a fundraiser. As indicated by the minutes of this meeting, Forman suggests, 'Let's discuss whether we should have someone from our own ranks or hire someone for lots of money. This person should have "internal drive," should be someone who feels fundraising is very important, who is willing to learn and who can move into cities and move the people there, who will attend to details, who will travel, who won't dump the program because of a commitment to be in the South. Ivanhoe could do this.' The minutes continue: 'Some discussion on the person to fill this job. T. Brown asked if it had to be a male and suggested Prathia [Hall]. John Lewis suggested we refer the names to a committee but Forman thought it was too important a question to be referred to a committee. Forman mentioned that male would be better since job involved living virtually out of a suitcase.'[22]

Although the restrictions involved gender-based assumptions, there was a general belief that women were capable of doing the job but that they should not do it. Though SNCC was not minister led, it was male dominated. Many respondents stated that women did not want to be in the office but preferred to work in the field. One respondent recalls, 'If you had a title, you were in the office.'[23] Titled positions, for women, often translated into less power. This was not true for men such as Julian Bond or James Forman, whose titled positions often translated into greater power to make decisions. If a woman was titled, this usually meant that her duties would be restricted to clerical activities. On the other hand, when she participated without a title, her activities could stretch beyond the bounds of her otherwise stated duties. In other words, it was unsuitable for a woman to hold a titled position with an undue amount of power. So women, cognizant of the fact that titles restricted one's leadership opportunities, chose to participate in a different context.

Women preferred to do fieldwork, though here, too, they did not often hold titled positions. Still such a position allowed for more autonomy. They worked at canvassing in local communities and, on a day-to-day basis, were able to make decisions within the local community. Canvassing included (1) seeing what was on people's minds – what kinds of things they would like to see done; (2) getting individuals to register to vote; and (3) recruiting individuals for local demonstrations.

Few women were able to become project directors though more were appointed as SNCC expanded and the need for experienced leaders increased. Between 1964–65, of the 50 staff members in Mississippi, there were 12 women. In Mississippi, Southwest Georgia, and Alabama, there were 29 project directors and only five were women, which included Muriel Tillinghast in Greenville, Mississippi; Mary Lane in Greenwood, Mississippi; Willie Ester McGee in Itta Bena, Mississippi (she worked alongside Stokely Carmichael who was the district director); Mary Sue Gellatly in Shaw, Mississippi; Lois Rogers in Cleveland, Mississippi; and Gwen Robinson in Laurel. Women project directors did not generally supervise more than one fieldworker, while most men supervised three or more.[24]

The fact that women's participation options as titled staff members were limited does not reduce the importance of their activities. Likewise the women interviewed did not perceive their activities as limited. Women felt themselves to be an important and integral part of the movement. Bernice Reagon, a member of SNCC, stated, 'So that one of the things that happened to me through SNCC was my whole world was expanded in terms of what I could do as a person. And I'm describing an unleashing of my potential as an empowered human being. I never experienced being held back. ... And I think if you talked to a lot of people who participated in the movement, who were in SNCC, you find women describing themselves being pushed in ways they had never experienced before.'[25]

This idea was echoed by most of the women interviewed. All felt their experiences in the movement to be liberating rather than constrained by their gender. Rather than focusing upon their limited positions within the movement, women shifted their leadership efforts toward bridging the movement to communities.

This gender bias within the civil rights movement was, of course, a reflection of the times. It did, however, create a specific effect. Since women, because of gender exclusion, could not be formal leaders, they more readily became bridge leaders. It was not the case that all bridge leaders were women, only that bridging was the primary area of leadership available to women. Nor was it the case that women were uniquely capable of performing such tasks. Rather, the effect of gender exclusion, which prevented strong leaders from becoming formal leaders, produced a remarkably capable tier of leadership that strengthened the mobilization of and recruitment to the movement.

Notes

1. See King Papers, Boston University (box 6, ser. I, file 38, MIA folder). This includes numerous documents of women's committee positions during the boycott and within the Dexter Avenue Baptist Church.

2. Interview with Johnnie Carr by telephone, 26 January 1990.
3. Interview with Hazel Gregory by telephone, February 15, 1990; King Papers, King Center, MIA document (box 16, file 25).
4. Interview with Dorothy Cotton, January 20, 1990.
5. See Hazel Gregory Papers, King Center (box 1, file 21); MIA Newsletters 1956–60, King Center.
6. See SCLC Papers, King Center (subgroup D, ser. 9, box 120, file 19); SCLC Newsletter November 1959 and SCLC Papers May 28, 1959 (sub. D, ser. 8, box 129, file 1).
7. See Ella Baker Transcript, p. 10, Civil Rights Documentation Project.
8. See Septima Clark Oral History Project, King Center, transcript 17, p. 39.
9. See SCLC Executive Staff Meeting minutes, August 26–28, 1965, SNCC Papers (sub. A, ser. 1, box 3, file 37); Seventh Annual Convention, September 24–27, 1963 (sub. D, ser. 13, box 130, file 2); Staff Meeting, September 16, 1964 (sub. E, ser. 1, box 137, file 4); SCLC Conference, November 10–12, 1964, Erna Dungee Papers (box 2, file 22); Annual SCLC Meeting, September 27–29, 1961 (sub. D, ser. 13, box 129, file 12); SCLC Conference, September 25–28, 1962 (sub. D, ser. 13, box 129, file 31); SCLC Convention 1963 (sub. D, ser. 13, box 130, file 2); Letter from Martin Luther King, Jr., to the presidents of affiliates, February 3, 1962, King Papers, King Center (box 29, file 1); SCLC Board Meeting Minutes, 1960, 1961, 1962, King Papers (box 29, file 1); SCLC Board Meeting Minutes, September 24, 1963 King Papers (box 29, file 2); SCLC Board Meeting Minutes, August 9, 1965, King Papers (box 29, file 5). For the years 1958 and 1960–66, there is only one press release from the SCLC that mentions a woman (ser. D-9, box 120, file 6). Dorothy Cotton, the one woman, is also mentioned several times in newsletters. Some women are recognized for graduating from the Citizenship Education Classes and going back to start schools in their communities (SCLC newsletters [sub. D, ser. 9, box 120, files 20–21 and box 122, file 19]).
10. Martin Luther King, Jr., to the associate editor of E. P. Dutton, 2 July 1962, King Papers, King Center (box 29, file 18).
11. Carole Hoover to Martin Luther King, Jr., King Papers, King Center (box 34, file 5).
12. Minutes of SCLC Executive Staff Meeting, August 26–28, SNCC Papers (sub. A, ser. 1, box 3, file 37). The view that King was ambivalent toward women is presented throughout Coretta Scott King's *My Life with Martin Luther King, Jr.*
13. See SNCC Papers, Chairman's Files 1960–65 (sub. A, ser. 1, boxes 1–5); Executive and Central Committees 1961–65 (ser. 2, box 6); Staff Meetings, 1960–65 (ser. 3, box 7); Executive Secretary Files, 1959–65 (ser. 4, boxes 8–24); and State Project Files, 1960–65 (ser. 15, boxes 94–105).
14. Marion Michaels to James Forman, April 5, 1962, SNCC Papers (sub. A, ser. 4, box 16, file 221).
15. Julian Bond to Marion Michaels, April 10, 1962, SNCC Papers (sub. A, ser. 4, box 16, file 221).
16. Interview with Fay Bellamy, 7 February 1990.
17. See Persons working out of the Atlanta office, SNCC Papers (sub. A, ser. 6, box 28, file 21).
18. Interview with Fay Bellamy, 7 February 1990.
19. See Persons working out of the Atlanta office, SNCC Papers (sub. A, ser. 6, box 28, file 21).
20. See Job Description, SNCC Papers (sub. A, ser. 4, box 28, file 17).
21. See Office Staff Meeting Minutes, 16 February 1964, SNCC Papers (sub. A, ser. 4, box 7, file 1).

22. Executive Committee Minutes, 4 September 1964, SNCC Papers (sub. A, ser. 3, box 6, file 4).
23. Interview with 'Anonymous' by telephone, 16 March 1989.
24. See Persons working out of the Atlanta office, SNCC Papers (sub. A, ser. 6, box 28, file 21).
25. Interview with Bernice Reagon by telephone, 30 November 1992.

'I May Not Get There with You': The True Martin Luther King, Jr

Michael Eric Dyson.

It is a scene that is too painful to conjure for many of Martin Luther King Jr.'s supporters. After spending his last night delivering one of the most brilliant speeches in his career – a moment comparable to Michael Jordan's fending off a swarming opponent to sink the winning shot in the Chicago Bulls' sixth championship series and thus immortalizing the image of his last play before his final departure from basketball and his team's certain disintegration – King allegedly rendezvoused with two women at different points of the night and in the early morning fought with a third female 'friend' before being gunned down later that evening at the Lorraine Motel. The source of this shattered image of King's Memphis martyrdom is not J. Edgar Hoover, Jesse Helms or Ronald Reagan. It is none other than Ralph David Abernathy.

If Martin Luther King was the civil rights movement's Michael Jordan, then Abernathy was surely King's Scottie Pippen (Jordan's superstar teammate). At midcentury, King and Abernathy formed a formidable one-two lineup in the agitation for freedom. When King was jailed, Abernathy was jailed. When King spoke, Abernathy often introduced him. When King couldn't speak, Abernathy often spoke for him. When King headed the SCLC, Abernathy was chosen by King to succeed him. When King stayed up late at night, Abernathy often kept him company. When King traveled to Norway to collect his Nobel Peace Prize, Abernathy was there. They ate in each other's homes, kept each other's kids, preached in each other's pulpits, and built each other up over nearly fifteen years of friendship and professional fraternity. And when King breathed his last breath in Memphis, it was in the arms of Abernathy, who also officially identified King's body at the

From *I May Not Get There with You: The True Martin Luther King, Jr* (New York: The Free Press, 2000), pp. 155–67.

morgue and presided over his friend's funeral a few days later. The two shared ideas back and forth until it was nearly impossible to discern where one man's thinking began and the other's ended. On this score, Abernathy is hardly accorded the credit he deserves for his contributions to King and to the cause they both championed. If King was the movement's most valuable player, then Abernathy was, by King's own account, a sturdy source of comfort and 'the best friend that I have in the world.'

When Abernathy, in his 1989 best-selling autobiography, *And the Walls Came Tumbling Down*, divulged secrets about Martin Luther King, Jr.'s, sex life that had until that moment rested with him in his grave, he was widely viewed by movement veterans as a traitor to King's memory. All along, there had been rumors among civil rights cognoscenti that Abernathy loved King even as he was jealous of his more famous friend. In their eyes he waited until King could no longer defend himself before offering damaging details of King's Promethean trysts. To be fair to Abernathy, he faced a difficult choice in telling the story of the movement and his friendship with King. In an introduction to the paperback edition of his autobiography, Abernathy answers his critics. He argues that in writing his book, he wanted to 'let Americans – particularly black Americans – in on a secret: Martin Luther King, Jr. was not just a great public hero but an extremely attractive human being as well – a man whom they would have loved to have as a friend.' Besides the portrait of a great defender of justice, Abernathy 'wanted to show the private man as well,' the 'mimic who was so funny he could render his friends helpless with laughter,' the 'young soldier who loved life and was afraid to die, but went into battle anyway,' and the man 'who on the last day of his life worried about hurting the feelings of a tired waitress who had brought the wrong order.' Abernathy thinks that controversy greeted his book because he 'wanted to portray Martin as a believable human being.' Therefore, he 'had to deal with certain personal weaknesses (which others had already written about).' Abernathy believes that it is important to tell the whole story so that future generations can truly appreciate King's genuine greatness as an epic hero on the order of 'Washington, Lincoln, and a handful of other leaders.' Since his friend has become a legend, Abernathy wants to set the record straight so that King's legend will be useful to Americans in the centuries to come. Abernathy argues that 'legends are important to give people a sense of who they are and what, in their best moments, they can become.' But Abernathy wants 'to let everyone know that this legendary figure was also a human being, and that his humanity did not detract from the legend but only made it more believable for other human beings.'

If we take Abernathy at his word, King's memory will not be besmirched by his best friend's revelations. Moreover, even King's severest critics cannot prevent his ascent to the pantheon of American heroes, figures whose clay feet and singular flaws have not prevented a nation from strongly embracing their legacies. But even if we doubt Abernathy's motives – he only obliquely referred to his own philandering, an alleged instance of which produced the famous photo of King having his youthful arm twisted by the police as he seeks to support his best friend in court against a charge of cuckolding – we can still endorse his belief that the more honestly we confront King's moral lapses, the more we are able to extract from his failings a sense of his authentic humanity and a fuller grasp of his towering achievements. To avoid exploring King's weaknesses is to deny him the careful consideration that should be devoted to any historic figure. And to pretend King didn't sin is to subvert the healthy critical distance we should maintain on all personages, the lack of which leads to charges of uncritical black hero worship. As Abernathy suggests, King 'will grow in the hearts of future Americans regardless of what I or other biographers have to say about him.'

If Abernathy is right, the charge of plagiarism cannot blot King's achievements from the pages of history. Neither can King's adultery reduce his reputation to the shape of a bed. Only advocates of moral perfection will seek to deny King his high place in history because of his sexual sins. This does not mean that we cannot or should not criticize King for his rampant womanizing and his relentless infidelity (although one is tempted to cry with Alfred Lord Tennyson in his defense of fellow poet Lord Byron: 'What business has the public to know of Byron's wildnesses? He has given them fine work and they ought to be satisfied'). But as with the good things in King's life, we must place the bad things in context as well. King was certainly reared in a preacherly culture where good sex is pursued with nearly the same fervor as believers seek to be filled with the Holy Ghost. And the war against white supremacy in which King participated was thoroughly sexist and often raucous; men who had a symbolic, and sometimes literal, bounty on their heads mistreated female soldiers and sought refuge in the fleeting pleasures of the flesh. But in the comparative moral context in which we inevitably view history, their sins were far less grievous than the racial apartheid that led figures like King to spend most of the year away from home, making them more vulnerable to their weaknesses. White supremacy didn't cause their sins, but it surely gave King and others ample opportunity to succumb to temptations that they may have otherwise been spared.

King's true greatness can be understood only when we get rid of the false expectations of human perfection in our heroes and leaders. King was a spiritual and moral genius, but his genius had nothing to do with unrealistic notions of purity. King's was, paradoxically, an imperfect perfection. To paraphrase singer Grace Jones – who sang that 'I may not be perfect, but I'm perfect for you' – King may not have been perfect, but he was perfect for Americans who desired racial justice. His moral aim of transforming

America was perfectly suited for the times and places in which he acted with decisive courage. And if King was pure, it was in the biblical sense of being 'pure in heart' – that is, obsessively single-minded about the greatest good: loving God and one's neighbour: King was so committed to that good that he died for it, a death that revealed the astonishing oneness of his speech and his life. To be sure, the sense of hurt, even betrayal, evoked by King's shortcomings partially underscores just how morally useful he has been in our culture. King is for many whites the ideal expression of black identity – whether that means speaking 'standard' English, refusing to hate bigoted whites, refraining from listening to violent rap music, or shunning Louis Farrakhan. The early King also symbolizes for many whites how black folk should behave in the aftermath of the racial revolution that King helped to ignite. Never mind, of course, that many of these same whites opposed King and the civil rights river as it began to flow. They have now been baptized in its redeeming currents and have had the sins of their resistance washed away. King reigns, then, as the Black Moral Messiah, the prophetic figure whose loving insurgence led many whites to a new faith in blacks.

As great as King's achievements are, they fail to silence his severest critics. King's good works are lost on those who were never satisfied with his moral goals or who rabidly opposed the civil rights movement. These critics are easily dismissed as bigots, folk who, in Howard Thurman's revealing definition of the term, 'make an idol of their commitments.' Then there are critics who believe that King's failures symbolize his essential perversion. In their eyes, King's theft of other men's words and their wives revealed his deep moral corruption. Although there are bigots in this group, it contains many others who simply believe that one can never be a good person if one is an adulterer or plagiarist. These folk are less easily dismissed. For one reason, King often spoke against the sins he committed, at least against adultery, and he insisted that ethical means and ends must hang together in a meaningful moral universe. Still other critics claim that one or another of King's sins is the defining feature of his character. And then there are those who oppose King out of civic duty. They claim that King was a hypocrite who is undeserving of national honor because he failed to, as the gospel song phrases it, live the life he sang about in his song. Some of these claims are surely repulsive, self-righteous, and overly simplistic, but they should nevertheless be met head-on with a sober grasp of King's successes and failures. In making a mature and balanced moral judgment of King, we have to acknowledge the enormous odds that were stacked against King and his colleagues throughout their lives. As King's life heroically suggests, morality is sized up and situated within messy personal and historical borders. The contours of a good life never trace the anatomy of perfection. The outlines of a life well spent are more likely composed of jagged edges and interrupted lines silhouetted against a backdrop of moral aspiration. Indefensible as it is, even King's philandering may suggest more than rakishness or depravity because of the unique conditions under which he conducted his career.

We have known for a while that King was at once a guilt-stricken, grief-engulfed, and, paradoxically, vigilant adulterer. Jesse Helms and J. Edgar Hoover (the latter's double life as gay, cross-dressing 'Mary' was a bigger and longer-held secret than King's philandering, and was no doubt the spur of Hoover's self-hating puritanism) tried to soil King's legacy by publicizing his peccadilloes. David Garrow has brilliantly documented the FBI's evil assault on King's life and reputation, including the use of illegally acquired electronic evidence of King's 'compulsive sexual athleticism' to dissuade King from his civil rights leadership. The FBI's immoral and relentless pursuit of King – at first on the grounds of his alleged communist activity, next for nonexistent financial malfeasance, and finally for nothing short of a voyeuristic campaign to discredit King and destroy the civil rights movement – reflected the highly conflicted emotions of segments of white society around the issue of black sexuality. Andrew Young, King's trusted lieutenant and former Atlanta mayor, Georgia congressman, and UN ambassador, argues that 'the campaign against Martin and the movement was less about sex than about fear of sexuality.' Young powerfully summarizes this fear when he writes:

> Deeply buried but intense sexual fear of black males, illustrated by the sexual nature of the attacks on black men by whites who seek to control or destroy black aggressiveness, has been a persistent pattern in the South since the advent of slavery. From the systematic destruction of the black family during slavery to contemporary barriers for black males attempting to protect and provide for their families via the imposition of strong societal and economic proscriptions, there is a recurrent theme: controlling black men. The theme was ever-present at lynchings of black men for allegations of rape or for flirtation with white women, and is always evident somewhere in the heavy punishment awaiting black men who assert or advocate the interests of their people. The FBI campaign was very much consistent with this neurotic white Southern racist tradition.

At the same time, there is little doubt that, like his habits of verbal borrowing, King's sexual practices were nourished within a powerful pocket of the church. His sexual habits grew in part out of a subculture of promiscuity that is rampant among clergy and religious figures in every faith. As David Levering Lewis remarks, sexual license is a 'chronic avocation among evangelical divines, black and white.' As surely as King learned from the black church the use of brilliant rhetorical strategies that would help change America, and as surely as he was shaped in its crucible of biblical interpretations of social sin and suffering, he learned in the same setting about the delights of the flesh that were formally forbidden but were in truth the sweet reward of spiritual servants. As the writer Marcia L. Dyson observes, there is a tradition in Christian churches of ministers who 'exploit this power [over women] and even take it for granted, as if it were an entitlement – sometimes preying on vulnerable and lonely women, at other times seeking out accomplices in sexual misconduct who are quite willing or, at best, self-deceived.' King was no exception. But it must be said that as an internationally famous figure, King was a sexual magnet for women of every race, from every walk of life, who longed to bask in his limelight and in his affectionate, lustful embrace.

Undeniably one of the great ironies of King's sexual failings is how they embodied the conflicted uses of black privacy. King fought against the ruthless restrictions imposed on black public life, which led black folk to use their private spaces as both incubators of political activism and protection from the tyranny of apartheid. King opposed the lethal limits that denied blacks full citizenship and equality before the law. Thus, black private and public spaces acquired heightened importance and took on multiple uses under segregation. These spaces were at once outlet and refuge, providing sanctuary and solace from the bruising public humiliations brought on by white supremacy. These spaces were a site for refining the moral narratives of social rebellion that black folk expressed in the white public. They also provided blacks a place to rebel against black immobility in the white world.

In King's case, the varied functions of black privacy were even more highly charged. During much of his career, King's private time was spent on the road in black homes or in the few black public accommodations, where he and his colleagues sharpened strategies for social change. King's time at home was severely curtailed by the inhuman demands of the movement. He spent nearly twenty-seven days of most months in pursuit of the prize of black liberation. Inevitably, this separation weakened King's sexual bonds with his wife and eroded the quality of time and affection he could devote to her and to their children. To be fair, King's habits of sexual adventure had been well established by the time he was married. His personal and public circumstances only amplified his sexual indiscretions.

It is clear that King was both tortured by his adultery and awkwardly comforted by its serial anonymities and episodic thrills. As a Christian minister, King was constantly reminded, if not by history or scripture then by circumstance, of the perilous traps of the flesh. In a remarkable 1966 interview with King conducted by Hugh Downs on NBC's *The Today Show*, King addressed what Downs termed the 'loose sex relations and problems of the quite young' with calm and balance. King suggested that in 'the past, too often the church has taken a kind of prohibitive attitude on the whole question of sex, a hush-hush attitude, rather than trying to honestly discuss sex and deal with the problems surrounding it.' King said that the 'only answer is for the church through its channels of religious education and other methods to bring this issue out into the open, and reaffirm once more than what God creates is good and that it must be used properly and not abused.' Although ostensibly addressing the evils that young folk face, King was surely thinking during the interview of his own compromised situation. King perhaps provides a poignant glimpse into his own psychic and moral struggles when he argued:

> I think it is also necessary to bring out this point that sex is basically sacred when it is properly used and that marriage is man's greatest prerogative in the sense that it is through and in marriage that God gives man the opportunity to aid him in his creative activity. Therefore, sex must never be abused in the loose sense it is often abused in the modern world. I think the other thing that is necessary to say here is that it is necessary to move to the causal basis of sexual promiscuity, the deep anxieties and frustration and confusion of modern life which lead to the abuses, and the church must not only work on the level of condemnation, but it must seek to get at the causal basis and work to remove these causes and deal with the psychological problems that bring the looseness into being, rather than making a general condemnation and not be concerned about the causal basis.

But the more recriminations he had over his sexual surrender – he said in a sermon that his congregation need not 'go out this morning saying that Martin Luther King is a saint' but that he was 'a sinner like all of God's children' – the more he was oddly driven to seek the satisfaction and relief that could come only from falling in sin and rising up to fight again. In his carnal escapades, King ritually reenacted the storyline of racial redemption: we attempt to do good, we fall, we rise again, we succeed for a while, we feel guilty for failing again, we get pleasure from our guilt, we feel remorseful for our pleasurable guilt, and we punish ourselves by reengaging the source of our suffering. King's private space provided him little relief from the unforgiving demands of representing the race. In his privacy, he was constantly consumed with how he might make a better world for blacks, even as he sought in vain to escape through sexual release the magnitude of his duty, the burden of his role, and the unrelenting pace of his quest for freedom.

King realized the moral schizophrenia produced by his prolific infidelities. He acknowledged them in a veiled way before his congregation at Ebenezer when he declared that 'each of us is two selves' and that the 'great burden of life is to always try to keep that higher self in command.' King admonished his hearers not to 'let the lower self take over,' but that occasionally one will 'be unfaithful to those you should be faithful to.' Of course, King realized that adultery was more than a failure to be faithful to one's partner. Because marriage is a profoundly sacramental relationship, it was also a repudiation of God's law. But to his glory, and grief, King could not resist representing God even in his most private domain at his most profane moment. King is said to have uttered during one of his sexual romps that 'I'm fucking for God,' suggesting that, in the lowest moment of moral alienation from his personal values, and when he was furthest from his vows of fidelity, King could not shake the consciousness of his representative duties: to his race, to the civil rights movement, and above all to God. Instead of bringing his duties and desires into conflict, King momentarily fused them. His attempt at such a union symbolized his temporary rejection of the idea that his duties and desires were incompatible. King's desperate hedonism was also a profound gesture of sanity making as he sought release into the forbidden realm of erotic excess as an escape from the unbearable heat of white hatred. It was perhaps a convoluted way of keeping in touch with his own flesh–flesh that was being ransomed to redeem racial justice as a condition of his commitment to black freedom. Indirectly, and unconsciously, King's exuberant extramarital affairs may have expressed anger at a God who would thrust such an onerous duty on him. At the height of his infidelity, King calls God's name in vain to bless his fleshly frolic as a way to call attention to his paradoxical predicament: by invoking the divine presence, he is both seeking sanction and inviting scorn on his divided soul. Even though he is breaking God's law in committing adultery, his reckless invocation of God is at once profane and the ultimate predicate of his existence. No matter what, King's theology reminds him that God 'promised never to leave me, never to leave me alone.'

King spiritualized his fleshly faults not so much to justify them as to bring them into even a tenuous relation to his higher urges. After all, David, a likely model for King, said in Psalm 139, 'if I make my bed in hell, behold thou art there.' King flipped the logic of representing God and took it to its literal climax: King explodes in orgasm to keep his spirit from exploding, since, as he claimed, 'fucking's a form of anxiety reduction.' But if he couldn't escape the heavenly hound, at least he might be able, through his sexual profligacy, to shift momentarily the burden of representing the race. King often attempted to drown in a sea of sensuality all the demands of being the good, upstanding Negro, the shining embodiment of black perfection, the exemplary exhorter of moral excellence – as he ejaculated during one encounter, 'I'm not a Negro tonight.'

Carl Rowan [an African American journalist] has also made disturbing claims about King's sex life. In his 1991 memoir *Breaking Barriers*, Rowan says that in the sixties, Congressman John Rooney informed him that 'a lot of congressmen had been inflamed by an alleged FBI tape recording' of what J. Edgar Hoover had termed an 'orgy' in King's suite at the Willard Hotel in Washington. This was one of the scenes of the scandalous FBI tape that had been sent to King as he departed for Europe to receive his Nobel Peace Prize. And there is a possibility that the tape that Rowan reports was exercising the congressmen was the very tape, or a version of it, sent to King. Rowan asked Rooney what was on the tape that had everyone up in arms.

'He looked at me as if doubting whether he should answer,' Rowan writes. 'He looked at his notes, which someone already had typed out for him. Then he replied: "Hoover played us a tape with sounds indicating that someone was having intercourse in one room of the King suite. But it clearly wasn't King, because we hear him saying to a man Hoover identified as Abernathy, "Come on over here, you big black motherfucker, and let me suck your dick." '

Rowan writes that he thought to himself that an 'FBI director who is suspected of being a homosexual has gone to Congress to try to destroy our greatest civil rights leader by portraying him as a homosexual!' Rowan says that he defended King to Rooney, arguing that he couldn't speak against a tape he hadn't heard. Rowan also argued that 'whenever black men gather in a party, the language, the back and forth, may have no relationship to reality.' Rowan suggested to Rooney that after a few drinks, black men and many others lie about their sexual prowess. 'They throw the word "motherfucker" around like "buddy" or "pal," ' Rowan writes. 'They talk about sucking dicks or cocks, which meant a vagina in Tennessee, the way they talk about eating a watermelon. And it may not have a damned thing to do with any behavior they intend to carry out.'

It is obvious that in Rowan's explanation of the behavior that he was told was captured on tape, he is quite uncomfortable with the possibility that King's alleged sexual activity involved another man. This is the vicious bind that Hoover's dirty tricks trap us in. If we decry his ruthless manipulation of the facts – after all, that is the point of spliced tapes – and if we protest his unprincipled use of private affairs, then it is reasonable to insist that painting King as a homosexual pervert is no worse than painting him as a heterosexual pervert. Of course, in the sixties, it was certainly the case that painting King as a homosexual was equal to labeling him a pervert. But what is also at work here is the deliberate attempt to smear a black leader's character by whatever means were available. In the sixties, it was King's sexuality – and in this case the implication that he engaged, or intended to engage, in gay sex – that had the desired effect of further damaging King's reputation. To defend King by suggesting that he was not gay, in this context, is not a knee-jerk homophobic response, but a desire to clarify his sexual practices on the basis of what we otherwise know about his sexual behavior. That information is important precisely because its source was not a disinterested observer of human behavior but a federal bureau out to do in a leader of global importance. Of course, the rush to disprove King's homosexuality may indeed indicate a homophobic streak. On the other hand, given the context of the repressive sixties, when sexuality was a highly charged issue that intersected in complex ways with race, the use of sexuality of whatever sort to stigmatize a black leader is simply wrong. Furthermore, the undeniable existence of homophobia does not mean that clarifying King's preferences for the sake of historical accuracy is a homophobic act. To extract the debate about King's sexuality from its racial and cultural context is to do a grave disservice to the causes of racial and sexual liberation.

In our attempt to get the facts of the case, we should not suppress any feature of the truth. It may be that FBI tapes, when they are unsealed and if they are proved to be reliable, will reveal that King did engage in a homosexual act. That will not make King a pervert, as the FBI forces wished to portray him, but it may also be revealed that King did not engage in a homosexual act, in which case his heterosexuality will be insufficient grounds to suggest his virtue. In a world where sexualities are equally valued, sexual preference will never automatically indicate one's perversity or purity. But in a world where sexuality, like race, continues to mark human identity in strange and powerful ways, we must pay attention to how those identities are manipulated by destructive forces. This is true today; it was even truer in the sixties. Even if Rowan's motivation for offering a plausible explanation of King's behavior is homophobic, it does not mean that his explanation is not legitimate. In other words, black men who have been drinking often lie about their sexual powers and engage in same-sex references for comic effect. Even if the reason for saying that is driven by homophobia, the truth is that the facts of the case remain unchanged. What is changed is the context of our interpretation of those facts. Such a context was provided by Hoover: King is an unrepentant pervert. A counterargument can appeal to King's true sexual preferences and practices without necessarily falling into the trap of homophobia.

Neither should Rowan's possible homophobia obscure an essential element of his defense of King: that the government was illegally listening in on King for no other purpose than to destroy him by destroying his reputation and, ultimately, his family life. 'All this stuff about King's sexual appetite is of trifling consequence,' Rowan says, 'compared with the still-chilling reality that under Hoover the nation's highest law enforcement agency tried unlawfully to destroy his reputation in hopes of thwarting the movement toward racial equality in America.' Besides, as Rowan said, it is impossible to speak against something one has not heard. And Rowan's explanation about black male humor, whatever the motivations that underlie his makeshift apologia, should remind us that as with anything else, context and circumstance are crucial in understanding and explaining behavior. To rely on J. Edgar Hoover as even an informal ethnographer of black sexuality is surely misleading.

In the end, King's adulterous liaisons are both a sign of his deeply flawed sexual ethics and a product of his unique role as the most renowned twentieth-century crusader for racial justice. If we read King's sexual practices merely as a response to his enhanced opportunity for licentious behavior, we ignore the keen moral sensitivity that made him conscious of his shortcomings. But if we deny that King's courageous pursuit of freedom and equality led him to live most of his life on the road, away from hearth and home and, hence, a loving environment where he might nurture marital fidelity, then we deny history and truth. King's fight against white supremacy not only cost him his life but a great deal more: his privacy, as he was recklessly pursued by an out-of-control government agency; quiet time to collect his soul and share his life with his family and friends; the enjoyment of the normal course of human events, since his mission to mold America into a greater nation intruded on nearly every waking moment of his life; and the constant threat and fear of death, for simply, plainly, and honestly striving to make democracy a reality for all of this country's citizens. In such a context, King's failures are not the greater evils, but the racial fascism and economic violence that made his career a necessary risk and, in the end, an unavoidable sacrifice for this nation's best interests.

For critics who insist that King's plagiarism and promiscuity signal a tragic lapse in judgment, they may be right. But critics who insist that his sins signal a *fatal* flaw in character – so that the good that King did is nullified by his failures – are absolutely wrong. The debate about character must be wrested away from *virtuecrats* who espouse a narrow view of character and the qualities that feed it. Character cannot be understood through isolated incidents or a fixation on the flaws of a human being during a selected period in life. Assessment of character must take into account the long view, the wide angle. Character is truly glimpsed as we learn of human beings negotiating large and small problems that test moral vision, ethical creativity, and sound judgment. Character cannot be grasped in disjointed details or sporadic facts. Character can only be glimpsed in a sustained story that provides plausible accounts and credible explanations of human behavior. Of course we can and often do draw inferences about a person's character based on a phrase here and an action there. These reactions may certainly be useful in casual relationships, but they are shaky grounds for choosing a life partner or, for that matter, a president. Character is undeniably an important ingredient in judging the worth of public figures like King. But character is hardly reducible to personal life. Personal matters surely count in assessing character, but so do courage, integrity, sacrifice, and love as they are expressed on the battlefield of public conscience. King possessed these traits in abundance, and arguably, they are the character traits most relevant to judging his effectiveness in the public realm. I am not suggesting that we jettison considerations of private virtue or personal character. I am arguing, however, that we should have a more encompassing vision of character, one that embraces personal and social features, as we judge the worth of a human being's life.

Notes

"*There is a Civil War going on Within All of Us*". David J. Garrow, *Bearing the Cross: Martin Luther King, Jr., and the Southern Christian Leadership Conference* (New York: William Morrow, 1986), p. 376.

a moment comparable to Michael Jordan fending off Jet. June 29, 1998, p. 53.

"*King allegedly rendezvoused with two women*": In 1993 Adjua Abi Naantaanbuu brought a defamation of character suit against the estate of Ralph David Abernathy, Harper & Row Publishers, and editor Daniel Bial. Naantaanbuu claimed that she was libeled by Abernathy's suggestion that she had an affair with Martin Luther King, Jr., the night before he was assassinated. Naantaanbuu was the woman at whose house King had dinner the night before his death. Abernathy's description of that night suggested that an unnamed woman and King had been intimate. The U.S. District Court for the Southern District of New York ruled that Naantaanbuu was "a private rather a public figure with respect to the present lawsuit," but that "there was no showing" that the defendants had "acted in a 'grossly irresponsible manner' as required for liability under New York law." The court concluded that Naantaanbuu "has not produced sufficient information to demonstrate the possibility that Abernathy acted with some degree of culpable conduct, if in fact his version of events was false. She has come forward with information to make it a genuine issue of fact as to whether Abernathy was telling the truth about the events of the evening of April 3. That is, she produced her own affidavit and that of her sister, both of which contradict Abernathy's version of events." In short, the truth or falsity of Abernathy's claims was not resolved, but the court found that he had no malicious intent to harm Naantaanbuu and therefore found Abernathy inculpable of the charge of libel. *Naantaanbuu v. Abernathy*, 816 F. Supp. 218 (S.D.N.Y. 1993), 218, 229–230.

A formidable one-two line-up: David L. Lewis, *King: A Critical Biography* (Urbana: University of Illinois Press, 1970); Stephen B. Oates, *Let the Trumpet Sound: The Life of Martin Luther King, Jr.* (New York: Harper & Row, 1982); Adam Fairclough, *To Redeem the Soul of America: The Southern Christian Leadership Conference and Martin Luther King, Jr.* (Athens, University of Georgia Press, 1987); Taylor Branch, *Parting the Waters: Martin Luther King and the Civil Rights Movement, 1954–63* (New York: Simon & Schuster, 1988); Taylor Branch, *Pillar of Fire: America in the King Years, 1963–65* (New York: Simon & Schuster, 1998); James A. Colaiaco; *Martin Luther King, Jr.: Apostle of Militant Nonviolence* (London: Macmillan, 1988); Andrew Young, *An Easy Burden: The Civil Rights Movement and the Transformation of America* (New York: HarperCollins, 1996).

"*best friend that I have in the world*": King, "I See the Promised Land," in James M. Washington, *A Testament of Hope: The Essential Writings of Martin Luther King, Jr* (San Francisco: HarperSanFrancisco, 1986).

best-selling autobiography: Ralph David Abernathy, *And the Walls Came Tumbling Down* (New York: Harper & Row, 1989).

Abernathy loved King even as he was jealous: Garrow, *Bearing the Cross*, p. 366; Branch, *Parting the Waters*, pp. 898–899, and *Pillar of Fire*, pp. 540–543; Young, *An Easy Burden*, pp. 174, 281, 320, 461–462.

"let Americans – particularly black Americans": Abernathy, "Introduction to the Paper back Edition, in *And the Walls Came Tumbling Down*, p. xiv.

"wanted to show the private man": Ibid.

"wanted to portray Martin": Ibid.

"Washington, Lincoln, and a handful": ibid., p. xv.

"legends are important": Ibid.

to his own philandering: Branch, *Parting the Waters*, pp. 237–240. Abernathy neglects to mention this incident or even refute Branch's story in his own autobiography. As historian Jimmie Franklin concludes, one "has to assume reasonably that such a serious charge would have drawn a sure rebuttal in this book if it were false" (Jimmie Lewis Franklin, "Auto-biography, the Burden of Friendship, and Truth," *Georgia Historical Quarterly*, 74, p. 97). Franklin argues that since Abernathy "has judiciously refused to stand witness to much of his own past," his omission raises "difficult questions about the author's intent and about historical truth," suggesting that such "careful selectivity places the alert historian on guard" (ibid.). Franklin's point is compelling, especially since, as he pointed out earlier in his review of Abernathy's book, the latter's decision to tell about King's infidelity, as opposed to th egoings on at the Willard Hotel where *both* ministers were under FBI surveillance, is problematic. Legitimate questions about Abernathy's believability and motives for telling that the "truth" about King's affairs can be usefully raised. However, to dismiss Abernathy out of hand as a liar (or traitor) because he has revealed uncomfortable apsects of his closest friend's sex life is equally troublesome. We should treat Abernathy's revelations as possibly, even plausibly, true, given his closeness to King and his intimate knowledge of King's personal life. Moreover, Abernathy's depiction of King is on balance a touching, moving, generous portrait of the man who in Abernathy's book comes off as a scarificial, courageous, humane, and *human* leader. As Bernice Reagon wites: "It is time for society to reckon with the fallacy of turning our heroes and heroines into godlike inhuman figures. Martin Luther King, Jr., needs to become—through our work as historians—the human being he was. ... I think all of us already know somewhat inside ourselves that those in human history who carry the mantle of being outstanding are also always flawed. However, popular and academic chronicles have a way of reshaping reality so that the warts and pimples get smoothed off" (Bernice Johnson Reagon, " 'Nobody Knows the Trouble I See:' or 'By and By I'm Gonna Lay Down My Heavy Load' " *Journal of American History*, 78 (June 1991), p. 111).

"will grow in the hearts of future Americans": Abernathy, *And the Walls Came Tumbling Down*, p. xx.

"What business has the public": Darrell McWhorter, "Images of King," *St. Louis Dispatch*, January 21, 1991, p. 1D; *reared in a preacherly culture where good sex:* Marcia L. Dyson, "Where Preachers Prey," *Essence*, May 1988, pp. 120–2, 190, 192, 194; Michael Eric Dyson, *Race Rule: Navigating the Color Line* (Reading, MA: Addison-Wesley, 1996); *it surely gave King and others ample opportunity:* Abernathy, *And the Walls Came Tumbling Down*, p. 471; Dyson, Race rules, p. 102.

"pure in heart": Matthew 5:8.

"make an idol of their commitments": Howard Thurman, "The Dilemma of Commitment," a sermon preached at Riverside Church, New York City, Aug. 7, 1965.

King often spoke of the sins he committed: Michael Friedly and David Gallen (eds), *Martin Luther King, Jr.: The FBI File* (New York: Carroll & Graf, 1993), pp. 453–4; Garrow, *Bearing the Cross*, p. 577.

double life as a cross-dressing "Mary":   Anthony Summers, *Official and Confidential: The Secret Life of J. Edgar Hoover* (New York: G. P. Putnam's Sons, 1993).

David Garrow has brilliantly documented: David J. Garow, *The FBI and Martin Luther King, Jr.: From "Solo" to Memphis* (New York: W. W. Norton, 1981); Gerald D. McKnight, *The Last Crusade: Martin Luther King Jr., the FBI and the Poor People's Campaign* (Denver, CO: Westview Press, 1998); Friedly and Gallen, *The FBI File*.

"compulsive sexual athleticism": Garrow, *Bearing the Cross*, p. 375.

"the campaign against Martin and the movement": Young, *An Easy Burden*, p. 471.

Deeply buried but intense sexual fear: Ibid,

"chronic avocation among evangelical divines":   David Levering Lewis, "Bearing the Cross," *Journal of American History*, 74 (September 1987), p. 482.

the sweet reward of spiritual servants: Dyson, *Race Rules*, pp. 100–104.

"exploit this power [over women]": Dyson, "When Preachers Prey," p. 120.

King was a sexual magnet for women: Garrow, *Bearing the Cross*, p. 375; Abernathy, *And the Walls Came Tumbling Down*, p. 471; Oates, *Let the Trumpet*, p. 283.

private and public spaces acquired heightened importance: Black Public Sphere Collective (ed.), *The Black Public Sphere: A Public Culture Book* (Chicago: University of Chicago Press, 1995).

He spent nearly twenty-seven days: Garrow, *Bearing the Cross*, p. 375; Oates, *Let the Trumpet*, p. 282. In a brief preface to a January 1965 *Playboy Magazine* interview he conducted with Martin Luther King, Alex Haley noted that King "works twenty hours a day, travels 325,000 miles and makes 450 speeches a year throughout the country" (*"Playboy* Interview: Martin Luther King, Jr.," in King, *A Testament*, p. 341).

both tortured by his adultery. Branch, *Pillar of Fire*, p. 557; Garrow, *Bearing the Cross*, p. 375.

"loose sex relations and problems": Friedly and Gallen, *The FBI File*, p. 453.

"the past, too often": ibid.

I think it is also necessary to bring: Ibid., pp. 453–454.

"go out saying this morning saying":   King, "Unfulfilled Dreams," in Clayborne Carson and Peter Holloran (eds.), *A Knock at Midnight: The Great Sermons of Martin Luther King, Jr* (New York: Warner Books, 1999); Richard Lischer, *The Preacher King: Martin Luther King, Jr. and the Word that Moved America* (New York: Oxford University Press, 1995). Unlike David Garrow, Richard Lischer doesn't see such comments by King as veiled confessions of his sexual sins. "In the sexual realm," Garrow writes, "King viewed himself as a sinner, a theme he sometimes touched upon in his sermons" (Garrow, *Bearing the Cross*, p. 587). Lischer writes that if King "was laboring under a burden of shame because of his secret sins and the contradiction between his public and private life, the sermons do not indicate it. With the exception of a few oblique references to 'habits' that destroy personality and relationships, the sermons give little evidence that he was engaged in a moral struggle with his own infidelity or the casual sex practiced by many of the Movement's leaders, including the preachers" (Lischer, *The Preacher King*, p. 169). I fall between Garrow and Lischer. Although King made no explicit confession in his sermons, he certainly wrestled with his libido and his conscientious duty to God and his family. It is certainly reasonable to expect that such a struggle might seep into his homilies, in much the same way that adultery became for King a metaphor of racial apartheid. King was quoted in the *Time* magazine story that named him Man of the Year as saying that segregation "is the adultery of an illicit intercourse between injustice and immorality," and it "cannot be cured by the Vaseline of gradualism" (*Time*, Jan 3, 1964).

"each of us is two selves": Garrow, *Bearing the Cross*, p. 376.

"I'm fucking for God": Branch, *Pillar of Fire*, p. 207. Branch explains that this quotation, as well as the quotation on the next page, are from FBI surveillance tapes of King. In interviews that Branch conducted with three FBI officials, he says that they reported having heard the bugging tapes. They claim to have heard King make the statements quoted here. Branch

himself did not hear the tapes, which are sealed along with other FBI surveillance until 2027.

"promised never to leave me": King, "Unfulfilled Dreams," in Carson and Holloran, eds., *A Knock at Midnight*, p. 199.

"if I make my bed in hell": Psalm 139:8, King James Version.

"fucking's a form of anxiety reduction": Garrow, *Bearing the Cross*, p. 375.

"I'm not a Negro tonight": Branch, *Pillar of Fire*, p. 207.

"He looked at me as if doubting": Ibid.

"an FBI director who is suspected of being a homosexual": Ibid.

"whenever black men gather": Ibid.

what we otherwise knew about his sexual behavior: Another indication of the possible insinuation of homoerotic behavior involving King occurs in a discussion in John William's book on King, *The King God Didn't Save: Reflections on the Life and Death of Martin Luther King, Jr* (New York: Coward-Macann, 1970). At the same time, the passage seems to suggest that King did not engage in the same-sex activity implied by circumstantial evidence. In the second part of his book, Williams quotes several anonymous sources by labeling them as Person A, Person B, and so on. Williams quotes Person C as saying the following: "There were two pictures. One showed me sitting on the floor beside the bathtub in which Martin sat, naked. From the angle of the photo, it looks as though I was doing something. The other photo showed me sitting on the bed beside Martin, who's laying there, nude. Now in both cases, I was conferring with Martin in the only time available to me. Nothing, absolutely nothing took place" (p. 190). Later, Person C is quoted as being in Scnadinavia with King (on his Nobel Peace Prize tour of Europe) and of being summoned to quash a potential controversy: "I was sleeping when they called me from downstairs and said that I had to come down to the desk at once. I pulled on my robe and went down. The police were there with a woman later said to be the biggest whore in town. And they had caught her coming out of the hotel with watches and wallets belonging to some of the people in our party. Well, she was there. There had been other women running through the hotel like chickens without their heads, looking for Martin. And all the guys were putting it to them that, if the girls gave them some pussy first, they'd see that she got to Martin. The whore? I thought it better to let her go with everything she had rather than embarrass ourselves and our hosts" (p. 198). From what we know about King's tour of Europe to collect his Nobel Peace Prize, Bayard Rustin coordinated the trip (Garrow, *Bearing the Cross*, p. 357; Oates, *Let the Trumpet*, p. 318; Branch, *Pillar of Fire*, pp. 524–525; Jervis Anderson, *Bayard Rustin: Troubles I've Seen: A Biography* (Berkeley, CA: University of California Press, 1997), p. 275). Further, we know that in Scandinavia, Bayard Rustin was summoned "as the group's coordinator," to "put a stop to some of the wilder activities" (Garrow, *Bearing the Cross*, p. 366). Apparently some of King's entourage had become involved with what Garrow termed "several scantly clad women," identified by Branch as "Norwegian prostitutes," who had attempted to rob the men after partaking in fleshly delight (Garrow, *Bearing the Cross*, p. 367; Branch, *Pillar of Fire*, p. 543). In fact, the women had "been promised Martin Luther King himself in exchange for favors to his unscrupulous associates" (Branch, *Pillar of Fire*). Rustin alerted hotel security, who quickly moved to take them into custody and return the stoken goods to their owners, including King's brother, A. D. Rustin demurred. He didn't "want these girls talking, let them have it. As far as I'm concerned, they've earned it. And get them out" (Garrow, *Bearing the Cross*, p. 367). In the light of Garrow and Branch's corroboration of the activities described by Williams, it seems likely that Rustin was Person C. Rustin was gay (Anderson, *Bayard Rustin*, Garrow, *Bearing the Cross*, p. 66; Branch, *Pillar of Fire*, pp. 172–173). His sexuality is of interest here because if, as I surmise, Rustin is Person C, then his disclaimers about King hold weight. Person C/Rustin claims that nothing took place between King and him on either occasion that phots (from surveillance cameras?) were taken. In each case, King was nude, and presumably Person C/Rustin was clothed. Still, as Person C/Rustin's comments suggest, the photos by themselves may be misleadingly interpreted—hence his assertion that "nothing absolutely nothing took place." If that is true—and there is no reason to doubt Rustin's word—it seems to suggest that King's sexual transgressions. at least in this case (and in every case about which there is corroborating evidence), were heterosexual in nature.

the context of the repressive sixties: Martin Duberman: *Cures: A Gay Man's Odyssey* (New York: Dutton, 1991); Samuel Delaney, *The Motion of Light in Water: Sex and Science Fiction Writing in the East Village, 1957–1965* (New York: Arbor House/William Morrow, 1988). I am referring here to the repression of gay sexuality, even as the liberation of heterosexuality from its Victorian principles flourished in the sixties.

when they are unsealed: The FBI surveillance tapes on King have been legally sealed until 2007. See my discussion, in Chapter 11, of Reagan's (and Jesse Helm's) mistaken belief that the tapes contian politically damaging—and not merely sexually explicit—materials.

Lie about their sexual powers: Lawrence Levine, *Black Culture and Black Consciousness: Afro-American Folk Thought from Slavery to Freedom* (New York: Oxford University Press, 1977); Henry Louis Gates, *The Signifying Monkey: A Theory of African-American Literary Criticism* (New York: Oxford University Press, 1988); Roger D. Abrahams: *Deep Down in the Jungle Negro Narrative Folklore from the Streets of Phildelphia* (Chicago: Aldine, 1970).

"All this stuff about King's sexual appetite": Carl T. Rowan, *Breaking Barriers: A Memoir* (Boston, MA: Little, Brown, 1991).

live most of his life on the road: Dyson, *Race Rules*, p. 102. In his sermon, "Standing by the Best in an Evil Time," King confessed that "I'm tired of all this traveling I have to do. I'm killing myself and killying my health, and aways away from my children and my family" (Cited in Lischer, *The Preacher King*, p. 167).

must be wrested away from virtuecrats: I have in mind here figures like Bill Bennett who have extracted virtue from a discussion of the complicated forces that shape the moral life and ener-gize our notions of the good, the just, and the beautiful. Bennett forgets that "the develop-ment of virtues, and the attendant skills that must be deployed in order to practice them effectively, is contingent upon several factors: where and when one is born, the conditions under which one mut live, the social and communal forces that limit and define one's life, etc. These factors color the character of moral skills that will be acquired, shape the way in which these skills will be appropriated, and even determine the list of skills required to live the good life in different communities" (Michael Eric Dyson, *Reflecting Black: African-American Cultural Criticism* (Minneapolis: University of Minnesota Press, 1993), p. 108, n. 13).

Character can only be glimpsed in a sustained story: Alasdair MacIntyre, *After Virtue: A Study in Moral Theory* (Notre Dame, Ind.: University of Notre Dame Press, 1984); Nancy Sherman, *Making a Necessity of Virtue: Aristotle and Kant on Virtue* (New York: Cambridge University Press, 1997); Ronald Thiermann, *Constructing a Public Theology: The Church in a Pluralistic Culture* (Westminster: John Knox Press, 1991).

8 Radicalism: Martin Luther King, Jr's Final Years, 1965–8

Introduction

Although historians now challenge the Montgomery-to-Memphis national narrative of the civil rights struggle, at one time that narrative competed for recognition against an even shorter 'Montgomery-to-Selma' narrative – a history of the civil rights movement that terminates with King's successful Selma campaign and the passage of the 1965 Voting Rights Act, and then skips the final few years of King's life to the coda of his 1968 assassination. The most high profile example of this is the Blackside, Inc. 1987 television series *Eyes on the Prize: America's Civil Rights Years, 1954–1965* and the same-titled accompanying book by Juan Williams. A 1990 series *Eyes on the Prize II: America at the Racial Crossroads, 1965–1985* updated the story of the ongoing struggle for freedom and equality since the mid-1960s.

Since then, more coverage has been given to King's final years. The authors of the two selections in this chapter, David J. Garrow and Adam Fairclough, were among the first historians to give these years the attention that they deserve. Both of these selections demonstrate why these years were initially glossed over. In contrast to the more tangible goals and discernible victories of the movement between 1954 and 1965, the years between 1965 and 1968 witnessed King and the civil rights movement tackling more complex issues with more ambiguous results. King's development in these years challenges the earlier characterization of him as a 'moderate' who worked hand-in-hand with the white establishment.

In the first selection, David Garrow charts the trajectory of King's final years and offers a useful summary of post-movement developments up until the early 1980s. Starting in 1965, Garrow points to the legislative victories

of the 1964 Civil Rights Act and 1965 Voting Rights Act that the movement had gained up to that point, but notes that these victories against segregation and disfranchisement did little to address the economic disparities
between the African American and white populations of the United States.
This was particularly evident in areas such as employment and housing. It
was in his final years that King's focus moved toward these issues. Over the
summer of 1965, King and the SCLC embarked upon their first campaign
in a major northern city. Chicago, however, offered a different set of problems than the smaller southern towns and cities that King and the SCLC's
non-violent direct action protests had previously targeted. Informal and less
overt forms of discrimination there proved more difficult to attack. Instead
of the steadfast intransigence of white southern politicians, seasoned urban
politicians like Mayor Richard Daley appeared more accommodating to
African American demands in public while remaining just as intractable as
southern whites at the negotiating table. The urban African American community in Chicago proved a different proposition too. They responded less
to King and the SCLC's distinctly southern and religious sensibilities. Some
local African American leaders viewed their own and the Chicago African
American population's best interests as being served by working with white
politicians rather than with civil rights activists. In 1966, Open Housing
marches through exclusively white neighbourhoods successfully highlighted
the problem of housing discrimination, but subsequent negotiations
achieved little in addressing the problem. According to Garrow, King and
the SCLC left Chicago without winning 'substantive gains nor . . . strategic
improvements'.

In June 1966, while King was still in the midst of the Chicago campaign,
he was called upon to participate in the 'Meredith March Against Fear'
through Mississippi. On the march, new SNCC chair Stokely Carmichael
popularized the 'black power' slogan, a new expression of the discontent of
the African American young and poor, both urban and rural, who felt
excluded from many of the movement's existing gains. The experience of
Chicago and the emergence of black power convinced King that 'a radical
reconstruction of society itself is the real issue to be faced.' King's final campaign, a planned Poor Peoples March on Washington DC to highlight the
continuing problems of America's poor, not just those affecting African
Americans but also those affecting other minorities and some whites, looked
to escalate non-violent direct action to mass civil disobedience. However,
before King had a chance to implement these plans, he was assassinated in
Memphis, Tennessee, while supporting striking sanitation workers in that
city. The PPC went ahead but failed to achieve its aims. Garrow finishes his
article with an assessment of post-movement developments from the perspective of the mid-1980s, in which he sees ongoing African American
struggles in politics and against 'racism, militarism and economic injustice' –
a picture that has changed remarkably little in the intervening years.

In the second selection, Adam Fairclough acknowledges the growing radicalism of King in his later years and focuses specifically on the question: 'Was Martin Luther King a Marxist?' This is far removed from August Meier's 'conservative militant' argument in Chapter 2, yet Fairclough maintains that the question is not as easily dismissed as one might initially think. When King's personal papers were made accessible to researchers in the 1980s, more radical private opinions than those voiced in King's more guarded public utterances were discovered. King had read Marx and Marx-influenced scholars during his academic studies and was impressed, if not wholly convinced, by their arguments. The three key founders of the SCLC, Bayard Rustin, Ella Baker and Stanley Levison all had backgrounds that linked them with the radical Left, as did many other activists of their generation. This was enough to raise the suspicions of the FBI, which regularly accused King and the movement of being infiltrated by communist agents, a suspicion only fuelled by the Cold War context of the times. King's experiences in Chicago and his growing criticism of the war in Vietnam increased his scepticism about capitalism being able to deliver social and economic justice.

Nevertheless, Fairclough points out that King's debt to Marx always came with a qualification. In the final analysis, King's ideas were based primarily upon his faith and his religious beliefs. Although King could identify with elements of Marxism, his perception of its 'rejection of spiritual values, a shallow economic determinism, and the absolute supremacy of the state' prevented King from ever entirely embracing its ideas. This meant that, according to Fairclough, King's 'hostility to excessive materialism, and his concern for the poor and the oppressed, owed more to the Social Gospel than to Marxist ideology.'

Questions for Discussion

1. Why did King believe that 'a radical reconstruction of society itself is the real issue to be faced' in the final few years of his life?

2. How did the Poor People's Campaign differ from previous campaigns run by King?

3. Why did King take a stand against the war in Vietnam in April 1967?

4. Did King's more radical stand in his final years help or hinder the civil rights movement? Was he right to broaden the focus of the movement beyond race-based issues?

Further Reading

Biographies by Adam Fairclough, *To Redeem the Soul of America: The Southern Christian Leadership Conference and Martin Luther King, Jr* (Athens, GA: University of Georgia Press, 1987), David J. Garrow, *Bearing the Cross: Martin Luther King, Jr and the Southern Christian Leadership Conference* (New York: William Morrow, 1986) and Taylor Branch, *At Canaan's Edge: America in the King Years, 1965–1968* (New York: Simon and Schuster, 2006) all do a good job of charting developments in King's final years. Vincent Harding, *Martin Luther King: The Inconvenient Hero* (Maryknoll, NY: Orbis Books, 1996) makes the persuasive case that for many years King's more radical legacy was conveniently but unjustly over-looked. For more specific readings on different aspects of King's final years see the Bibliography at the end of this book.

From Reformer to Revolutionary

David J. Garrow

Many years have passed since Martin Luther King, Jr. was assassinated in Memphis on the cool spring evening of April 4, 1968 – more time than the twelve years of his own life that King gave to 'The Movement' between the onset of Montgomery, Alabama's famous bus boycott in December, 1955 and that sudden accurate rifle shot from the bathroom window of a flophouse.

So much had changed in those twelve years. Racism had been confronted as a central theme of American life. Public segregation – of lunch counters, water fountains, city parks, and city buses – had largely vanished from the South. The Movement had evolved from the student sit-ins, the Freedom Rides, and Bull Connor's Birmingham to the divisive controversy over 'Black Power' and the unsuccessful effort to use southern activists and techniques to launch a 'Freedom Movement' in Chicago's ghettos. Martin King had grown from a naive optimist who had told Montgomery's protesters that their passive withdrawal from the buses would persuade white southerners of segregation's immorality to a sagacious, worn down realist who knew that the central injustice of American society lay not simply in its racial practices but in its entire economic structure. Toward the end of his journey, he began to see that only by confronting 'class issues . . . the

From *Reflections on the Legacy* (Democratic Socialists of America, 1983): 27–36.

problem of the gulf between the haves and the have nots,' and by openly advocating democratic socialism, could 'The Movement' begin to combat the widespread economic injustice that underlay American racism, American militarism, and American materialism.

Up through the summer of 1965 'The Movement' had won the enactment of two of the greatest legislative milestones in American political history: the Civil Rights Act of 1964 and the Voting Rights Act of 1965. At first glance, those two statutes promised to make real the transformation of the South.

Then, over some six months' time, Martin King came to a deep and very painful realization, a realization he had had inklings of before, but that never had crystalized: those acts of Congress, no matter how comprehensive, really did very little to improve the daily lives of poor black people across the rural South. Those bills did little, if anything, to provide better jobs, better housing, or greater economic power for the millions of people north and south who long had been the exploited victims of the American economy. Long time activist Bayard Rustin had been arguing for three years that the Movement had to turn away from a singular focus on race, and confront the basic issues of wealth and poverty in America, but his voice had largely been drowned out. The great 1963 pilgrimage had been titled 'The March on Washington for Jobs and Freedom', but Rustin's and A. Philip Randolph's insistence on an economic focus had been replaced by a preoccupation with winning congressional approval of John Kennedy's civil rights bill. Only in the early fall of 1965, as Martin King gradually realized that the 1964 and 1965 Acts had given neither economic independence to rural southern blacks nor anything at all to northern ghetto dwellers, did the economic issue move to the forefront of his mind.

The Chicago Freedom Movement, begun late in 1965 in an effort to unite King's symbolic authority with an interracial coalition of local activists eager for such support, was the first attempt by King's Southern Christian Leadership Conference (SCLC) to confront the economic issue and to mount a campaign outside the South. Initially, the Chicago effort intended to concentrate on organizing 'unions' of slum dwellers rather than on street demonstrations or protests. It would be precisely the sort of grass roots organization building that the southern movement's real shock troops, the Student Nonviolent Coordinating Committee (SNCC), had long advocated, but which King and SCLC intentionally had forsaken in order to pursue 'direct action' protests geared to evoke newsworthy violence from reactionary segregationists. That pragmatic strategy had propelled the 1964 and 1965 Acts through a previously reluctant Congress, but it had done little to generate tangible gains or to create ongoing political organizations for the citizens of those southern towns where SCLC had mounted its protests. Now, in Chicago, King knew that something different was called for.

The Chicago problem was neither legalized segregation nor formal exclusion from the political system and elections. Black elected officials had long been a part of the city's political 'machine', and even if blacks were distinctly unwelcome, even as visitors, in many of the city's totally segregated white residential neighborhoods, there was little of the total segregation of public life that only slowly was disappearing from the South. Instead, 'the Chicago problem', as Martin King succinctly put it, 'is simply a matter of economic exploitation'. Be it delapidated rental housing, overpriced food, or lack of job opportunities, 'every condition exists simply because someone profits by its existence'. Protest tactics which had worked admirably in the South, because of the 'general pattern of state and local resistance', would be far less effective against forces of economic exploitation that did not need police dogs or fire hoses to keep their victims supine. 'In Chicago', King acknowledged, 'we are faced with the probability of a ready accommodation to many of the issues in some token manner, merely to curtail the massing of forces and public opinion around those issues'. Organizing the victims of that ongoing exploitation into enduring, self-directed groups would be a more effective strategy for combatting that economic oppression.

Unfortunately, for King, for Chicago, and for all of America, the black slum dwellers did not respond in sizeable numbers to SCLC's southern staff workers, to King's rhetorical challenges, to the fervent church rallies, or to the dedicated local activists. Organizing Chicago's ghettos block by block proved a far tougher enterprise that recruiting several hundred ready marchers in Selma or St. Augustine. After six frustrating months of trying, King and his assistants adopted a new target and new tactics for the Chicago movement. 'Open housing' was the goal, and street marches through Chicago's totally segregated and virulently racist neighborhoods were the means of attack. Discriminatory housing practices contributed to the maintenance of the city's slums, and street protests would draw attention to that aspect of northern racism. King's calculation proved accurate, and the summer months of 1966 witnessed almost daily white assaults upon the movement's marchers as they nonviolently made their way into the most racist Chicago neighborhoods. News reports depicted cars being overturned and burned by white mobs, and a stunned King struggling to regain his footing after being struck in the head with a rock. Threatened with a movement plan to march into an even more violent white stronghold, Cicero, city officials and business leaders offered King a modest agreement full of promises that Chicago would attack housing discrimination and other forms of racism. Eager to salvage some sign of success from an increasingly frustrating enterprise, King accepted the settlement and proclaimed victory. Some activists publicly attacked him for settling for so little, and many King supporters admitted in private that it was a barely palatable outcome. King himself did not need to be told that the Chicago effort was far from a success. It had generated neither the substantive gains nor the strategic improvements he had desired. Much of his own time, and much of his staff's energy, had been drawn away from Chicago by the suddenly-improvised mass march through Mississippi in mid-June to protest the shooting of James Meredith. Out of the 'Meredith March' and the growing tensions between SCLC and SNCC had come a new rhetorical call, 'Black Power', whose powerful appeal to many black activists was matched only by the emotional overreactions of many white commentators to the phrases' uncertain but threatening connotations.

King thought SNCC chairman Stokely Carmichael's trumpeting of 'Black Power' and its anti-white implications a serious tactical mistake for the movement, though he firmly agreed with the calls for black cultural pride and political empowerment. Within the context of the movement's need, and King's own need, to find a method for attacking the entire economic structure of America, the rhetorical controversy over 'Black Power' was necessarily a secondary issue. King knew that, but after the disappointment of Chicago he did not know how the movement could get a clear handle on America's pervasive economic injustice. 'I am still searching myself; I don't have all the answers', he confided to his staff. The movement to date had done much for the black middle class, but little for the black under class, and the time had come for that to change. 'We are now dealing with class issues ... with issues that relate to the privileged as over against the underprivileged ... Something is wrong with the economic system of our nation', King stated, and 'something is wrong with capitalism ... There must be a better distribution of wealth, and maybe America must move toward a democratic socialism.'

Throughout early 1967, much of King's time and energy were consumed by his courageous new determination to speak out strongly against America's destructive involvement in Vietnam and the imperialist values which led Lyndon Johnson and his cohorts to pursue that violent enterprise with such a vengeance. Then, in August, 1967, he began to articulate for the first time a plan for bringing about 'a radical redistribution of economic and political power' in America. His idea would require the movement to admit that it had passed from an era of reform to 'a new era, which must be an era of revolution', and that the movement itself had to change from a 'reform movement' to a 'revolutionary movement'. Now, King said, 'we are called upon to raise certain basic questions about the whole society ... We must see now that the evils of racism, economic exploitation, and militarism are all tied together, and you really can't get rid of one without getting rid of the others ... The whole structure of American life must be changed.'

Almost four years earlier, in the wake of the September, 1963, bombing of Birmingham's Sixteenth Street Baptist Church in which four young black girls had been killed, two of the movement's most creative activists, SNCC's Diane Nash and SCLC's Jim Bevel, had proposed to their colleagues and to

King that the movement respond to this tragic outrage by taking mass direct action to a new height: civil disobedience by thousands of protesters, designed to completely close down Alabama's capital city of Montgomery. 'People were highly aroused, frustrated, and sad, eager to do something, but no one knew what to do', Diane Nash wrote in describing the situation and in explaining why complete but nonviolent disruption of Montgomery was the appropriate scale of action for the movement to adopt. When she spoke to King, however, he 'looked at her and laughed', one close friend of King's recalled. Why? 'Because she suggested we go out and throw our-selves under trains and the wheels of airplanes, and he just chuckled. He said; "Oh, Diane. Now wait, wait. Now, let's think about this'. It was a joke, really – and she was for real'. By August of 1967, however, Martin King had come to realize that massive nonviolent disruption was something to be practiced rather than laughed at. Furthermore, the best place to prac-tice it was not in Alabama but in Washington, DC, the one city where mass civil disobedience would be able 'to cripple the operations of an oppressive society'. It was a radical vision, King knew, a vastly different type of political action than what he had advocated twelve years earlier in Montgomery or even four years earlier at the seemingly triumphant March on Washington. But now, in 1967, Martin King appreciated how naive he and most of his movement colleagues had been throughout the ten years from 1955 to 1965. 'We really thought we were making great progress', he confessed at a meeting in Chicago. 'We somehow felt that we were going to win the total victory, before we analyzed the depths and dimensions of the problem', In the beginning he had thought that 'a great number of white southerners are ready to do what is right' if the movement would simply confront their con-sciences. Twelve years later he knew he had been wrong. 'There aren't enough white persons in our country who are willing to cherish democratic principles over privilege', he remarked less than three weeks prior to the final cool evening in Memphis. 'Truly America is much, much sicker', King confided to one close aide, 'than I realized when I first began working in 1955'. So much had changed in those twelve years in America, in the South, and in 'The Movement'. So much had changed in Martin King, too, in his beliefs about the fundamental alterations that America would have to undergo and the tactics that would have to be employed to coerce the society toward greater racial and economic justice. American life would have to be transformed. The 'radical reconstruction of society itself is the real issue to be faced.' A concern with eliminating human suffering would have to replace an obsession with military might. A commitment to others, 'to the least of these', would have to replace a society-wide pursuit of selfish materialism.

So much had changed in those twelve years leading up to April 4, 1968 in Memphis. So little, in all truthfulness, has changed in the years since. Yes, King's exhausted SCLC colleagues did carry through with the idea of a

'Poor People's Campaign' in Washington in the late spring of 1968, but it was a very faint shadow of what King privately had envisioned. The articulated goals were vague and modest, and bespoke nothing of transforming American life or restructuring the American economic order. The tactics too were tame, far tamer than the mass disruption that King had spoken of before his assassination. Neither the radical goals nor the nonviolently disruptive tactics that King himself had come to believe necessary were put forward or tested.

Some things, of course, have changed over these past years. Prominent examples from all across the South show the electoral strength that black citizens now possess in many places in the region. Talented black politicians have been elected mayors of Atlanta, New Orleans, and even Birmingham. In many smaller cities, and in some rural counties, blacks have won positions on local governing boards. Some of the changes seem dramatic, even touching: the influential black minority that sits on Selma's city council, the election of former SNCC activist Charles Sherrod, southwest Georgia's original 'outside Agitator', to the governing body of Albany, GA, once the scene of the movement's most frustrating southern campaign.

But the transformation of the South oftentimes is overstated. Yes, Selma, Albany, and Birmingham are vastly different places than they were twenty years ago. In many small towns and rural counties, however, local activists and a small band of dedicated voting rights attorneys are still attempting to win meaningful electoral influence for black citizens whose potential political power is heavily diluted or completely frustrated by 'at large' election schemes that allow white majorities to prevent the election of any black candidate. Even more importantly, neither in the South's larger cities nor in the rural areas has there been even the beginnings of the sort of shift of economic power and wealth needed to put black citizens on a par with their white neighbors.

Electing black mayors and other local officials, in the South or in the North, no more marks full empowerment for black people than did the passage of the 1964 and 1965 Acts mark the supposedly all but total success of the movement. On the surface, both sets of developments appear to be precisely what long was sought. Truthfully, however, electing black officials in the 1980s is the same sort of incomplete and potentially misleading victory that the Civil Rights Act and the Voting Rights Act handed King and the movement in the 1960s.

Nowhere is this presently more clear than in the urban battleground that brought Martin King face-to-face with America's most deep-seated economic injustices, Chicago. Mayor Harold Washington's victory in Chicago was rightfully celebrated by progressive Americans of all races all across the country. Particularly ironic was the fact that Washington's campaign manager, Al Raby, was the very same man who in 1965 had headed up the coalition of local activists that had persuaded King and

SCLC to come to Chicago. In the immediate aftermath of Washington's surprising win, Raby understandably was ecstatic. 'Martin Luther King said he wouldn't see the promised land, but that we would. In Chicago we have come to see that promised land', one news report quoted Raby as exclaiming.

Washington's election, however, will not, by itself, constitute the promised land that Martin King had in mind. Indeed the unrelenting racial machinations of white Chicago politicians who tried unsuccessfully to deny Washington his victory in the general election vividly revealed just how much anti-black hostility still exists in that city many years after the white mobs stoned Dr King. Washington's victory should be celebrated, but the significance of any single electoral triumph should not be exaggerated. Whether Chicago has a good mayor or a bad mayor, a black mayor or a white mayor, will not bring about the radical transformation that would represent Martin King's real 'promised land'.

Martin Luther King, Jr., in 1968 was speaking out in the strongest terms against the racism, militarism, and economic injustice that pervaded all of American society. How much have any of those preeminent evils abated in the years since April 4 in Memphis? Very little, I'm afraid. Racism? Look at the transparent political maneuvering in Chicago, at recent news reports from places like Boston or Miami, at the latest stories about the 1950s-style civil rights policies being promulgated by Ronald Reagan's Justice Department. Militarism? Look at the Reagan defense budget and the incredibly excessive and wasteful military appropriations currently being advocated by the administration. Look everywhere in America, at the unemployment lines in Alabama as well as in Michigan and California, at the urban slums in any major city, at the drafty shacks you still can find in virtually any county in the South, at the people huddled over sidewalk heating grates in those parts of the country whose spring evenings are cool, too cool to spend the night outside.

Yes, little of what Martin King wanted to change in American society as of 1968 had been altered since his death. The pervasive evils that he denounced then are little weaker, and some perhaps considerably stronger. The 'radical restructuring' of American society that he so fervently sought has not even begun.

If racism, militarism, and economic injustice have changed little over the past two decades, one thing that has changed drastically is the image many Americans have of Martin Luther King, Jr. himself. Unfortunately, King today oftentimes is portrayed as simply a prototypically successful American reform leader whose message and achievements comport perfectly with the most reassuring myths about American society and politics. If King is not pictured as the gentle minister who achieved desegregated seating on Montgomery's buses, then it is his 'I Have a Dream' oration that is cited to represent him. The incessant implication is that America in the 1960s made

King's dream come true. Rarely quoted, if ever, is a line that King used many times between 1966 and his death: 'the dream I had in Washington back in 1963 has too often turned into a nightmare'.

Frequently nowadays it seems as if the last two and one-half years of Martin King's life conveniently have been forgotten, that the civil rights movement ended when Lyndon Johnson signed the Voting Rights Act of 1965 into law, just before Watts, before Martin King went north to Chicago, before Martin King spoke out against the Vietnam war, and before Martin King began speaking about democratic socialism and massive nonviolent disruption. King was very serious about how the movement, and he himself, had to move forward from 'reform' to 'revolution', and challenge American society at its core rather than simply at its most flagrantly unjust edges. Martin King's goal was not simply to win thoroughgoing racial integration throughout American society, it was to transform that society from the ground up. That would entail both a 'radical restructuring' and very basic changes in American values, the creation of a society and an economy 'more person-centered than property-centered and profit-centered'. 'Let us', he emphasized, 'not think of our movement as one that seeks to integrate the Negro into all existing values of American society'.

In recent years, King's challenge has rarely been confronted and only infrequently pursued. That ability to forget, to avoid uncomfortable reminders, to lose commitment, was an ability that King himself wholly lacked. 'I'm tired of marching', he confided one evening in Chicago, 'tired of marching for something that should have been mine at first ... I must confess I'm tired ... I don't march because I like it, I march because I must'.

Was Martin Luther King a Marxist?

Adam Fairclough

Martin Luther King, Jr, has seldom figured in the Left's pantheon of Socialist heroes. To many of his contemporaries he seemed a typical product of the 'black bourgeoisie': a middle-class preacher from a middle-class family who pursued middle-class goals. Although an eloquent and courageous crusader for racial justice, his ultimate vision – as expressed for example in his famous 'I Have A Dream' oration – seemed to be the integration of the Negro into the existing structure of society; capitalism was

From *History Workshop Journal* 15 (Spring 1983): 117–25.

not at issue. When he talked about the need for cleanliness, godliness and thrift, he sounded like Booker T. Washington, that epitome of bourgeois values who, at the turn of the century, had exhorted blacks to pull themselves up by their own bootstraps. King's own admiration for Washington, whom many blacks viewed as an arch 'Uncle Tom', was widely-known and openly advertised. By the mid-1960s, at the height of his fame and success, King struck many of his contemporaries as an essentially conservative figure. He was always 'amenable to compromise', wrote one commentator, 'with the white bourgeois political and economic Establishment'. Lawrence Reddick, King's friend and biographer, had anticipated such verdicts years earlier. 'Neither by experience nor reading is King a political radical', he wrote in 1959. 'There is not a Marxist bone in his body.' True, King adopted a much more radical stance during the last two years of his life, but he never seemed to wander very far from the political mainstream. To the student radicals of the 'New Left', as well as to the angry advocates of 'Black Power', King remained a staid, unexciting figure, the ineffectual exponent of an outdated brand of liberalism.[1]

It seems scarcely credible, then, that King was, as the Federal Bureau of Investigation maintained, a self-confessed Marxist. Did the FBI's ubiquitous wiretaps really record the civil rights leader saying, 'I am a Marxist', and that he would profess this publicly but for the knowledge that it would destroy his position? In view of the notorious conservatism of the FBI, which branded the mildest of social critics 'subversive', this allegation might be dismissed as a paranoid fantasy, or perhaps a product of the racism that permeated the Bureau under its chief, J. Edgar Hoover. Hoover's own loathing for King, and his malevolent campaign to destroy him, have been thoroughly documented in Congressional investigations and a recent book by David J. Garrow.[2]

Yet the FBI's perception of King as a radical threat to American institutions was not as far-fetched as it may seem, for King did, in fact, express admiration for Marx and argue that the United States should move towards Socialism. King's placid exterior, his orotund manner, and his sober clerical mien tended to disguise his deep political radicalism. In addition, he expressed his political beliefs far more frankly and explicitly in private than he did in public. Only recently, when Mrs Coretta King allowed researchers access to the records of the Southern Christian Leadership Conference (the organization that her husband headed) has the real scope of King's radicalism become apparent. By 1966 he had become a passionate enemy of Western capitalism and an advocate, in his own words, of 'democratic socialism'.[3]

King's intellectual attraction to socialism pre-dated his career as a civil rights leader. In 1949, as a student at Crozer Theological Seminary, he read *Capital, The Communist Manifesto*, and some interpretive works on the thinking of Marx and Lenin. Although he rejected the materialist conception of reality, King was clearly enamoured by much of what he read. The *Communist Manifesto*, he later wrote, 'was written by men aflame with a passion for social justice.' Marx had raised 'basic questions', and 'in so far as he pointed to weaknesses of traditional capitalism, contributed to the growth of a definite self-consciousness in the masses, and challenged the social conscience of the Christian churches, I responded with a definite "yes".' Later, as a doctoral student at Boston University, King read and admired the writings of Reinhold Niebuhr, who combined Christian ethics with a Marxian analysis of history and society, and whose seminal work, *Moral Man and Immoral Society*, had a profound and continuing impact on him. King's radical views while a student did not please his conservative father: as 'Daddy' King later wrote, 'Politically, he ... seemed to be drifting away from the bases of capitalism and Western democracy that I felt very strongly about. There were some sharp exchanges; I may even have raised my voice a few times.'[4]

In December 1955 King was thrust into a position of leadership that he had neither sought nor wanted. Elected to serve as president of the Montgomery Improvement Association, a group formed to boycott the segregated buses in Montgomery, Alabama, King soon became the internationally-recognized symbol of the emerging civil rights movement. When black clergymen from across the South met to found a new civil rights organization, the Southern Christian Leadership Conference (SCLC), they automatically chose King to act as president. Interestingly, they decided to include the word 'Christian' in their name partly to avoid being labelled as a 'Red' organization.

Nevertheless, the three New Yorkers – two blacks and one white – who organized SCLC on King's behalf were all firmly on the Left. Bayard Rustin, Ella Baker and Stanley Levison were much older than King; their political involvement went back to the 1930s. Rustin had joined the Young Communist League before the war but, like so many others, broke with the party over its subservience to Moscow. He subsequently worked for various pacifist organizations, and helped set up the first London-to-Aldermaston march against nuclear weapons. He also tried, without much success, to popularize Gandhian civil disobedience as a means of fighting racial discrimination. He remained a Socialist, however, and had the long-term goal of moving blacks into a radicalized labour movement. Ella Baker lacked Rustin's interest in pacifism, but otherwise moved in the same political milieu. 'I had been friendly with people who were in the Communist Party and all the rest of the left forces', she would recall. Levison's political allegiance was more ambiguous. Ostensibly a liberal Democrat, he had been active in such groups as the businessman's committee for the re-election of Roosevelt (1944) and the American Jewish Congress. But he was also close to leading members of the beleaguered Communist Party and may have, in the early 1950s, offered them financial advice and assistance. Baker simply remembered that he, too, 'had come out of the New York left'. All three recognized that mass civil disobedience, especially in the context of the American South, was a tactic that had far-reaching potential. Excited by the Montgomery bus boycott – an entirely spontaneous protest – they offered the inexperienced King help and advice, and constructed SCLC as a vehicle for mass action throughout the South. Interestingly, Baker soon fell out with King because, in part, she deemed him insufficiently radical. Rustin and Levison, on the other hand, worked with him until his death in 1968, acting as unofficial advisers and behind-the-scenes organizers.[5]

Because of his association with these two, the FBI depicted King, from 1963 until his death, as either a conscious 'fellow traveller', or, at best, a naive dupe. Levison, the Bureau asserted, was a particularly subversive influence: a man who manipulated King in the interests of the Communist Party. Years after King's death, Levison, who was white, attributed this canard to the FBI's 'racist contempt for the intellect of the black man. No one with a modicum of sense ... could have concluded that a man with the force of intellect and fierce independence that Martin King had could have been dominated by anybody ... And if there had been any domination in the relationship, the greater probability was that he would influence or perhaps dominate me.' Levison raised funds for SCLC, helped King with his speeches and writings, and proffered common-sense advice that remained, in David Garrow's words, 'wholly innocuous'. Rustin assisted King in similar ways and, far from being a dangerous radical, drifted steadily to the right, eventually attaching himself to the Johnson-Humphrey wing of the Democratic party.[6]

With his religious cast of mind, King tended to reject political ideology. Interested first and foremost in combating racism, he accepted assistance from whatever quarter it came. As for his staff, all he asked was that they accept nonviolence – as a tactic if not a philosophy – and be fully committed to the civil rights movement. On rare occasions, however, he succumbed to political pressure, and he distanced himself from both Rustin and Levison for a time because of their allegedly 'tainted' political pasts. In the case of Levison the pressure came from the White House itself. Later, King reproached himself for moral cowardice, and reestablished a close relationship with both of them. 'There's nothing to hide,' he told Levison. 'And if anybody wants to make anything of it, let them try.' By 1965, King had concluded that 'anti-communism' provided a handy cloak for opposition to social progress. By making continual allegations about 'communist infiltration' of the civil rights movement, he charged, J. Edgar Hoover aided and abetted the 'Southern racists and the extreme right-wing element.' Radicalism among blacks grew out of 'impatience with the slow pace of establishing justice.' America's fear of communism, he concluded, was 'morbid', 'irrational' and 'obsessive'.[7]

Until 1965, King's radicalism was more intellectual than emotional. He had approached the struggle for racial justice in a non-ideological way, hoping to overcome bigotry and prejudice through an appeal to idealism and Christian principles. Perhaps because his parents had shielded him from the worst effects of racial oppression, he viewed racism as a Southern anachronism which would, in the course of a decade or two, wither away and die. After that, he believed, blacks would have to 'work desperately to improve their own conditions and their own standards ... The Negro will have to engage in a sort of Operation Boot-strap.' By 1966, however, he categorically rejected the idea of piecemeal reform within the existing socio-economic structure: a massive redistribution of wealth, not self-help, was the most urgent necessity.[8]

Two factors hastened this process of radicalization: King's belated realization that racism was endemic in American society; and his horror of America's military role in Vietnam. When he took SCLC North, to Chicago, he had to abandon his assumption that racism outside the South was a secondary, residual phenomenon. When blacks demanded an end to discrimination in housing, education and jobs, white support for the civil rights movements melted away. Routine police brutality pushed black frustration to the boiling-point, yet government, both federal and local, responded to the eruption of rioting with repression rather than root and branch reform. By the end of 1966 King's optimism had been shattered. Only 'a minority of whites,' he wrote, 'genuinely want authentic equality'. To black audiences, and to his staff, he put it more bluntly: 'the vast majority of white Americans are racists'.[9]

More and more, King saw racism as an instrument of class privilege, a means of dividing the working-class by giving whites marginal economic advantages and encouraging their psychological pretensions to superiority. Both black and white labour was thus more easily exploited and cheapened. With his top aide James Bevel, King viewed the black ghettos as 'internal colonies', a segregated market where goods and services were deliberately restricted in order to boost the profits of the capitalists who provided them. At an SCLC retreat in November 1966, he warned that demanding an end to the ghetto meant 'getting on dangerous ground because you are messing with folk then. You are messing with Wall Street. You are messing with the captains of industry'. He told his staff not to be afraid of the word 'socialism', for 'something is wrong with capitalism' and 'the Movement must address itself to the restructuring of the whole of American society'. Sweden, he pointed out, had 'grappled with the problem of more equitable distribution of wealth'; it had free health care, and no slums, poverty or unemployment. Institutional racism could only be eliminated through a radical redistribution of economic power; 'privileged groups will have to give up some of their billions'. America, too, he argued, 'must move toward a Democratic Socialism'.[10]

The war in Vietnam reinforced King's disenchantment with American capitalism. His opposition to the war has often been interpreted as a purely moral concern, an expression of his dogmatic commitment to non-violence. Not so: he did not take a politically agnostic position, but roundly condemned the United States as the aggressor. Time and again he insisted that Ho Chi Minh was leading a popular nationalist revolt against a corrupt dictatorship, and that the United States had taken the wrong side. Again, King expressed his views more plainly and frankly when talking to black audiences, to friends, and to his own staff. During an SCLC retreat in May 1967, he left his staff in no doubt about his admiration for Ho Chi Minh – nor his utter contempt for the rulers of South Vietnam. He scornfully dismissed the notion that the South was being 'invaded' by the North: 'the Vietcong came into being in the South as a movement to resist the oppression of Diem.' Besides, he argued, the division of Vietnam had been imposed from without: 'how can somebody invade himself?' When America supported the South, it was 'as if the French and the British had come over here during the Civil War to fight with the Confederacy'. Speaking to an SCLC-sponsored conference of black ministers in early 1968, he cited the recent Tet offensive as conclusive proof that 'the vast majority of the people in Vietnam are sympathetic with the Viet Cong. That is a fact.'[11]

King did not see America's involvement in Vietnam as an isolated aberration, but as part of a wider 'pattern of suppression' that embraced Africa and Latin America in addition to Southeast Asia. America bolstered the racist regimes in South Africa and Rhodesia; American arms and personnel helped to fight rebels and guerrillas in Venezuela, Guatemala, Columbia, and Peru. Why, he asked, had 'the Western nations that initiated so much of the revolutionary spirit of the modern world' become 'the arch anti-revolutionaries' of the twentieth century? Ultimately, he believed, the answer lay in the very nature of Western capitalism: 'individual capitalists of the West' invested 'huge sums of money in Asia, Africa and South America, only to take the profits out with no concern for the social betterment of the countries'; multinational cartels stripped underdeveloped nations of their resources 'while turning over a small rebate to a few members of a corrupt aristocracy'. The historic freedom accorded to capital in the United States had made government the servant of private profit:

A nation that will keep people in slavery for 244 years will 'thingify' them, make them things. Therefore they will exploit them, and poor people generally, economically. And a nation that will exploit economically will have to have foreign investments ... and will have to use its military might to protect them.

This 'need to maintain social stability for our investments' explained the alliance with the landed gentry in Latin America; the support for colonial and white settler regimes in Africa; and the sponsorship of puppet dictators in Southeast Asia. The United States had become the world's foremost neo-colonial power.[12]

During the last two years of his life, King became convinced that capitalism was the common denominator that linked racism, economic exploitation and militarism. These 'triple evils' of the modern era were 'incapable of being conquered' when 'profit motives and property rights are considered more important than people.' If hostility to capitalism coloured his writings and speeches so strongly, could he, then, be described as a 'Marxist'? In private, King readily acknowledged his intellectual debt to Marx and commended his critique of capitalism. Yet he always coupled such praise with qualifications. King, echoing the conventional definitions of the day, associated Marxism with the rejection of spiritual values, a shallow economic determinism, and the absolute supremacy of the state. All this he emphatically rejected. He summed up his feelings about Marx, both positive and negative, in a talk to the SCLC staff in 1966:

> I always look at Marx with a yes and a no. And there were some things that Karl Marx did that were very good. Some very good things. If you read him, you can see that this man had a great passion for social justice ... [But] Karl Marx got messed up, first because he didn't stick with that Jesus that he had read about; but secondly because he didn't even stick with Hegel.

As always, King then went on to talk about Jesus as his primary inspiration:

> Now this is where I leave Brother Marx and move on toward the Kingdom [of God] ... I am simply saying that God never intended for some of his children to live in inordinate superfluous wealth while others live in abject, deadening poverty.

That King should have stated 'I am a Marxist,' without these qualifications and in such bald terms, is, in the opinion of this writer, unlikely in the extreme. His hostility to excessive materialism, and his concern for the poor and the oppressed, owed more to the Social Gospel than to Marxist ideology.[13]

Regardless of the influences that helped shape his political analysis, King made no bones about his radical opposition to American capitalism. 'For years,' he told one reporter, 'I labored with the idea of reforming the existing institutions of the society, a little change here, a little change there. Now I feel quite differently. I think you've got to have a reconstruction of the entire society.' He did not openly advocate 'socialism', but talked instead of a 'synthesis' between capitalism and communism; a 'socially conscious democracy which reconciles the truths of individualism and collectivism.' As he admitted in private, however, such definitions were really euphemisms for democratic socialism. In public, the best he could hope for was to encourage questioning and doubt. 'Why are there 40 million poor people in America?' he asked at the SCLC convention in August 1967:

> When you begin to ask that question, you are raising questions about the economic system, about a broader distribution of wealth. When you ask that question, you begin to question the capitalistic economy. And I'm simply saying that more and more, we've got to begin to ask questions about the whole society. We are called upon to help the discouraged beggars in life's market place. But one day we must come to see that an edifice which produces beggars needs restructuring ... You see, my friends, when you deal with this, you begin to ask the question, 'Who owns the oil?' You begin to ask the question, 'Who owns the iron ore?'[14]

King clearly found the gap between his own deepening radicalism and the political unsophistication of his followers frustrating. He hoped that black clergymen could, through education and training, be oriented toward his own radical values, enabling them to occupy the vanguard in a struggle for economic justice just as they had been in the forefront of the civil rights movement in the South. 'We must develop their psyche,' he told a planning meeting of SCLC's Ministers Leadership Training Program. 'Something is wrong with capitalism as it now stands in the United States. We are not interested in being integrated into *this* value structure ... a radical redistribution of power must take place.' As Louis Lomax wrote, this vision of the clergy was, perhaps, 'the most ethereal dream he ever entertained'.[15]

By the end of 1967, King believed that he had found a more viable alternative; an interracial alliance of the poor. His last major project, the 'Poor People's Campaign', was an attempt to translate this concept into political reality. America, he argued, already had 'socialism for the rich'; if the government could hand out massive subsidies to affluent farmers, giant corporations and wealthy individuals, then it could guarantee jobs and a decent income for all. He did not define his goal as 'socialism'; instead, he called it 'poor people's power'. King proposed to lead thousands of the poor to Washington where, if necessary, they would engage in mass civil disobedience in order to stimulate government action. 'We will be confronting the very government, and the very federal machinery that has often come [to] our aid', he warned his staff. Many old allies and supporters were aghast at the plan. His old friend Bayard Rustin publicly opposed it. Even colleagues in SCLC had grave doubts. King nevertheless showed every intention of going ahead. In the midst of the preparations for the campaign he went to Memphis to support striking sanitation workers in their fight for union recognition. 'In a sense,' he told a reporter shortly before his assassination there, 'you could say we are engaged in the class struggle, yes'.[16]

Notes

1 August Meier, 'On the Role of Martin Luther King', in Melvin Drimmer (ed.), *Black History: A Reappraisal*, Garden City, NY, 1968, p. 444; L. D. Reddick, *Crusader Without Violence*, NY, 1959, p. 233. On King's admiration for Washington, and his praise of thrift and self-help, see Martin Luther King. Jr, *Stride Toward Freedom,* London, 1959, p. 213; Robert Penn Warren, *Who Speaks for the Negro?* NY, 1966, pp. 209–10; 'An Interview with Martin Luther King', *Playboy*, January 1965, p. 76. Reddick also wrote, however, that Marx did have an appeal for King – 'his dialectic, his critique of monopoly capitalism, and his regard for social and economic justice' (Reddick, p. 22).

2 'Testimony of Charles D. Brennan', in US Congress, House Select Commission on Assassinations, *Martin Luther King, Jr.: Hearings*, 95th Cong., 2nd sess., vol. VI, p. 346; David J. Garrow, *The FBI and Martin Luther King, Jr.*, New York, 1981. For briefer summaries of the FBI's anti-King campaign, see Mark Lane and Dick Gregory, *Code Name 'Zorro': The Murder of Martin Luther King, Jr.*, Englewood Cliffs, NJ, 1977. pp. 60 111, US Congress, Senate Select Committee to Study Governmental Operations with Respect to Intelligence Activities, *Final Report: Book III*, 94th Cong., 2nd sess., 1976; *Report of the House Select Committee on Assassinations: Findings and Recommendations*, 95th Cong., 2nd sess., 29 March 1979, pp. 432–9.

3 The SCLC records, which extend to more than 140 linear feet, were opened to researchers in the summer of 1981, in Atlanta.

4 King, *Stride Toward Freedom*, pp. 86–93; 'How Should a Christian View Communism?' in King, *Strength to Love*, New York, 1963, pp. 114–23; Martin Luther King. Sr., with Clayton Riley, *Daddy King: An Autobiography*, New York, 1980, pp. 141–2; Garrow'. p. 213. King's widow recalled Martin saying, when still a student, that while 'I could never be a Communist', he could not be a 'thoroughgoing capitalist' either; 'I think a society based on making all the money you can and ignoring other people's needs is wrong': see Coretta Scott King, *My Life with Martin Luther King, Jr.*, New York 1969, p. 71. In a 1959 speech, King cited Marx (along with Jesus, Einstein and Freud) as outstanding examples of men who creatively used their intellectual and moral freedom: see 'Address at Meeting of Mississippi Christian Leadership Conference', 23 September 1959, handwritten manuscript. King Papers, Boston University, file drawer XI, folder 8 (collection hereafter cited as BU). In writing *Stride Toward Freedom*, King resisted suggestions from his editors at Harper and Row that he tone down his criticisms of American capitalism; see Stephen B. Oates, *Let The Trumpet Sound: The Life of Martin Luther King, Jr.*, London, 1982, p. 131.

5. Ella J. Baker (John H. Britton interview, 19 June 1968). Civil Rights Documentation Project, Moorland-Springarn Research Center, Howard University, pp. 10–23 (collection hereafter cited as HU); Stanley D. Levison (James Mosby interview, 14 February 1970), HU, pp. 16–17; Don Oberdorfer, 'King adviser says FBI "used" him', *Washington Post*, 15 December 1975; Milton Viorst, *Fire in the Streets: America in the 1960s*, New York, 1979, pp. 119–23, 200–11; Thomas R. Brooks 'A Strategist without a Movement', in August Meier and Elliott Rudwick (eds), *Black Protest in the Sixties*, Chicago 1970, pp. 339–41.

6. Victor Navasky, *Kennedy Justice*, New York, 1971, pp. 141–9; Garrow, pp. 44–77 and *passim*; Roger Wilkins, ' "King" Disappoints NBC and Some Civil Rights Leaders'. *New York Times*, 19 February 1978, III, p. 19. FBI memos concerning Levison's alleged influence over King were legion; for a sample of the more important ones (although Levison's name is deleted), see House Select Committee on Assassinations, *King: Hearings*, vol. VI, pp. 131, 143–4, 187, 263–4. Only days before King's death, the FBI prepared a request to reinstall wiretaps in the SCLC offices, citing Levison as the reason. Levison had been the pretext for installing taps on King's own phone, as well as SCLC's offices in Atlanta and New York, in 1963. Unlike Rustin, Levison encouraged King to speak out against the Vietnam war; the evidence that he worked for the Communist Party, however, or succeeded in establishing an irresistible influence over King, is completely absent. Yet in 1978 one of Hoover's top assistants still insisted that King, by virtue of his friendship with Levison, was a Communist; see 'Testimony of Cartha D. De Loach', Assassinations Committee, *King Hearings*, VII, p. 49.

7. Navasky, pp. 141–6; M. S. Handler, 'Negro Rally Aide Rebuts Senator', *New York Times*, 16 August 1963, p. 10; 'Dr. King Hits Communist Charges in Stanford Speech', SCLC press release, 23 April 1964, SCLC collection, Martin Luther King. Jr. Centre for Nonviolent Social Change, Atlanta (collection hereafter cited as SCLC); King, hand-written notes, n.d. [late March/early April 1965] King papers, King Center; 'Joint statement of Rev. Dr. Martin Luther King, Jr. . . . and John Lewis', 30 April 1965, SCLC, box 27, folder 55; James Forman, *The Making of Black Revolutionaries*, New York, 1972, pp. 367–9; King, *Where Do We Go From Here: Chaos or Community?* New York, 1968, p. 211 (hereafter cited as *Where?*); 'Honoring Dr. Du Bois,' *Freedomways*, second quarter 1968, p. 109.

8. King, 'No More Room in the Negro's Soul', *Honolulu Advertiser*, 20 February 1964; Warren, pp. 209–10. Stanley Levison, on the other hand, believed that King's affluent background accentuated his concern for the poor and underprivileged: 'Martin was always aware that he was privileged . . . and this troubled him. He felt that he didn't deserve this. One reason he was so determined to be of service was to justify the privileged position he'd been born into'; see Jean Stein and George Plimpton, *American Journey: The Times of Robert Kennedy*, New York, 1970, pp. 108–9.

9. King, *Where?*, p. 13; 'Dr. King's speech, Frogmore, November 14, 1966', SCLC, 28, 26, pp. 5–6; speech to voter registration rally. Louisville, Kentucky, 2 August 1967, pp. 1–3; 'America's Chief Moral Dilemma', speech to Hungry Club, Atlanta, 5 October 1967, pp. 4–5; King Papers.

10. 'Dr. King's speech. Frogmore', pp. 14–20; King interview by John Herbers, *New York Times*, 2 April 1967, pp. 1, 76. King first referred to 'internal colonialism' in 'The Chicago Plan', 7 January 1966, SCLC press release. Earlier hints of a class analysis of racism could be seen in King, *Why We Can't Wait*, New York, 1964, p. 138; and in the famous speech King delivered after the Selma-to-Montgomery march in 1965; see 'Selma to Montgomery speech', 25 March 1965, TLS, SCLC, 27, 54.

11. King. 'Beyond Vietnam', speech to Clergy and Laymen Concerned About Vietnam, Riverside Church, New York City, 4 April 1967, SCLC recording. Atlanta (reprinted in *Freedomways*, Spring 1967); 'Conscience and the Vietnam War', *The Trumpet of Conscience*, New York, 1968, pp. 21–34; 'Speech at staff retreat, Frogmore, SC', May 1967, pp. 10–20; 'America's Chief Moral Dilemma', 5 October 1967, pp. 8–12. King Papers; 'Speech to Ministers Leadership Training Program', 18 February 1968, TLS, p. 17, SCLC, 28, 51. See also King's comments about the lack of popular support for the government of South Vietnam, and his scathing remarks about the performance of the South Vietnamese army, in 'The Domestic Impact of the War in Vietnam', speech to National Labor Leadership Assembly for Peace, Chicago, 11 November 1967, SCLC recording. Many of King's speeches on Vietnam were drafted by Stanley Levison.

12. King, *Where?*, pp. 202–19; 'Beyond Vietnam', *Current*, May 1967, p. 38; 'President's Address to the Tenth Anniversary Convention of the Southern Christian Leadership Conference', 16 August 1967, reprinted in Wayne L. Brockriede and Robert L. Scott (eds), *The Rhetoric of Black Power*, New York, 1971, p. 163; 'The Casualties of the War in Vietnam', speech at the *Nation* Institute, Los Angeles, 25 February 1967, King Papers, pp. 5–7; 'Dr. King Advocates Vietnam', *New York Times*, 26 February 1967, pp. 1, 10. In 'Honoring Dr. Du Bois', delivered at Carnegie Hall, New York, on 23 February 1968, King spoke of 'our brother of the Third World' being 'the victim of imperialist exploitation'; see *Freedomways*, second quarter, 1968, pp. 110–11.

13. King, *Where?*, p. 216; 'Dr. King's speech: Frogmore, November 14, 1966', pp. 20–1, 29; 'What is Man?' in *Strength To Love*, p. 109. The fullest discussion of King's thought from a theological point of view is Kenneth L. Smith and Ira G. Zepp, *Search for the Beloved Community: The Thinking of Martin Luther King, Jr.*, Valley Forge, PA, 1974. David Garrow, on the other hand, believes that King, in certain narrow contexts, might have stated 'I am a Marxist' in private conversation (Garrow, p. 213; and correspondence with this writer, 2 February 1982).

14. David Halberstam, 'The Second Coming of Martin Luther King', *Harper's*, August 1967, pp. 47–8; King, *Where?*, p. 217; 'President's Address', 16 August 1967, in Brockriede and Scott, pp. 161–2. The 'synthesis' idea appeared in his earliest published writings, but it was only in 1965 and after that he began equating this nebulous concept with democratic socialism of the Swedish model.

15. Minutes of national advisory committee, SCLC training program, 24 November 1967, p. 6, SCLC, 48, 11; Louis Lomax, 'When "Nonviolence" Meets "Black Power",' in C. Eric Lincoln (ed.), *Martin Luther King, Jr.: A Profile*, New York, 1970, p. 172; 'King Aide Seeks to Organize Negro Ministers in 15 Cities', *Atlanta Constitution*, 23 January 1968, p. 6. The programme was financed by the Ford Foundation. The FBI 'briefed' the Vice President of the Ford Motor Company 'as to the subversive backgrounds of King's principal advisers' in an unsuccessful attempt to stop the grant; see G. C. Moore to W. C. Sullivan. 29 November 1967, in Assassinations Committee, *King Hearings*, VI, pp. 277–8.

16. King, 'Speech to Mississippi Leaders on the Washington Campaign', 15 February 1968, p. 6; King Papers; 'A Proper Sense of Priorities', speech to Clergy and Laymen Concerned About Vietnam, 6 February 1968, SCLC recording; 'Nonviolence and Social Change', *The Trumpet of Conscience*, pp. 53–64; 'Showdown for Nonviolence', *Look*, 16 April 1968, pp. 23–35; 'Why We Must Go To Washington', talk to SCLC staff meeting. Atlanta, 15 January 1968, pp. 11–17, King papers. For opposition to the Poor People's Campaign from two of King's close friends and advisers, see Marian Logan to King, 8 March 1968,

TLS memo, SCLC, 40, 3; and Bayard Rustin, 'Memo on the Spring Protest in Washington, DC', January 1968, in Bayard Rustin, *Down The Line: The Collected Writings of Bayard Rustin* (Chicago 1971), pp. 202–5. For opposition from some of King's top aides, notably James Bevel and Jesse Jackson, see minutes of executive staff meeting, 27 December 1967, pp. 8–9, SCLC, 49, 13.

9 Assassination: Conspiracy or Lone Gunman?

Introduction

King's assassination has been the subject of much controversy and many conspiracy theories. The official line is that career criminal and known racist James Earl Ray shot and killed King on the evening of 4 April 1968 while King stood on the balcony outside his room in the Lorraine Motel in Memphis, Tennessee. In 1977–8 the US Congress House Select Committee on Assassinations concluded that 'there is a likelihood' that Ray did not plan the assassination alone. In 1997, King's son, Dexter Scott King, met with Ray and declared that he believed that Ray was innocent of the crime. The following year, US Attorney General Janet Reno opened a limited investigation into events without finding evidence of a conspiracy. In December 1999, a Memphis jury awarded the King family token damages of $100 in a 'wrongful death' civil lawsuit. The jury concluded that King's death had been the result of a conspiracy.

Academic scholars have in the main avoided becoming entangled in the details of the King assassination and examining conspiracy theories. Much of the literature has been written by those directly involved in events, by investigative journalists, and by those writing popular histories directed at a mass market. This has only served to further fuel the sensationalism surrounding an already contentious topic. The first selection here is written by international lawyer William F. Pepper, the man who has led the court battle to prove that King's death was part of a wider conspiracy. Pepper's article 'The Children of Vietnam', which appeared in *Ramparts Magazine* on 1 January 1967, is generally credited as being one of the key turning points in convincing King to speak out against the war. Pepper knew King through their mutual involvement in the antiwar movement. In 1977, Ralph Abernathy, who succeeded King as president of the SCLC, asked Pepper to arrange a meeting with James Earl Ray to try to assuage Abernathy's doubts about the assassination. The meeting only convinced Abernathy and Pepper that Ray was not the assassin. In 1988, Pepper agreed to act as Ray's lawyer in an attempt to have him tried for the murder of King. At the initial hearings in 1968, Ray had entered a guilty plea and was sentenced to 99 years in prison without a trial. After failing to get Ray a trial on appeal through the US courts, Pepper arranged a trial by television sponsored jointly by US broadcaster HBO and British Thames Television. 'The Trial of James Earl Ray' was televised in 1993. The jury found Ray not guilty. In 1995, Pepper published *Orders to Kill: The Truth Behind the Murder of Martin Luther King*, where he presented the evidence he had accumulated in his investigations to press further for a trial in the US courts. The case was bolstered by support from King's family members who voiced their doubts about Ray's guilt. However, Ray's death in 1998 finally ended the possibility of a trial. The King family instead took out a civil suit for 'wrongful death' against Lloyd Jowers, the owner of 'Jim's Grill', located on the ground floor of the building across from the Lorraine Motel, and whom Pepper had implicated in the conspiracy to kill King.

The first selection here is from Pepper's updated 2003 book about the King assassination called *An Act of State: The Execution of Martin Luther King*. Pepper explains how he became involved in the case and the reasons why he believes King was killed. Principally, these involve King's increasing radicalism, his critique of US capitalism and his opposition to the war in Vietnam. Pepper concludes that King's assassination was part of a much wider conspiracy and a cover-up that 'ultimately expose[s] the dark underbelly of American government and the covert activities of its military and intelligence organizations and their fealty to corporate interests and organized crime'.

In the second and third selections, Gerald Posner asserts that there is 'no doubt that James Earl Ray shot and killed Martin Luther King, Jr'. Posner, a former Wall Street-based corporate lawyer and now an investigative journalist and freelance writer, has written a number of popular histories including a book on the Kennedy assassination *Case Closed: Lee Harvey Oswald and the Assassination of JFK* (1993) which is a companion piece to his book on the King assassination, *Killing the Dream: James Earl Ray and the Assassination of Martin Luther King, Jr* (1998). In both books, Posner takes the same line, claming that Oswald and Ray acted essentially alone in their endeavours and that no extensive conspiracy exists in either case.

The first selection written by Posner comes from the epilogue to his book on the King assassination. Posner claims that Ray killed King for three principal reasons. Firstly, because of Ray's desire for notoriety and recognition. Secondly, because of Ray's inherent racist beliefs and practices.

Thirdly, for cold hard cash – Posner believes that Ray thought he would pick up a bounty for King's assassination. An 'elaborate plot' seems unlikely since Ray did not seek to cover his tracks in the lead-up to the assassination and he was not a likely candidate for a hitman. 'If there was ultimately a conspiracy behind King's death,' Posner concludes, 'a crude family plot seems more likely than a sophisticated operation involving the mafia or some government agency.' The second selection written by Posner, an addendum to his study after Ray's death in prison, does little to alter his previous analysis but it does suggest the reasons why many, including King's family, remain suspicious about King's murder. In particular, revelations about the harassment of King by J. Edgar Hoover and the FBI link a federal agency with constant direct and indirect personal attacks on King of an often scandalous nature. Therefore, while still sticking to his 'lone gunman' thesis, Posner concedes that 'While it may not have pulled the trigger, the government did however, by such outrageous conduct, create an atmosphere where racists thought it was safe to shoot a black leader in the South and think they could get away with it.' In short, although the government and its agencies had no direct role in King's assassination, they helped to create a climate whereby this became a distinct possibility – a different claim to Pepper's, though still a damning one.

In the fourth selection, Kenneth O'Reilly sketches out the sort of harassment that King received from the FBI in an extract from a larger study of the FBI's covert surveillance of African Americans in the 1960s and early 1970s. After the 1963 March on Washington, Hoover's and the FBI's attention increasingly focused upon King. Wiretaps were placed in King's home and office, and bugs in his hotel rooms, as part of a surveillance operation aimed at discrediting him and the movement. This surveillance also extended to King's close associates such as his advisor Stanley Levison. Initially, the FBI sought to discredit King and other movement activists by labelling them communist dupes. When that failed, the focus turned to a more personal attack on King's standing. Hoover publicly labelled King 'the most notorious liar in the country' in a squabble over comments King had previously made about the inactivity of FBI agents when civil rights demonstrators faced white violence. A more scandalous private attack came when William Sullivan, head of the FBI's Division Five, charged with smearing left-wing leaders, collated a 'highlights' package of covert surveillance, purported to contain 'dirty jokes and bawdy remarks . . . plus the sounds of people engaging in sex' in King's hotel room. Sullivan sent the tape to King along with a threatening letter inviting him to either commit suicide or to withdraw from public life, with the threat to make the tape public if he refused. Coretta Scott King, who collected and opened the package and listened to the tape, dismissed it as 'just a lot of mumbo jumbo'. Attempts by the FBI to pass the tape on to the national press met with rebuffs from editors. The desperate and perfidious techniques used by the FBI to discredit King do little to allay suspicions about the role played by government agencies in King's death – although, of course, they do not prove their involvement either.

Questions for Discussion

1. What elements do you find particularly convincing or unconvincing about the case for a conspiracy, and why?

2. What elements do you find particularly convincing or unconvincing about the case for a lone gunman, and why?

3. What difference would solving the case make? To who, and why?

4. Should governments have the right to engage in the covert surveillance of their citizens? In what cases do you think this would be acceptable (if at all)?

Further Reading

Among the first to publish conspiracy theories about King's assassination were William Bradford Huie, *He Slew the Dreamer: My Search with James Earl Ray for the Truth about the Murder of Martin Luther King* (Montgomery, AL: Black Belt Press, 1970), Gerold Frank, *An American Death: The True Story of the Assassination of Dr. Martin Luther King, Jr and the Greatest Manhunt of Our Time* (London: Hamilton, 1972), and Mark Lane and Dick Gregory, *Code Name 'Zorro': The Murder of Martin Luther King, Jr* (Englewood Cliffs, NJ: Prentice-Hall, 1977) which was revised and updated in *Murder in Memphis: The FBI and the Assassination of Martin Luther King* (New York: Thunder's Mouth Press, 1993). William F. Pepper, *Orders to Kill: The Truth Behind the Murder of Martin Luther King, Jr* (New York: Carroll and Graf, 1995), revised and updated in *An Act of State: The Execution of Martin Luther King* (London: Verso Books, 2003), puts forward the most recent case. James Earl Ray, *Who Killed Martin Luther King, Jr? The True Story by the Alleged Assassin* (New York: National Press Books, 1992) is the convicted assassin's own account of events and a plea of innocence before his death in 1998. Gerald Posner, *Killing the Dream: James Earl Ray and the Assassination of Martin Luther King, Jr* (New York: Random House, 1998), dismisses the notion of any significant conspiracy (his book *Case Closed: Lee Harvey Oswald and the Assassination of JFK* (New York: Random House, 1993) does the same for the Kennedy assassination).

On the FBI, David J. Garrow (ed.), *The Martin Luther King, Jr File* (Frederick, MD: University Publishers of America, 1984) provides copious primary material of King's surveillance and Garrow's book *The FBI and Martin Luther King, Jr: From 'Solo' to Memphis* (New York: W. W. Norton, 1981) is the best monograph on the subject. Kenneth O'Reilly, *Racial Matters: The FBI's Secret File on Black America, 1960–1972* (New York: Free Press, 1989) places the story of King's surveillance in a wider context as does John Drabble, 'To Ensure Domestic Tranquillity: The FBI, COINTELPRO-WHITE HATE and Political Discourse, 1964–1971', *Journal of American Studies* 38 (August 2004): 297–328.

An Act of State: The Execution of Martin Luther King

William F. Pepper

. . .

When one assesses this awesome array of private established, non-governmental, institutional power, it is eminently reasonable to consider those in government decision-making positions as being compelled to listen to, protect and serve the unified interests of this corporate establishment. When business speaks with one voice, as it did in respect of the [Vietnam] war or the purported extreme threat of war at the time when Martin King set himself up in opposition, the relevant government agencies and their officials become mere footsoldiers for the mighty economic interests. Out in front in time of war are the armed forces, the intelligence and law enforcement communities. Not far behind are the executive, the legislative and the judicial legitimizers, who sanction the necessary actions, and the media conglomerates who, as the publicists of government policy, posing as independent voices of the people, vigorously support and defend the official policy in serious national security instances of significant concern to the corporate establishment.

Virtually unanimously, and with one voice, the mass media condemned Dr King's opposition to the war. In the shadows were the forces they serve.

When one understands this context and those times, more than three decades ago, it is understandable that when Martin King began to crusade against the war, he would cast a long shadow over the economic forces of

From *An Act of State: The Execution of Martin Luther King* (London: Verso Books, 2003), pp. 6–10.

America. Little wonder that they shuddered at the possibility that his efforts might result in the tap of the free-flowing profits being turned off. Should the American people come to demand an end to the war and should the war end, the losses were not something they could accept.

Perhaps it was for this reason alone that King had to be stopped.

If this was not reason enough Dr King gave these awesomely powerful forces another inducement to eliminate him. He had been wrestling with the problem of economic injustice for some time. It was, he said, one thing to gain the civil right to eat at a formerly segregated lunchroom counter but quite another to be able to pay the bill. This was the next and, in a capitalist society, an essential component of freedom and equality, and one which was the essence of the movement for social justice. The war had made things worse. Not only were a disproportionate number of blacks being sent 10,000 miles from home to serve as cannon fodder, but the cost of the war increasingly required that essential social services and programs in their communities be curtailed. The poor knew better than anyone that President Johnson's commitment to 'guns and butter' could not be fulfilled. In effect there was an undeclared cease in the 'war on poverty.'

So, for Martin King, opposition to the war against the people of a poor, non-white ancient culture was in harmony with, and a natural extension of, the civil rights struggle against oppression and the denial of basic freedoms and essential services at home.

By mid-1967, he began to formulate a strategy to address the widening gap between the rich and the poor. The project gradually took the form not of a march by itself but the extensive Poor People's Campaign and mobilization culminating in an encampment in the shadow of the Washington Memorial. The projection was for the establishment of a tent city of some 500,000 of the nation's poorest and most alienated citizens, who would regularly lobby their elective officials for a range of socio-economic legislation. They would remain as long as it took to get action from the Congress.

If the wealthy, powerful interests across the nation would find Dr King's escalating activity against the war intolerable, his planned mobilization of half a million poor people with the intention of laying siege to Congress could only engender outrage – and fear.

They knew that it was not going to be possible for the Congress to satisfy the demands of the multitude of poor, alienated Americans led by Dr King, and they believed that the growing frustration could well lead to violence. In such a situation with the unavailability of sufficient troops to control that mass of people, the capital could be overrun. Nothing less than a revolution might result. This possibility simply could not be allowed to materialize, and neither could Martin King's crusade against the war be permitted to continue.

When the National Conference for New Politics (NCNP) convention was held on Labor Day weekend, many of us believed that nothing less than the nation's rebirth was on the agenda. But a small, aggressive group had urged each arriving black delegate to join an obviously planned Black Caucus which at one point threatened to take Dr King hostage. He made a spirited speech, calling for unity and action, after which I had to arrange for him to leave the stage quickly under guard for his own safety. Black Caucus delegates voted en bloc. There were walkouts, hostilities, and splits. Though we didn't admit it at the time, the NCNP died as a political force that weekend. We had not realized the power of the forces ranged against us to divide the emerging coalition and to infiltrate and manipulate movement organizations.

Dr King stepped up his anti-war efforts and threw himself into developing the Poor People's Campaign which was scheduled to bring hundreds of thousands of the nation's poor blacks, Hispanics, whites, and intellectuals to Washington in the spring of 1968. He would, of course, not live to see it.

Since their plight was the very epitome of the condition of the wretched of America, Dr King lent his support to the Memphis sanitation workers' strike by predominantly black non-union workers. On March 18 1968 he addressed a meeting at the Mason Temple and called for a general work stoppage in Memphis. He agreed to return to lead a march and did so on March 28. Chaos descended, and the march was disrupted. Because he was determined to lead a peaceful march, it was rescheduled for April 5. He returned to Memphis on April 3, checking into room 306 at the Lorraine Motel. At 6:01 PM the next evening, he was shot dead on the motel balcony.

The FBI hunt led to fingerprints on a map of Atlanta found in a room in the city hired by a man calling himself Eric S. Galt. They matched those of a fugitive from a Missouri penitentiary – James Earl Ray. He fled to England, but eventually, on Saturday June 10, he was arrested at Heathrow Airport and extradited to the United States.

The case never came to trial because James Earl Ray entered a plea of guilty on Monday, March 10 1969. He was subsequently sentenced to 99 years in the state penitentiary. Within three days of arriving there, Ray had written to the court requesting that his guilty plea be set aside and that he be given a trial.

Any reservations I had about another lone-assassin explanation for the removal of a progressive leader were sublimated by the combined feelings of grief, sadness and disgust with all politics.

During the next nine years, I had virtually nothing to do with the civil rights and anti-war movements. I had no hope the nation could be reconstructed without Martin King's singular leadership. Then, in late 1977, Ralph Abernathy, who had succeeded Dr King as the President of Southern Christian Leadership Conference (SCLC) but had been replaced in 1976 by the Reverend Joseph Lowery, and who had been a close friend of Dr King, told me that he had never been completely satisfied with the official explanation of King's murder. He wanted a face-to-face meeting with the alleged assassin. Although I was surprised by his interest I told him that I had assumed that the right man was in prison and that I knew very little about the case. If I was to help him, I would need time to catch up on the facts.

In the absence of a trial, the prosecution's scenario had been put out to the world as the final word, bolstered by books written by publicists of the official story and media coverage. To the general public, Ray was a loner, motivated by race hate, who sought to make his mark in history.

The state claimed Ray began stalking Dr King on the weekend of March 17 in Los Angeles, arriving in Memphis on April 3 with the murder weapon and booking into a seedy rooming house above Jim's Grill. It had a bathroom overlooking the Lorraine Motel balcony, where Dr King was standing when he was killed. Ray, according to the state, locked himself in and fired the fatal shot.

Then, in haste, he neglected to eject the spent cartridge. Straight afterwards, he gathered up a few belongings from his room and ran down the front stairs, allegedly seen by rooming house tenant Charles Stephens who became the state's chief prosecution witness. Supposedly seeing a police car parked near the sidewalk of the fire station, Ray allegedly dropped the bundle in the recessed doorway of the Canipe Amusement Company on South Main before jumping into his white Mustang and heading for Atlanta, where he ditched the car. He then made his way to Canada. His prints were found on the gun, scope, binoculars, beer can, and copy of the Memphis *Commercial Appeal* dropped in the bundle.

During this period, the House Select Committee on Assassinations (HSCA) had been set up to investigate the murders of President Kennedy and Dr King. Following Ralph's request, I began to read everything I could about the killing. Meanwhile in early June 1977 after a failed escape attempt, James Earl Ray was returned to his cell at Brushy Mountain Penitentiary.

Finally, on October 17 1978, with Ralph Abernathy and a body language specialist in attendance, I met Ray. He told us he had been set up, his actions leading up to the assassination coordinated through a shadowy figure called Raul. He had met this man in the Neptune bar in Montreal in August 1967 while on the run, looking for a way to leave North America.

At the end of the interview, Abernathy and I agreed. Ray was not the shooter. As we left the prison, Ralph Abernathy told waiting journalists that Ray's answers to questions convinced him more than ever a conspiracy had led to Martin Luther King's death and Ray should get a trial. I was troubled by the discrepancy between the public image of James Earl Ray and the person we interviewed, as well as by the unanswered questions of which I became aware. The more I thought about the issues, the more concerned I became. I decided to quietly probe the official story. It was the beginning of a quest that was to last more than a quarter of a century and which would ultimately expose the dark underbelly of American government and the covert activities of its military and intelligence organizations and their fealty to corporate interests and organized crime.

Killing the Dream: James Earl Ray and the Assassination of Martin Luther King, Jr

Gerald L. Posner

. . .

There is no doubt that James Earl Ray shot and killed Martin Luther King, Jr. The more puzzling questions are what motivated him, and whether he acted alone or as part of a conspiracy. As for motivation in something as complex as a political murder, the shooter is often driven by several different factors, with no single one predominating. For instance, when Oswald killed John Kennedy, his radical political beliefs were part of the reason he shot at the president, but his primary incentive appears to have been his desire for glory, the almost psychotic craving of a nobody to suddenly become someone. With Ray, there is some of that same yearning for fame and acknowledgment, at least among his criminal peers – as seen in his oft-stated belief, even wish, that the FBI would place him on its ten most-wanted list. Certainly killing King would accomplish that in an instant. Ray relished that newfound notoriety, even taking the risk, while on the run, of visiting a local bar in Toronto in order to watch the popular television program *The F.B.I.* on the night he was placed at the top of the Bureau's most-wanted list. After his arrest, he constantly asked the policemen assigned to guard him about the publicity over the case and how he was portrayed in the press.

But fame alone does not explain why Ray killed King. Another reason was likely his demeaning and dismissive view of blacks. There are prominent incidents in Ray's life – from his refusal to be transferred to an integrated honor farm while in prison, to his bar fights with black sailors while in Mexico, to his repeated attempts to flee to segregationist Rhodesia after killing King – that demonstrate that he is a committed racist. His racism alone would have made it easier for him to murder Martin Luther King, Jr. After all, to Ray he would only be killing a black man in the South. Racists

From *Killing the Dream: James Earl Ray and the Assassination of Martin Luther King, Jr* (New York: Harcourt Brace, 1998), pp. 333–5, 337–9.

like him would think he was heroic. King was a troublemaker, thought Ray, and no one worthwhile would miss him.

However, his desire for notoriety, even combined with his racism, does not provide a complete and satisfactory answer to why he went to Mrs. Brewer's rooming house on April 4, 1968. Since Ray was a career criminal, driven primarily by the desire to make money, it would seem that he had to believe there was a profit in killing King. Ray's love of quick money, mixed with the racism with which he was raised, was a combustible blend in the volatile political and social climate of the late 1960s.

That he was driven primarily by money does not necessarily mean that he was hired to commit the crime. He might well have learned about a bounty on King, especially the $50,000 offer from St. Louis, and thought he could collect it by committing the murder.

Although Ray had previously bragged to other convicts, and to his brothers, that he might one day kill King, he does not appear to have become serious about those threats until after his December 1967 trip to New Orleans. Following his return to Los Angeles, he took certain actions – having plastic surgery and sending out photos of himself that might create confusion in case of a large manhunt – that appear to be precautions a professional criminal would undertake in preparing for a major crime.

As for a conspiracy, there are several persuasive arguments against Ray's having been brought into an elaborate plot. The crime did not take place for another three and a half months after his visit to New Orleans, during which Ray returned to a leisurely lifestyle in Los Angeles; no plotter could afford to let him in on such a high-profile crime months in advance of the operation. Also, while some conspiracists have speculated that racist Southern businessmen contracted with the New Orleans mob to kill King, it would be an unprecedented assignment for organized crime. Professor Robert Blakey, the Select Committee's chief counsel, as well as the author of the key crime-fighting tool against the mob, RICO (Racketeer Influenced and Corrupt Organizations Act), told the author, 'It would not at all be a characteristic of the mob. Except for the CIA/mob effort on Castro, I know of no single instance in which they ever took an assignment from outsiders to kill someone else. It's not what they do. They are a parasite on the body politic and they do not survive by killing the hand that feeds it. [Carlos] Marcello was clearly a racist, but he would not take the assignment because it was not what he did for business, and it involved far too many potential risks.'

There is also the perplexing question of why anyone with a substantial contract on King would hire Ray, a person who had no reputation for killing, and had never demonstrated he had the capability or nerve to carry out such an assignment. A professional hit man would surely have been hired.

However, if the St. Louis offer of $50,000 to kill King became known to John and Jerry Ray – which, despite their adamant denials, appears possible – a plan to collect the bounty could have been set in motion. A Orleans rendezvous could have been a chance for one of the brothers to pass the idea on to James. Fifty thousand dollars was a lot of money, and certainly worth considering, even if they were not ready to commit murder.

If there was ultimately a conspiracy behind King's death, a crude family plot seems more likely than a sophisticated operation involving the mafia or some government agency. That James Earl Ray has lived thirty years after the murder is persuasive evidence that professional conspirators were not involved, since if they had been, they would have disposed of him. They could never be safe so long as Ray lived, and he would have little incentive not to turn them in to authorities in order to win his own coveted freedom. However, if the conspirators included family members – a charge that all Ray's relatives have persistently denied – then he would have an incentive to stay silent. The special bond among the Rays would prevent James from turning in the only people he ever trusted.

The ultimate answers, of course, reside with Ray. He has not helped resolve the crime's mysteries but instead has relished adding confusion and controversy by maintaining steadfast silence on some matters while giving often changing stories about others. He obviously wants to take his secrets to the grave. But he has failed. Whether he acted with the foreknowledge or assistance of his brothers, or whether he was offered money before the murder or merely had heard about an offer and acted on his own, James Earl Ray is the reason that Martin Luther King, Jr., is dead. A four-time loser looking for a big score killed the dreamer, and put himself in the history books.

A Final Analysis: Author's Note Written for This Edition

Gerald L. Posner

. . .

On April 23, 1998, three weeks after the publication of the hardcover book, James Earl Ray died in a Tennessee prison of liver failure at the age of 70. There was no death bed confession, no indication he was burdened by his conscience and had decided to free the King family and many concerned Americans from the web of deceit he had spun over the decades. Rather, Ray passed defiantly, protesting to the very end that he was merely a patsy in a convoluted conspiracy led by someone he knew only by the name Raoul. Ray also died with the satisfaction that during the last year of his life he had pulled one of the grandest cons of his long criminal career – he had duped the King family into publicly endorsing his innocence.

There was never any question that the Kings had their hearts in the right place as they searched for absolute answers in the assassination. In the years following the murder, they had learned the shocking details of J. Edgar Hoover's obsessive war against Dr. King and were therefore legitimately suspicious that the government might have been involved in the killing. Into this setting entered Ray and his last lawyer, William Pepper, who presented the Kings with purported new witnesses and evidence, persuading them that the assassination was a massive plot that ran all the way up to Lyndon Johnson. This was a tragic turn of events since the Kings accepted the Ray team's evidence without aggressively investigating it.

Once convinced of a gigantic conspiracy, they dug in their heels, and did not want to consider other answers. Although I sent copies of this book to several family members, they refused to read it. They boycotted shows on which I appeared. King family associates attacked me publicly while also refusing to read the book. While this book covers most of Ray's 'new' evidence in detail – and reveals it to be bogus – Coretta Scott King and her son, Dexter, instead asked President Clinton to establish a new, full inquiry into the case. To their disappointment, the Justice Department finally agreed to only a limited investigation.

While Ray's death prompted the Kings to accelerate their effort at obtaining a new murder inquiry, the Ray brothers – Jerry and John – fell back to old habits and started to think of ways to profit from the turn of events. Jerry (who alternately referred to me in widely distributed letters as an 'FBI pimp' or a 'slimeball.' and once caused the police to be called at one of my book signings he disrupted in Memphis) bragged about an 'explosive' book he intended to write. He also unsuccessfully lobbied the District Attorney General in Memphis to release to him the murder weapon and other personal items belonging to James, all of which could fetch high prices on the auction block. Although Jerry had spent some ten years working with the arch-racist and convicted church bomber, J. B. Stoner, and himself had written heatedly about 'Nigger beasts,' he continued his calculated campaign to become an ally of the Kings. Not only did he brag about Dexter King's embrace of him before James's death, but at the memorial service for James, Jerry sat next to Isaac Farris, Jr., a nephew of Dr. King who represented the King family. 'They are not a dumb family,' Jerry Ray told me. 'They know what really happened.'

As for John Ray, who had remained silent for years about the assassination, he announced four months after James's death that he would 'solve the whole case' if the government gave him a 'six-figure' payoff. Nobody took up his offer.

The results of the latest Justice Department investigation are not expected until sometime in 1999, and most observers, including this author, expect that none of the so-called new evidence will amount to anything substantive. This will leave the King family, and many others who share their opinions, unsatisfied.

However, if those convinced of a widespread plot are willing to approach this murder with an open mind, there can be closure. After thirty years, there is ample credible evidence to determine who shot Dr. King, and what the most likely reasons were for the murder. Two separate events took place in the late 1960s. On the one hand, the government waged an illegal war against Dr. King. Its purpose was to ruin his reputation and career and leave him without honor in his own community. At the same time, a racist named James Earl Ray, almost certainly motivated by the lure of big money, and possibly helped by a small conspiracy of like-minded bigots, moved toward killing King. I have little doubt that some government officials celebrated King's death and would have pinned a medal on Ray. But my investigation shows the government was not behind Ray.

While it may not have pulled the trigger, the government did however, by such outrageous conduct, create an atmosphere where racists thought it was safe to shoot a black leader in the South and think they could get away with it. To that extent, the government bears moral responsibility for the death of Dr. King. But the ultimate responsibility – for the sake of justice and history – must be placed squarely on the man with blood on his hands, James Earl Ray. To say otherwise, in light of the overwhelming evidence of his guilt, is to let Ray have the final laugh, and to mock the great memory of Dr. King.

'Racial Matters': The FBI's Secret File on Black America, 1960–1972

Kenneth O'Reilly

. . .

The FBI's domestic political intelligence activities clearly centered on Dr King. 'King is no good,' as Hoover put it back in February 1962. The ferocity of the Bureau's pursuit does suggest a vendetta, an overreaction to a new and potent social force. But King's targeting was quite rational. He was the available man, the most well-known, effective, and charismatic civil rights leader. After the March on Washington, King and the movement were inseparable in the public mind. If King could be damaged, the movement could be damaged. King was vulnerable to a subversion charge, FBI

From *'Racial Matters': The FBI's Secret File on Black America, 1960–1972* (New York: The Free Press, 1989), pp. 125–55.

officials reasoned, because of his associations with [Stanley] Levison, [Jack] O'Dell, and others. Beyond that, as the FBI discovered first through the wire-tapping of Clarence Jones's telephone, King's personal life made him vulnerable on another front. The ease with which the FBI slid from the communist issue to the morality issue indicates that the director and his aides were looking for something – anything – that might work to discredit King. It also paralleled the typical racist belief in the sexual prowess of the black male and the threat to white society that posed. Hoover's fears were deeply personal.

No matter how promising, the FBI drew a blank on the Levison-Moscow connection – despite 'electronic surveillances on Levison dating back to 1954' and forward to the first of the Nixon years, and at least twenty-nine entries (burglaries) into Levison's business office in New York between 1954 and 1964. The Jones tap and then the bugs in King's hotel and motel rooms, however, provided another connection to exploit. If King could not be ruined by publicity charging him with subversion, perhaps he could be ruined with publicity charging him with adultery. 'Hoover was a strict Presbyterian-brought-up individual,' Crime Records Division agent Lawrence Heim said. 'If the Ten Commandments said 'Thou Shalt Not Covet Thy Neighbor's Wife,' that meant [exactly that].' Years later, after the tragedy in Memphis, the director initially suspected that King's assassin had been a vengeful husband.

Hoover dreamed of destroying Dr King and replacing him with 'a manageable black leader,' another former Crime Records agent, Harold Leinbaugh, said. And a few of the more confident FBI officials, William Sullivan included, tried to find one. In January 1964, when Sullivan proposed to remove King from his pedestal, he suggested that the Bureau replace King with the 'right kind' of black leader. John F. Malone, the FBI's man in New York, nominated [NAACP Executive Secretary] Roy Wilkins. Division Five agents also favored Wilkins ('a man of character'), but in this instance Sullivan overruled his men – offering instead Samuel R. Pierce, Jr., a talented, conservative attorney who joined the Ronald Reagan cabinet seventeen years later as secretary of housing and urban development. Both men, Wilkins and Pierce, were unaware of the plans of their Bureau cheerleaders.

The FBI campaign to take King off his pedestal went on and on, finally cresting in the late fall and early winter of 1964. Upon learning on October 14 that King would receive the Nobel Peace Prize, Hoover sent a flood of reports to the White House, the Department of Justice, the State Department, the US Information Agency, and American embassies across Europe concerning King's character. Then, during a November 18 meeting with a group of women reporters, the director labeled King 'the most notorious liar in the country.' [Cartha] DeLoach passed Hoover three notes asking him to retract the statement or at least request the reporters to consider it off-the-record, but the director threw each note in the trash and finally told the assistant director to mind his own business. Needless to say, the notorious-liar quote was the one item that stuck out during Hoover's three-hour oration. 'The girls,' DeLoach noticed, 'could hardly wait to leave to get to the telephone.' King learned of the remark while vacationing in Bimini, and he responded in kind, labeling his sixty-nine-year-old adversary senile and expressing his 'sympathy for this man who served his country so well.'

Hoover's specific reference in calling Dr King a liar was a year-old statement the civil rights leader had made to the *New York Times*. A reporter asked King if he agreed with a report on the Albany, Georgia, protests prepared by the historian Howard Zinn for the Southern Regional Council. One of the statements in the report charged FBI agents assigned to civil rights cases in the South with racism, and King said he agreed with Zinn. Too many agents were 'white Southerners who have been influenced by the mores of the community.' Southern agents were 'friendly with the local police and people who are promoting segregation,' he added. 'Every time I saw FBI men in Albany, they were with the local police force.'

This was a serious charge. It could not be answered with a file check on Howard Zinn or explanations about how blacks considered black agents 'finks' because they worked in law enforcement. Hoover ignored the racism issue, concentrating instead on the accuracy of King's statement – specifically, the notion that all agents assigned to the Albany office were southerners. Only one was a native southerner. The other four were from New York, Indiana, Minnesota, and Massachusetts. If wrong on the specific question, King was quite correct on the larger issue. Calling him a liar was not 'simply a matter of calling a spade a spade,' as DeLoach, in an incredible choice of words, told CORE's Val Coleman. Any FBI agent assigned to the Deep South would have to confront his own 'psychological needs,' Albany movement attorney C. B. King said. 'He wants social approbation. He wants his wife to be accepted as the wife of a regular fellow in this community. He wants her to have friends to be invited to dinner. And the only people who are relevant to him are white people.' In the end, the agent would likely be a reformed Yankee, just another 'local redneck with an FBI tag.'

Many of the FBI's agents supported civil rights, Bayard Rustin said, but the executives in Washington did not send in 'flaming liberals. By and large they did what they could to send in people who were not going to be helpful.' The one native southerner assigned to the Albany FBI office, Marion Cheek, whose family had once owned a large piece of land in DeKalb County, just north of Atlanta, land that Sherman's troopers had once camped on and tore up, found himself at the center of the entire controversy. Arthur Murtagh, the Atlanta agent who sometimes worked out of the Albany office and whose waistline exceeded Hoover's notion of what the proper girth of a G-man should be, said he considered Cheek 'a friend, but on the question of race I could not discern much difference between his view and the view of the Ku Klux Klansmen that I would have occasion to interview from time to time.' Hoover spoke to Cheek only once in Cheek's twenty-six-year Bureau career, to advise him that Martin Luther King was trying to 'get you transferred out of there.'

Division Five responded aggressively as Hoover's mostly one-sided feud with King moved into the public realm after the March on Washington. The Division had the FBI lab make a composite tape of the 'highlights' of the various microphone surveillances (mostly 'dirty jokes and bawdy remarks . . . plus the sounds of people engaging in sex' in King's room at Washington's Willard Hotel), and in November 1964 William Sullivan himself drafted a ghastly note recommending suicide as a way out:

> King, look into your heart. You know you are a complete fraud and a great liability to all of us Negroes. . . . King, like all frauds your end is approaching. You could have been our greatest leader. . . . But you are done. . . . No person can overcome facts. . . . The American public, the church organizations that have been helping – Protestant, Catholic and Jews will know you for what you are . . . So will others who have backed you. You are done . . . there is only one thing left for you to do. You know what this is. You have just 34 days in which to do (this exact number has been selected for a specific reason, it has definite practical significant [sic]). You are done. There is but one way out for you. You better take it before your filthy, abnormal fraudulent self is bared to the nation.

On November 21, thirty-four days before Christmas, Sullivan put the tape and letter in an unmarked package, gave the package to one of his agents, Lish Whitson, and instructed him to fly to Miami. Once in Miami, Whitson called headquarters, and Sullivan (or one of his men) told him to address and mail the package to the SCLC office in Atlanta.

Three days later, on November 24, Hoover again went public with his attack on King, with an indirect reference in a speech at Loyola University in Chicago to 'pressure groups' headed by 'Communists and moral degenerates.' In the meantime, DeLoach offered a copy of a King microphone surveillance transcript to Benjamin Bradlee, *Newsweek* Washington bureau chief. When Burke Marshall and Nicholas Katzenbach learned of this, they asked President Johnson to look into the matter. Johnson did so by warning the FBI about Bradlee. He was unreliable, the president said, and was telling the story all over Washington.

These and other FBI efforts to smear Martin Luther King led to a series of meetings between Bureau officials and various civil rights leaders intent on making peace. Roy Wilkins approached Cartha DeLoach first, shortly after the director's Loyola speech. According to the assistant director, however, Wilkins was on the Bureau's side and willing to assist in the planned removal of 'King from the national picture.'

> I told [Wilkins] that the Director, of course, did not have in mind the destruction of the civil rights movement as a whole . . . [but] if King wanted war we certainly would give it to him. Wilkins shook his head and stated there was no doubt in his mind as to which side would lose if the FBI really came out with all its ammunition against King. I told him the ammunition was plentiful and that while we were not responsible for the many rumors being initiated against King, we had heard of these rumors and were certainly in a position to substantiate them.

'The monkey was on his back and that of the other Negro leaders,' DeLoach reiterated. Wilkins promised to 'tell King that he can't win in a battle with the FBI,' that 'the best thing for him to do is to retire from public life.' With that comment, the meeting concluded. Not surprisingly, Wilkins described DeLoach's account of what was said at their meeting as 'self-serving and filled with inaccuracies.' Hoover passed along that account, nonetheless, to President Johnson.

Wilkins's assessment of what actually transpired in his meeting with DeLoach is no doubt closer to the truth. Indeed, Hoover abruptly (if briefly) cut off Wilkins a few months later. 'I don't want anything given to [him] . . . in view of [his] visit to the President demanding my dismissal because of what I had to say re King.' Edwin Guthman, who went back to his office and typed up a memo for the files after every one of his meetings with DeLoach, had the opportunity to compare his recollections with the assistant director's several years later. 'It was like we were at two different meetings,' he said. Even within the Bureau, neither field agents nor his fellow executives completely trusted DeLoach. 'Many FBI colleagues observed that [he] seemed to fulfill the role of a son to Hoover,' Sanford Ungar wrote. 'Others thought it was more like a hatchet man.' In either case, Hoover trusted DeLoach absolutely. Born poor in Claxton, Georgia, DeLoach had been with the FBI since 1942, when he dropped out of the Stetson College School of Law in Florida to sign up, and since 1951 he had been under the director's wing at headquarters. In meeting with Wilkins, DeLoach did exactly what Hoover wanted him to do.

Another Big Six civil rights leader who had a close relationship with the FBI, [CORE National Director] James Farmer, met with DeLoach on December 1, in the back seat of a limousine while driving around Washington. According to DeLoach, the two men discussed 'warfare' between Hoover and King. 'I told him that if this war continued that we, out of necessity, must defend ourselves. . . . Farmer got the point without any difficulty whatsoever. He immediately assured me that there would be no further criticism from him. He stated he felt certain there would be no further criticism from King.' Farmer also disputed DeLoach's recollection. He did not remember DeLoach saying anything about 'warfare,' and he did not make any commitment to stop sniping at the FBI. Farmer said he knew what DeLoach and Hoover were up to. 'They wanted to isolate King.'

Later in the day, Martin Luther King himself, accompanied by Ralph Abernathy, Andrew Young, and Walter Fauntroy, met with Hoover and the ever-present DeLoach. The civil rights leaders discovered what everyone who had ever been in the same room with the director already knew – as Robert Kennedy once put it, 'You know, he talks a hell of a lot, J. Edgar Hoover.' When King did say something, the director maintained, it was generally 'laudatory about the Bureau's work.' DeLoach described the meeting as 'a love feast,' and for once the civil rights leaders agreed with him. 'You would have thought you were watching a mutual admiration society,' Young said, calling it 'a completely nonfunctional meeting.'

While Hoover and DeLoach met with King and the other civil rights leaders, William Sullivan planned the secret convening of a group of prominent black leaders – Roy Wilkins and two or three other movement leaders (Farmer and Randolph), 'top Negro judges' (James B. Parsons and William Henry Hastie), 'top reputable ministers' (Robert Johnson of the Washington City Presbytery), and 'other selected Negro officials from public life such as the Negro Attorney General from one of the New England states.' Division Five intended to enlist these men in the campaign to topple King and to promote 'the stature of Roy Wilkins.' The group could learn 'the facts' about the FBI's many civil rights accomplishments, the truth about King's sexual and political transgressions. While trying to make the necessary arrangements, Division Five blackballed Carl Rowan, director of the US Information Agency, and Ralph Bunche, undersecretary-general of the United Nations, on the grounds that 'they might feel a duty to advise the White House of such a contemplated meeting.' In this case, the proposal was simply too incredible. The meeting with 'reputable Negroes' never happened.

William Sullivan's Division Five and Cartha DeLoach's Crime Records Division remained active on other fronts and they sometimes acted in concert. They wanted to be certain King's rivals in the civil rights movement had the facts, so DeLoach offered the microphone recordings that Sullivan's agents had compiled to various civil rights leaders. C. Sumner Stone, Jr, editor of the *Chicago Defender* and later in the year a special assistant to New York Congressman Adam Clayton Powell, Jr, said a fair number of movement people 'claimed to have heard the tapes. Whitney Young heard them. Roy Wilkins heard them.' And of course King himself heard them. The Division Five package mailed on November 24 had sat in the SCLC office in Atlanta until January 5, when Coretta King stumbled over it. She listened to a brief portion ('just a lot of mumbo jumbo'), read the accompanying letter, and then called her husband, who had returned from Oslo only the week before. A Nobel laureate to the world, to the FBI, in Sullivan's words, King was 'a dissolute, abnormal moral imbecile,' 'an evil, abnormal beast.'

FBI interest in Martin Luther King's private life was not unprecedented. Some of the older movement people had a clear sense of *déjà vu*. What Jesse Jackson called the director's 'Peeping Tomism,' his 'sick interest of the white male in black sexuality,' was arguably present in his predecessors as well. (Heavyweight boxing champion Jack Johnson had his troubles with the FBI and 'the Mann' in 1912.) In December 1964, only a few days after he met with King, Hoover told *US News and World Report* publisher David Lawrence that the White Slave Traffic Act was 'supposed to protect the virtue of womanhood.' His interest in interracial sex and the morality of individual black activists was nothing if not consistent. The old General Intelligence Division of 1919 focused on the specter of miscegenation, but so did the Domestic Intelligence Division of 1953. 'It is interesting to note that one of [the Communist party's] "concrete demands" . . . advocated "the removal of all legal restrictions and social censorship of intermarriage in the Southern States." ' For the director, interracial sex, extramarital sex, premarital sex, homosexuality, bisexuality, and sexual deviancy was all something that could be used to discredit political adversaries. And it was something to which Martin Luther King – and in a broader sense the civil rights movement as a whole during the 1960s – appeared to be particularly vulnerable.

FBI interest in Dr King as 'the "top alley cat"' accompanied a parallel interest in the sex lives of virtually anyone interested in the subject of racial justice. New York agents tried to find out who the Communist party's top black functionaries were 'carrying on' with, while Washington agents worked up a memo on a Civil Rights Division attorney who had gone off on an interracial date. Division Five investigated 'the moral character' of Andrew Young and Jesse Jackson and looked into a rumor about Stanley Levison 'having a paramour.' In the meantime, Hoover discussed the 'immoral conditions' within the black family with the ubiquitous David Lawrence, told the House Appropriations Subcommittee that Bayard Rustin (who was in fact homosexual) had once been 'convicted for sodomy,' and flooded the White House with memos concerning the 'personal behavior' of Community Relations Service workers. 'He spread garbage about us,' Roger Wilkins charged, 'and he spread garbage about everybody in the civil rights movement.'

Having documented 'the depraved nature and moral looseness' of Dr King and other black activists, FBI officials' attempts to use the information uncovered met with little success. Sumner Stone said 'Hoover was a real prude – he misjudged the morality of the average American.' When DeLoach offered transcripts based on the King buggings to a variety of newspaper reporters, columnists, and editors, nobody accepted the offer. Jim Bishop of the Hearst chain even claimed to have seen photographs, snapped by the FBI 'through a one-way mirror,' of King chasing 'White women . . . in motel rooms.' 'The old man,' Bishop concluded, 'saw the preacher as a buffoon' and 'could barely mention the name without bubbling at the lips.'

Hoover could not even convince the Catholics to do anything. The Chicago archdiocese published a pamphlet describing King as being 'like Jesus,' and Marquette University, a Jesuit school, invited him to receive an honorary degree. (Since World War II the FBI recruited heavily at Jesuit schools, and by the 1960s Protestant agents considered themselves a distinct minority, members of a 'PU' – a Protestant underground.) In this last case the FBI claimed to have convinced a source at Marquette that King was unworthy, and King did not receive the degree – but the excuse was that he was unable to attend the ceremonies and Marquette had a policy against awarding honorary degrees in absentia. The FBI agent who approached University officials, nonetheless, received a monetary award from his superiors. All this was quite minor compared to King's plans to meet with the Pope. That audience had to be 'nipped in the bud,' so the director sent New York SAC John Malone off to brief Francis Cardinal Spellman and to have Spellman alert the Vatican. 'Hoover always . . . kept a Cardinal in the background,' Harold Leinbaugh remembered, and Malone said the King matter had been handled. But it did not do any good. 'I am amazed that the Pope gave an audience to such a degenerate,' Hoover responded, upon discovering that Malone and Spellman had failed.

Hoover's obsession with the sexual habits of Martin Luther King and other civil rights activists posed an irony. The suspicion that the director himself was homosexual followed him for most of his career. Not even the FBI's own agents were quite sure about Hoover, a result of his 'strange relationship' with Clyde Tolson, his second in command, with whom he took all his meals and vacationed over a period of thirty years. 'I don't think anybody really knows,' Leinbaugh concluded.

Notes

1. James F. Bland to William C. Sullivan, 3 February 1962, no. 135, Stanley Levison File, Federal Bureau of Investigation Files (collection hereinafter cited as FBI Files). The FBI Files include Freedom of Information Act and other releases, including partial releases.
2. Director to Assistant Attorney General, 18 December 1975, no. X65, File 62–117166; Director to Attorney General, 1 October, 1969, no. 353, FBI–Stanley Levison File.
3. Lawrence J. Heim, interview with author, 23 July 1986; James Alonzo Bishop, *The Days of Martin Luther King* (New York: G. P. Putnam's Sons, 1971), p. 83.

4. Special Agent in Charge (SAC) New York to Director, 14 October 1963, no. 34–502, FBI–Counterintelligence Program, Communist Party of the United States File (hereinafter cited as FBI–COINTEL (CPUSA) File); Victor Navasky, 'The FBI's Wildest Dream', *The Nation*, 17 June 1978, pp. 716–18; Harold P. Leinbaugh, interview with author, 24 July 1986.

5. Statement, re. J. Edgar Hoover, 19 November 1964, Box 27.41, Southern Christian Leadership Conference Papers, King Center, Atlanta, GA; US Congress Senate Select Committee to Study Governmental Operations with Respect to Intelligence Activities, *Final Report – Book III, Supplementary Detailed Staff Reports on Intelligence Activities and the Rights of Americans*, 94th Cong., 2d sess., 1976, 162 (hereinafter cited as US Congress, *Final Report – Book III*); David J. Garrow, *The FBI and Martin Luther King, Jr.: From 'SOLO' to Memphis* (New York: W.W. Norton, 1981), pp. 122–3.

6. Garrow, *FBI and Martin Luther King*, pp. 54–5; Howard Zinn, *Albany* (Atlanta, GA: Southern Regional Council, 1962). King had been on record as a critic since 4 February 1961.

7. Hoover had monitored the percentage of southern-born agents assigned to civil rights cases since the mid-1950s.

8. Cartha D. DeLoach to John P. Mohr, 19 November 1964, number not recorded, FBI–Martin Luther King, Jr. File; Victor Navasky, *Kennedy Justice* (New York: Atheneum, 1971), p.122.

9. Marion E. Cheek, interview with author, 2 July 1986 (phone); US Congress House Select Committee on Intelligence, *Hearings on Domestic Intelligence Programs*, Pt 3, 94th Cong., 1st sess., 1975, 1047; US Congress House Select Committee on Assassinations, *Hearings on Investigation of the Assassination of Martin Luther King, Jr.*, vol. 6, 95th Cong., 2d sess., 1978, 92–6; Bayard Rustin, interview with author, 22 January 1987 (phone, New York).

10. Garrow, *FBI and Martin Luther King*, pp. 125–6, 133–4; David J. Garrow, *Bearing the Cross: Martin Luther King, Jr. and the Southern Christian Leadership Conference* (New York: William Morrow, 1986), pp. 373–4.

11. US Congress, *Final Report – Book III*; Garrow, *FBI and Martin Luther King*, p 127

12. DeLoach to Mohr, 27 November 1964, no. 16, and Hoover to the President, 30 November 1964, no. 15, FBI Roy Wilkins File; US Congress, *Final Report –Book III*, pp. 162–3, US Congress Senate Select Committee to Study Governmental Operations with Respect to Intelligence Activities, *Hearings –Federal Bureau of Investigation*, vol. 6., 94th Cong., 1st sess., 1975, 172; Garrow, *Bearing the Cross*, pp. 687–8; Garrow, *FBI and Martin Luther King*, p. 271.

13. Edwin O. Guthman, interview with author, 14 January 1987 (phone, Philadelphia, PA); Sanford J. Ungar, *FBI* (Boston: Little, Brown, 1975), p. 281; Fred J. Baumgardner to Sullivan, 15 February, 1965, no. 312, and 5 March 1965, no. 319, FBI–COINTEL (CPUSA) File.

14. Ungar, *FBI*, pp. 279–95; Athan Theoharris, *The Boss: J. Edgar Hoover and the Great American Inquisition* (Philadelphia: Temple University Press, 1988), p. 105.

15. US Congress, *Final Report – Book III*, 168–71; James Farmer, *Lay Bare the Heart: An Autobiography of the Civil Rights Movement* (New York: Arbor House, 1985).

16. Leon Howell, 'An Interview with Andrew Young', *Christianity and Crisis*, 16 February 1976, p.16; Robert F. Kennedy and Burke Marshall, interview by Anthony Lewis, 4, 6, and 22 December 1964, Robert F. Kennedy and Burke Marshall Oral Histories, John F. Kennedy Library, Boston, MA.; Hoover to Clyde Tolson, Alan H. Belmont, John P. Mohr, Cartha D. DeLoach, and Alex Rosen, 1 December 1964, no. 3, and DeLoach to Hoover, 2 December, 1964, no. 634, FBI – King File.

17. Joseph A. Sizzo to Sullivan, 1 December 1964, no. 3, King Folder, FBI – J. Edgar Hoover Official and Confidential Files. Carl T. Rowan and Ralph Bunche, nonetheless, received derogatory information on King from time to time.
18. C. Sumner Stone, Jr., interview with author, 29 August 1986 (phone, Philadelphia, PA); Garrow, *FBI and Martin Luther King*, pp. 125–6, 133–4; Garrow, *Bearing the Cross*, pp. 373–4. The King flap continued to occupy a good deal of the FBI's time. On 30 March, after Edwin C. Berry of the Urban League in Chicago criticized the director, SAC Marlin Johnson gave him a 90-minute going over in the chambers of federal judge James B. Parsons, a Bureau ally. Another Chicago resident, Rev. Archibald Carey, met with DeLoach in May in a futile attempt to end the King–Hoover feud. Afterward, Hoover gave DeLoach the ultimate accolade ('Well handled. H.'), though, in this case, it was a bit gratuitous. Carey had once named the director, along with the entire 'Jewish community', as one of the ten living whites who had done the most to help black America. D. C. Morrell to DeLoach, 31 March, 1965, number not recorded, FBI – National Urban League File; Archibald J. Carey, Jr., to [deleted] 3 March 1964, no. 27, and DeLoach to Mohr, 19 May 1965, no. 30, FBI – Archibald Carey File.
19. Hoover to Tolson, Mohr, and DeLoach, 8 December 1964, no. 127, FBI–David Lawrence File; Randy Roberts, *Papa Jack: Jack Johnson and the Era of White Hopes* (New York: Free Press, 1983); *Chicago Defender*, 11 and 15 August 1970.
20. Hoover's prurient interests extended beyond blacks. His old General Intelligence Division held a file on birth-control crusader Margaret Sanger; in the late 1930s his agents investigated several condom manufacturers on the grounds that their products were 'often found in the possession of high school students'; and throughout his 48-year tenure his senior staff remained on alert for "sex deviates" among the faculty and staff of his alma mater, George Washington University.
21. FBI Report, 'Communist Party and the Negro', 1953, p. 10.
22. Sexism within the movement should not be exaggerated, but it did exist – as evidenced by Stokely Carmichael's casual remark: 'The only position for women in SNCC is prone.'
23. Director to SAC New York, 11 May 1960, no. 1649, and Director to SAC Atlanta, 19 August 1964, number not recorded, FBI–COINTEL (CPUSA) File; Navasky, *Kennedy Justice*, 16; Hoover to Tolson, Mohr, and DeLoach, 8 December 1964, no. 127, FBI–David Lawrence File; Director to SAC New York, 25 August 1966, number not recorded, and Director to SAC New York, 14 September 1966, no. 1964, FBI–Stanley Levison File; US Congress House Committee on Appropriations, *Hearings*, 87th Cong., 1st sess. – 92d Cong., 1st sess., 1961–71 (1966), p. 296; Roger Wilkins, interview with author, 8 August 1986 (phone, Washington, DC); SAC Chicago to Director, 16 April 1968, no. 2116, FBI–SCLC File; US Department of Justice, *Report of the Department of Justice Task Force to Review the FBI Martin Luther King, Jr., Security and Assassination Investigations* (Washington, DC: Government Printing Office, 1977), p. 136.
24. Stone interview; Jim Bishop, *A Bishop's Confessions* (Boston: Little, Brown, 1981).
25. Leinbaugh interview; Baumgardner to Sullivan, 4 March 1964, no. 312, 31 August 1964, no. 450, 17 September 1964, no. 479, and UPI ticker, 9 November 1963, no. 264, FBI–Martin Luther King, Jr. File; Hoover to Tolson, 2 June 1967, number not recorded, FBI–Clyde Tolson Memo File; Garrow, *FBI and Martin Luther King*, p.121.
26. Leinbaugh interview.

10 Commemoration: The King Holiday and Street Naming

Introduction

Soon after King's 1968 assassination there were calls to create a paid federal holiday in his honour, which would grant him equal status with similarly honoured white American historical heroes such as Christopher Columbus and President George Washington. A long campaign, headed by African American Congressman John Conyers (Democrat, Michigan) with the backing of King's family, and especially King's widow Coretta Scott King, finally culminated in the passage of a Federal Holiday Bill in 1983. The first Martin Luther King, Jr Holiday was celebrated in 1986 on the third Monday of January.

The first selection by William H. Wiggins, Jr is taken from a book that looks at the larger question of African American emancipation celebrations, of which the King Holiday forms the latest chapter. Wiggins notes that African Americans have for many years struggled for national recognition of their history and achievements. For example, since 1858 African Americans in Massachusetts have celebrated Crispus Attucks Day, commemorating the first casualty of the American Revolution in the 1770 'Boston Massacre' (Attucks was a seaman of African and Native American descent). Since 1865 African Americans in Texas have celebrated 'Juneteenth' on 19 June to mark emancipation from slavery, a celebration that has spread to other states and to other countries. 'National Freedom Day' was the idea of former Pennsylvania slave and post-Reconstruction leader Major Richard Robert Wright, Sr, signed into law by President Harry S. Truman in 1948, a year after Wright's death. Celebrated on 1 February, the day marks President Abraham Lincoln's signing of the US Constitution's Thirteenth

Amendment that abolished slavery and it is dedicated to the ideals of American freedom for all. None of these days, however, is a paid federal holiday.

The struggle to have the King Holiday recognized as such revisited many of the controversies and debates covered elsewhere in this book. Opponents of the holiday – mostly white – charged that King was a man of violence and civil unrest rather than a man of non-violence, that he defied the law and the legal process, and that his alleged communist links made him unpatriotic and thus undeserving of national commemoration. They also argued that a federal holiday in King's honour would be too expensive, that it was too soon after his death to see if his legacy would stand the 'test of time', and that other African American historical figures would be more deserving of the accolade. When such arguments failed, opponents attempted to make the holiday a commemorative holiday rather than a paid federal holiday.

Even after the legislative victory, the struggle over the meaning of the King Holiday continued. President Ronald Reagan, who signed the bill into law, also refused to dismiss allegations about King being a communist sympathizer. Several southern states still allow a choice over whether to celebrate King or various Confederate Civil War heroes who opposed the abolition of slavery. Other states attempted to bypass King's name by terming the day something else instead. In Utah, for example, it was called 'Human Rights Day'. Not until 2000 did all states celebrate a 'Martin Luther King, Jr Holiday' as a paid holiday for all federal and state employees in one form or another. At a county level, Greenville County, South Carolina, was the last to succumb in 2006.

The King Holiday has not been the only site of struggle over King's commemoration. Whereas the struggle for a King Holiday was mainly (although not exclusively) a racialized debate between African American activists and white opponents, local forms of commemoration, such as naming streets after King, reveals that King's memory is not only contested between African Americans and whites but also within the African American community itself. This has been manifested in a number of ways. For example, there have been disagreements over whether to honour King or local and state figures symbolizing African American achievement. In some instances, this has been the result of ongoing ideological conflicts, whereby local African American communities believe that local leadership and efforts were in fact more important than King's national campaigns of protest. This revisits the SCLC/SNCC 'top-down' versus 'bottom-up' debate outlined in Chapter 2. In some cases there have been personality clashes involved. One of the most infamous examples of this was Chicago's Rev. Joseph H. Jackson, a former president of the African American National Baptist Convention and a long-time critic of King's, who changed the entrance to his church so that it would not bear King's name on the street address.

In the second selection, Derek H. Alderman deals with the phenomenon of street naming as a form of commemorating King. He frames the debate within the concept of 'scaling'. This operates at several levels. Firstly, there is the size of the street named after King. Alderman argues that how long or short, or wide or narrow, the street named after King is, directly relates to the scale and importance of community commemoration. The longer and wider the street, the greater the degree of accessibility and visibility it will have, and therefore the greater its commemorative impact. Secondly, there is the question of the prominence of the street and where it stands in the hierarchy of streets in a particular village, town or city. The more prominent the street, the more effective it will be as a marker of commemoration. This involves factors such as the amount of people who use the street, the exposure it has to the wider community and its overall visibility in day-to-day life.

Thirdly, there is the location of the street. Should it be in a poor or rundown neighbourhood or in a rich and affluent one? Should it run through a predominantly African American neighbourhood or a predominantly white neighbourhood? Should it reflect contemporary usage of the street or should it reflect the sites of key community struggles of the past? The symbolic relevance here is not always straightforward. If the street is in a poor and rundown neighbourhood – and given the increasingly racially separate nature of America's residential patterns and the correlation of race and poverty, it is more likely to be an African American neighbourhood – does it appropriately reflect King's concerns with the poor and his roots within the African American community, or does it further marginalize the poor, the African American community, and King? If it is located in an affluent – usually, but not exclusively white – neighbourhood, is it then divorced from the very people that King represents and who would most be interested in commemorating him?

The struggle to commemorate King demonstrates precisely why ongoing controversies and debates, both scholarly and popular, remain relevant today. They form part of an ongoing battle to determine the significance of King and the civil rights movement that simultaneously defines their historical legacy and situates their relevance in the context of America's present and future dialogue on race relations.

Questions for Discussion

1. Should the Martin Luther King, Jr Holiday be a paid national holiday?

2. Is street-naming a useful way of commemorating historical figures? What issues does it raise and why?

3. Can you think of other appropriate ways for national heroes to be commemorated, apart from holidays and street-naming? What advantages and disadvantages do they have?

4. Is King simply a 'race hero' or is his legacy relevant to all Americans – or indeed to all people?

Further Reading

Relatively little secondary material exists on the Martin Luther King, Jr Holiday. Apart from Wiggins's chapter, Mary C. Lewis, 'Origins: How the Holiday was Born', *American Visions* 1 (1986): 44–9 is a good starting point and Thomas J. Shields, 'The "Tip of the Iceberg" in a Southern Suburban County: The Fight for a Martin Luther King, Jr, Holiday', *Journal of Black Studies* 33 (2003): 499–519 looks at the local dimensions of the struggle to observe King's birthday in Henrico County, Virginia. The *Journal of Blacks in Higher Education* has monitored the observation of the King Holiday in successive articles on the subject: 'Colleges and Universities That Don't Observe the Martin Luther King, Jr Holiday', 19 (Spring 1998): 26–7; 'The Martin Luther King, Jr Holiday Remains Unobserved at Some Prestigious College Campuses', 27 (Spring 2000): 48–9; and 'Yale and Penn Sign on to Observe the Martin Luther King, Jr Holiday', 33 (Autumn 2001): 33–4. William J. Starosta, 'A National Holiday for Dr King: Qualitative Analysis of Arguments Carried in the *Washington Post* and *New York Times*', *Journal of Black Studies* 18 (March 1988): 358–78 examines the debates in two leading national newspapers. Clarence G. Williams (ed.), *Reflections of the Dream, 1975–1994: Twenty Years Celebrating the Life of Dr. Martin Luther King, Jr at the Massachusetts Institute of Technology* (Cambridge, MA: MIT Press, 1995) contains speeches delivered at MIT annual observances of King's birthday.

Several historians have written essays on the subject in popular magazines such as Robert Weisbrot, 'Celebrating Dr King's Birthday', *New Republic*, 30 January 1984: 10–16; David J. Garrow, 'The Helms Attack on King', *Southern Exposure* 12 (March–April 1984): 12–15; and Taylor Branch, 'Uneasy Holiday', *New Republic* 3 February 1986: 22–7.

Derek H. Alderman has written extensively on the subject of using King's name as a form of public commemoration, including: 'Creating a New Geography of Memory in the South: The (Re)Naming of Streets in Honor of Martin Luther King, Jr', *Southeastern Geographer* 36 (1996): 51–69; 'A Street Fit for a King: Naming Places and Commemoration in the American South', *Professional Geographer* 52 (2000): 672–84; 'School Names as Cultural Arenas: The Naming of US Public Schools after Martin

Luther King, Jr', *Urban Geography* 23 (2002): 601–26; 'Street Names as Memorial Arenas: The Reputational Politics of Commemorating Martin Luther King, Jr in a Georgia County', *Historical Geography* 30 (2002): 99–120. Jonathan Tilove, *Along Martin Luther King: Travels on Black America's Main Street* (New York: Random House, 2003) uses streets named after King as a basis for an exploration of African American life in the early twenty-first century. There are also a number of useful newspaper articles about the ongoing battles over King street naming: see, for example, Larry Copeland, 'Streets Named MLK at Crossroad', *USA Today*, 18–20 January 2002, 3A, and Abby Goodnough, 'Honor for Dr King Splits Florida City, and Faces Reversal', *New York Times*, 10 May 2004, 1A.

O Freedom! Afro-American Emancipation Celebrations

William H. Wiggins, Jr

. . .

Celebrations of Dr King's birth date have evolved in four stages. In the first stage the celebrations were primarily spontaneous and mostly informal affairs, such as the one attended by Dr L. Harold De Wolf, a former teacher of Dr King at Boston University. He testified: 'I was in the congregation of Ebenezer Baptist Church one Sunday morning when, at the close of an evangelistic service, his [Dr King's] father led in observing the birthday of the martyred leader. Patriotic songs were sung, and the procession to the nearby tomb was led by the bearer of an American flag.'[1]

In the second phase the celebrations became quasi-legal holidays in which Afro-American workers did not work and some black community businesses were closed in honor of Dr King's memory. Congressman John Conyers, Jr, gave this testimony on how the black auto workers in Detroit observe January 15th. 'I have been told by people in plant after plant in Detroit that on January 15th, if it is not in the bargaining contract, one does not come to work anyway. It is a holiday already.'[2] A Philadelphia business executive noted a similar trend among small businesses in his city. 'Recently, [an] increasing number of small businesses in the Philadelphia area where First Pennsylvania Corporation is headquartered have joined in memory of Dr King by closing their doors on January 15.'[3]

From *O Freedom! Afro-American Emancipation Celebrations* (Knoxville: University of Tennessee Press, 1987), pp. 134–51.

In the third stage the celebrations were granted legal sanction by some business or governmental institutions. Black union members have had some success securing Dr King's birthday as a paid legal holiday. An American Federation of State, County and Municipal Employees official testified that 'Since 1968, AFSCME International has established January 15th, Dr King's birthday, as a paid legal holiday and has encouraged AFSCME local unions and councils to seek inclusion of Dr King's birthday as a paid holiday in all contract negotiations.'[4] Likewise Ms Pat Brown, an Indianapolis public schoolteacher and chairperson of the NEA Black Caucus, testified: 'In our city teachers have negotiated a contract that will allow us to close down schools on Martin Luther King's birthday.'[5] Celebrants of Dr King's birthday, like celebrants of Juneteenth (Texas), Crispus Attucks Day (Massachusetts) and National Freedom Day (Pennsylvania), were also successful in getting an impressive number of state governments to recognize this date in some official way. Mrs Coretta Scott King testified: 'To get a complete appreciation of the official support for the legislation [Dr King holiday bill], we must take note of the fact that seventeen states, at least seventeen states, as well as the District of Columbia and the Virgin Islands now observe a day for Martin Luther King, Jr, as a legal, public holiday.'[6] These state observances include Pennsylvania's 'commemorative' day,[7] Virginia's celebrating Dr King's birthday on New Year's Day,[8] and South Carolina's optional holiday observance. Senator Strom Thurmond (R-S.C.) testified: 'In my State of South Carolina Martin Luther King, Jr's birthday is not [sic] observed as an optional holiday. The people in the state can observe his birthday, or Robert E. Lee's, whichever they prefer.'[9] Senator Thurmond's reluctant observance of Dr King's birthday contrasts sharply with this enthusiastic remembrance of Mr David Clarke, chairman of the [Washington] DC City Council, who recalled that when the District was granted home rule in 1975, a King holiday bill 'was the second bill that we passed, and I think that now we have established a traditional way to celebrate the day that should serve as a model for the rest of the nation.'[10]

The fourth stage in the holiday's evolution was the agitation for the passage of a federal holiday bill. The following resolution of the Coalition of Black Trade Unionists (CBTU) is representative of other resolutions sent to Washington by the United Auto Workers (UAW), the AFL-CIO, NEA, and other national labor unions. The CBTU's resolution concludes:

Whereas: His [Dr King's] commitment to Black citizens in his struggle for human right [sic], dignity, justice and freedom cost him his life. . .
Now, Therefore, Be It Resolved:
That this CBTU convention go on record urging national legislation be passed making Martin Luther King's birthday (January 15) national holiday.[11]

Because of this impressive groundswell of support, leaders of the Martin Luther King, Jr, holiday movement took the next step and began the long and tedious legislative process to get the bill signed into law. Congressman Conyers, a chief architect of the bill, cited this growing popular support for the King holiday bill during the first hearings held on the subject. He told the subcommittee:

> The support for the notion of making a public legal holiday of his birthday is one that can be measured by the increasing support that it receives every year. May I say to my colleagues on this subcommittee that I have received more mail as the originating sponsor of this bill than on any other legislative proposal. I had intended to bring over the six US mailbags of mail that have come to me in the form of letters and petitions since 1968. It is enormous.
> It still comes in. People are still writing, and asking, and I am sure that you and the members of this subcommittee have also received a great deal of mail and encouragement in this matter.[12]

Mrs King, another major organizer of the holiday-bill movement, mentioned yet another example of popular support from the American people for making her husband's birthday a national holiday. She told the subcommittee: 'In the days after my husband's assassination Congress was inundated with petitions calling for a holiday for Martin Luther King, Jr. I know, for example, that one radio station in Newark, New Jersey, collected over 250,000 signatures endorsing a national holiday in honor of Martin's life and work.'[13]

. . .

This thoughtful exchange over the relative merits of Emancipation Day and Martin Luther King, Jr, Day raised the curtain on eight years of congressional hearings on the Martin Luther King, Jr, Holiday Bill. During the debate in US Congress, House and Senate committee chambers were transformed into political stages on which an endless cast of witnesses attacked and defended this piece of legislation with all the acrimony, humor, restrictive reason, effusive eloquence, pathos, and theatrics of an accomplished road company. Heroes (a white Congressman who originally opposed the bill and later became one of its staunch defenders) and villains (a black Communist who gives strong testimony against the passage of the bill) that would stretch the credibility of any casting director performed a seemingly endless series of playlets based upon one or more of the following themes: violence, extravagance, history, and patriotism.

Opponents of the legislation, such as E. Stanley Rittenhouse, a legislative aide for the conservative Liberty Lobby, and Congressman Larry P. McDonald (D-Ga.), a right-wing Congressman, constantly launched diatribes based on this convoluted logic: Because his acts of civil disobedience often led to violence, Dr King was really an advocate of violence and not a man of nonviolence. Mr. Rittenhouse played to the conservative right-wing segment of the drama's audience:

> Mr Chairman [Senator Strom Thurmond], Liberty Lobby believes that S. 25 is a thoroughly bad piece of legislation. It would sanctify and justify a man who deliberately brought violence to American streets, a subversive who was called 'the most notorious liar in America' by J. Edgar Hoover – who was in a position to know – It is a very one-sided, racist legislation.[14]

Congressman McDonald stepped from the wings to second this notion that Dr King was a man of violence. 'Mr Chairman [Senator Edward M. Kennedy], I submit that Rev. Martin L. King, Jr, was not the caliber of person suitable to be made into a national hero . . . his teaching of contempt for the law and the legal process makes it most unsuitable for his anniversary to be made a national holiday.'[15]

Congressman McDonald was challenged by a Mr. Williams, an aide of Senator Birch Bayh (D-Ind.):

> *Mr Williams:* If there is a law that goes against those principles [life, liberty, and the pursuit of happiness], would you consider that a bad law?
> *Mr McDonald:* As determined by whom, individual? That would be anarchy.

And later:

> *Mr Williams:* Well, would you agree that laws that have as their intent segregating the American people on the basis of race, or religion, are bad laws?
> *Mr McDonald:* Well, I guess there is a great deal of consternation in our society today over the things such as affirmative action on the Bakke Case, and so forth, where one group is selectively penalized to the benefit of another group, and I think that type of thing has created turmoil.[16]

The holiday's $195 million price tag also spawned passionate debate among the drama's players. Liberty Lobbyist E. Stanley Rittenhouse, restating similar lines of such key actors as Senator Thurmond and Congressman McDonald, opposed the holiday bill on the grounds that 'it would be very costly to the citizens and taxpayers of America.'[17] Senator Bayh replied that the King holiday has a symbolic value which far exceeded its monetary cost:

The cost? What are the costs of a national holiday? Perhaps more rightly, what are the costs of not having a holiday? What are the costs of second-class citizenship? What are the costs of a little black boy or a little black girl or a little brown boy or a little brown girl not having the opportunity to share in a national holiday of some great leader that happens to look like them, to come from the same heritage that they came from?[18]

Mrs King's rebuttal was based upon the economic exploitation of slavery:

. . . it would be hard to imagine how American industry could have financed its expansion without the enormous pool of unpaid agricultural labor that was available until the Emancipation Proclamation in 1863. I am not asking for reparations to the black community. No amount of money can compensate for the brutal injustice of slavery in the United States. But, given the hundreds of years of economic sacrifice and involuntary servitude of American blacks, is it too much to ask that one paid holiday per year be set aside to honor the contributions of a black man who gave his life in an historic struggle for social decency?[19]

An attempt to make Dr King's birth date a commemorative holiday instead of a paid legal holiday was a subplot of these cost debates that drew a wide range of responses. Congressman William Dannemeyer (R-Calif.) and the Speaker of the House, the Honorable Tip O'Neill (D-Mass.) debated this issue:

Mr Dannemeyer: Mr Speaker, in December 1979, the House voted to a vote of 207 to 191 to honor the memory of Dr. Martin Luther King by observing the third Sunday in January as a day of prayer and remembrance. . .

My question to you is what do you think is the difference between making the day of remembrance a Sunday, which is a non-work day, as opposed to the sense of the proponents of a commemorative resolution is, to hold it on a workday.

What is the difference really?

Mr O'Neill: Oh, I think that there is a tremendous difference. You know, we have a Mother's Day, a Father's Day, an Uncle's Day, a Grandmother's Day. It is a day of remembrance.

Mr Dannemeyer: Mother's Day is on a Sunday, is it not?

Mr O'Neill: Yes, it is on Sunday. Other than Mother's Day, who adheres to those? Very few. Here is a man whose place is in history. His place is in history, because he changed America. . .

I think that a man of beauty, that a man of a minority race of this country – we have honored the great leaders. And he is a great leader that we should honor.

And I just feel that a Sunday of remembrance. There are so many Sunday remembrances. It is Cap Day in Boston for the Red Sox. That is a remembrance. Let us not put things in categories like that. Let us give this man the homage that is due his greatness. And that would be a national holiday.[20]

The question-and-answer session that followed this conversation produced two divergent responses to Congressman Dannemeyer's question. Congressman Mickey Leland (D-Tex.) improvised this cutting bit of sarcasm off of House Speaker O'Neill's reference to a baseball Cap Day not beginning to approach the significance of Dr King's holiday. Congressman Leland made the same point with this Super Bowl anecdote, whose bittersweet humor is reminiscent of jokes told by Juneteenth celebrants in his home state of Texas:

In the last session, one of my more conservative colleagues, who had a thread of sensitivity, I think, particularly for those of us who are black in the Congress, came to me and said:

'I think that I have the compromise worked out, I think that what we ought to do is put Dr King's celebration and memorial service on Super Bowl day when the Super Bowl is to be played.

That way, all Americans would be watching television, and even at the Super Bowl they could have some kind of demonstration to memorialize Dr King.'[21]

But Congressman Louis Stokes (D-Ohio) shunned Leland's technique of comic understatement, and instead delivered a passionate speech of opposition to the establishment of a mere commemorative holiday for Dr. King:

Various substitutes . . . have been proposed to recognize Dr King. These substitutes have included the placing of a statue or a bust of Dr Martin Luther King in the Capital, or designating some Sunday as his day of recognition. But the life that Dr King gave was not a substitute. It was not a facsimile thereof. It was the genuine thing: his own and his only life. I cannot accept therefore, Madame Chairwoman [Honorable Katie Hall, D-Ind.], a substitute tribute, an ersatz award, for this man who was true to humanity, true to the causes of freedom and justice, true to his commitment to nonviolence, true to his belief in the basic integrity of the American people, true to his dream.[22]

Opponents of the legislation also argued that it was too soon after the death of Dr. King to honor him; they argued that only the test of time would justify such an honor. The testimony of Mr Clifford J. White, III, the national director of Young Americans for Freedom, is an excellent example of similar testimonies given by Senator Thurmond, Congressman McDonald, and a host of other bit players in this tense American freedom drama. Mr White said:

> National holidays are important occasions for all Americans. When an individual is recognized – or rather almost canonized – through a national holiday in his honor, it is understood that the individual had a unique and indispensable impact on this Nation's history. So great a recognition is this that only Christopher Columbus and George Washington have in this way been honored. To so recognize Martin Luther King, a patriotic American to be sure, would be to classify him along with Washington – and above Lincoln, Jefferson and Adams. We would do this without the benefit of being able to put his memory under the test of time.[23]

Proponents of the legislation responded in a variety of ways. Congressman Leland once again drew spirited applause from Afro-American spectators when he lashed out with a justification of Dr King's greatness shared by many other Afro-Americans.

> . . . I would like to remind the gentleman [Congressman William Dannemeyer, R-Calif.] that Mr Lincoln advocated the freedom and the liberation of only those slaves that were held within the dissenting States, the Confederate States of this country, and not the liberation of all human beings, as did Dr Martin Luther King.
> That advocacy puts Dr King at least one step above Mr Lincoln in terms of our honoring him.[24]

While Reverend Joseph E. Lowery, president of the Southern Christian Leadership Conference argued that Dr King was as important an American figure as the Founding Fathers:

> *Dr Lowery:* While it is regrettably true that in our more than 200-year history, we have not so honored a black American, the designation of Dr King's birthday as a national holiday would transcend the issue of race and color.
> Martin Luther King's leadership gave all Americans, white, black, yellow, red, and brown, a new sense of worth and purpose . . .
> His leadership brought together a coalescence of communities and disciplines that demonstrated the unity in diversity that portends a

greatness unparalleled in nationhood – under God. If Columbus discovered America, Martin helped America discover itself.

If Washington established a Nation, Martin led the Nation to understand that there can be no nationhood without brotherhood.

His leadership personified the spirit of a people whose historic dedication to liberty caused them to tread the unknown, dare to do the dangerous, pioneer into the perilous – knowing that the reward of liberty is more precious than the price the struggle compels us to pay.

Willing to pay that price Martin Luther King, Jr, sought freedom for all God's children knowing that those who mind the chains that bind [others] are also bound.

Senator Kennedy: You are beginning to preach a little bit here.

Dr Lowery: Yes. I am about to take an offering. [*Laughter.*]

His leadership taught us that revolutionary change can occur within the context of nonviolence, when a people inspired and motivated by a sense of justice and the efficacy of love are so determined.

Yes, the designation of Dr King's birthday as a national holiday will do deserved honor to him, and will likewise honor the Nation and the family of man, and I respectfully urge and support its immediate implementation.[25]

Opponents of the legislation further argued that Dr King was not the Afro-American who most deserved to be honored with a national holiday. A subcommittee hearing dialogue between Senator Thurmond and Congressman McDonald typifies this line of reasoning:

Senator Thurmond: Congressman McDonald, I just have a few questions to propound to you.

Since you oppose the designation of another Federal legal holiday for Martin Luther King, Jr, do you think there are any other Americans who should be considered for such a legal holiday, if one is going to be named for Martin Luther King?

Mr McDonald: One would be George Washington Carver; the second would be Booker T. Washington, and I think the man would be shocked at the thought if he were here today – if he could be here today, he would certainly argue against it, but a man who pointed out that he could come from poverty in Florida, whose mother, I believe, ran a school so that he could gain some of the things of life. A family who, as Senator Bayh stated, clawed and worked its way up from poverty, from a poor background, was Gen. Chappy James, as you know, as a member of the Senate Armed Services Committee, passed away perhaps a year ago. I do not think we have had a more dedicated, finer American on the scene than Gen. Chappy James.[26]

Proponents of the legislation were quick to respond to these objections. Mr Williams leaped to interrogate Congressman McDonald on the issue.

> *Mr Williams:* . . . I would like to know, what is it that Booker T. Washington did that he could be considered instead of Martin Luther King, what were his characteristics; what was it about that man?
> *Mr McDonald:* I am glad you asked that question. As you know, he is the author of the book, *Up from Slavery*. He pointed out to the Negro Americans, to black Americans that, 'Yes, we have come up from slavery, the bottom level of the ladder, and we should not be, perhaps, so preoccupied with trying to become instant leaders. But we should gain knowledge of two four-letter words.' We live in a time when four-letter words are very popular among some segments of our society, but in the case of Booker T. Washington I think they were most apropos because he said the two words 'wash' – w-a-s-h – and 'work.' Intimating that you can be poor, but you can also be clean and work by standards of personal cleanliness, and also work to make yourselves productive citizens in the new land, and gain respect of your fellow members of the community. Out of that respect you will find that your children and their children will be able to move up to all levels of American society.[27]

Mrs King, on the other hand, managed to refute Congressman McDonald's arguments in this straightforward manner.

> It may be argued that throughout American history, there have been many black historical figures other than Martin who deserve to be honored with a holiday in their name – Crispus Attucks to Harriet Tubman to Booker T. Washington – to name just a few. But it should be remembered that previous black leaders necessarily addressed issues that tended to concern blacks exclusively, while Martin Luther King, Jr spoke to us all.[28]

But opponents of the legislation countered Mrs King's claim that Dr King's appeal was universal contending that Dr King was not a true patriot; in their eyes, he was at best a Communist sympathizer. Mr Rittenhouse testified: 'Enemies, enemies everywhere and not a patriot to be found around Martin Luther King, Jr. The fact is he aided the Communist cause; he abetted it constantly, continuously. Since when does a Nation honor a man who honored its enemy?'[29] Mr. Alan Stang, a 'professional journalist and writer,' asserted that 'Martin Luther King collaborated intimately with the Communists from the very beginning of his career to its end.'[30] While Ms Julia Brown, a black American who was a former member of the Communist Party, told Senator Thurmond: 'Mr Chairman, while

I was in the Communist Party as a loyal American Negro, I knew Martin Luther King to be closely connected with the Communist Party. If this measure is passed honoring Martin Luther King, we may as well take down the Stars and Stripes that fly over this building and replace it with a Red flag.'[31]

Supporters of the legislation did not let these accusations go unchallenged. Mr Karl Prussion, a former Communist and FBI double agent, was closely cross-examined by Mr David Boies, chief counsel and staff director of the Senate subcommittee, and Mr Williams, aide to Senator Birch Bayh, after he had given similar testimony. The former's cross-examination had all the tension of a courtroom drama.

> *Mr Boies:* Mr Prussion, I believe you said that you had never been at a Communist meeting with Dr King; is that correct?
> *Mr Prussion:* That is correct, sir.
> *Mr Boies:* Have you ever been at a Communist meeting in which a member of the Communist Party asserted to you that Dr King was a Communist?
> *Mr Prussion:* No, sir; but I have been to many meetings where he was referred to as a good leader for Communist-directed activities.

And later:

> *Mr Boies:* Perhaps my question was not clear. What I was asking was, whether you were ever told by a member of the Communist Party – since you had never talked to Dr King yourself – but I was asking whether you were ever told by a member of the Communist Party that Dr King was being directed by the Communist Party.
> *Mr Prussion:* That was common knowledge in the Communist Party.
> *Mr Boies:* Were you ever told that, and if so by whom, sir, and under what circumstances and when?
> *Mr Prussion:* This was common talk within the Communist Party, and I cannot recall by whom. Within the Communist activities there is much conversation, many Communists. It was generally known within the Communist Party, but I have no recollection which particular member told me that.[32]

Mr Williams's questioning of Mr Prussion increasingly resembled the style of a detective interrogating a murder suspect in a whodunit:

> *Mr Williams.* Did you, as an individual, ever attend a Communist meeting when Martin Luther King, Jr, was there?

Mr Prussion: Never, no. I never attended a meeting where he was there. However, the evidence was presented . . .

Mr Williams: No, did you attend a meeting?

Mr Prussion: Not in his presence . . .

Mr Williams: You never saw Martin Luther King attend Communist meetings. Thank you.[33]

. . .

During the finale of this Afro-American freedom drama a seemingly endless line of Americans stepped upon the congressional stage to spell out the three-part symbolic significance of the Martin Luther King, Jr, national holiday bill. Some portrayed it as a day of recognition of Dr King's greatness. Others perceived the holiday as a just official recognition of Afro-American's contributions to America. While still others saw the day symbolizing democracy and brotherhood, two cornerstones of the American ethos.

Notes

1. US Cong., House, Subcommittee on Census and Population of the Committee on Post Office and Civil Service, *Designate the Birthday of Martin Luther King, Jr., as a Legal Public Holiday*, 94th Cong. 1st sess., H.R. 1810 (Washington, D.C.: GPO, 1975), 21.
2. House Subcommittee on Census and Statistics, 42.
3. House subcommittee on Census and Population, 26.
4. House Subcommittee on Census and Statistics, 73.
5. US Cong., Senate, Committee on the Judiciary, and House, Committee on Post Office and Civil Service, *Martin Luther King, Jr., Holiday Bill*, 96th Cong., 1st sess., S. 25 (Washington, D.C.: GPO, 1979), 31.
6. House Subcommittee on Census and Statistics, 9.
7. House Subcommittee on Census and Population, 26.
8. Senate Committee on the Judiciary, and House Committee on Post Office and Civil Service, 81.
9. Ibid., 72.
10. Edward D. Sargent, '100 Give Thanks for Passage of Holiday Measure,' *Washington Post*, 20 October 1983, p. A17.
11. House Subcommittee on Census and Statistics, 77.
12. House Subcommittee on Census and Population, 4–5.
13. Senate Committee on the Judiciary, and House Committee on Post Office and Civil Service, 19.
14. Senate Committee on the Judiciary, and House Committee on Post Office and Civil Service, 34.
15. Ibid., 59.
16. Ibid., 67.
17. Ibid., 34.

18. Ibid., 7.
19. Ibid., 19.
20. House Subcommittee on Census and Statistics, 21.
21. Ibid.
22. Ibid., 67.
23. Senate Committee on the Judiciary; and House Committee on Post Office and Civil Service, 75.
24. House Subcommittee on Census and Statistics, 24.
25. Senate Committee on the Judiciary, and House Committee on Post Office and Civil Service, 27–8.
26. Ibid., 72.
27. Ibid., 73.
28. Ibid., 21.
29. Ibid., 36.
30. Ibid., 41.
31. Ibid., 43.
32. Ibid., 49.
33. Ibid., 48.

Street Names and the Scaling of Memory: The Politics of Commemorating Martin Luther King, Jr within the African American Community

Derek H. Alderman

. . .

Importance of Scale to Commemoration

The naming of streets for Martin Luther King is part of a larger movement in the United States to affirm the historical importance of minority groups and challenge traditional, white-dominated conceptions of the past that frequently ignore these contributions (Rhea 1997). With the establishment of federal and state holidays in his honour, King has become an official icon of the civil rights movement and black heritage in general – sometimes at the

From *Area* 35 (2003): 163–73.

historical neglect of lesser-known activists, particularly women (Dwyer 2000). The movement to memorialize King and the civil rights movement is affecting not only the names attached to streets, but also the geography of statues, museums, preserved sites, heritage trails and festivals (Gallagher 1995; Armada 1998). O'Meally and Fabre noted a significant need for research that identifies and analyses African American 'sites of memory' (1994, 3–4) or places where blacks invest the past with great symbolic and political significance. Analysing King streets is an important entry point to understanding how blacks struggle to incorporate their achievements into the nation's collective memory.

Scale is an intrinsically important facet of memorializing the past and bringing significant public attention to the historical contributions of African Americans (Alderman 1996). The geographic scale at which memory is produced (or commemoration is carried out) determines, in large measure, the populations who will be touched by the memorial meanings being communicated. By expanding the scale of memory or increasing the geographic extent of commemoration, social actors and groups hope to make images of the past retrievable or available to a larger array of publics. As suggested by Schudson, retrievability is an essential factor in shaping the ultimate power or influence of a cultural object or practice: 'If culture is to influence a person, it must reach the person' (1989, 160). Street naming is a potentially powerful form of commemoration because of its capacity to make certain visions of the past accessible to a wide range of social groups. In contrast, a restriction in the scale of commemoration can decrease the retrievability and accessibility of the past, thus limiting the extent to which traditional historical interpretations and valuations can be challenged and changed. As Smith argued, scale has a 'double-edged nature' and can be constructed to both constrain identities as well as enlarge them (1993, 114). King streets have a similar double-edged nature. Depending on the location and spatial extent of these streets, they can represent an expansion of African American influence and cultural expression or a reinforcement of the boundaries that have traditionally constrained black identity and power.

Defining the notion of scale – as it relates to streets and roads – can be difficult. Howitt identified three facets of geographic scale – size, level and relation. He noted that while geographers generally recognize scale in terms of 'size' and 'level within a hierarchy', they have not fully explored the idea of 'scale as a relation between geographic totalities' (1998, 50–2). In terms of size, the scaling of commemoration can refer to the length or width of the named street. In many instances, the size of a street determines the sheer number of residences and businesses identified, by address, with a commemorated person or event. Addresses are essential to daily activities and represent an important way of inscribing commemorative meanings into a multitude of urban practices and narratives (Azaryahu 1996). The scaling of memory through street names can also be defined in terms of level, specifically the street's level of prominence within a city's hierarchy of roads. As Azaryahu pointed out, there is often a positive correlation between 'the strategic importance of a thoroughfare and the prestige of the associated commemoration' (1996, 325). A prominent, frequently travelled street would represent a larger and more significant scale of memorialization than a small side road because of differences in the amount of public exposure and visibility that each road brings to a memorial cause.

African American activists hold strong views about constructing the geographic scale of King's commemoration relative to the size of the named street and the street's perceived level of prominence. In Sylvester, Georgia (USA), two black city council members voted against a street-naming proposal when they learned that King's name would be placed in a poor, deteriorating neighbourhood (Towns 1993). In Athens, Georgia (USA), African Americans living along Reese Street opposed identifying King with their street, which they described as 'unknown' and 'drug infested' (Alderman 1996). In March of 2002, African American activist Torrey Dixon petitioned the city council of Danville, Virginia (USA), asking that Central Boulevard, a major commercial thoroughfare, be renamed in honour of King. He considered the thoroughfare an 'appropriate street' to rename because its central location and high volume of traffic would ensure that King's name would be seen by many people. The proposal failed and officials suggested renaming a smaller street that had served as a focal point for members of the local civil rights movement when King had visited Danville in 1963. The leader of the street-naming campaign rebuked this counter-proposal and was quoted as saying: 'I think Dr King should have a major road . . . I think having a road in a low-class neighborhood named after King is offensive' (quoted in Davis 2002, 3A). In this case, the commemoration of King at an inappropriate scale of prominence represented a degradation of his memory, even when the street in question had a strong historical association with the civil rights leader.

The geographic scale of commemorative street naming can also be defined in relational terms or the extent to which a named street creates associations or linkages between different people and places in the city. Street names have a connectivity that allows them to touch the consciousness of social actors and groups who may or may not identify with the person or event being remembered. However, because cities often develop (intentionally and unintentionally) in segregated patterns, not all streets cut across and connect diverse populations, thus reducing the scale of public identification and interaction with a commemorative naming. When commemorating King, African Americans are often concerned about the location of the named street in relation to the white community and the extent to which the street serves as a geographic bridge between races. Accompanying the importance of naming a long and prominent thoroughfare is the equally important desire to name a street that reaches beyond the confines of the black community. This was certainly the case in Keysville, Georgia (USA). African American leaders found little opposition when they renamed a street for King within the city limits of Keysville. However, they encountered intense resistance when they sought to have the road renamed across the entire county from one boundary to another. Ultimately, county commissioners voted against the extension of Martin Luther King Road. This decision limited the geographic scale of King's commemoration, specifically the scale of race relations that would be embodied along the renamed road. The city of Keysville is largely African American (more than 75 per cent) and the larger county is almost 50 per cent white. Keysville's mayor, Emma Greshman, reacted to the county commission vote by saying: 'The whites who protested the new name need a little more knowledge about what Dr King meant not only to his race but to America' (quoted in *Atlanta Constitution* 1989, A18). As indicated by Greshman, the scaling of memory through street naming is inherently political because people hold multiple and sometimes conflicting ideas about the public relevance of King's achievements.

Differences in African American Memory and Activism

Debates over where to commemorate Martin Luther King are not just between whites and African Americans. As the case study in the next section will illustrate, black leaders may disagree with each other about what constitutes an appropriate scale of memorialization. To conduct an analysis of these struggles requires a critical understanding of African American memory and activism. Kelley (1994) and Goings and Mohl (1996) emphasized the importance of seeing blacks as active cultural and political agents who mobilize to reclaim streets and other public spaces as a means of redefining social and political identity. These scholars also pointed to the important role that divisions and contestation play within the black community.

As Tuck (2001) recently noted in retracing the history of the civil rights movement in Georgia (USA), the struggle for racial equality does not follow one normative pattern. Black activism, according to him, can be defined and carried out in different and conflicting ways. In some instances, integration takes a back seat to blacks developing their community institutions and a sense of psychological empowerment. Even Martin Luther King holds a complex and sometimes contradictory place in African American history and culture. During the civil rights demonstrations of the 1960s, black leaders in Savannah, Georgia (USA) tried to bar King from preaching in the city.

They feared that the civil rights leader's presence might antagonize local authorities and disrupt an already successful protest movement. The marginalization of King has even been inscribed into Savannah's civil rights museum. Although located on Martin Luther King Boulevard, the museum says little about King's accomplishments and stresses, instead, local activists and struggles during the Movement.

An African American commemorative culture existed long before the emergence of King as a national icon. Clark (2000) has examined, for example, Emancipation Day celebrations in the years immediately following the Civil War. These ceremonies represented more than a shared affirmation of the importance of black freedom. They also 'provided crucial forums for African Americans to reflect, debate, and enact their own versions of history and plans for the future' (Clark 2000, 125–6). In speaking about the memory of slavery and the evolution of black progress, a range of African American voices could be heard at these gatherings from conservative, accommodationist views to more radical calls for change. Following the lead of Clark (2000), the commemoration of King can be interpreted as a forum or arena for African Americans to present and debate their interpretations of his legacy as they articulate future political visions for the black community.

King's legacy – like all historical reputations (Fine 1996; Schwartz 1997) – is open to competing interpretations and constructions, even amongst his most devoted supporters. This competition became evident immediately after the civil rights leader's assassination in 1968. While the SCLC (Southern Christian Leadership Conference) sought to honour their fallen leader through increased social activism and protest, Correta Scott King placed more emphasis on establishing the King Center in Atlanta, Georgia (USA) and establishing a holiday in her husband's memory. The two parties even differed on when to commemorate the civil rights leader. SCLC focused on April 4, the date of King's death. The King family preferred the birth date on January 15 (Daynes 1997). Jacqueline Smith is a more recent example of intra-racial division over how best to memorialize King. She has spent over a decade protesting the conversion of the Lorraine Motel – the site of King's assassination – into the National Civil Rights Museum. Smith was the last resident of the Lorraine before its closure. She argues that the museum does not embody or truly commemorate the ideals and beliefs of King, who would have never allowed low-income people to be displaced for the purpose of building a memorial and tourist attraction (Jones 2000). While the museum focuses largely on King's contribution to racial integration, Smith emphasizes the civil rights leader's concern, later in his life, for issues of poverty and economic inequality. According to her, the Lorraine should have been converted into a centre to offer housing, job training, education, health services and other aid to the poor.

In assessing the commemoration of African American memory, Ruffins (1992) made a distinction between interior and exterior views of the past.

Interior interpretations of the past are those produced by African Americans about their own experiences. Exterior interpretations originate from outside the black community. While this duality between interior and exterior helps us understand how blacks and whites remember and represent the past differently, it can also shed light on commemorative complexities within the African American community. As Ruffins (1992) pointed out, African Americans are bicultural, living in two American cultures – one white and one black. Consequently, the remembrance of Martin Luther King operates on at least two different levels within the black community.

On the one hand, African Americans participate in an exterior or external mode of commemoration in which King's image is fashioned for consumption by non-blacks as well as blacks. The goal is to educate a larger, white-dominated American culture about the historical importance of King and his social philosophies. The exterior or external mode is characterized by an emphasis on using King's memory to challenge prevailing, race-bounded views of history and society. On the other hand, African Americans also participate in an interior or internal mode of commemoration in which King's image is used to inspire fellow blacks and give them a sense of racial pride and identity. From this perspective, remembering the civil rights leader is more about constructing a role model for the African American community rather than presenting a multicultural lesson for non-blacks. Indeed, Rhea (1997) asserted that the growing movement to commemorate minority historical contributions is not only about achieving cultural recognition within the larger society but also about (re)educating minorities in their own heritage and cultural worth.

A potential tension underlies commemoration as African Americans negotiate between interior and exterior uses of memory. Implicit in each perspective are ideas about what constitutes an 'appropriate' scale at which to memorialize the past. Essential to enacting an 'exterior' view of King's contributions is constructing his commemoration at a geographically expansive scale. By the same token, while an 'interior' view does not necessarily relegate the civil rights leader's memory to obscure places, it does emphasize the importance and value of spatially focusing commemorative activities within the confines of the black community. The following case study illustrates how the tension between these two memory/scalar perspectives can drive the politics of naming streets for Martin Luther King.

Street Naming in Eatonton, Georgia (USA)

Eatonton is a town of 6764 people (2000) in Putnam County, which is located in the central part of the state of Georgia (USA). Although seemingly small and obscure, Eatonton is actually representative of many other towns that have engaged in the street-naming process. Well over three-quarters of all Martin Luther King streets are located in the American South, and Georgia – King's home state – led the nation with the largest number of such streets (72) in 1996. King street naming occurs in small towns as well as large cities in the South (Alderman 2000). Indeed, 41 per cent of these streets are in places with populations ranging from 2500 to 9999. In Georgia, the median population size of a place with a King street is only 5595. Street naming in the southeastern United States occurs most often in places where African Americans constitute at least 30 per cent of the total population (Alderman 2000). Blacks comprise 59 per cent of Eatonton's population and 30 per cent of the population of Putnam County.

Eatonton is noted for being the birthplace of authors Joel Chandler Harris and Alice Walker, both of whom made significant contributions to the representation of black culture and history in the United States. Joel Chandler Harris (1848–1908), a white author, is best known for writing the *Uncle Remus Tales.* Harris retold the 'trickster' folktales and fables of plantation slaves, which were acted out by animal characters such as 'Brer Rabbit' and 'Brer Fox'. Uncle Remus, the elderly narrator of these tales, embodies the docility and humorous innocence of the Sambo stereotype. Harris' writing took on even greater popularity and stereotypical proportions when Walt Disney adapted it into an animated film titled *Song of the South* (Kesterson 1989). African American author Alice Walker (born 1944) constructed a different and perhaps more complex image of rural black life in her book, *The Color Purple.* While the Remus Tales were told by a gentle black man and dealt with racial struggle in sublime, metaphorical terms, Walker's protagonist (Celie) and central characters were women and her work dealt directly with issues of violence, abuse and sexuality (Gaffney 1989). *The Color Purple*, also made into a widely popular film, challenged Americans to think more critically about divisions and struggles within the black community.

The city of Eatonton named a road for Alice Walker in 1985, five years before dedicating a street to Martin Luther King. The naming of a street for Walker further establishes the symbolic importance that African Americans attach to place naming as a means of making their accomplishments visible on the landscape. Public recognition of Walker represented an attempt to rewrite Eatonton's symbolic landscape. From monuments and museums to festivals and business names, the landscape is permeated with references to the legacy of Joel Chandler Harris and Uncle Remus. The establishment of Alice Walker Drive is also significant because it exposed a commemorative tension within the African American community. This tension resurfaced and became more clearly defined when selecting a street to name for King. The black activists involved in honouring Walker – many of whom participated in King's commemoration – disagreed over whether the author's name should adorn a street restricted to the black community or one that reminds the entire city of her accomplishments. As would become the case with King, Alice Walker was identified with a residential road populated largely by African Americans. Interesting enough, Alice Walker Drive closely parallels Martin Luther King, Jr. Drive, although there is no direct evidence to suggest that the honouring of Alice Walker influenced the location of King's street.

The idea of naming a street in memory of Martin Luther King made its formal appearance during an Eatonton city council meeting on 4 September 1990. Black city councilman Ulysses Rice, then vice-chairman of the local chapter of the NAACP (National Association for the Advancement of Colored People) and a former college classmate of King, discussed the possibility of renaming Concord Avenue for the civil rights leader (Eatonton City Council Minutes, 4 September 1990). Concord was a main residential artery in the African American community as well as located near an elementary school, a funeral home owned by Rice, an American Legion post and the Ebenezer Baptist Church. In January of the previous year, the road had taken on great symbolic importance as part of the route for a 'Freedom March' held on the Martin Luther King holiday. Participants assembled at the Ebenezer Baptist Church, marched to the county courthouse and then returned to the church for a three hour memorial service in which a pastor re-enacted King's 'I Have a Dream' speech (Eatonton Messenger 1989). To mobilize support behind the renaming of Concord after King, Rice and other members of the NAACP distributed a questionnaire to residents along the street asking if they were in favour of the name change. Results of this questionnaire, which indicated almost unanimous support for the name change, were submitted to the city council in support of the request made by Rice (Eatonton City Council Minutes, 7 October 1990). On 7 November 1990, the city council officially changed the name of Concord Avenue to Martin Luther King, Jr. Drive (Eatonton City Council Minutes, 7 November 1990).

In the case of Eatonton, geographic scale figured directly in how activists conceptualized and carried out the campaign to commemorate King through street naming. For example, in explaining his support for renaming Concord Avenue, councilman Rice emphasized the size of the street. He stated, 'Concord ran all the way through the county to Pea Ridge Road near Highway 441.' Indeed, Martin Luther King Drive stretches over four miles, connecting black residential areas of varying value with rural dairy farms. To emphasize the relative prominence of King Drive, Rice added, 'most of the houses (along King Drive) are fairly decent by black standards' (Rice 1998). This emphasis on the street being evaluated by 'black standards' is important to our discussion because Rice advocated that the geographic scale of Martin Luther King Drive be limited largely to the spatial confines of the black community.

From Rice's point of view, the scale of the named street was appropriate for what he envisioned as its political and social purpose. Promoting an interior interpretation and use of the past, Rice showed great concern for how King's commemoration would focus and inspire the black community: 'If naming the street after King hasn't done anything else, it has pulled people together who want to live in a decent neighborhood. Black people have a place to be proud of' (Rice 1997). He represented the renaming of Concord Avenue as a way of focusing the black public, particularly children, on King's importance and the larger achievements of African Americans. On this point, he said:

> Helping to keep King alive in Eatonton was a way of showing a person the great opportunities that await black people. Black kids would have an opportunity to drive down the street [King Drive] and remember the things that black people can achieve. Even little children, who could care less. Everyday they ride down that street, it gets drilled in them. When programs are held at the school, if they don't know anything else about Dr King, they know his name is on a street nearby. (Rice 1998)

Although the naming of Concord for King progressed rather quickly, it did not go unchallenged. The primary opponents were not local white citizens or other city council members, but were from within the African American community. On 15 October 1990, a group of African Americans led by Fannie Pearle Farley – former vice-president of the American Legion Auxiliary – requested that King's name be attached to a road more prominent than Concord Avenue (Eatonton City Council Minutes, October 1990). She asserted that King was an important symbol and that placing his name on a major road would project a more positive image to those living in the town and to the larger outside world. Like Rice, Farley is a prominent leader in the Putnam County African American community. In 1981, the NAACP voted her one of the ten most influential women in Middle Georgia. Farley had a history of being heavily involved in commemorative issues. For example, in 1986, her American Legion Auxiliary erected a monument on the courthouse lawn to honour veterans (*Eatonton Messenger* 1986). In 1990, not long before the emergence of the King street-naming issue, Farley presented the city with a flag that had been flown over the United States Capitol (Eatonton City Council Minutes, 5 March 1990). Because of Farley's previous leadership in commemorative issues, she felt compelled and justified to approach the city council to express an alternative vision of how best to commemorate King.

In challenging the attachment of King's name to Concord Avenue, Farley offered two alternatives. The first was Jefferson Avenue, one of the town's major thoroughfares and a national highway. The second was the then-uncompleted Highway 441 bypass, which now runs around the western edge of the town. The renaming of Jefferson Avenue was quickly dismissed by the city council because of the unlikelihood of gaining the support of the street's white population. In fact, one white city councilman responded by stating: 'I don't want to shove this (renaming a street) down anybody's throat if they don't want it' (quoted in *Eatonton Messenger* 1990, 1). This view reflects an assumption found in many communities that residents and businesses located along the street in question should have a disproportionately strong influence on the approval or revocation of a name change. Left out of this perspective are the voices of people who identify with and use the street by simply working, shopping and driving along it. As Berg and Kearns pointed out, the politics of naming places are 'both a politics of space (deciding who names and controls space) and a spatialized politics (whereby the spatial defines who has legitimacy to speak)' (1996, 111). The spatialized politics embodied in place naming can have a dramatic effect on the geographic scale at which King is ultimately commemorated, since it is unlikely that all (if not most) of the stakeholders on a large, racially diverse street would agree to a renaming. Responding to resistance toward the Jefferson proposal, Farley suggested that naming the new bypass would avoid some of the political controversy that results from *re*naming a street. Yet, the bypass proposal also failed because of plans to name the highway after a still living and very popular city official, James Marshall. Debating the merits of naming the bypass for King was further complicated by the fact that Marshall was well liked by the black community in Eatonton. Ultimately, Farley was unsuccessful in convincing the city council to place King's name on a different and, as she saw it, a more appropriate street for King.

While Ulysses Rice argued that a largely African American street was an appropriate geographic scale for commemorating King and representing the achievements of blacks, Fannie Pearle Farley countered by suggesting that the geographic scale of street naming should extend beyond the black community. In building her conception of an appropriate scale at which to commemorate King, Farley advocated an exterior use of memorialization, emphasizing the importance of naming a street that would be visible to and touch white residents and visitors. She stated:

> Signs are important. The problem with Concord Avenue [King Drive] is people going through Eatonton can't see it. Where it is now, people don't know it's there. The magnitude of King demands that a prominent street be named after him, not one stuck in the black area of town. After all, King did not fight just for blacks but for everyone. (Farley 1997)

From Farley's perspective, street naming was a way of bringing the importance of King to the attention of whites, who, in her opinion, benefited from the civil rights leader's achievements along with blacks. Unlike Rice, her notion of geographic scale is concerned less with the size or length of street *per se* and more with its ability to transcend racial boundaries and hence create relations between different groups of people within the city. While Rice is advocating a scale of commemoration that honours the traditional lines of residential segregation, Farley is advocating that the scale of King's commemoration should be constructed in such a way as to break down what Rhea (1997) called the 'segregation of memory'. When asked whether she thought the street-naming campaign had been a success, Farley stated

> No it wasn't because having Martin Luther King Drive where it is does not give the community [the black community] full credit for its achievements. The street should have gone through a major thoroughfare. (Farley 1997)

In this respect, street naming in Eatonton was characterized by a tension among African Americans between using the geographical scaling of King's memory as a device for challenging and changing the historical consciousness of whites versus using it as a means of consolidating and focusing the black community ideologically.

Concluding Remarks

Street names are important memorial landscapes that play a key but under-analysed role in the contested process of attaching meaning to the past. Streets named for Martin Luther King, Jr represent one of the most widespread and controversial products of the ongoing US movement to recognize the historical contributions of minorities, particularly African Americans. I have suggested that geographic scale is an important factor in shaping political struggles over public commemoration in general and King's commemoration in particular. Recognizing that differences and divisions exist in African American memory and activism, I also suggested that black leaders hold multiple and sometimes competing views about the civil rights leader's legacy and hence the most appropriate scale at which to honour him through street naming. As illustrated in the case of Eatonton, African Americans may advocate interior or exterior scalar constructions of King's commemoration depending upon their immediate political goals. This is not to minimize the importance of examining commemorative struggles between black and white Americans and those occurring within the white community. However, this study sought to challenge some basic assumptions about how heritage and history are divided along racial lines. As with any historical figure, King's legacy is open to redefinition not only by opponents to his political/social philosophy but also people who unquestionably embraced and benefited from this philosophy.

References

Alderman, D. H. 1996 Creating a new geography of memory in the South: (re)naming of streets in honor of Martin Luther King, Jr, *Southeastern Geographer* 36: 51–69.

Alderman, D. H. 2000 A street fit for a King: naming places and commemoration in the American South, *Professional Geographer* 52: 672–84.

Armada, B. 1998 Memorial agon: an interpretive tour of the National Civil Rights Museum, *Southern Communication Journal* 63: 235–43.

Atlanta Constitution 1989 Whites' in Burke County win fight over renaming road, 13 January A18.

Azaryahu, M. 1996 The power of commemorative street names, *Environment and Planning D: Society and Space* 14: 311–30.

Berg, L. D. and Kearns, R. A. 1996 Naming as norming: 'race', gender, and the identity politics of naming places in Aotearoa/New Zealand, *Environment and Planning D: Society and Space* 14: 99–122.

Clark, K. 2000 Celebrating freedom: Emancipation Day celebrations and African American memory in the early reconstruction South, in Brundage, W. F. (ed.), *Where these memories grow: history, memory, and southern identity* (University of North Carolina Press, Chapel Hill) pp. 107–32.

Davis, T. 2002 Council rejects MLK road proposal, *Danville Register & Bee*, 6 March, 1A 3A.

Daynes, G. 1997 *Making villains, making heroes: Joseph R. McCarthy, Martin Luther King, Jr. and the politics of American memory* (Garland Publishing, New York).

Dwyer, O. J. 2000 Interpreting the civil rights movement: place, memory, and conflict, *Professional Geographer* 52 660–71.

Eatonton City Council Minutes, 4 September 1990; 15 October 1990; 7 November 1990; 5 March 1991.

Eatonton Messenger 1986 Monument dedication set, 2 January, 16.

Eatonton Messenger 1989 Freedom march, 19 January, 1.

Eatonton Messenger 1990 Group asks to have street renamed for King, 18 October, 1.

Farley, F. P. 1997 Telephone interview with author, 4 September.

Fine, G. A. 1996 Reputational entrepreneurs and the memory of incompetence: melting supporters, partisan warriors, and images of President Harding, *American Journal of Sociology* 101: 1159–93.

Gaffney, E. 1989 'Walker, Alice' in C. R. Wilson and W. Ferris, *Encyclopedia of Southern culture* (University of North Carolina Press, Chapel Hill), p. 898.

Gallagher, V. J. 1995 Remembering together: rhetorical integration and the case of the Martin Luther King, Jr. Memorial, *Southern Communication Journal* 60: 109–19.

Goings, K. W. and Mohl, R. A. (eds) 1996 *The new African American urban history* (Sage, Thousand Oaks).

Howitt, R. 1998 Scale as relation: musical metaphors of geographical scale, *Area* 30: 49–58.

Jones III, J. P. 2000 The street politics of Jackie Smith, in G. Bridge and S. Watson, *The Blackwell companion to the city* (Blackwell, Oxford), pp. 448–59.

Kelley, R. D. G. 1994 *Race rebels: culture, politics, and the black working class* (Free Press, New York).

Kesterson, D. B. 1989 'Harris, Joel Chandler' in C. R. Wilson and W. Ferris, *Encyclopedia of Southern culture* (University of North Carolina Press, Chapel Hill), pp. 885–86.

O'Meally, R. and Fabre, G. 1994 Introduction in G. Fabre and R. O'Meally (eds) *History and memory in African-American culture* (Oxford University Press, New York), pp. 3–17.

Rhea, J. T. 1997 *Race pride and the American identity* (Harvard University Press, Cambridge, MA).

Rice, U. 1997 Interview with author, 5 September.

Rice, U. 1998 Interview with author, 15 March.

Ruffins F. D. 1992 Mythos, memory, and history: African American preservation efforts, 1820–1990 in I. Karp, C. M. Kreamer and S. D. Lavine (eds) *Museums and communities: the politics of public culture* (Smithsonian Institution Press, Washington), pp. 506–611.

Schudson, M. 1989 The present in the past versus the past in the present, *Communication* 11: 105–13.

Schwartz, B. 1997 Memory as a cultural system: Abraham Lincoln in World War I. *International Journal of Sociology and Social Policy* 17: 22–58.

Smith, N. 1993 Homeless/global: scaling places in J. Bird, B. Curtis, T. Putnam, G. Robertson and L. Tucker (eds) *Mapping the futures: local culture, global change* (Routledge, London), pp. 87–119.

Towns, H. R. 1993 Back streets get King's name, *Atlanta Journal-Constitution* 30 October A3.

Tuck, S. G. N. 2001 *Beyond Atlanta: the struggle for racial equality in Georgia, 1940–1980* (University of Georgia Press, Athens, GA).

Bibliography

Primary Sources

King's Published Work

King, Martin Luther, Jr, *Stride Toward Freedom: The Montgomery Story* (New York: Harper & Row, 1958).

King, Martin Luther, Jr, *The Measure of a Man* (Philadelphia, PA: Christian Education Press, 1959).

King, Martin Luther, Jr, *Strength to Love* (New York: Harper & Row, 1963).

King, Martin Luther, Jr, *Why We Can't Wait* (New York: Harper & Row, 1964).

King, Martin Luther, Jr, *Where Do We Go From Here? Chaos or Community?* (New York: Harper & Row, 1967).

King, Martin Luther, Jr, *The Trumpet of Conscience* (New York: Harper & Row, 1968).

King's Published Papers

Clayborne, Carson, Ralph E. Luker and Penny A. Russell (eds), *The Papers of Martin Luther King, Jr,* Vol. I: *Called to Serve, January 1929–June 1951* (Berkeley, CA: University of California Press, 1992).

Clayborne, Carson, Ralph E. Luker, Penny A. Russell and Peter Holloran (eds), *The Papers of Martin Luther King, Jr,* Vol. II: *Rediscovering Precious Values, July 1951–November 1955* (Berkeley, CA: University of California Press, 1994).

Clayborne, Carson, Susan A. Carson, Peter Holloran, Dana L. Powell and Stewart Burns (eds), *The Papers of Martin Luther King, Jr,* Vol. III: *Birth of a New Age, December 1955–December 1956* (Berkeley, CA: University of California Press, 1997).

Clayborne, Carson, Susan A. Carson, Adrienne Clay, Virginia Shadron and Kieran Taylor (eds), *The Papers of Martin Luther King, Jr,* Vol. IV: *Symbol of the Movement, January 1957–December 1958* (Berkeley, CA: University of California Press, 2000).

Clayborne, Carson, Tenisha Armstrong, Susan A. Carson, Adrienne Clay and Kieran Taylor (eds), *The Papers of Martin Luther King, Jr,* Vol. V: *Threshold of a New Decade, January 1959–December 1960* (Berkeley, CA: University of California Press, 2005).

Edited Collections

Carson, Clayborne (ed.), *The Autobiography of Martin Luther King, Jr* (New York: Warner Books, 1998).

Carson, Clayborne and Holloran, Peter (eds), *A Knock at Midnight: The Great Sermons of Martin Luther King, Jr* (New York: Warner Books, 1999).

Carson, Clayborne and Shepard, Kris (eds), *A Call to Conscience: The Landmark Speeches of Dr Martin Luther King* (New York: Warner Books, 2001).

Washington, James M., *A Testament of Hope: The Essential Writings of Martin Luther King, Jr* (San Francisco, CA: HarperSanFrancisco, 1986).

Oral History

Hampton, Henry and Steve Freyer (eds), *Voices of Freedom: An Oral History of the Civil Rights Movement from the 1950s through the 1980s* (New York: Vintage, 1994).

Morrison, Joan and Robert K. Morrison (eds), *From Camelot to Kent State: The Sixties Experience in the Words of Those Who Lived It* (New York: Times Books, 1987).

Raines, Howell (ed.), *My Soul is Rested: Movement Days in the Deep South Remembered* (Harmondsworth: Penguin, 1983).

Rodgers, Kim Lacy, 'Oral History and the Civil Rights Movement', *Journal of American History* 75 (1988–9): 567–76.

Selected Biographies and Memoirs

Abernathy, Ralph David, *And the Walls Came Tumbling Down* (New York: Harper & Row, 1989).

Carmichael, Stokely with Eknueme Michael Thelwell, *Ready for Revolution: The Life and Struggles of Stokely Carmichael [Kwame Ture]* (New York: Charles Scribner's, 2003).

Farmer, James, *Lay Bare the Heart: An Autobiography of the Civil Rights Movement* (New York: Arbor House, 1985).

Forman, James, *The Making of Black Revolutionaries* (New York: Macmillan, 1972) revised and reprinted (Washington, DC: Open Hand Publishing, 1985).

Henry, Aaron, with Constance Curry, *Aaron Henry: The Fire Ever Burning* (Jackson: Mississippi University Press, 2000).

King, Christine Farris, *My Brother Martin: A Sister Remembers Growing Up with Rev. Dr. Martin Luther King, Jr* (New York: Simon and Schuster, 2003).

King, Coretta Scott, *My Life with Martin Luther King, Jr* (New York: Holt, Rinehart and Winston, 1969).

King, Dexter Scott, *Growing Up with King: An Intimate Memoir* (New York: Warner Books, 2003).

King, Martin Luther, Sr., with Clayton Riley, *Daddy King: An Autobiography* (Boston, MA: William Morrow, 1980).

Lewis, John, *Walking with the Wind: A Memoir of the Movement* (New York: Simon and Schuster, 1998).

Mays, Benjamin E., *Born to Rebel: An Autobiography* (Athens, GA: University of Georgia Press, 1987).

Wilkins, Roy, *Standing Fast: The Autobiography of Roy Wilkins* (New York: Viking, 1982).

Young, Andrew, *An Easy Burden: The Civil Rights Movement and the Transformation of America* (New York: HarperCollins, 1996).

Secondary Sources

Historiography

Chafe, William H., 'The God's Bring Threads to Webs Begun', *Journal of American History* 86: 4 (March 2000): 1531–51.

Eagles, Charles C, 'Toward New Histories of the Civil Rights Era', *Journal of Southern History* 66: 4 (Nov. 2000): 815–48.

Fairclough, Adam, 'Historians and the Civil Rights Movement', *Journal of American Studies* 24 (1990): 387–98.

Hall, Jaquelyn Dowd, 'The Long Civil Rights Movement and the Political Uses of the Past', *Journal of American History* 91: 4 (March 2005): 1233–63.

Kirk, John A., 'State of the Art: Martin Luther King, Jr', *Journal of American Studies* 38 (2004): 329–47.

Lawson, Steven, 'Freedom Then, Freedom Now: the Historiography of the Civil Rights Movement', *American Historical Review* 96: 2 (1991): 456–72.

Payne, Charles, 'The Social Construction of History', in *I've Got the Light of Freedom: The Organizing Tradition and the Mississippi Freedom Struggle* (Berkeley: University of California Press, 1995), pp. 413–41.

Robinson Armstead L. and Patricia Sullivan (eds), *New Directions in Civil Rights Studies* (Charlottesville, VA: University of Virginia Press, 1991).

Rodgers, Kim Lacy, 'Oral History and the History of the Civil Rights Movement', *Journal of American History* 75: 2 (September 1988) 567–76.

Biographies of King

Bennett, Lerone, Jr, *What Manner of Man: A Biography of Martin Luther King, Jr* (Chicago: Johnson Publishing, 1964).

Bishop, James Alonzo, *The Days of Martin Luther King* (New York: G. P. Putnam's Sons, 1971).

Branch, Taylor, *Parting the Waters: Martin Luther King and the Civil Rights Movement, 1954–63* (New York: Simon and Schuster, 1988).

Branch, Taylor, *Pillar of Fire: America in the King Years, 1963–65* (New York: Simon and Schuster, 1998).

Branch, Taylor, *At Canaan's Edge: America in the King Years, 1965–1968* (New York: Simon and Schuster, 2006).

Burns, Stewart, *To the Mountaintop: Martin Luther King Jr's Sacred Mission to Save America, 1955–1968* (San Francisco, CA: Harper SanFrancisco, 2003).

Colaiaco, James A., *Martin Luther King, Jr: Apostle of Militant Nonviolence* (London: Macmillan, 1988).

Downing, Frederick L., *To See the Promised Land: The Faith Pilgrimage of Martin Luther King, Jr* (Macon, GA: Mercer University Press, 1986).

Fairclough, Adam, *Martin Luther King, Jr* (Athens, GA: University of Georgia Press, 1990).

Fairclough, Adam, *To Redeem the Soul of America: The Southern Christian Leadership Conference and Martin Luther King, Jr* (Athens, GA: University of Georgia Press, 1987).

Garrow, David J., *Bearing the Cross: Martin Luther King, Jr and the Southern Christian Leadership Conference* (New York: William Morrow, 1986).

Kirk, John A., *Martin Luther King, Jr* (London: Pearson Longman, 2005).

Lewis, David L., *King: A Critical Biography* (Urbana, IL: University of Illinois Press, 1970; reprinted as *King: A Biography*, 1978).

Ling, Peter J., *Martin Luther King, Jr* (London: Routledge, 2002).

Lokos, Lionel, *House Divided: The Life and Legacy of Martin Luther King* (New Rochelle, NY: Arlington House, 1968).

Miller, William Robert, *Martin Luther King, Jr: His Life, Martyrdom and Meaning for the World* (New York: Weybright and Talley, 1968).

Oates, Stephen B., *Let the Trumpet Sound: The Life of Martin Luther King, Jr* (New York: Harper & Row, 1982).

Reddick, Lawrence D., *Crusader without Violence: A Biography of Martin Luther King, Jr* (New York: Harper & Bros., 1959).

White, John, *Martin Luther King, Jr and the Civil Rights Movement* (Durham: British Association of American Studies, 1991).

Williams, John A., *The King God Didn't Save: Reflections on the Life and Death of Martin Luther King, Jr* (New York: Coward-Macann, 1970).

Cold War Contexts

Anderson, Carol, *Eyes Off the Prize: The United Nations and the African American Struggle for Human Rights, 1944–1955* (New York: Cambridge University Press, 2003).

Borstelmann, Thomas, *The Cold War and the Color Line: American Race Relations in the Global Arena* (Cambridge, MA: Harvard University Press, 2002).

Dudziak, Mary L., *Cold War Civil Rights: Race and the Image of American Democracy* (Princeton, NJ: Princeton University Press, 2000).

Dudziak, Mary L., 'Desegregation as a Cold War Imperative', *Stanford Law Review* 41 (November 1988): 61–120.

Dudziak, Mary L., 'Josephine Baker, Racial Protests, and the Cold War', *Journal of American History* 81: 2 (September 1994): 543–70.

Horne, Gerald, *Black and Red: W. E. B. Du Bois and the AfroAmerican Response to the Cold War, 1944–1963* (Albany, NY: State University of New York Press, 1985).

Horne, Gerald, *Communist Front? The Civil Rights Congress, 1946–1956* (London: Associated University Press, 1988).

Krenn, Michael L. (ed.), *Race and US Foreign Policy during the Cold War* (New York: Garland Publishing, 1998).

Krenn, Michael L. (ed.), *The African American Voice in U.S. Foreign Policy since World War II* (New York: Garland, 1999).

Krenn, Michael L., *Black Diplomacy: African Americans and the State Department, 1945–1969* (Armoruk, NY: M. E. Sharpe, 1999).

Plummer, Brenda Gayle, *Rising Wind: Black Americans and US Foreign Affairs, 1935–1960* (Chapel Hill, NC: University of North Carolina Press, 1996).

Romaro, Renee, 'No Diplomatic Immunity: African Diplomats, the State Department, and Civil Rights, 1961–1964', *Journal of American History* 87: 2 (September 2000): 546–79.

Skrentny, Jon David, 'The Effect of the Cold War on African-American Civil Rights: America and the World Audience, 1945–1968', *Theory and Society* 27 (April 1998): 237–85.

Brown v. Board of Education, 1954

Balkin, Jack (ed.), *What Brown v. Board of Education Should Have Said* (New York: New York University Press, 2001).

Bass, Jack, *Unlikely Heroes: The Dramatic Story of the Southern Judges Who Translated the Supreme Court's* Brown *Decision into a Revolution for Equality* (New York: Simon and Schuster, 1981).

Irons, Peter, *Jim Crow's Children: The Broken Promise of the Brown Decision* (New York: Viking Penguin, 2002).

Klarman, Michael, *From Jim Crow to Civil Rights: The Supreme Court and the Struggle for Racial Equality* (New York: Oxford University Press, 2004).

Kluger, Richard, *Simple Justice: The History of* Brown v. Board of Education *and Black America's Struggle for Equality* (New York: Alfred A. Knopf, 1976).

Patterson, James T., *Brown v. Board of Education: A Civil Rights Milestone and Its Troubled Legacy* (New York: Oxford University Press, 2001).

Wilkinson, J. Harvie III, *From Brown to Bakke: The Supreme Court and School Integration: 1954–1978* (New York: Oxford University Press, 1979).

The Murder of Emmett Till, 1955

Hudson-Weems, Clenora, *Emmett Till: The Sacrificial Lamb in the Civil Rights Movement* (Troy, MI: Bedford Press, 1994).

Metress, Christopher (ed.), *The Lynching of Emmett Till: A Documentary Narrative* (Charlottesville, IL: University of Virginia Press, 2002).

Whitfield, Stephen J., *A Death in the Delta: The Story of Emmett Till* (New York: Free Press, 1988).

The Montgomery Bus Boycott, 1955–6

Barnes, Catherine, *Journey from Jim Crow: The Desegregation of Southern Transit* (New York: Columbia University Press, 1983).

Brinkley, Douglas, *Mine Eyes Have Seen the Glory: The Life of Rosa Parks* (New York: Viking Press, 2000).

Burns, Stewart (ed.), *Daybreak of Freedom: The Montgomery Bus Boycott* (Chapel Hill, NC: University of North Carolina Press, 1997).

Carson, Clayborne, Susan A. Carson, Peter Holloran, Dana L. Powell and Stewart Burns (eds), *The Papers of Martin Luther King, Jr,* Vol. III: *Birth of a New Age, December 1955–December 1956* (Berkeley, CA: University of California Press, 1997).

Chappell, Marisa, Jenny Hutchinson and Brian Ward, '"Dress modestly, neatly ... as if you were going to church": Respectability, Class and Gender in the Montgomery Bus Boycott and the Early Civil Rights Movement', in Peter J. Ling, and Sharon Monteith (eds), *Gender in the Civil Rights Movement* (New York: Garland Publishing, 1999: 69–100).

Fields, U. J., *The Montgomery Story: The Unhappy Effects of the Montgomery Bus Boycott* (New York: Exposition Press, 1959).

Garrow, David J. (ed.), *The Walking City: The Montgomery Bus Boycott, 1955–1956* (Brooklyn, NY: Carlson Publishing, 1989).

Glennon, Robert Jerome, 'The Role of Law in the Civil Rights Movement: The Montgomery Bus Boycott 1955–57', *Law and History Review* 9 (Spring 1991): 59–112.

Graetz, Robert, *A White Preacher's Memoir: The Montgomery Bus Boycott* (Montgomery, AL: Black Belt Press, 1999).

Gray, Fred D., *Bus Ride to Justice: Changing the System by the System: The Life and Works of Fred D. Gray, Preacher, Attorney, Politician: Lawyer for Rosa Parks* (Montgomery, AL: Black Belt Press, 1999).

King, Coretta Scott, *My Life with Martin Luther King, Jr* (New York: Holt, Rinehart and Winston, 1969).

King, Martin Luther, Jr, *Stride Toward Freedom: The Montgomery Story* (New York: Harper & Row, 1958).

Morris, Aldon D., *Origins of the Civil Rights Movement: Black Communities Organizing for Change* (New York: Free Press, 1984).

Parks, Rosa, with Jim Haskins, *Rosa Parks: My Story* (New York: Dial Books, 1992).

Robinson, Jo Ann, with David Garrow, *The Montgomery Bus Boycott and the Women Who Started It* (Knoxville, TN: University of Tennessee Press, 1989).

Seay, Solomon S., *I was There by the Grace of God* (Montgomery, AL: S. S. Seay Educational Foundation 1990).

Thornton, J. Mills, *Dividing Lines: Municipal Politics and the Struggle for Civil Rights in Montgomery, Birmingham, and Selma* (Tuscaloosa, AL: University of Alabama Press, 2002).

Thornton, J. Mills, 'Challenge and Response in the Montgomery Bus Boycott of 1955–1956', *Alabama Review* 33: 163–235.

Webb, Clive, 'Closing Ranks: Montgomery Jews and Civil Rights, 1954–1960', *Journal of American Studies* 32 (1998): 463–82.

White, John, '"Nixon was the One"! Edgar Daniel Nixon, the MIA and the Montgomery Bus Boycott', in Brian Ward and Tony Badger (eds), *The Making of Martin Luther King and the Civil Rights Movement* (London: Macmillan, 1996): 45–63.

The Little Rock Crisis, 1957

Anderson, Karen, 'The Little Rock School Desegregation Crisis: Moderation and Social Conflict', *Journal of Southern History* 70 (August 2004): 603–36.

Arkansas Historical Quarterly 61 (Autumn 1997). Special edition on the Little Rock School Crisis.

Bates, Daisy, *The Long Shadow of Little Rock: A Memoir* (New York: David McKay Company, Inc., 1962).

Freyer, Tony, *The Little Rock Crisis: A Constitutional Interpretation* (Westport, CT: Greenwood Press, 1984).

Jacoway, Elizabeth and C. Fred Williams (eds), *Understanding the Little Rock Crisis* (Fayetteville, NC: University of Arkansas Press, 1999).

Kirk, John A., *Redefining the Color Line: Black Activism in Little Rock, Arkansas, 1940–1970* (Gainesville, FL: University Press of Florida, 2002).

Stockley, Grif, *Daisy Bates: Civil Rights Crusader from Arkansas* (Jackson, MS: University of Mississippi Press, 2005).

The Founding of the SCLC, 1957–1960

Fairclough, Adam, 'The Preachers and the People: The Origins and Early Years of the SCLC, 1955–1959', *Journal of Southern History* 52 (August 1986): 403–523.

Grant, Joanne, *Ella Baker: Freedom Bound* (New York: John Wiley and Sons, 1998).

Ling, Peter J., 'Gender and Generation: Manhood at the Southern Christian Leadership Conference', in Peter J. Ling and Sharon Monteith (eds), *Gender in the Civil Rights Movement* (New York: Garland Publishing, 1999): 101–30.

Morris, Aldon D., *Origins of the Civil Rights Movement: Black Communities Organizing for Change* (New York. Free Press, 1984).

Sellers, Clyde, *The River of No Return: The Autobiography of a Black Militant and the Life and Death of SNCC* (New York: William Morrow, 1973).

Wofford, Harris, *Of Kennedy's and Kings: Making Sense of the Sixties* (New York: Farrar, Straus, Giroux, 1980).

The Sit-Ins and SNCC, 1960

Carson, Clayborne, *In Struggle: SNCC and the Black Awakening of the 1960s* (Cambridge, MA: Harvard University Press, 1981).

Chafe, William H., *Civilities and Civil Rights: Greensboro, North Carolina and the Black Struggle for Freedom* (New York: Oxford University Press, 1980).

Greenberg, Cheryl (ed.), *A Circle of Trust: Remembering SNCC* (New Brunswick, NJ: Rutgers University Press, 1998).

Halberstam, David, *The Children* (New York: Random House, 1998).

Morris, Aldon D., *The Origins of the Civil Rights Movement: Black Communities Organizing for Change* (New York: Free Press, 1984).

Stoper, Emily, *The Student Nonviolent Coordinating Committee: The Growth of Radicalism in a Civil Rights Organization* (Brooklyn, NY: Carlson Publishing, 1989).

Wolff, Miles, *Lunch at the Five and Ten, The Greensboro Sit-Ins: A Contemporary History* (New York: Stein and Day, 1970).

Zinn, Howard, *SNCC: The New Abolitionists* (Boston, MA: Beacon Press, 1965).

The Sit-Ins and King, 1960

Garrow, David J. (ed.), *Atlanta, Georgia, 1960–1961: Sit-Ins and Student Activism* (Brooklyn, NY: Carlson Publishing, 1989).

Kuhn, Clifford M., '"There's a Footnote to History!": Memory and the History of Martin Luther King's October 1960 Arrest and Its Aftermath', *Journal of American History* 84: 2 (September 1997): 583–95.

Wofford, Harris, *Of Kennedy's and Kings: Making Sense of the Sixties* (New York: Farrar, Straus and Giroux, 1980).

The Freedom Rides and CORE, 1961

Arsenault, Raymond, *Freedom Riders: 1961 and the Struggle for Racial Justice* (New York: Oxford University Press, 2006).

Barnes, Catherine, *Journey from Jim Crow: The Desegregation of Southern Transit* (New York: Columbia University Press, 1983).

Brauer, Carl M., *John F. Kennedy and the Second Reconstruction* (New York: Columbia University Press, 1977).

Carson, Clayborne, *In Struggle: SNCC and the Black Awakening of the 1960s* (Cambridge, MA: Harvard University Press, 1981).

Farmer, James, *Lay Bare the Heart: An Autobiography of the Civil Rights Movement* (New York: Arbor House, 1985).

Forman, James, *The Making of Black Revolutionaries* (Washington, DC: Open Hand Publishing, 1985).

Lewis, John, *Walking with the Wind: A Memoir of the Movement* (New York: Simon and Schuster, 1998).

Meier, August and Elliott Rudwick, *CORE: A Study in the Civil Rights Movement, 1942–1968* (New York: Oxford University Press, 1973).

Niven, David, *The Politics of Injustice: The Kennedys, the Freedom Rides, and the Electoral Consequences of a Moral Compromise* (Knoxville, TN: University of Tennessee Press, 2003).

The Albany Campaign, 1961–2

Brauer, Carl M., *John F. Kennedy and the Second Reconstruction* (New York: Columbia University Press, 1977).

Carson, Clayborne, *In Struggle: SNCC and the Black Awakening of the 1960s* (Cambridge, MA: Harvard University Press, 1981).

Forman, James, *The Making of Black Revolutionaries* (Washington, DC: Open Hand Publishing, 1985).

Journal of South-West Georgia History (Fall 1984).

Lewis, David L., *King: A Critical Biography* (Urbana, IL: University of Illinois Press, 1970).

Morris, Aldon D., *The Origins of the Civil Rights Movement: Black Communities Organizing for Change* (New York: Free Press, 1984).

O'Reilly, Kenneth, *Racial Matters: The FBI's Secret File on Black America, 1960–1972* (New York: Free Press, 1989).

Raines, Howell (ed.), *My Soul is Rested: Movement Days in the Deep South Remembered* (Harmondsworth, UK: Penguin, 1983).

Ricks, John. A., 'De Lawd Descends and is Crucified: Martin Luther King, Jr in Albany, Georgia', *Journal of Southwest Georgia History* 2 (Fall 1984): 3–14.

Tuck, Stephen G. N., *Beyond Atlanta: The Struggle for Racial Equality in Georgia, 1940–1980* (Athens, GA: University of Georgia Press, 2001).

Watters, Pat and Reese Cleghorn, *Climbing Jacob's Ladder* (New York: Harcourt, Brace and World, 1967).

Watters, Pat, *Down to Now: Reflections on the Southern Civil Rights Movement* (New York: Pantheon Books, 1971).

Zinn, Howard, *SNCC: The New Abolitionists* (Boston, MA: Beacon Press, 1965).

The Birmingham Campaign, 1963

Bass, Jonathan S., *Blessed Are The Peacemakers: Martin Luther King, Jr, Eight White Religious Leaders, and the 'Letter from Birmingham City Jail'* (Baton Rouge, LA: Louisiana State University Press, 2001).

Brauer, Carl M., *John F. Kennedy and the Second Reconstruction* (New York: Columbia University Press, 1977).

Connerly, Charles E., *The Most Segregated City in America: City Planning and Civil Rights in Birmingham, 1920–1980* (Charlottesville, VA: University of Virginia Press, 2005).

Eskew, Glenn T., *But For Birmingham: The Local and National Movements in the Civil Rights Struggle* (Chapel Hill, NC: University of North Carolina Press, 1997).

Forman, James, *The Making of Black Revolutionaries* (Washington, DC: Open Hand Publishing, 1985).

Gaillard, Frye, *Cradle of Freedom: Alabama and the Movement that Changed America* (Tuscaloosa, AL: University of Alabama Press, 2004).

Garrow, David J. (ed.), *Birmingham, Alabama, 1956–1963: The Black Struggle for Civil Rights* (Brooklyn, NY: Carlson, 1989).

Jacoway, Elizabeth and David R. Colburn (eds), *Southern Businessmen and Desegregation* (Baton Rouge, LA: Louisiana State University Press, 1982).

King, Martin Luther, Jr, *Why We Can't Wait* (New York: Harper & Row, 1964).

Lee, Spike (dir.), *4 Little Girls* (HBO Home Video and 40 Acres and a Mule, 1997).

Mannis, Andrew M., *A Fire You Can't Put Out: The Civil Right's Life of Birmingham's Fred Shuttlesworth* (Tuscaloosa, AL: University of Alabama Press, 1999).

McWhorter, Dianne, *Carry Me Home: Birmingham, Alabama – The Climatic Battle of the Civil Rights Revolution* (New York: Simon and Schuster, 2001).

Thornton, J. Mills, *Dividing Lines: Municipal Politics and the Struggle for Civil Rights in Montgomery, Birmingham, and Selma* (Tuscaloosa, AL: University of Alabama Press, 2002).

Ward, Brian, *Radio and the Struggle for Civil Rights in the South* (Gainesville, FL: University of Florida Press, 2004).

Westin, Alan and Barry Mahoney, *The Trial of Martin Luther King* (New York: Thomas Y. Crowell, 1974).

The March on Washington for Jobs and Freedom, 1963

Anderson, Jervis, *Bayard Rustin: Troubles I've Seen: A Biography* (Berkeley, CA: University of California Press, 1997).

Barber, Lucy G., *Marching on Washington: The Forging of an American Political Tradition* (Berkeley, CA: University of California Press, 2003).

Bass, Patrick Henry, *Like a Mighty Stream: The March on Washington, August 28, 1963* (Philadelphia, PA: Running Press, 2002).

Carson, Clayborne, *In Struggle: SNCC and the Black Awakening of the 1960s* (Cambridge, MA: Harvard University Press, 1981).

Fairclough, Adam, 'Civil Rights and the Lincoln Memorial: The Censored Speeches of Robert R. Moton (1922) and John Lewis (1963)', *The Journal of Negro History*, 82 (Autumn, 1997): 408–16.

Farmer, James, *Lay Bare the Heart: An Autobiography of the Civil Rights Movement* (New York: Arbor House, 1985).

Forman, James, *The Making of Black Revolutionaries* (Washington, DC: Open Hand Publishing, 1985).

Gentile, Thomas, *March on Washington, August 28, 1963* (Washington, DC: New Day Publications, 1983).

Hansen, Drew D., *The Dream: Martin Luther King, Jr and the Speech that Inspired a Nation* (New York: HarperCollins, 2003).

Levine, Daniel, *Bayard Rustin and the Civil Rights Movement* (New Brunswick, NJ: Rutgers University Press, 2000).

Lewis, John, *Walking with the Wind: A Memoir of the Movement* (New York: Simon and Schuster, 1998).

Sandage, Scott A., 'A Marble House Divided: The Lincoln Memorial, the Civil Rights Movement, and the Politics of Memory, 1939–1963', *Journal of American History* 80: 1 (June 1993): 135–67.

Weiss, Nancy J., *Whitney M. Young, Jr and the Struggle For Civil Rights* (Princeton, NJ: Princeton University Press, 1989).

Wilkins, Roy, *Standing Fast: The Autobiography of Roy Wilkins* (New York: Viking, 1982).

Young, Andrew, *An Easy Burden: The Civil Rights Movement and the Transformation of America* (New York: HarperCollins, 1996).

The St Augustine Campaign, 1964

Colburn, David R., *Racial Change and Community Crisis: St Augustine, Florida, 1877–1980* (New York: Columbia University Press, 1985).

Garrow, David J. (ed.), *St Augustine, Florida, 1963–1964: Mass Protest and Racial Violence* (Brooklyn, NY: Carlson, 1989).

Jacoway, Elizabeth and David R. Colburn (eds), *Southern Businessmen and Desegregation* (Baton Rouge, LA: Louisiana State University Press, 1982).

The Civil Rights Act, 1964

Brauer, Carl M., 'Women Activists, Southern Conservatives, and the Problem of Sex Discrimination in Title VII of the 1964 Civil Rights Act', *Journal of Southern History* 49 (February 1983): 37–56.

Deitch, Cynthia, 'Gender, Race, and Class Politics and the Inclusion of Women in Title VII of the 1964 Civil Rights Act', *Gender and Society* 7 (June 1993): 183–203.

Findlay, James F., 'Regional and Politics in the Sixties: The Churches and the Civil Rights Act of 1964', *Journal of American History* 77: 1 (June 1990): 66–92.

Graham, Hugh D., *The Civil Rights Era: Origins and Development of National Policy, 1960–1972* (New York: Oxford University Press, 1990).

Halpern, Stephen C., *On the Limits of the Law: The Ironic Legacy of Title VI of the 1964 Civil Rights Act* (Baltimore, MD: Johns Hopkins University Press, 1995).

Hart, John, 'Kennedy, Congress and Civil Rights', *Journal of American Studies* 13 (1979): 165–78.

Loevy, Robert D., *To End All Segregation: The Politics of the Passage of the Civil Rights Act of 1964* (Lanham, MD: University Press of America, 1990).

Loevy, Robert D. (ed.), *The Civil Rights Act of 1964: The Passage of the Law That Ended Racial Segregation* (Albany, NY: State University of New York Press, 1997).

Minchin, Timothy J., 'Black Activism, the 1964 Civil Rights Act and the Racial Integration of the Southern Textile Industry', *Journal of Southern History* 65 (November 1999): 809–44.

Orfield, Gary, *The Reconstruction of Southern Education: The Schools and the 1964 Civil Rights Act* (New York: Wiley-Interscience, 1969).

Watson, Denton L., *Lion in the Lobby: Clarence Mitchell, Jr's Struggle for the Passage of Civil Rights Laws* (New York: William Morrow and Co., 1990).

Watters, Pat, *Down to Now: Reflections on the Southern Civil Rights Movement* (New York: Pantheon, 1971).

Whalen, Charles W. and Barbara Whalen, *The Longest Debate: A Legislative History of the 1964 Civil Rights Act* (Cabin John, MD: Seven Locks Press, 1985).

Freedom Summer and the Mississippi Freedom Democratic Party (MFDP), 1964

Ball, Howard, *Murder in Mississippi: United States v. Price and the Struggle for Civil Rights* (Lawrence, KS: University Press of Kansas, 2004).

Belfrage, Sally, *Freedom Summer* (London: Deutsch, 1965).

Burner, Eric R., *And Gently Shall He Lead Them: Robert Parris Moses and Civil Rights in Mississippi* (New York: New York University Press, 1994).

Cagin, Seth and Philip Dray, *We Are Not Afraid: The Story of Goodman, Schwerner and Chaney and the Civil Rights Campaign for Mississippi* (New York: Macmillan, 1988).

Dittmer, John, *Local People: The Struggle for Civil Rights in Mississippi* (Urbana, IL: University of Illinois Press, 1994).

Grant, Joanne, *Ella Baker: Freedom Bound* (New York: John Wiley and Sons, 1998).

Hamer Fannie Lou Hamer, *To Praise Our Bridges: An Autobiography* (Jackson, MS: KIPCO, 1967).

Huie, William Bradford, *Three Lives For Mississippi* (London: Heinemann, 1965).

King, Mary King, *Freedom Song: A Personal Story of the 1960s Civil Rights Movement* (New York: William Morrow, 1987).

Lee, Chana Kai, *For Freedom's Sake: The Life of Fannie Lou Hamer* (Urbana, IL: University of Illinois Press, 1999).

Locke, Mamie E., 'Is This America? Fannie Lou Hamer and the Mississippi Freedom Democratic Party' in Vicki L. Crawford, Jaqueline Anne Rouse, and Barbara Woods (eds), *Women in the Civil Rights Movement* (Brooklyn, NY: Carlson Publishing, 1990), pp. 27–37.

Marsh, Charles, *God's Long Summer: Stories of Faith and Civil Rights* (Princeton, NJ: Princeton University Press, 1997).

McAdam, Doug, *Freedom Summer* (New York: Oxford University Press, 1988).

McMillen, Neil R., 'Black Enfranchisement in Mississippi: Federal Enforcement and Black Protest in the 1960s', *Journal of Southern History* 43 (August 1977): 351–73.

Mills, Kay, *This Little Light of Mine: The Life of Fannie Lou Hamer* (New York: E. P. Dutton, 1994).

Mills, Nicolaus, *Like a Holy Crusade: Mississippi 1964 – The Turning Point of the Civil Rights Movement in America* (Chicago: I. R. Dee, 1992).

Moody, Anne, *Coming of Age in Mississippi* (New York: Dell, 1968).

Morris, Willie, *The Ghosts of Medgar Evers: A Tale of Race, Murder, Mississippi, and Hollywood* (New York: Random House, 1998).

Moye, J. Todd, *Let the People Decide: Black Freedom and White Resistance Movements in Sunflower County, Mississippi, 1945–1986* (Chapel Hill, NC: University of North Carolina Press, 2004).

Nossiter, Adam, *Of Long Memory: Mississippi and the Murder of Medgar Evers* (Reading, MA: Addison-Wesley, 1994).

Parker, Frank, *Black Votes Count: Political Empowerment in Mississippi after 1965* (Chapel Hill, NC: University of North Carolina Press, 1990).

Payne, Charles, *I've Got the Light of Freedom: The Organizing Tradition and the Mississippi Freedom Struggle* (Berkeley, CA: University of California Press, 1995).

Rachal, John R., '"Long Hot Summer": The Mississippi Response to Freedom Summer, 1964', *Journal of Negro History* 84 (Fall 1999): 315–19.

Ransby, Barbara, *Ella Baker and the Black Freedom Movement: A Radical Democratic Vision* (Chapel Hill, NC: University of North Carolina Press, 2002).

Rothschild, Mary Aickin, *A Case of Black and White: Northern Volunteers and the Southern Freedom Summers, 1964–1965* (Westport, CT: Greenwood Press, 1982).

Sinsheimer, Joseph A., 'The Freedom Vote of 1963: New Strategies of Racial Protest in Mississippi', *Journal of Southern History* 55 (May 1989): 217–45.

Street, Joe, 'Reconstructing Education from the Bottom-Up: SNCC's 1964 Mississippi Summer Project and African American Culture', *Journal of American Studies* 38 (2004): 273–96.

Sutherland, Elizabeth (ed.), *Letters from Mississippi* (New York: McGraw-Hill, 1965).

Vollers, Maryanne, *Ghosts of Mississippi: The Murder of Medgar Evers, the Trials of Byron De La Beckwith, and the Haunting of the New South* (Boston, MA: Little, Brown and Company, 1995).

The Selma Campaign, 1965

Carson, Clayborne, *In Struggle: SNCC and the Black Awakening of the 1960s* (Cambridge, MA: Harvard University Press, 1981).

Chestnut, J. L., Jr, with Julia Cass, *Black in Selma: The Uncommon Life of J. L. Chestnut, Jr* (New York: Anchor Books, 1991).

Fager, Charles, *Selma, 1965: The March that Changed the South* (New York: Charles Scribner's Sons, 1974).

Fleming, Cynthia Griggs, *In the Shadow of Selma: The Continuing Struggle for Civil Rights in the Rural South* (Lanham, MD: Rowman and Littlefield, 2004).

Forman, James, *The Making of Black Revolutionaries* (Washington, DC: Open Hand Publishing, 1985).

Garrow, David J., *Protest at Selma: Martin Luther King, Jr, and the Voting Rights Act of 1965* (New Haven, CT: Yale University Press, 1978).

Hamilton, Charles V., *The Bench and the Ballot: Southern Federal Judges and Black Voters* (New York: Oxford University Press, 1973).

Lawson, Steven F., *Black Ballots: Voting Rights in the South, 1944–1969* (New York: Columbia University Press, 1976).

Lawson, Steven F., *Running For Freedom: Civil Rights and Black Politics since 1941* (New York: McGraw-Hill, 1991).

Leonard, Richard D., *Call to Selma: Eighteen Days of Witness* (Boston, MA: Skinner House Books, 2002).

Longenecker, Stephen L., *Selma's Peacemaker: Ralph Smeltzer and Civil Rights Mediation* (Philadelphia, PA: Temple University Press, 1987).

Stanton, Mary, *From Selma to Sorrow: The Life and Death of Viola Liuzzo* (Athens, GA: University of Georgia Press, 1998).

Thornton, J. Mills, *Dividing Lines: Municipal Politics and the Struggle for Civil Rights in Montgomery, Birmingham, and Selma* (Tuscaloosa, AL: University of Alabama Press, 2002).

Webb, Sheyan and Rachel West Nelson, *Selma, Lord, Selma: Girlhood Memories of the Civil Rights Days* (Tuscaloosa, AL: University of Alabama Press, 1980).

The Voting Rights Act, 1965

Davidson, Chandler and Bernard Grofman (eds), *Quite Revolution in the South: The Impact of the Voting Right Act, 1965–1990* (Princeton, NJ: Princeton University Press, 1994).

Grofman, Bernard and Lisa Handley, 'The Impact of the Voting Rights Act on Black Representation in Southern Legislatures', *Legislative Studies Quarterly* 16 (February 1991): 111–25.

Joubert, Paul E. and Ben M. Crouch, 'Mississippi Blacks and the 1965 Voting Rights Act', *Journal of Negro History* 46 (Spring 1977): 157–67.

Knickrehm, Kay M. and Devin Bent, 'Voting Rights, Voter Turnout, and Realignment: The Impact of the 1965 Voting Rights Act', *Journal of Black Studies* 18 (March 1988): 283–96.

The Chicago Campaign, 1965–6

Anderson, Alan B. and George W. Pickering, *Confronting the Color Line: the Broken Promise of the Civil Rights Movement in Chicago* (Athens, GA: University of Georgia Press, 1986).

Cohen, Alan and Elizabeth Taylor, *American Pharaoh: Mayor Richard J. Daley, His Battle for Chicago and the Nation* (Boston, MA: Little, Brown, 2000).

Garrow, David J. (ed.), *Chicago 1966: Open Housing Marches, Summit Negotiations, and Operation Breadbasket* (Brooklyn, NY: Carlson, 1989).

Hirsch, Arnold R., 'Massive Resistance in the Urban North: Trumbull Park, Chicago, 1953–1966', *Journal of American History* 82: 2 (September 1995): 522–50.

Hirsch, Arnold R., *Making the Second Ghetto: Race and Housing in Chicago, 1940–1960* (Chicago, IL: University of Chicago Press, 1998).

Meyer, Stephen Grant, *As Long As They Don't Move Next Door: Segregation and Racial Conflict in American Neighborhoods* (Lanham, MD: Rowman and Littlefield, 2000).

Ralph, James R., Jr, *Northern Protest: Martin Luther King, Jr, Chicago, and the Civil Rights Movement* (Cambridge, MA: Harvard University Press, 1993).

Royko, Mike, *Boss: Richard J. Daley of Chicago* (London: Barrie and Jenkins, 1971).

Sugrue, Thomas J., 'Crabgrass-Roots Politics: Race, Rights and Reaction Against Liberalism in the Urban North, 1940–1964', *Journal of American History* 82: 2 (September 1995): 551–78.

The Meredith March Against Fear and Black Power, 1966

Acham, Christine, *Revolution Televised: Prime Time and the Struggles for Black Power* (Minneapolis, MN: University of Minnesota Press, 2004).

Allen, Robert, *A Guide to Black Power in America: An Historical Analysis* (London: Gollancz, 1970).

Carmichael, Stokely and Charles V. Hamilton, *Black Power: The Politics of Liberation in Black America* (New York: Random House, 1967).

Haines, Herbert M., *Black Radicals and the Civil Rights Mainstream, 1954–1970* (Knoxville, TN: University of Tennessee Press, 1989).

Hill, Lance, *The Deacons for Defense: Armed Resistance and the Civil Rights Movement* (Chapel Hill, NC: University of North Carolina Press, 2004).

King, Martin Luther, Jr, *Where Do We Go From Here? Chaos or Community?* (New York: Harper & Row, 1968).

Meredith, James, *Three Years in Mississippi* (Bloomington, IN: University of Indiana Press, 1966).

Muse, Benjamin, *The American Negro Revolution: From Nonviolence to Black Power, 1963–1967* (Bloomington, IN: Indiana University Press, 1968).

Ogbar, Jeffrey O. G., *Black Power: Radical Politics and African American Identity* (Baltimore, MD: Johns Hopkins University Press, 2005).

Tyson, Timothy B., *Radio Free Dixie: Robert F. Williams and the Roots of Black Power* (Chapel Hill, NC: University of North Carolina Press, 1999).

Tyson, Timothy B., 'Robert F. Williams, "Black Power", and the Roots of the African-American Freedom Struggle', *Journal of American History* 85: 2(September 1998): 540–70.

Van DeBurg, William L., *New Day in Babylon: The Black Power Movement and American Culture, 1965–1975* (Chicago, IL: University of Chicago Press, 1992).

Williams, Robert F., *Negroes with Guns* (Detroit, MI: Wayne State University Press, 1962, reprinted 1998).

Woodard, Komozi, *Nation Within a Nation: Amiri Baraka (LeRoi Jones) and Black Power Politics* (Chapel Hill, NC: University of North Carolina Press, 1999).

King and Vietnam, 1967

Aptheker, Herbert, *Dr Martin Luther King, Vietnam and Civil Rights* (New York: New Outlook Press, 1967).

Fairclough, Adam, 'Martin Luther King, Jr and the War in Vietnam', *Phylon* 45 (1984): 19–39.

Fairclough, Adam, *Martin Luther King* (Athens, GA: University of Georgia Press, 1995).

Hall, Simon, 'The Response of the Moderate Wing of the Civil Rights Movement to the War in Vietnam', *The Historical Journal* 46 (September 2003): 669–701.

Hall, Simon, *Peace and Freedom: The Civil Rights and the Antiwar Movements in the 1960s* (Philadelphia, PA: University of Pennsylvania Press, 2005).

The Poor People's Campaign, 1968

Freeman, Ronald L., *The Mule Train: A Journey of Hope Remembered* (Nashville, TN: Rutledge Hill Press, 1998).

King, Martin Luther, Jr, *The Trumpet of Conscience* (New York: Harper & Row, 1968).

King, Martin Luther, Jr, *Where Do We Go From Here? Chaos or Community?* (New York: Harper & Row, 1968).

Lackey, Hilliard and Lawrence, Marks, *Martin and the Mule Train* (Jackson, MS: Town Square Books, 1998).

McKnight, Gerald D., *The Last Crusade: Martin Luther King Jr, the FBI, and the Poor People's Campaign* (Denver, CO: Westview Press, 1998).

The Memphis Sanitation Workers' Strike, 1968

Appleby, David, Allison Graham and Steven Ross (dirs), *At the River I Stand* (California Newsreel, 1993).

Biefuss, Joan Turner, *At the River I Stand: Memphis, the 1968 Strike, and Martin Luther King* (Memphis, TN: B & W Books, 1985).

Honey, Michael, *Black Workers Remember. An Oral History of Segregation, Unionism and the Freedom Struggle* (Berkeley, CA: University of California Press, 1999).

Selected Websites

Martin Luther King, Jr Papers Project, Stanford University, California
http://www.stanford.edu/group/King/

The King Center Atlanta, Georgia
http://www.thekingcenter.org/

National Park Service: King National Historic Site, Atlanta, Georgia
http://www.nps.gov/malu/

Martin Luther King, Jr National Memorial, Washington, DC
http://www.mlkmemorial.org/

National Civil Rights Museum, former Lorraine Motel, Memphis, Tennessee
http://www.civilrightsmuseum.org/

Birmingham Civil Rights Institute, Birmingham, Alabama
http://www.bcri.org/index.html

We Shall Overcome: Historic Places of the Civil Rights Movement
http://www.cr.nps.gov/nr/travel/civilrights/

The Seattle Times: Martin Luther King, Jr and the Civil Rights Movement
http://seattletimes.nwsource.com/mlk/

Time Magazine: One Hundred Leaders Profile
http://www.time.com/time/time100/leaders/profile/king.html

Public Broadcasting Service (US) Website for the documentary film Citizen King (2004)
http://www.pbs.org/wgbh/amex/mlk/

The FBI Website (contains some of the declassified documents on King)
http://foia.fbi.gov/foiaindex/king.htm

The New Georgia Encyclopaedia: Introductory article on King's Life
http://www.georgiaencyclopedia.org/nge/Article.jsp?id=h-1009

Index

Druck:
Canon Deutschland Business Services GmbH
im Auftrag der KNV-Gruppe
Ferdinand-Jühlke-Str. 7
99095 Erfurt